Europe in the Eighteenth Century

Europe in the Eighteenth Century

ARISTOCRACY AND THE BOURGEOIS CHALLENGE

GEORGE RUDÉ

Harvard University Press
Cambridge, Massachusetts
1985

Library of Congress Cataloging in Publication Data

Rudé, George F. E.
    Europe in the eighteenth century.

    Reprint. Originally published: London: Weidenfeld
and Nicolson, c1972.
    Bibliography: p.
    Includes index
    1. Europe—Social conditions—18th century. 2. Social
history—18th century. I. Title.
HN373.R83   1985   940.2′53   84-19735
ISBN 0-674-26921-7

CONTENTS

MAPS

INTRODUCTION

The author of a book on eighteenth-century Europe is faced with numerous pitfalls, and I certainly do not claim to have avoided them with greater skill than anybody else. For one thing, he must be continually aware that the great French Revolution, whatever his feelings about it, looms large at the end of the road. So he is in continual danger of presenting the history of pre-Revolutionary Europe as a sort of backdrop to revolution or a history of the *ancien régime* in France writ large, in which all roads lead inexorably and inevitably to Paris in the summer of 1789. The truth is, of course, that some roads led there while others, equally decidedly, did not; so the author, unless he is to prove himself guilty of a major optical illusion, must refrain from putting all his eggs into one basket, and make a choice between the two. What my own choice has been in this matter I have tried to explain in a concluding chapter.

In some ways this is a pity, as the author, if he is to avoid a bare country-by-country recital of events, has to give his book a pattern; and the 'all-roads-lead to revolution' pattern, even if it is basically unsound, has the undoubted virtue of being neat and simple. So what is he to put in its place? In this respect, some ages appear to be more fortunate than others: patterns and titles like an Age of Revolution, or of Elegance, Expansion or Reform, spring readily to mind. Here no such tidy label lies at hand: my own sub-title of *Aristocracy and the Bourgeois Challenge* is at best a convenient piece of shorthand that lays no claim to fill the gap. The age has many features and these, though among the most significant, are only two. Others, which the reader will pick out from some (though not all) of my chapter-headings, are the population 'explosion', the agrarian and industrial revolutions, the growth of a wealthy bourgeoisie, Enlightenment and 'enlightened despotism', the challenge to monarchy and aristocracy, popular protest, commercial expansion and colonial wars. Such a presentation – by broad themes rather than by countries or events – has certain obvious disadvantages: some countries and some activities tend to be neglected or to be left out in the cold. In

I

this volume such casualties are Denmark, Spain, Turkey-in-Europe, Italy and Poland; and I further plead guilty to having paid more attention to internal conflicts than I have to wars and the relations between states. I have, however, attempted to compensate for such neglect by adding two appendices, giving the names of rulers and the principal events.

A further problem that arises from this type of presentation is how to stress movement – which is the very stuff of history – as well as conditions, 'structure' and continuity. It is one thing to enumerate and analyse the elements composing the 'society' or 'portrait' of an age; it is quite another to present that age in terms of the changes and conflicts that mark its progress. As an example of what happens when historians neglect the one for the other, one may cite the case of the eighteenth-century British constitution as it emerges, virtually unchanged, from the pens of certain writers of our time. Here I have attempted to avoid this pitfall and solve the problem in two ways: first, by stressing change as well as continuity in handling each of the constituent parts, society, population, institutions, economic activity and ideas; and secondly, by focusing attention on change and conflict in a separate section of the book.

Yet it is not simply a question of continuity and change in general. In every period of history, certain turning-points are more significant and more pregnant with further change than others. In eighteenth-century Europe, it is remarkable how many changes took place about the late 1750s and early 1760s: thus the century, prior to the French Revolution, falls into two unequal parts. The first, though it has its full share of dynastic and colonial wars, is marked, particularly in the West, by a certain steady social development and social peace. The second half, on the contrary, is more explosive: it is the time of the first phase of the industrial revolution in Britain, of the population 'explosion', the economic crisis of 1763, of enlightened despotism (though it started earlier in Prussia), of the rising challenge of both middle classes and aristocracy, of substantial administrative reforms, of Britain's contest with the American colonists, of London radicalism, and of that rising tide of popular protest which M. Godechot (I believe mistakenly) has seen as a sort of generalised curtain-raiser to the revolutionary events in France. Yet, whether one accepts M. Godechot's view or not, it is clear that the tempo of political and social change in Europe was given a great forward thrust in the course of these thirty years. It is a phenomenon which the historian must not only note but try to explain.

Another problem is that posed by Britain. Lying on the periphery of Europe, it is not surprising that she should have followed a different course from her continental neighbours and, in some respects at least, have been the odd man out. Like other writers, I have drawn attention to the peculiar nature of her government and institutions, to her greater degree of social mobility, the wealth and maturity of her middle classes and her technical advance, and have tried to explain why for these and other reasons she alone went through an industrial revolution at this time. But has the uniqueness of the British experience been stressed too much? Was she really quite so different as she has seemed? Historians have begun to question the point, some arguing that her society was not all that more 'open' than the French, others that her technical superiority by the 1780s was not far ahead of that of Belgium, Switzerland or France. Here the recent direction of political research in England, with its emphasis on the unique and unchanging nature of her institutions, has perhaps closed more doors than it has opened. For even if Parliament was (with the exception of the Swedish Riksdag) quite unique, was the attitude to the state of her landed classes, who controlled it, so vastly different from what it was in France or Sweden, or even Poland? If we take a view of Europe as a whole there may appear to be a certain affinity (though on a more muted plane) between George III's attempt to assert his authority over the old Whig party leaders in 1761 and the assumption of power by Gustavus III at the expense of the Swedish nobility in 1772. And while a great deal has been made of the 'aristocratic anarchy' practised by the Swedes and Poles in their 'golden age' or 'age of freedom', very little has been said of the implications of Christopher Wyvill's remark after the 1784 general election in England that a victory for the Fox–North coalition would have 'changed our limited Monarchy into a mere Aristocratical Republic'. It may have been an exaggeration, but it is still one of those problems that need to be explored in greater depth.

Finally a word needs to be said of the assumptions and prejudices that go into a work of this kind. Every generation of historians has its quota of in-built assumptions and *parti-pris*. For long it was fashionable, for example, for English Whigs or liberal-minded historians to take the aristocratic Parliamentary leaders at their word and champion the 'liberties' they proclaimed against the 'tyranny' of George III. Yet curiously enough, when they turned to France they tended to reverse the roles and the reforming ministers of royal 'despotism' (men like Maupeou, Turgot and Brienne) were cast as heroes, while the *parlementaires*, who talked as insistently of 'liberties' as their counterparts in Britain, were written off (and still continue to be so) as the villains of the piece. More recently British historians, under the impact of Sir Lewis Namier and his school, have tended to look more critically at the 'liberal' pretensions of the Newcastles, Rockinghams and Burkes; while others (like M. Egret in France) have begun to accord a degree of sympathy to the French Parlements that they were denied before. This is partly the result of a conservative swing of the pendulum away from the

3

Whig–liberal interpretations of the past. Yet there is more to it than that; for the new interest in economic factors, in radicalism and protest-movements 'from below' has tended to shift the emphasis away from the actors at the centre of the stage and, consequently, to reduce them to less one-sidedly heroic, or villainous, proportions and take the steam out of the old debate. Thus many old heroes and villains have been reduced in size, and none more thoroughly than those former favourites among the 'enlightened despots', Catherine of Russia and Frederick the Great (while the stock of Joseph II has, for other reasons, shown a tendency to rise).

For my part I do not claim any immunity from these trends in historical fashion; and the discerning reader will note, for example, that I have been inclined to be severe with Turgot, to be critical of Frederick and Catherine the Great and to show greater tenderness for Joseph II than for any of his fellow 'despots'. Yet these are matters of relatively small importance that tell the reader something of the author's personal choices and antipathies but very little of the basic assumptions that underlie his work. But in reading these chapters he will note, besides, that a great deal of attention has been paid to social classes, to the institutions and ideas they generate and to the tensions and conflicts that arise between them. These, in turn, are presented as an important element in the historical process and, in consequence, as having played a significant part in the events leading up to the revolution in France. Such a view commends itself to some historians but not to others; so it will not be to everybody's taste. But as the proof of the pudding may lie in the eating, the reader will no doubt first read the book and then decide for himself whether assumptions of the kind enlighten or obscure the history of Europe in the eighteenth century.

I

PEOPLE AND SOCIETY

CHAPTER 1

COUNTRIES AND POPULATION

It is a truism that the eighteenth century was an age of rapid social and political change; it could hardly have been otherwise in the case of a century that ended in the industrial revolution in England and the great political revolution in France. One factor, however, remained stubbornly constant: the physical contours of Europe, its mountains, its rivers, its soil and its climate. Then as now, there were remarkable contrasts between north and south, between the sandy soil of Brandenburg-Prussia and the rich black soil in the Russian Ukraine, the mountainous regions of Switzerland and Norway and the rich alluvial wheatlands of France and the more favoured regions of Italy and Spain. Equally striking were the regional contrasts to be found within some countries: in Russia, between the sandy north and the black-soil south; and, in Spain, between the deep black soils of the Guadalquivir or the orange groves of Valencia and the limestone and granite soils of the central tableland of Castile. Spain was, in fact, a classic example of such contrasts, as was noted by Richard Ford, a contemporary observer: 'The north western provinces [he wrote] are more rainy than Devonshire, while the central plains are more calcined than those of the deserts of Arabia, and the littoral south or eastern coasts altogether Algerian.'[1]

Then as now, it was a matter of debate how far such natural divergences affected the material wealth and the political evolution of states. Before the industrial revolution threw other values into the scales, opinion would probably have agreed with Montesquieu, and with earlier writers like Bodin, that climate and soil were of paramount importance in determining a country's history and national character, the evolution of its laws and institutions and its material and political power.[2] France was an obvious case in point: her great natural wealth and the diversity and equability of her climate appeared to assure her of a stable agriculture, of relatively stable institutions and of a continuing role as the leading power in Europe. Yet as the century advanced it became evident that there were also other, social, factors to be taken into account, such as the remarkable tenacity and vigour of the Prussians

7

despite the sandy Brandenburg soil, the commercial enterprise of the English, and the continuing failure of the Spanish to take advantage of their natural opportunities – a failure characterised by a recent historian as 'the drag of a reluctant society' which proved 'too much for a feeble state'.[3]

If the physical map of Europe remained constant, it did little to ensure the constancy of its political boundaries or to determine how or where they should be drawn. The 'natural' frontiers of states were the exception rather than the rule. The sea, of course, afforded a certain guarantee of permanence, as in the case of Spain and Portugal and the British Isles and of the coastlines of France and the Netherlands. Continental France, too, where her land-frontiers adjoined those of other states, had the natural frontier of the Rhine south of Strasbourg, of the Rhône and the Var adjoining Savoy and of the Alps and the Pyrenees as its boundaries between Switzerland and Spain; but even she, for all her wealth and resources, had German princes encamped inside her province of Alsace and the further enclaves held by the Pope at Avignon and in the Comtat-Venaissin. In other parts of Europe the drawing of boundaries according to nature or nationality hardly arose at all. Norway was a part of the Kingdom of Denmark (later to be transferred to Sweden). Prussia had a large new enclave within Poland and would soon take over Silesia. The Ottoman Empire sprawled across parts of Asia and Africa and, in Europe, occupied the bulk of the territories later known as the Balkan States. The King of England was Elector of Hanover; most of Italy was divided into a number of Spanish and Austrian dominions; and Germany (or 'the Empire') still had no national identity whatsoever and was splintered into more than 360 principalities and (largely) petty states.

The main delineation of Europe's land-frontiers in the early eighteenth century had been made by a series of dynastic and commercial wars, terminating in three sets of treaties, which had unscrambled the settlements effected by the treaties of Westphalia, the Pyrenees and the North half a century before. These new treaties were the treaties of Utrecht, Rastadt and Baden (1713–14) which concluded the war in the west; the treaties of Nystad, Stockholm and Frederiksborg (1719–21) which ended the war in the north; and the treaties of Karlowitz (1699) and Passarowitz (1718) which ended the Austro-Turkish wars in the southeast. This recasting of the old settlements of 1648–60 put the stamp of legality on the conquests of the recent past and marked a notable shift in the balance of power brought about by the diplomacy, wars and economic expansion of the intervening years. Through these treaties, England increased her colonial empire at the expense of France and Spain and gained a virtual trading monopoly in large parts of the world. The United Provinces (the future Holland), though protected against

French expansion by regaining her 'barriers' in the southern Low Countries, had ceased to be a great power. By Rastadt and Utrecht, Austria acquired the old Spanish Netherlands (the future Belgium) in the north and the former Spanish principalities of Milan, Sardinia and Naples in Italy; and, by Karlowitz and Passarowitz, she recovered Transylvania and Hungary and gained parts of Bosnia and Serbia from the Turks. Russia (at first temporarily) gained Azov from Turkey and, by the treaty of Nystad, extended her frontiers westward at the expense of Sweden and Poland. Meanwhile the Electorate of Brandenburg had emerged as the Kingdom of Prussia and added new lands both east and west, and would soon add to them further by the conquests of Frederick the Great.

More significant than the addition or exchange of territories were the political results of the treaties and the new power-relationships that flowed from them. Great Britain (as England had become with the addition of Scotland in 1707) had, with her conquests of Gibraltar and Minorca, Acadia (Nova Scotia), Newfoundland and Hudson's Bay and her acquisition of the lucrative *Asiento des Negros*, become the leading colonial and commercial power, yet her ascendancy in Europe, which followed the Utrecht treaty, was short-lived. Austria, having largely enriched herself at Spain's expense, had considerably extended her power and dominion (though these were soon to be challenged by the rising power of Prussia). Turkey, while she was soon to recover a part of her losses in Serbia and Wallachia (treaty of Belgrade, 1739), continued to decline, was now destined to fight only rearguard actions to defend her shrinking frontiers, and was already showing symptoms that would, a century later, qualify her for the role of 'the sick man of Europe'. Among other former great powers, Sweden, Spain and the United Provinces were also in decline; and their places were taken (or would shortly be taken), with dramatic suddenness, by Russia in the east and Prussia in the centre. Neither had been considered a serious contender in the previous century: Brandenburg-Prussia had been a poor client-state of France; and Russia, before Peter the Great, had appeared as a kind of Asian curiosity of which Samuel Pepys had contemptuously written, 'Not a man that speaks Latin, unless the Secretary of State by chance'. Alone among the powers, France's position remained virtually unchanged. Though she had been defeated in the recent wars and had lost part of her overseas empire, it had required the combined power of Britain, the Netherlands and the Habsburg Empire to reduce her. Moreover, the setback was momentary and she still had the greatest military might and the largest population; her court at Versailles was the envy of every despot or aspirant to despotism in Europe; a Bourbon grandson of Louis xiv sat on the throne of Spain; and she still retained the bulk of her overseas possessions. Yet, of course, these relations

9

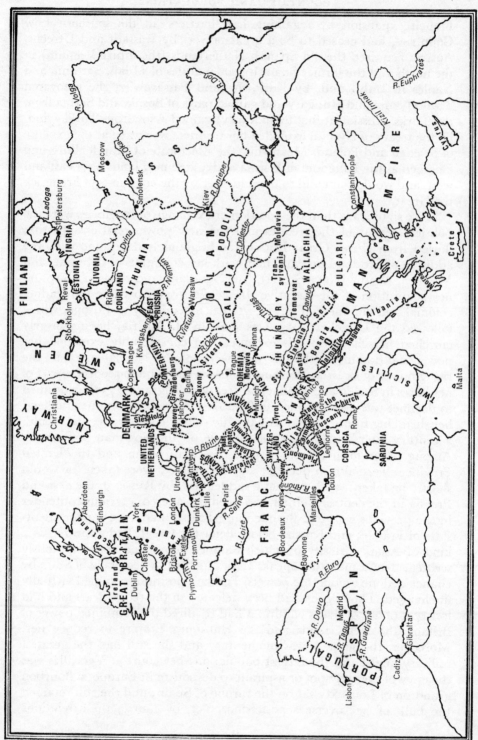

1 Europe in 1721

between the powers were anything but stable and we shall note important changes in the later chapters of this book.

Another important factor that was to have considerable influence in the future was the growth of Europe's population; indeed, historians have written of the eighteenth century as an age of 'demographic revolution'. This had certainly not been the case with the seventeenth century, when, with few exceptions, populations either fell or stagnated. Among the exceptions were Germany, whose population leapt ahead at the end of the Thirty Years War, and England and Wales, where in the 1690s Gregory King noted a 0·4 per cent increase a year and where London had a population explosion that far exceeded that of the century that followed. Yet in neither century can one speak with any conviction of anything but trends, as statistical calculations were notoriously deficient. During the eighteenth century, where such calculations were made, they were of two kinds, of which the first was the more frequent but less likely to be reliable than the second: they were either based on the parish registers of births, marriages and deaths (which, nominally at least, often excluded minority religious groups) or on a census, a counting of heads, which was a rare phenomenon before the early 1800s. Parish registers went back in England and France to the 1530s, in Norway and Sweden to the 1680s and in Romania (then a part of the Ottoman Empire) to the seventeenth century in the case of Protestants and to the eighteenth in the case of Orthodox Greeks. The first known national counts, based on the registers, were those taken in Austria in 1695 and Prussia in 1725. But the Swedes, by a law of 1748, were the first to put them on a regular annual (later triennial) footing; and an Englishman, William Coxe, noted, as he travelled through the northern countries thirty years later, that 'the population is perhaps more accurately ascertained in Sweden than in any other part of Europe': he ascribed it to 'the peculiar attention of government to obtain a correct register of the marriages, births and deaths'.[4] The French followed the Swedes, in Controller General Terray's time, in 1772. Yet the modern type of census, or the actual counting of *heads*, was a more sophisticated and elaborate affair, and this was delayed for some time to come. The delay was due not only to a lack of technical knowledge, but as much to the opposition of those who feared that a census would endanger national security, public morality or individual liberty, or a combination of all three. Thomas Thornton, for example, an English Member of Parliament, who successfully opposed its introduction in Britain in 1753, told the Commons: 'As to myself, I hold the project to be totally subversive of the last remains of English liberty, and, therefore, though it should pass into law, I should think myself under the highest of all obligations to oppose its execution.'[5]

However, such objections were eventually overcome and the first regular census appeared in France and Britain in 1801; it was followed by that in Prussia in 1810, the Netherlands (Holland and Belgium) in 1829, Sweden and Norway in 1840, Italy in 1861 and Russia in 1867.

So the accurate counting of heads was a product of the nineteenth rather than of the eighteenth century. This being so it is not surprising that in the period which concerns us here the wildest notions were held of the national population. Even official calculations varied widely and it was commonly believed in France and Britain, prompted no doubt by memories of the famine of 1709 and the recurrent food crises of the subsequent decades, that the population was falling dangerously. In England, Dr Richard Price claimed that the population of England and Wales had declined by one and a half million since 1688, and in France Montesquieu, Voltaire and the Marquis de Mirabeau were all persuaded that numbers were falling, while Mirabeau's estimate of a population of fourteen million (made in 1748) probably fell short of the actual figure by nearly a third. The pessimists obviously exaggerated the position, yet there were parts of Europe where the population continued to stagnate until the middle years of the century (notable exceptions were Russia, Sweden and Finland), after which it generally leapt ahead; so that what has been called 'the demographic revolution' dates more properly from 1750 than from 1700.

In brief, from the inadequate information available it appears that the population of Europe (excluding the territories within the Ottoman Empire) rose from 100–120 million in 1700 to 120–140 million in 1750 and to 180–190 million in 1800, in other words, that the rate of growth accelerated in the course of the century and doubled during the last fifty years. Every country contributed, to a greater or lesser degree, to this expansion. Among the larger states that contributed most were Russia, whose population rose from nineteen million in 1762 to twenty-nine million in 1766 (without taking account of the territories added by Catherine II after 1762); England and Wales, expanding from six million in 1750 to nine million in 1800; Prussia from three and a half to six million (but in this case including the Polish territory acquired in 1772); and the Habsburg Empire (excluding its Belgian and Italian possessions) from twelve and a half million to twenty-three million (but including Galicia's three million after 1772). Others developed more slowly, notably France from perhaps twenty-two to twenty-seven million, Spain from nine to eleven million and Italy from fifteen and a half to eighteen million. If these figures can be taken as being even remotely accurate (of which there is considerable doubt),* the percentage increase of those countries whose boundaries remained constant,

* In the case of France, Messrs. Braudel and Labrousse refuse to go further than to say that the increase between 1720 and 1790 may have been between twenty and forty per cent (*Histoire économique et sociale de la France*, pp. 18–19).

or may be assumed to have been so, ranged from about sixteen for Italy, twenty-two for Spain and twenty-three for France to fifty in the case of England and Wales and fifty-three in the case of Russia.[6]

While the actual figures are debatable, historians and demographers have been generally agreed that an expansion of this kind took place. What they have failed to agree on are the reasons why it happened, and particularly on the order of priorities to accord to the various explanations put forward. Was it primarily due to a fall in mortality or to a rise in the number of births? And were these in turn due to improved conditions of health or living, to a decline in plagues, or wars or famines, to earlier marriage or greater fertility, to immigration or to an industrial or agrarian revolution? All these explanations have been presented and debated, but naturally they have been argued with greater conviction and with different orders of priorities in relation to some countries than to others and have varied with the type of evidence consulted.[7] For a fuller discussion the reader is referred to the Appendix at the end of this chapter (on page 15).

What were the discernible effects of such a general rise in Europe's population? Contemporary opinion was divided as to whether it would be beneficial or detrimental to the national interest. Malthus, as is well known, took a distinctly pessimistic view. In his *Essay on Population* (1798) he argued that, failing wars, plagues and famines and without the exercise of such further 'preventive checks' as emigration and voluntary abstinence, the swelling numbers of new mouths would rapidly exhaust the nation's ability to feed itself and would lead to famine and disaster. He was not the first to hold such gloomy views. In 1761, a Scottish economist, Robert Wallace, expressed the fear that, but for wars and vices, mankind would double itself every thirty years; and, also before Malthus, a number of Italian writers – Ortès, Ricci, Beccaria, Briganti and Filangieri – were voicing similar apprehensions. Others argued, on the contrary, that a rising population would redound to human happiness and that it was the decline rather than the expansion of population that should cause concern. The Russian Possochkov, for example, in his *Poverty and Wealth*, written in 1724, claimed that a rising population, by increasing the number of labourers, must be an absolute good. His opinion was shared by several of the *philosophes* in France and by writers like Richard Price in England. We have already noted that the mistaken belief that the population was in a state of sharp decline had filled Voltaire, Montesquieu and Price with considerable alarm. More positively, French Physiocrats like Quesnay, Gournay and Dupont de Nemours, who believed that land was the source of all wealth and that the more hands that were available to till and cultivate it the better, welcomed the rise in population which they saw as an essential ingredient of prosperity.

These prophecies of well-being or disaster, consequent upon the eighteenth-century growth in population, would have to wait until the next century for their fuller realisation; so in general they lie well beyond the scope of this volume. In the immediate future, there was nothing to justify the jeremiads of Malthus; there seemed perhaps to be more to support the Physiocrats in their belief that prosperity and a rising population inevitably went hand in hand. The economic effects were to be seen in the increasing consumption of food and raw materials, the improvements in agricultural methods, as in Britain and Belgium, and in large extensions of the area of cultivation – reaching even beyond the boundaries of Europe, as in the case of Russia. There were other economic and social results as well. It may be, for example, that M. Goubert is right in claiming that peasants in the south-west of France took to contraception because of the growing pressure on their land, and it seems likely that similar considerations prompted Scots and Swiss to emigrate in ever larger numbers. No doubt, too, the rising population helped to tip the military scales in favour of some countries at the expense of others by providing a ready source of manpower for their armed forces; Frederick the Great may well have had this in mind in encouraging immigration, for the greater the numbers of foreign labourers and craftsmen, the greater the number of his prison population that could, following the practice of the day, be released for service in his armies. It is also, presumably, no coincidence that France retained her ascendancy in Europe as long as her population exceeded that of any other major power, and that she was still able to draw on vast resources of manpower to man and equip her armies and sustain her victories during the Revolutionary and Napoleonic wars; whereas, after this last great effort, as her birth rate fell and her population declined relatively to those of Britain, Russia and the Austro-German states, she lost her ascendancy in the century that followed.[8] Other social and political consequences affecting the immediate as well as the more distant future are perhaps more disputable. Did the greater longevity of the nation at large, and not only of small privileged groups, tip the balance, in the long run, in favour of a greater democracy? Did a rising population, within the cities as well as on the land, cause intolerable tensions and promote social protest as well as emigration? Was the demographic factor – the pressure of population in the villages, if not in Paris, Rouen or Lyons – a major cause of the revolution in France? Some have argued that it was; others have been less easily convinced. Perhaps later chapters will throw some light on these and other related problems.

Appendix

What were, briefly, the reasons for the 'population explosion' in the latter half of the eighteenth century? In the first place, it appears to be generally accepted that, in many European countries, the death rate began to fall in about 1740 or 1750; though exactly when this was, how long it lasted, or why and to what extent it happened, or which classes and age-groups were most significantly affected, is either not known or has been seriously contested. In the case of England, it has been argued (by Armengaud and others) that the death rate, having risen from 28–29 per thousand to 35–36 per thousand between 1701–10 and 1731–40, dropped back to 26–27 per thousand in 1791–1800. In Sweden, according to these experts, the death rate began to fall appreciably in about 1750 and continued to do so for the rest of the century; whereas in Norway mortality remained constant throughout this period. The French pattern was similar to the Swedish and the English; and here, as in England, there was a particularly sharp decline in infant and juvenile mortality, which, in turn, increased the expectation of life. The death rate also fell in Belgium and Switzerland, though it generally rose in eastern Europe (with the possible exception of Poland): in Bohemia, for example, it rose steadily from 30·4 per thousand in 1785–9 to 39·5 per thousand in 1805–9. Meanwhile, life expectation varied considerably as between countries and classes. In patrician Geneva, for instance, the expectation at birth of upper-class families rose from 41·6 years in the first half of the century to 47·3 years in the second; in Sweden, where it seems to have been higher than anywhere else for the population as a whole, more general figures suggest that, between 1750 and 1800, it was 33·7 years for men and 36·6 years for women; whereas in France the average for both sexes taken together was no more than 29.

The fall in the death rate, which was such a common feature in the countries of western Europe, has been attributed to a number of factors, including the decline of such disasters as famines, plagues and mass-killings in wars, to better health and medical facilities and to an improvement in the general conditions of living. Some of these explanations have been more generally acceptable than others. Wars, which played an equally significant part in the history of the eighteenth century, have for obvious reasons not been placed very high on the list of priorities except in the case of Germany where, as we saw, an end of the blood-letting of the Thirty Years War (in 1648) led to a rapid rise in population. The dramatic decline in gin-drinking in the early 1750s may have contributed substantially to the hopes of survival of many English men, women and children, particularly in London and other cities; and it is evident that the heaviest gin-drinking corresponded very closely with those years – 1725–9, for instance – when mortality in Britain reached its most alarming proportions. (It has been suggested, however, that this may be putting the cart before the horse and that it was the high mortality that occasioned gin-drinking rather than the reverse.) An explanation that has a far more general validity is that, at a time when bread was the basic essential of the working man's diet, the bad harvests and food crises so much in evidence in earlier decades in France, Belgium and Switzerland (and to a lesser extent in Britain) contributed substantially to the high mortality in those countries in the first half of the century and that, conversely, the improvement in the supply and quality of food contributed to its decline in the second. In eastern Europe, on the other hand, where the death rate either rose or remained constant, famines persisted and continued to claim their toll of victims; in Bohemia, for example, the famine of 1771–2 killed off one-tenth or more of the population.

A widely-held view is that the fall in the death rate in certain countries owes a great deal to a greater resistance to disease: specifically, in England, France, Switzerland and parts of Germany; and that this followed from the agricultural improvements of the late seventeenth and early eighteenth centuries. Epidemics, it is true, persisted and by no means disappeared overnight: in 1719, for instance, smallpox killed 14,000 persons in Paris alone and ravaged most of Europe's large cities in 1770. Spain had malaria epidemics in 1784–7 and again in 1790–2; and in Sweden whooping cough is reported to have caused the death of 40,000 children between 1749 and 1764. But in western Europe at least, there was a general decline in the incidence and virulence of epidemics in the course of the century, and the dreaded bubonic plague which had been such a scourge in the past did not, for reasons that have never been adequately explained, recur after 1720. What did the advance in medicine and hygiene and in the general standards of health contribute to these results? There is little doubt that there was a growing concern with problems of health and hygiene, particularly after the 1760s. To cite two comparatively minor examples from France: it was forbidden to bury the dead within the limits of cities after 1777; and Louis XVI had an English-style water closet (the first of its kind in France) erected for his use on the occasion of his coronation at Rheims in 1774. Of greater general significance, of course, were the active measures taken, notably but not solely in Britain, to combat disease by the use of quinine against fevers, inoculation and vaccination against smallpox, the building of large new hospitals and dispensaries for the poor and the more scientific methods of diagnosis. Some of these improvements and innovations undoubtedly contributed to a decline in 'killer' diseases like smallpox and typhus (and there is plenty of contemporary evidence to support this), though it has been argued that the new hospitals, by herding people together under unhealthy conditions, may in some cases have killed off more patients than they cured; this is, however, more likely to be true of the early nineteenth century than of the latter part of the eighteenth. Among sceptics, Professors McKeown and Brown have insisted that the impact of medicine and public health measures on the death rate can only have been of minimal significance at this time; and that, even in Britain, they only began to play a major part as late as the 1870s. They have therefore argued, after examining all the other explanations that have been advanced, that the fall in mortality and the decline in disease must, in the case of England at least, be sought in the general improvements in environment and the 'quality of life' that followed from improved farming methods and the provision of more nutritive foods, including the long-despised potato.

Some writers, including Professor Habbakuk and Dr Krause in England, have directed more attention to the rising birth rate than to the declining death rate as the key factor in determining the increase of population; and it seems obvious enough that, as they are intimately related, no serious conclusions can be arrived at without striking some sort of balance between the two. So, as a generalisation, it may be said that, in late eighteenth-century Europe, there was a marked tendency for the birth rate to rise and the death rate to fall and, above all (even where the birth rate remained constant), for the number of births to exceed the number of deaths. The latter point is presented by Professor Habbakuk as follows:

It is probable that in most parts of Europe outside the great towns there was an excess of births over deaths in a year which was free from epidemics and war and in which the yield of the harvest was normal. Any run of years which was fortunate in these respects was therefore likely to enjoy an increase of population. The second half of the eighteenth century seems to have been such a period. The fluctuations in the number of deaths were less violent in the second half of the eighteenth than in the first.[9]

But, of course, not only did the balance between births and deaths fluctuate in response to such influences as the state of harvests or the prevalence of epidemics, but there was also a considerable variation in the birth rate between one country and another and even between one generation and the next. As an example of the first we may cite the example of the Scandinavian countries. Finland had a birth rate during this period of 41·3 per thousand inhabitants, compared with Denmark's 31, Norway's 32·4 and Sweden's 33·6; and, as the death rate varied only slightly between the four (ranging from 25 per thousand in the case of Norway to 28·2 in the case of Denmark), Finland, by virtue of its higher birth rate, had a considerably greater natural increase of population than its neighbours. As an example of the second, there was the case of France, whose birth rate (these again are M. Armengaud's figures) dropped from 36–37 per thousand in 1770–89 to 35 in 1792 and to 33 per thousand during the Napoleonic Empire.

This raises a further question: what determined such variations in the birth rate? Again, several explanations have been put forward, among them the age and rate of marriage, the expectation of life of married couples, their state of health and fertility, the incidence of celibacy, temporary migrations, the abundance or scarcity of land and the practice of voluntary birth control. Some of these, such as the age and rate of marriage, are clearly of greater relevance than others. Thus in Venice, the age of first marriage for women was about twenty-nine years of age and, in France, about twenty-five, both of which are relatively high, whereas women married far younger in Ireland, where, as Sir William Petty had written, they married 'upon the first capacity'. Though the age at which French women married was high (and this, in turn, had a bearing on fertility), to offset this the marriage rate in France – meaning the proportion of adults marrying yearly – rose appreciably during the century as a whole. It was also high in Belgium, in Catalonia and in parts of Italy; but it was low in Scandinavia, particularly in Norway, and in Sweden it actually declined during the latter part of the century. Clerical celibacy and the maldistribution of land appear to have played a part in checking population growth in Spain; and, in some countries, birth control, which today serves as the most conspicuous of all checks on a rising population, had already made an appearance. The French, it has been argued, were the first to bring it into general practice and both M. Sauvy and M. Goubert hold the view that this alone can adequately account for the dramatic decrease in the birth rate in France during the 1780s and 1790s and particularly during the Revolutionary years. M. Goubert writes of these years: 'I do not know if the "Révolution de 1789" was a "bourgeois revolution", but I am sure it witnessed a demographic revolution in large areas of the nation'; and he attributes the practice to a combination of causes, such as the decline in religious belief and peasant reluctance to divide land among a superfluity of sons.[10] But contraception appears to have been practised in other communities as well. The Genevan bourgeoisie have been shown to have practised it already a century before; and, in the case of Sweden, M. Armengaud concludes from a study of the declining numbers of births between the 1760s and 1800 'that it is too great to be explained by late marriages, and . . . that voluntary birth control must have been practised at least by some Swedish couples during the second half of the eighteenth century'.[11]

Two further factors need to be noted. Whether migration served to stimulate the birth rate (as it has been claimed) or not, it obviously helped to increase the population in some countries while depleting it in others. Migration overseas or to an adjoining continent was presumably a total loss, unless it can be said to have been compensated by leaving more land for the non-emigrants to cultivate (which was often true enough); so that the yearly emigration of Englishmen, Frenchmen and Germans to the British colonies in America and the 575,000 Russians who, in the course of the century, moved into Siberia may be treated as a drain of Europe's 'surplus' population. But, in the meantime, there was a parallel exchange of population between the European countries, which might cancel out or lead to an increase or a decline. Frederick the Great, for example, who believed that 'a country's wealth is the number of its men', attracted 300,000 immigrants into more than 900 villages in Prussia. Yet this addition was offset by the large numbers of Germans (many of them Prussians) brought to Russia by Catherine ii or who settled in Poland and the Baltic states. Again France, although it had the largest population of any country in Europe, drew in thousands of migrants as mercenaries for her armies and as specialist workers for her industries, and there were said to be 50,000 foreigners in France in 1775; yet these, in turn, have to be offset by the larger number of Frenchmen who emigrated to Catalonia and other continental states. Two peoples at least were continuously depleted by emigration: the Scots and the Swiss. The Swiss in particular, for in this century alone 300,000 Swiss left their country to serve as mercenaries under foreign rulers in the armies of Russia, France and Spain.

Finally, there was a factor that affected Britain more than any other country: the rapid growth of the economy and the industrial revolution that began with the 1760s. This, it has been argued, may have substantially increased the birth rate by stimulating a demand for labour, making children profitable and thus encouraging early and prolific marriages. Among contemporaries holding such views was the Rev. Thomas Malthus, who wrote: 'What is essentially necessary to a rapid increase in population is a great and continued demand for labour.'[12]

CHAPTER 2

LAND AND PEASANTS

In the eighteenth century land was still the prime source of wealth for every state in Europe and it was from the land that the great majority of Europeans gained their livelihood. Peasant families accounted for seventy-five per cent or more of the population of Prussia and Poland, for eighty per cent of the population of France and maybe for nine in ten of that of Russia; and even in England towards the end of the previous century, three-quarters of the working population had been employed on the land; in 1770 Arthur Young estimated that where £37 million were drawn from commerce and industry, £66 million were drawn from the soil. This preponderance of agriculture in a nation's economy was therefore a factor common to all; but the types and methods of cultivation, the degree of sophistication displayed in their exercise, the system of landholding and tenancy, and the status and conditions of the cultivators varied widely from one country and from one part of Europe to the next.

The agricultural landscape, as one writer has termed it,[1] varied with soil and climate and geographical situation; but it also varied, though in some areas more conspicuously than in others, with social and political organisation and the response of the farming communities to a rise or fall in prices. For convenience this 'landscape' may be divided into four main areas of cultivation, broadly distinguished by the nature of their crops or livestock and the types of agriculture they pursued. In northern Europe, there were the Scandinavian countries and a continental belt extending from east of Brittany to the curve in the River Elbe and bounded on the south by the northern Rhineland and Westphalia in Germany. This great region may, in turn, be divided into the predominantly forest and mountainous areas of the north and the plains, lower plateau and slopes and valleys of the south. In the first, notably in Norway and Sweden, the prevailing crop was barley while in the south it was more often rye, with some areas given over to hops and vines (in Alsace) and (more widely) to hemp and flax. Livestock breeding prevailed in both, by long tradition on the forest fringes in the north, and

20

spreading in the course of the century to the southern plains, where cattle-fattening and dairy-farming became the main source of the agricultural prosperity of Denmark, Mecklenburg and Schleswig-Holstein.

Another great region was the region of plains and gentle hills stretching from central Germany east of the Elbe across Hungary, Poland and Russia. This was essentially a region of cereal production, particularly of rye and, compared with the north, livestock played a comparatively insignificant part except in Hungary, Moravia and southern Poland; here, too, it had its ups and downs depending on the rise and fall of agricultural prices, which, in Poland, had slumped heavily in the latter part of the previous century. A third region is that which spreads along the Atlantic seaboard, reaching southward to the Alps and the southern slopes of the Massif Central and embracing the northern Rhineland and Westphalia in Germany, the Netherlands, the British Isles, the north and west of France and the northern parts of the Iberian Peninsula. It is a highly diverse region and here, more than in any other, nature favours a great diversity and flexibility of cultivation. In Britain, for example, a damp and relatively mild climate favoured experiment and made it easier to switch, when occasion demanded, from tillage to animal husbandry and vice-versa. The same was generally true of Friesland, the Netherlands and the north and west of France. But in no region was it so apparent that the type of agriculture actually pursued might owe as much to social organisation and human capacity to exploit opportunities offered as to purely natural factors such as climate and soil. So, with equally favourable conditions, Irish agriculture stagnated while English agriculture experimented and prospered; and the Flemish farmers, in particular, showed themselves masters of flexibility and responded more quickly than any others to new opportunities and to market conditions. They combined a diversity of livestock-breeding with a diversity of cultivation and were the first to go over to fodder crops for cattle and to develop the potato and tulip on scientific lines. They were among the first to experiment with and specialise in a wide range of industrial crops, such as hemp and flax for textiles, madder, woad and pastel for dyes, and barley and hops for beer. By contrast, agriculture in the south-west of France and west of Spain, less favoured by climate and more hidebound by tradition, followed traditional patterns in the cultivation of olives and vines, wheat and rye.

Finally, there were the countries lying along the Mediterranean coast, the greater part of Spain, Italy, Greece and the southern areas of France. This region divided naturally into three: between the areas of mountain (Alps, Apennines, Pyrenees and Sierras); the hillsides and foothills of Catalonia, the Rhône Valley and the Po Valley and centre of Italy; and the long coastline stretching from the east and south of Spain through Languedoc and Provence to Sicily and Greece. Here geography, soil and climate once more played the main determining role, while human ingenuity and response to changing social or market relations were less in evidence. So, in the mountainous areas, the main activity was, and remained, forestry and raising sheep and cattle: typical was the operation of the *Mesta*, the great sheep-breeding combine which pastured its vast (though now dwindling) flocks on the great Spanish central plateau. Along the coastal belt the main crops were vines, olives, citrus fruits, mulberries and almonds, occasionally cotton and sugar cane. The areas most favoured by nature were those on the inland slopes and hillsides, which grew wheat, alternating with corn, rye, barley and (in Italy) millet. Some of these were areas where tradition laid a less heavy hand on experiment and ingenuity; while the Po Valley and Lombardy were, as we shall see, among the areas which in earlier centuries had prepared the way for an 'agricultural revolution' in the eighteenth.

This then is one way of looking at the agricultural and rural map of Europe in the eighteenth century. For the social and political historian and the general reader, however, it is perhaps more fruitful to focus the vision more closely on the contrasting features between the developing West and the stagnating or more slowly developing East and South. Here the great dividing line was the Elbe, cutting central Germany from the great plains of the East; smaller dividing lines were formed by the Pyrenees, dividing France from Spain, and the Po, dividing Italy's extreme north from its centre and south. In a broad sense, every country, whichever side of these boundaries it lay, was faced with a similar challenge presented by the 'demographic revolution' of which we have spoken: how to extend its production of food in order to meet the pressure on land and subsistence of an increasing population. Some countries, like Russia and Spain, with their considerable expanses of undeveloped land, met it by spreading traditional methods over a wider area of cultivation; others, like Poland and much of Italy, failed to meet it and stagnated; while others again – and these were mainly among the more densely populated regions to the west of the Elbe and north of the Po and the Pyrenees – met it by adopting new methods of farming and more intensive cultivation. These countries and regions included Britain and the Netherlands, the Po Valley in northern Italy and parts of France; and it is in these countries only that anything like an 'agricultural revolution' may be said to have taken place in the seventeenth or eighteenth centuries.

The essence of the revolution was not, as in the case of the revolution in industry, the introduction of machinery, but of a more flexible rotation of crops, including roots, legumes, lucerne and clover, which both improved and enriched the general yield of the soil and provided more and better fodder for cattle. It involved other innovations as well, such as better implements, the clearance of land, the more extensive use of the horse for traction and the systematic breeding of fatter cattle and sheep. The main obstacle to improvement lay in the persistence of the old system of the 'open field', whereby land was divided into scattered strips and cultivated in common by the villagers in a two- or three-year cycle that left a large part of the arable to lie fallow for long periods at a time. The longer-term aim of the improvers was to replace the old open field by the 'enclosure' or fencing of the land and the creation of compact farms held in individual occupation; but the more immediate and com- pelling need was to find means to eliminate wastage by the substitution of a continuous rotation of crops. The need to do so had first become apparent in regions of dense settlement, especially in the proximity of towns; and the first move to abolish fallow farming had been made, as far back as the sixteenth century, in areas adjacent to certain German cities, in parts of Normandy and Provence and above all in the two largest areas of early urban civilisation, northern Italy and Flanders. The use of clover, which (like the turnip) played such a large part in these new developments, had first been introduced in Italy in the six- teenth century, and from there it had spread to Holland, and from Holland to England to which it was being regularly exported by 1620; forty years later, an Englishman, Andrew Yarranton, was writing that six acres of clover were worth thirty of open grass. It was an Italian, too, a little-known Venetian agronomist of the sixteenth century, who had first urged a course of cultivation including forage crops and the elimination of the fallow period; but these early innovators found few imitators north of the Alps until the next century, when the enterprising farmers of Flanders and Brabant adopted their methods on a far wider scale and found ready disciples in England, and later in France. So the real springboard of the agrarian revolution was the Low Countries, whose people communicated their practices and ideas to visiting Englishmen like Sir Robert Weston in the seventeenth century; while England, in turn, fed them back to France in the middle of the century that followed.

In England the revolution, which was largely promoted by private enterprise, followed four main lines of development.[2] These were the steps taken to improve the yield of the soil, to overcome the wastage of the 'open field', to reclaim moors and wasteland and to produce and feed fatter sheep and cattle. Among the pioneers were Jethro Tull, a Berkshire farmer, who wrote a book on 'Horse-hoeing Husbandry' and invented a mechanical seed-drill; Robert Bakewell, a farmer of Leicestershire, who successfully demonstrated how the quality of sheep and cattle could be improved by selective breeding and the improved use of grass crops; and Viscount Townshend, a former Secretary of State, who first demonstrated the large-scale cultivation of hay, clover and turnips as winter feed for cattle and popularised a new four-crop rotation (of oats, barley, wheat and sainfoin), which became known as the Norfolk course. Equally important was the intensive agitation carried on for many years by Arthur Young, the great advocate of enclosure and land-clearance for arable farming. Young's insistent refrain was the need to make profitable use of all available areas of cultivation and to replace such open fields as still existed – mainly in the south-east and midlands of England – by compact fields enclosed by hedges and fences. Partly as the result of Young's propaganda, enclosure acts followed one another in rapid succession after 1760, and Young became secretary of the Board of Agriculture set up in 1793. Two and a half million acres – over ten per cent of the total acreage of England – were enclosed by act of Parliament between 1760 and 1801. Enclosures undoubtedly brought profits to many and advantages to many more; but whether the cost, in terms of hard cash[3] or in human suffering, was fully justified has been disputed ever since. Young himself lived to deplore the speed with which enclosures were carried through and the almost total disregard shown for the interests of the small yeoman-cultivator, who was being progressively robbed of his original means of livelihood if not actually driven from the soil. 'I had rather,' he wrote at the end of the century, 'that all the commons were sunk in the sea than that the poor should in future be treated on enclosing as they have generally been hitherto.'

Where in England the initiative for improvement had come largely from the enterprising farmers and stock-breeders, in France it came from the combined efforts of innovating noblemen eager to make profits, Physiocrats who believed that the soil was the source of all wealth and the government itself which in 1761 set up a Department of Agriculture and encouraged the formation of local societies to promote the new ideas. Among public bodies supporting the changes were the provincial Estates of Béarn, which issued a strong declaration in their favour in 1754, while the Academy of Bordeaux, the year after, drew public attention to the causes of blight in wheat. Among reforming ministers there was Bertin, Controller General from 1759 to 1763 and later Secretary of State, and among administrators d'Ormesson, Intendant of Finance in the Controller General's department and the main driving force in agricultural affairs during the 1760s and 1770s. Between 1769 and 1781 edicts were issued authorising the partition of the commons in the Three Bishoprics, Lorraine, Alsace, the Cambrésis, Flanders, Artois, Burgundy and the généralité of Auch and Pau. In Brittany, heathland was thrown open for purchase by landlords and speculators. Land-clearance schemes were pushed forward which promoted the interests of wealthy buyers at the expense of the collective traditions of the past. Similarly, encroachments were made on collective grazing and legal restrictions were imposed on the communal use of pastures by the Parlements of Toulouse, Paris and Rouen. In 1767, d'Ormesson persuaded the government to follow suit by restricting or abolishing two ancient customs of the village communities which prohibited enclosure and 'intercommoning' (or the banding together of villages to prevent grazing rights being relaxed). So between 1767 and 1777 a number of edicts granted freedom to enclose in an impressive list of provinces and regions, including the Three Bishoprics, the Barrois, Hainaut, Flanders, the Boulonnais, Champagne, Burgundy, Franche Comté, Roussillon, Béarn, Bigorre and Corsica; while between 1768 and 1771, 'intercommoning' was forbidden in most of these as well. Most of these measures were carried through by 1771, after which they came virtually to a dead stop. Why was this? It seems to have been for a variety of reasons, the most simple being that a great many Frenchmen, either from apathy, fear of peasant revolt or that their own interests would be injured, ignored or resisted the innovations. Peasant hostility had certainly to be reckoned with: the abolition of grazing rights and 'intercommoning' was a serious threat to established and treasured village practice, while the division of the commons, although favouring some (including many poor, land-hungry villagers), injured others, including some landowners and wealthy farmers. Moreover, there may be substance in Arthur Young's suggestion that existing wheat prices were so favourable to growers that they were not willing to risk their future by measures that, whatever their longer-term effects, might in the short-term reduce their acreage and production. But basically, Marc Bloch believes, it was the tenacity of the small and middling independent proprietor, the *laboureur*, to preserve the old ways against dangerous innovation that tipped the scales and made the government stop in its tracks. So in France the reforms of the 1760s and 1770s, unlike the changes carried out in England, left comparatively little mark; and it was only in parts of Hainaut and the Boulonnais in the north, where the agricultural revolution coincided with a changeover from arable to grass, that the appearance of the countryside became radically changed. And, as regards enclosure, the government hesitated to follow the energetic example set by the British Parliament. It proceeded by persuasion and achieved comparatively slim results; so that, outside Normandy, the end of the *ancien régime* saw fallow farming still firmly established on the great majority of peasant holdings.[4]

In a handful of other countries besides, there were pockets of improvement. This was notably the case with Denmark, where immigrant Dutch dairymen brought with them the improved methods of feeding and breeding pigs and poultry; the new enterprises, called 'Hollaenderier' after their creators, laid the foundation for the prosperous Danish dairy-farming of the future. In Germany there was a certain, though limited, reclamation of wastelands, but these were not, as in England, taken into unrestricted individual control; and in most districts the arable field continued to lie open, with its invariable succession of spring-sown corn (barley and oats), autumn-sown corn (wheat and rye) and fallow, and the parcels of the manorial lord intermingled, as in the past, with the parcels cultivated by their peasants. In Switzerland some successful attempts were made to cultivate the land more intensively by transforming heaths into orchards and meadows, draining bogs, introducing new crops and improving agricultural instruments; but these changes encountered peasant apathy and resistance and were on a comparatively minor scale.

Elsewhere, the methods and organisation of agriculture continued as before or even reverted to more primitive practice; they would not follow in the path of innovation until a century or two centuries later. This is not to say that nothing was attempted or that the measures adopted by English, the Belgians and Dutch did not inspire enthusiasm in other quarters. In fact, agricultural societies, in imitation of the West, abounded in Scandinavia and other countries east of the Elbe and south of the Pyrenees. Russia, for example, had its Society for the Promotion of Agriculture or Free Economic Society, patronised by Catherine ii, and made some limited experiments with maize. In Austria and Prussia candidates for posts in the civil service were required to take courses in agriculture. But the practical achievement was negligible owing either to ingrained habits and tradition, to the resistance of landlords who found that traditional methods served better to rivet the peasant to the land, or to the obstacles imposed by geology and climate. The latter was more conspicuously the case in Scandinavia north of Denmark. In Norway and Sweden, bears, wolves and foxes were a perpetual menace to livestock; agricultural implements continued to be of the most primitive kind; and William Coxe noted of Norway that 'tillage cannot generally be flourishing in a country which is in many parts so rocky as to defy the plough, where the climate is so severe that the hoar-frosts begin in September, and where the cold in the highlands prevents the maturity of the corn'.[5] Similarly unfortunate geographical conditions acted as a blight on agricultural progress at the other end of Europe, in the sun-parched districts of Sicily and southern parts of Spain, leading to the constant menace of famine or depopulation. In other parts of Europe, as in Russia and Poland and on the Italian mainland south of the Po, it was as much the perpetuation of outdated forms of social organisation as the obstacles imposed by nature that served as a barrier to progress. In central Muscovy, the main agricultural area of Russia at the time of Peter i, peasants were still in the early years of the century pursuing the old practice of burning down forests and sowing their crops among the ashes for thirty to forty years before moving on to

perform a similar operation elsewhere; and even where settlement was
permanent, the redistribution of strips every half-dozen or dozen years
removed all incentive to enrich the soil. In the Polish Duchy of Lithuania, Coxe noted with astonishment the primitive nature of peasant
equipment: 'Their carts are put together without iron; their bridles and
traces are generally plaited from the bark of trees, or composed of
twisted branches. They have no other tools but a hatchet to construct
their huts, their furniture, and their carts.'[6] Poland was in fact a
country whose agricultural production, which had known some prosperity in the sixteenth century, far from expanding in the age of agricultural revolution had for some time been contracting. Similarly, in
southern Italy and the Papal States, a combination of factors, including
maladministration and the survival of antiquated social and political
forms, led to an agricultural setback in the late seventeenth and early
eighteenth centuries, and even to a return to earlier methods of cultivation, causing a gradual reduction in the area given over to arable land
and a reversion to primitive pasture and afforestation.[7]

But there were also similar pockets of backwardness and resistance to
change in the countries of agricultural revolution themselves, notably in
France and the British Isles. Ireland was a notorious example. Here
rackrenting by stay-away landlords, who left the management of their
estates to their stewards and imposed heavy obligations on their tenants,
perpetuated backward rural conditions that had no counterpart in
England. Cereal production remained at a primitive level and the
change-over to animal husbandry during the century was slow and
painful, leaving the peasant exposed to shortage and famine (as in 1728)
– and leading, incidentally, to the cultivation of the potato which,
transferred to the more skilful hands of the Belgians, became a model for
other countries to follow. Arthur Young, who toured Ireland in 1780,
was appalled by much of what he saw; but he was equally appalled by
some of the things he saw in France on his visit there a few years later.
Two things in particular provoked his condemnation: the tendency to
subdivide the land into ever smaller parcels, as in Lorraine and Champagne; and the widespread system of *métayage*, or share-cropping, which
was most common south of the Loire but was also found scattered over
all the poorer soils of the country. He describes his arrival at a village in
'the miserable province of Sologne': 'a dead flat of irongray, sandy
gravel, with much heath . . . the poor people, who cultivate the soil
here, are *métayers*, that is, men who hire the land without ability to stock
it . . . a miserable system that perpetuates poverty and excludes instruction'.[8]

Broadly corresponding to these boundaries between the 'improving'
West and the traditional or stagnating East and South were those
separating the countries of small ownership from those of large landed

estates. East of the Elbe, the land was generally held in vast tracts by noble landowners, who exploited the unfree labour of serfs, whereas west of the Elbe, as in France, in south-west Germany, Switzerland and northern Italy, small properties (although there were notable exceptions) were the order of the day. Properties tended to become larger as one moved further east beyond this line and whereas a Brandenburg Junker might hold 5,000 acres (considered a large concentration in the West), a Polish or Russian or Hungarian magnate would have thought such a property of little account. In Hungary, after its recovery from the Turks in the early eighteenth century, large tracts of land equal in size to whole German principalities were handed over by a grateful Emperor to Hungarian nobles like the Grassalkovics, Janovics, Festetics and Fekele families; the income of Prince Esterhazy, the richest of the Hungarian magnates, exceeded 700,000 florins a year. A visitor to Bohemia in 1775 wrote of estates of 20,000 to 30,000 acres. In Russia, as often in Poland, landed wealth was reckoned more in terms of labour than of acres. 'I don't need land,' wrote A.I.Bezobrazov, a Russian landlord, to his steward, 'I need peasants.'[9] In the first half of the century to qualify as a rich man one needed to have a thousand serfs. But this was only a minimum requirement: Alexander Menshikov, Peter the Great's old favourite, had more than 100,000 serfs when he fell from power under Catherine I; under Anna, Prince Cherkasskii had 70,000, and the 140,000 serfs which Peter Sheremetev had acquired by marriage and inheritance towards the middle of the century had swollen to 185,610 in the possession of Count N.P.Sheremetev towards the end.

Both north and west of the Elbe, properties tended to be small. This was particularly true of south-west Germany, Switzerland, the Netherlands, northern Italy (Piedmont and Lombardy) and the Scandinavian countries. The small independent proprietors and farmers had played a large part in the new farming methods adopted in Holland and Belgium. The Norwegian peasant proprietors, though poor in comparison with English tenant farmers and the more prosperous of the *laboureurs* in France, had considerably increased their status and holdings since the middle of the previous century. The hundred years that followed were a period of unusual peasant prosperity, and the number of small proprietors rose in three of the largest districts of the Uppland (mountain country) from 918 in 1658 to 3,230 in 1760; and when in the 1720s both crown and noble properties came up for sale, peasants were among the principal buyers that came forward.

France too was essentially a country of small farms and properties. Even the largest landlords, with their stretches of forest in the south-west and their herds of cattle and sheep in Normandy or Lorraine, never owned more than 5,000 acres; and land directly held by the nobility rose in no province above forty-four per cent. It fell, in some, as low as nine per cent, with an overall share of perhaps one-quarter of the whole. The rest was distributed among the three other social groups roughly as follows: church, ten per cent; bourgeoisie, thirty per cent; and peasants (freeholders or perpetual leaseholders), thirty-five per cent. Moreover, as much of the land owned by the larger proprietors (whether noble, clerical or bourgeois) was leased out to small tenants or share-croppers, it is evident that the typical holding, unlike that in the East, was one of small-scale farming.

The exception to the rule, in fact, was not France but England. Here there were large magnates, almost on the scale of those in the East, and as rich as any in Europe, who held estates of 10,000, 20,000 or 50,000 acres – men like the Dukes of Bedford, Newcastle and Richmond, the Marquess of Rockingham and the Duke of Kingston whose scattered estates yielded a net income of nearly £14,000 in 1726, £19,000 in 1731, £22,000 in 1740 and considerably more after the 1760s. And as the agricultural revolution progressed, with its improved drainage and fencing and succession of enclosures, small men sold out and estates became both wealthier and larger. Much of this land was consolidated in the lord's domain and administered by his steward; but parts of it were leased in large portions to substantial tenants. So farms generally, whether farmed by the owner or his tenant, tended to become larger and more prosperous. And in the course of this process of 'revolution', consolidation and expansion, modern rural society was emerging, with the extinction of the yeoman freeholder and 'peasant' and its tripartite division into large landlord, well-to-do farmer and farm labourer.

Other exceptions to the neat geographical boundaries between regions of large and small estates were to be found south of the Po and south of the Pyrenees. In Italy small-scale and large-scale farming rubbed shoulders within the same state. The Papal States were evenly divided between the great properties of the Campagna, owned by Roman patricians and mostly let out to sheep-farmers for grazing, and the small farms of the Umbrian hillside tenanted by share-croppers. In Tuscany, too, large-scale and share-cropping farms existed side by side. In the southern Kingdom of The Two Sicilies, the emphasis was all on large estates – predominantly so in Sicily, where wealthy landowners, with bailiffs (*gabellottos*) as their intermediaries, exploited the labour of an impoverished rural proletariat. On the Neapolitan mainland these *latifundia*, held severally by noble landlords, church and municipalities, still predominated, but here they contrasted with small peasant properties and profit-sharing farms that still survived from earlier days along the coastal strip. Spain was a land of even greater contrasts. At one extreme there were the small tenant farms and properties of Galicia, Navarre and Asturias stretching into Catalonia, in the north; at the other the great *señorios* and *mayorazgos* (family estates) worked by day-labourers in Seville, Granada and Murcia, and reaching upwards into Estremadura and New Castile in the south; while between the two lay the medium and small cereal farms of Castile and León and what remained of the once great sheep-farming monopoly, the *Mesta*, which was now in rapid decline. The prototype of the small independent proprietor or tenant was the Basque farmer of Asturias, and it was of this region that a contemporary observer wrote: 'The majority of the houses and land attached to them are lived in and tilled by the owners themselves.' Very different was the picture painted by Joseph Townsend, a Wiltshire parson who toured through Spain in the 1770s describing the lives and properties of the great *señores* of the south. 'Three great lords [he wrote, with some exaggeration it is true], the dukes of Osuna, Alba and Medina Coeli, cover almost the whole province of Andalusia; and the last of these claims by inheritance the greatest part of Catalonia.'[10] More soberly the census of 1797, in setting out the proportions of owners, tenants and day-labourers in the various provinces of Spain, recorded that there were only five labourers to eighty-nine tenants and six owners in Asturias and twenty-six labourers to forty-eight tenants and twenty-six owners in Galicia; while in the southern provinces of Cordoba, Jaen and Seville, the proportion of labourers rose to eighty-one, eighty and eighty-six, with that of tenants shrinking to fourteen, seventeen and ten.[11]

But the size of properties, the numbers of large owners and small producers, the types of crops grown or livestock raised, the organisation and methods of farming, are only one side of the story. They tell us very little about the conditions of the rural community, of the grievances or the sort of lives led by the mass of small cultivators – whether freeholders, tenants, share-croppers or landless labourers – who generally (though not always accurately) went by the name of peasants. In view of the diversity of their functions, of their economic and social status and of the size and nature of their holdings, it is impossible to generalise and they cannot be treated, even within the confines of a single state, as a homogeneous social class. There was, for example, all the difference in the world both in function and in status between the yeoman freeholder (until enclosure eclipsed him) and the farm labourer in England; between *laboureur*, *métayer* and *manoeuvrier* (day-labourer) in France; between the Basque farmer and southern estate-labourer in Spain; between the peasant serfs and the new class of dairy farmers in Denmark and the north of Germany; as there was between small proprietors, tenants and labourers in Belgium, Switzerland or Norway. In fact, it was only in the East that there was a certain uniformity among the peasant population: in Brandenburg, Poland, Hungary and Russia there was a great and growing divide – certainly greater than elsewhere

– between the landowners, whether large or small, and the peasants who worked on their estates.

So it will be unwise to generalise, except on one point: the peasant's legal status, which had a great deal to do with his place in the community, even if it does not tell us much about the degree of his security or material wellbeing. Was he bond or was he free; and, if free, was he truly free to marry or inherit or to move around, or was his freedom hedged around by a variety of manorial or seigneurial obligations? Once more, the most obvious line of division was that formed by the River Elbe; in this case the boundaries of the Po and the Pyrenees are not involved. The great regions of serfdom or unfree labour lay in the East; and the countries where serfdom had ceased to exist, was a diminishing factor or survived only in nominal forms (though there were notable exceptions) lay in the West and South. Properly speaking, there was no serfdom in the British Isles, in Spain and Portugal, Switzerland, the Netherlands, Norway and Sweden and (once Ferdinand I had removed it soon after the mid-eighteenth century from his Neapolitan dominions) on the Italian mainland. (Yet, as Dr Anderson pertinently observes, how far a labourer in Connaught or Calabria – and, he might have added, on the *latifundia* of Andalusia – was a free man in any meaningful sense of the term is quite another matter.) In Savoy, Baden and Lorraine serfdom was abolished in the course of the eighteenth century. Yet pockets of serfdom remained even in the West; for, as Dr Anderson also reminds us, the East–West contrast should not be applied too mechanically. In France, after its disappearance from Lorraine, there were still serfs on certain mainly ecclesiastical estates in the eastern regions of Franche Comté and the Nivernais: these may have accounted for half a million peasants by the time of the Revolution where there may have been a million half a century before. In Germany west of the Elbe, the peasant had, as in France, generally commuted his old labour services or *corvées* for money payments and thus won his legal freedom. This was particularly true of the Rhineland, where serfdom no longer existed; but it still remained, in varying degrees of oppressiveness, in Bavaria, Saxony (west as well as east) and Holstein, and in Baden until its abolition in 1783.

The only major exception to this sharp East–West antithesis was the Kingdom of Denmark where, despite efforts to free the peasants (in Seeland, Laaland and on neighbouring islands) in 1702, serfdom continued until the end of the century. In fact, as in the East, it was on the increase rather than on the wane. This happened in two ways. By successive decrees in 1701 and 1733, male villagers between the ages of fourteen and thirty-six were forbidden to leave the parishes of their birth without the permission of their lords; moreover, crown tenants who had largely been spared compulsory labour on the royal estates found this exemption withdrawn when crown lands were sold, in large tracts, to speculators in 1768 and 1776. The peasants, we are told, resenting the change, gave expression to their feelings in a contemporary slogan, 'Better become poor by sleeping than by working'. Soon after, William Coxe, in his travels in Denmark, noted with some surprise and disapproval the servitude of the Danes which contrasted so sharply with the freedom and spirit of independence he had found in Norway and Sweden. Having first been to Russia and Poland and 'witnessed the slavery of the peasants in those two countries', coming to Sweden it was 'a pleasing satisfaction to find oneself again among freemen, in a kingdom where a more equal division of property prevails; where there is no vassalage, and where the lowest order enjoy a security of their persons and property'. And now, alas, in Denmark he found himself once more in a country where 'the slavery of the peasants is part of the remaining feudal system' and where there persisted 'a servitude no less disgraceful to the government than prejudicial to the community'. Yet he was gratified to note that the nobility were becoming more enlightened and 'the bonds of servitude' were becoming, or were soon likely to become, relaxed.[12]

Yet if with these exceptions personal bondage was a dwindling factor in the West, there still survived, and on a far larger scale, obligations and tributes attaching to the land which were remnants of an older feudal or seigneurial system of land settlement. (Some historians have objected to the use of the term feudalism in this context; yet it was a term that, far from losing ground, was being used with increasing insistence by its victims and critics in the eighteenth century.) In England and the greater part of the British Isles, they were non-existent: there was only the copyhold lease that remained as a by now almost meaningless survival of the difference between the free and unfree peasant (or villein) of the past. In Ireland, such survivals had greater substance in that the Irish peasant, though nominally free, was virtually committed to spend a great deal of his time working on the landlord's estate: a system described by Aldo de Maddalena as 'a well-nigh feudal system which in many ways resembled that in the *Grundherrschaft* territories east of the Elbe'.[13] Outside the British Isles, one of the most common feudal survivals was the *corvée*, or compulsory road-maintenance, which was a burden much resented by the peasants: it was practised in the Scandinavian countries, France, Germany, Italy, Switzerland and Spain. Other tolls or levies on the land included the obligation to pay tithe to the church (particularly resented in Belgium where other forms of tribute had ceased to be onerous), to pay quit-rents (a reminder of the personal services of the past), to concede hunting rights to the lord of the manor, or to pay him a fine on the inheritance or sale of a property or on the coming of age of a son or the marriage of a daughter. In Spain,

the *señorios* were a major source of income: the owners exacted a variety
of dues from their peasants, and many *señores* claimed the right to enforce old traditional rights, such as a monopoly of hunting and fishing
or of operating mill and oven, and demanded, as a tangible sign of their
lordship, a share of their crops and livestock either in money or in kind.

In no western country were such practices as widespread as in France,
and in none did they come to arouse such an accumulation of resentment – possibly, as we shall see in a later chapter, because the French
small proprietors and tenants included many who had tasted a new-won
freedom and a growing sense of prosperity and independence. The
French peasant, like peasants in other countries where there was an
established church, paid tithe to the church; he paid taxes – the *taille*,
vingtième, capitation and *gabelle* (salt tax) to the state; and to the *seigneur*,
whether lay or ecclesiastical, whether aristocrat or bourgeois, he paid a
varying toll of obligations, services and dues, ranging from the *corvée*
(exacted in cash or kind), the *cens* (feudal rent in cash) to the *champart*
(rent in kind) and *lods et ventes* (a charge on the transfer of property); or
he might, if not owning his land outright, have to pay for the compulsory use of his lord's mill, wine-press and bakery. The incidence of such
burdens, like the status of the peasant, varied, as in other countries,
widely according to the region where he lived; but in years of bad
harvests and depression, they proved – and this was to become a decisive
factor in the future – to be universally vexatious and intolerable.

East of the Elbe, however, the issue was not so much one of occasional
services and obligations as one of a continuous and almost total lack of
freedom, varying from personal bondage in the form of serfdom to the
status of a domain or household chattel. One or other of these conditions
was general in Brandenburg-Prussia, in Poland, Russia and in large
parts of the Austrian Empire – and, we should add, in the Balkan lands
still occupied by the Ottoman Turks. There were, of course, exceptions
– as in parts of northern Russia, with its poor soil and scanty population,
where labour service to a lord was still unknown. Yet the exceptions
were few and becoming more so; for, in most of these countries (this was
particularly the case with Russia, Poland and East Prussia) serfdom was
extending and not contracting and the remaining pockets of freedom
were being gradually mopped up.

The reasons for the deterioration in the status of the small cultivators
in the East were various, but generally they were associated with wars,
times of internal 'troubles', growing opportunities for developing grain
for export and the tendency of central government, either by choice or
necessity, to make concessions to the landed classes. In the Balkan
regions held by the Turks, most of these factors had been at work when
the smaller tenures previously favoured by the Ottoman rulers had been
replaced, from the sixteenth century onwards, by *latifundia*-type estates

33

owned by nobility, military and clergy and when serfdom reappeared in lands such as those in the Lower Danube where it had long been extinct. So there was a reversion, under the impact of wars and aristocratic pressure, to the conditions of a more feudal past. In Brandenburg, Saxony and East Prussia, the case was different. Here serfdom and large-scale estates run on feudal lines were a comparatively recent innovation; and whereas in western and south-western Germany (as in France) feudalism was on the wane and seigneurial justice, as well as the military and fiscal functions of the lords, were being rapidly absorbed by the state, in the east it was almost exactly the reverse. An increase in the landlord's authority had been favoured by a number of factors: their enterprise in reclaiming waste-lands from the sixteenth century onwards, the need to reconstruct after the devastation caused by the Thirty Years War, the general shortage of labour at the end of the wars and the lure of the grain trade through the Baltic which had, since the seventeenth century, opened up prospects of making greater profits from enlarged estates. In addition, the kings of Prussia had become ever more dependent on their Junkers to fill the higher posts in their army and administration; and, in return for these services, they had given them greater freedom, both as landlords and officials, to enlarge and administer their estates. So, over the years, peasants had been evicted from their holdings, granted new, but precarious and short-term, leases and bound to the lords' domain by *corvée* and labour service. The burden of this service varied from estate to estate and was seldom fixed by law; it appears that in East Prussia it might amount to as much as five or six days' work a week.

In the Austrian Empire serfdom had a longer history, though here, too, the deterioration of the peasant's status followed in the wake of the devastation, shortage of labour and social unrest consequent on the Thirty Years War and the long contest with the Turks; in Hungary and Bohemia it may, in addition, have been a convenient form of reprisal for the earlier peasant rebellions in 1514 and 1618. Basically, the tenurial system which bound the peasants to the land was the same in all the Austrian dominions, and remained so, with minor changes caused by the Emperor Joseph II's reforms, until 1848. The peasant was officially described not as a serf (*Leibeigener*) but as an 'hereditary subject' (*Erbunterthan*); yet in practice it made no difference. He was effectively bound to the land and compelled to pay his lord dues and services in cash, kind and labour, while the lord's exercise of his right of jurisdiction ensured that the tribute was paid. In addition, the peasant was required to pay a tax on relinquishing or exchanging his property, a death tax and a variety of tithes; and peasant boys at the age of fourteen were often recruited for compulsory service in the lord's house or on his domain. Of all the compulsory services and obligations the most vexatious and the most widely resented was the labour service, or *Robot*. Its incidence differed widely between manors and between states, depending on the whim of the landlord and the shifting policies of government. In Bohemia, as a protection for the peasant against arbitrary exaction, it was fixed at three days a week, with additional days at seed-time and harvest-time; but it was often more. In Hungary, in particular, though nominally peasant obligations were less onerous than elsewhere, the universal presence of the landlord on the magistrate's bench meant that in practice there was no effective limit. Towards the end of the century, however, the peasant in the Austrian dominions found a powerful pro-tector in the person of the Emperor himself. Earlier attempts had been made – in 1680, 1716 and 1738 – to set limits to the labour services exacted from the peasants of Silesia, Bohemia and Moravia. There had followed later the Empress Maria Theresa's *Urbarium* of 1767, which was intended to regulate the rights and duties of serfs in their relations with their lords within the Empire as a whole. But these were half-hearted palliatives compared with the purposeful attempts made by the Empress's son Joseph II, after he became Emperor in his own right in 1780, to deal with the peasant question. The attempt took shape in three laws which although not fully successful left a considerable impression. The first, the *Strafpatent*, limited the lord's right to punish the peasant; the second, the *Unterthanspatent*, abolished his personal serfdom by giving him the right to leave the estate and marry whom he wished; it did not abolish labour service but it restricted its extension; and the third ordered the substitution of a money payment for the *corvée* in kind – but this only applied to peasants paying a certain minimum tax and was hedged around with certain reservations. Unfortunately, for reasons that we shall consider in a later chapter, Joseph found himself compelled to withdraw or dilute a part of these reforms, a process that was carried further by his successor. So much remained to be done and the old feudal system of land tenure in Austria survived, in its essentials, until the revolution of 1848.

Even more servile than the condition of the peasant in Prussia and in the Austrian and Ottoman Empires was that of the eighteenth-century peasant in Poland and Russia. Poland was a classic case of a semi-feudal country in which chaos and the ineffectiveness of government left the rural population to the mercies of a landlord class that combined the ownership of large estates with the administration of local justice. So here, as in Hungary, though with even less chance of government inter-ference, labour dues and *corvées* could, on the landlords' estates, be extended at will. William Coxe, in his travels, however, noted that a minority of peasants, those attached to the crown, had the right to lodge complaints in the royal courts of justice, which afforded them some opportunity of obtaining redress. The rest, the great majority, had no such protection, and, up to 1768, he observed that a master who killed his serf would escape with a fine. He found a few nobles 'of benevolent hearts and enlightened understandings'; but he added that 'the generality are not inclined either to establish or give efficacy to any regulations in favour of the peasants, whom they scarcely consider as entitled to the common rights of humanity'.[14] In Russia, where there were similar distinctions between peasants attached to the crown and those belonging to the lords, he found the situation even more depressing; for here the latter class were 'the private property of the landholders, as much as implements of agriculture, or herds of cattle, and the value of an estate is estimated . . . by the number of boors, and not by the number of acres'.[15] This tendency to reduce the peasant or labourer of any kind to the condition of a chattel had been proceeding since the time of Peter I, when the poll-tax law of 1723 made the landowner responsible for the collection of the tax and for supplying recruits for the tsar's armies from his estates. Thus serfdom was no longer, as it had been in earlier times, a mere attachment to the soil; now it involved a personal attachment to the serf-owner as well. This new form of vassalage, amounting to virtual slavery, was given official recognition by an edict of Peter III in 1763, which empowered the lords to transfer serfs from one estate to another, and in this way deprived the peasant entirely of his old right to the land he cultivated. In addition, he could be sold by auction with his lord's estate or let out for hire, and (by an edict of 1760) he might be exiled to Siberia by his master when he proved lazy or rebellious. Moreover, serfdom was not only changing its form and becoming intensified; it was being extended over wider areas of the Empire. As the century progressed, under three Peters, Anna, Elizabeth and two Catherines, more territories, formerly Swedish, Polish or Turkish or hitherto unclaimed, came under the authority of the Russian tsar; and with each addition new groups of peasants, if not serfs already, were reduced to servile status. This was particularly the case in the expansionist reign of Catherine II, which witnessed a steep rise in the total serf population; and a visiting English scholar noted in 1784, with regret, that the formerly free peasants of the Ukraine 'have lately undergone a deplorable change and have been reduced, by an edict of the present Empress, to the condition of her other subjects'.

But if the status of the peasant in Russia, Hungary and Poland was inferior to that of the peasants in other European countries, does it follow that their general condition of living was worse, that their lives were more insecure or that they were more subject to hunger and deprivation? This is quite another problem, but it seems highly likely that their living conditions were no worse than those of the landless labourers of Sicily or Andalusia, who were nominally free but tied to the soil none the less, and beggared by low wages and unemployment. Yet such facts are hard to measure and the recurrent famines in Sicily were matched by those which ravaged Saxony and Bohemia in 1770-2, and every great city, with the possible exception of London, was, at times of bad harvests or rural distress, invaded by poor peasants from the villages around. Britain was, in fact, the only one of the great European states that by this time had no real fear of famine. But even so it was not only a matter of economic conditions: how measure, for example, in adequate terms the relative security of the peasant-serf on his lord's domain, however degraded his status, against the uncertain future of the English midlands yeoman or cottager, wrested by enclosure from his garden or field? On the other hand, it can certainly be argued that the great peasant rebellions of the East – the Silesian, Bohemian and Austrian revolts of the 1760s to 1780s and the Pugachev rebellion in Russia in 1773 – were eloquent indicators of a deeper discontent than was evident in the forms assumed by rural protest in the West. In Norway, there were the tax riots of the 1760s and the Lofthuus affair of the 1780s; in France, there were massive grain riots, particularly in 1775; and in England (as also in France) the countryside and market towns were swept by recurrent food riots as the century progressed: we shall return to them later. But these were relatively mild affairs compared with the great peasant conflagrations in the East. Yet, even so, we need to think twice before jumping to hasty conclusions. It was France, and not Russia or Poland or Hungary or Austria or Bohemia, that had a peasant revolution at the end of the century; and this must give food for further thought. Why this was so, and what factors were involved other than those we have considered already, will be discussed in the final chapter of this book.

CHAPTER 3

INDUSTRY AND TRADE

The end of the eighteenth century in Europe saw the beginnings of an industrial revolution that was to have far more dramatic and far-reaching effects than the agrarian revolution we considered in the previous chapter. Yet it was confined to one country and contemporaries were barely aware of its implications until the century that followed. So it is not surprising that even in Britain, where the revolution began, what impressed people most, until the end of the century at least, was not so much the wealth and ingenuity of her manufactures as the prosperity and extent of her overseas trade. In the world of business it was the merchant or the banker, and not the industrialist, who was king; and Gregory King, in his famous picture of the population of England in 1696, had not even deigned to give the manufacturer a mention. Few were the commentators who, like Daniel Defoe, in his tour of 'the Island of Great Britain' in the 1720s, actually told his readers where industries were located, how they were organised and what they produced. The Abbé Le Blanc, one of the many foreign visitors to England in the middle of the century, was no exception when he wrote: 'It must be owned that the natural productions of the country do not, at most, amount to a fourth part of her riches: the rest she owes to the colonies, and the industry of her inhabitants, who by the transportation and exchange of the riches of other countries, continually augment their own.'[1]

So the emphasis was all on trade and on the goods and bullion carried rather than on the goods produced; and it was as true of other countries as it was of Britain. The British, however, were in the exceptional position of having, since the War of the Spanish Succession, secured a firm advantage over the other colonial and maritime powers – France, Spain and Holland – and they continued to exploit it. The Dutch had, in the previous century, been the leading trading nation: their virtual monopoly of the carrying trade, in particular, had excited the envy and rivalry of others and had brought them into wars with France, and even, in Charles II's time, with England. Since the Spanish War, however, the United Provinces were not able to maintain the race against wealthier and more powerful rivals: both her small population and her lack of manufactures counted against her. So while continuing to hold her own in the Baltic trade and the East Indies, she gradually fell back in the developing trade with the Americas and West Indies; and, by 1739, it was noted that twice as many ships unloaded their cargoes in London as in Amsterdam. From now on, the main contest was between the English and the French. Their commercial rivalry extended over all the main sea routes in the world: over the trade in the Baltic and Mediterranean as well as in the Indian and Atlantic oceans. From their Mediterranean trade both nations brought back cargoes of silks, wines, oils, dried fruits, spices, tea and coffee, and paid for them with fish, textiles and hardware; and here France, with her long Mediterranean seaboard and her great port of Marseilles, had the undoubted advantage: this trade alone accounted for nearly a third of her exports and imports. Both nations, too, competed with the Dutch in importing wheat and naval stores from the Baltic and the North. From the southern Baltic ports of Danzig and Königsberg they shipped home quantities of wheat from the great granaries of Poland, Brandenburg and Pomerania; and from Sweden and Russia iron, copper, tar, pitch, hemp and timber to build masts and equip their navies. Here the Dutch for long held the major share; but by the 1770s they had lost it to the English and the Balts themselves, while the French were hardly in the race at all.

Another great theatre of trade and trade rivalry between the powers was India and south-east Asia. Here the Dutch, having secured the monopoly in the Spice Islands in the century before, started with a clear initial advantage; and Dutch traders, established in their East Indian capital of Batavia, carried on a trade in spices and coffee, extending their operations into India, Ceylon, the Islands and Persia. The French and the English, meanwhile, were confined to the Indian mainland, and in rivalry with the Dutch, drew calico from India, tea from China and coffee from the Red Sea ports. By the middle of the century, however, Dutch naval power was unable to match that of the English and the French and the Dutch lost their foothold on the Indian mainland. A few years later, with the Seven Years War, the French were also left 'without a foot of ground in India'; and the British remained in sole possession of the mainland, while the Dutch confined their activities to the Archipelago.

Finally, in the most lucrative and most expansive trade of all, that with the West Indies, Latin America and England's colonies across the Atlantic, the French and English carried on a duel that lasted for the greater part of the century. They drew precious metals from Spanish America, gold and coffee from Brazil, ginger, sugar, coffee and indigo from the West Indian islands and cotton from North America; and, in return, they sent out to the West Indian and American plantations their own manufactures and great shiploads of negro slaves levied among the west African tribes. By 1789, the volume of this trade amounted to one-third of all Britain's commercial operations and to little less in the case of France.

Meanwhile, from all these transactions the carrying capacity of both nations' merchant fleets and the volume of their trade had expanded to a remarkable degree. Unfortunately, comparative figures do not exist to show how far or at what stage one had leapt ahead of the other. We know, however, that England's merchant navy increased from 3,300 ships with a tonnage of 260,000 in 1702 to 9,400 ships with a tonnage of 695,000 in 1776; and that by 1800 her carrying capacity had risen to five or six times what it had been a century before. France, on the other hand, increased her trade with other European countries nearly four-fold between 1716 and 1788 and the value of her combined exports for this period rose from 120 million to 500 million livres; and most of this increase took place in the last twenty-five years. The expansion, in both cases, is reflected in the growing volume of shipping and prosperity in the great ports lying on both sides of the English Channel. At Le Havre, in the north of France, imports of sugar doubled and imports of coffee increased five-fold between 1768 and 1789. In 1788, out of 686 ships returning to France from the West Indian islands, 108 docked at Rouen and Le Havre, 131 docked at Nantes, 133 at Marseilles and 292 at Bordeaux. Bordeaux, in fact, had become the greatest of France's ports, handling a quarter of her overseas trade, with a merchant fleet that had trebled in sixty years; and Arthur Young, travelling in France at this time, was struck by the evident signs of prosperity of its merchant class and the magnificence of its buildings, which 'greatly surpassed' his expectations and which he considered superior to those of Liverpool, whose slave-traders at this time were reputed to be earning profits of £300,000 a year. Liverpool, for its part, with its two-way traffic in cotton and slaves, was rapidly overtaking Bristol, the long-established centre of the West Indian and American trade, and was, by the end of the century, receiving the lion's share of ships bringing raw cotton to the growing textile industries of Lancashire. There was also Hull, on the other side of the island, an old commercial centre, now prospering from the Baltic trade. It was of Hull that Defoe had written, back in 1724, that 'there is more business done . . . than in any town of its bigness in Europe'.[2]

But none of these ports, whether in England or in France, was the equal of London. At the end of the previous century, London had handled more than three-quarters of the combined foreign trade of the kingdom, its tonnage being then eight times that of its closest rival,

Bristol. This proportion declined as Bristol and Liverpool expanded and as Newcastle and Hull drew an increasing volume of the trade with the Baltic. But, in absolute terms, the volume of London's trade and shipping continued to expand. The tonnage of London-based ships engaged in foreign trade rose from 157,000 in 1705 to 235,000 in 1751 and 620,000 in 1794; and the opening of the wars at the end of the century saw her firmly established as the world's largest *entrepôt* and port.

Meanwhile, in the rest of Europe, some countries had a rapid commercial expansion while others declined. Among the losers were Venice and the north German trading cities of the Hanseatic League. The League was already long past its prime, and in 1763, closed down its great *entrepôt* at Bergen, in Norway. Venice, a once proud trading city, was in full decline and, after 1715, could no longer enforce her traditional control of shipping in the Adriatic. As Venice declined, her rivals Trieste and Ancona expanded, as did Leghorn on the other side of the peninsula. Among the old German ports, Hamburg and Bremen adapted themselves to new ways and did a thriving business. Hamburg, in particular, by trading freely with all comers, whether in peace or in war, rose to new heights of prosperity: every year 2,000 ships alone carrying raw materials from the French colonies unloaded at her docks. The Baltic trade brought prosperity to other northern ports as well. In 1787 Sweden had an expanding fleet of 1,200 merchantmen and Prussia nearly a thousand. Russia, from Peter the Great's time, rapidly extended her foreign trade, opened her Baltic ports ever wider to the West and became Europe's largest supplier of iron: by 1790 she was shipping almost 26,000 metric tons a year from her vast Ural deposits to Britain. Even Spain had a remarkable revival: in 1789, half the goods she sent to South America were home-produced where only one-eighth had been so at the end of the previous century.

As trade expanded, new methods had to be found to organise and direct it and to finance and channel its operations. As in the century before, the great chartered companies (the 'moneyed companies' as they were called in London) continued to play an important role. The oldest of these, the Dutch East India Company, still kept a tight fist on the lucrative trade in spices from the East Indies, handling rice from Java, nutmeg from Banda and cinnamon from Ceylon. The French and English East India Companies played a similar part in the India and China trade; in London there were, besides, the Russia, Africa, Levant, Hudson Bay and South Sea Companies, variously engaged in trade with the Baltic, west Africa, the near east and North and South America. Some of these companies were immensely wealthy, reaping profits from trade and from the loans they advanced to governments and individuals, both of their own and other countries; thus in the early 1720s the combined volume of bonds issued by the East India and South Sea Companies in London amounted to over £7 million. But the companies had chequered careers, both because they tended to be greedy and push their luck too far and because they naturally aroused the resentment of the wider business community whose operations their monopoly impeded. The South Sea Company went bankrupt over the South Sea 'Bubble' scare in 1720 and was only saved from extinction by the intervention of Sir Robert Walpole and the Bank of England; and the same year the crash of John Law's East and West Indies schemes in France brought temporary disaster to the *Compagnie des Indes*. Two years later, the Ostend Company, promoted by the Austrian Emperor Charles VI to open up trade through Antwerp in his newly-won Belgian dominion, failed owing to the stubborn resistance of the Dutch who were anxious to preserve the monopoly of Amsterdam, in which they received the support of England. In London, the African Company was wound up and given the more liberal status of a 'regulated' company in 1750, and the Levant Company was thrown open to all comers in 1753. Even the East India Company, from the 1760s onwards, was under continuous pressure, in and out of Parliament, to relax its control of India and to mend its ways; and its privileges were gradually whittled down. Its French sister-company was less fortunate and lost its charter in 1769. But even where the companies survived, their services to trade were patently a thing of the past, and new challengers – the rising class of 'interlopers' (like William Pitt's grandfather, 'Diamond Pitt', in England) and a group of international merchant houses, skilled in all financial operations – were waiting to take over. Among these international merchants, who assumed an increasing importance as the century went on, were men like Engel and Richey at Hamburg, specialists in the Atlantic and Baltic trade; Eichhorn and Moritz at Breslau; and Zetner at Strasbourg. At Amsterdam, Etienne le Jay traded in silks and English cloth; at Neufchâtel, Portalès specialised in calico; and, at Frankfurt-am-Main, von Bodeck traded in tissues and spices, Stadel in coffee, tea, pepper and cinnamon, while Meyer Amschel Rothschild, the founder of the great Jewish banking family, was trading in bullion and army equipment.

Some of these men, or men with similar financial inclinations, became specialists in various branches of the retail or wholesale trade, like the Italian firm of Brentano which took up residence in Germany. Others founded Stock Exchanges at Berlin, Hamburg and Vienna to add to those already established at London, Antwerp, Amsterdam and Lyons in the century before; while others again promoted a new service, marine insurance, for the greater protection of shipping; Lloyd's famous list of ships was first issued in a London coffee-house in 1734 and Lloyd's Register appeared there thirty years later; the example was soon followed at Hamburg and Genoa. Yet others, like the Rothschilds, became bankers, who advanced long- and short-term loans to governments and private clients and promoted international trade by offering credits at competitive rates of interest (settling around five per cent) and discounting commercial bills or letters of exchange. Some of these activities went back to the Middle Ages; others were of more recent growth. It was in the seventeenth century that central banks like the Banks of Amsterdam, Venice and Hamburg and the Bank of England were founded, while Child's (private) Bank was already carrying on a thriving business in the City of London. The new century saw a considerable further expansion in banking of both kinds. Among banks whose main purpose was to promote commercial ventures were the banks at Brunn (founded in 1751) and St Gall (1752), the Noble Bank in Russia (1754) and the Caisse Française de Commerce and the Caisse d'Escompte (1778) in France, not to mention the Banque Royale which the Scot, John Law, set up in Paris to finance his ill-starred operations of 1719 and 1720. In England, Lloyd's Bank was founded in 1765 and, in the City of London, the number of banks grew from thirty-five to forty in the 1760s to sixty in 1791 and seventy in 1795, many of them acting in turn as agents for English country banks, which also discounted bills and of which there were 150 by 1776 and 280 by the early 1790s. But in banking and international financial operations it was still the Dutch that held the lead and, until the Napoleonic Wars, it was still Amsterdam and not London that was the money market of the world. In 1777, the Dutch were reputed to own forty per cent of Britain's national debt. 'The bill on Amsterdam,' Professor Charles Wilson has written, 'was to the eighteenth century what the bill on London was to become to the nineteenth century.'[3]

So there was a general, though uneven, expansion of trade in the eighteenth century, in which France and Britain drew the major share but to which most other countries made some contribution: the most notable exceptions were countries in central and south-east Europe. Inevitably, such an expansion both reflected and stimulated a greater industrial activity as well; and here there was by no means, as we noted in the case of agrarian 'improvement', a more or less sharp dividing line between East and West. Britain, it is true, stood somewhat apart from the rest: how this was and why this was we shall consider later. Naturally enough, the pace of advance differed between one country and another, as did the nature and the quality of the goods produced and even, on occasion, the type of labour engaged in their manufacture; but the actual *methods* of production were everywhere much the same and it was only after the 1780s that contemporaries began to become aware that any radical changes were on their way.

These methods of production were broadly speaking of four main kinds. In the first place, there was the small workshop, which had emerged from the medieval city and been located within its walls and in which a master craftsman worked side by side with his apprentices and journeymen, whose numbers, like the quantity and quality of the goods they produced, were regulated by the gilds. The gilds had of course changed as society changed: they had lost a great deal of their old vigour and relevance and their regulations were seen increasingly as a restraint on trade rather than as a protection. Besides, the journeymen, losing hope of ever becoming masters, were organising in their own associations (as in the *compagnonnages* in France) to protect their own interests as workers and to raise their wages; so we find the Imperial Diet in Germany, when attempting to reform the gilds in 1731, listing among the 'abuses' in most urgent need of remedy that 'artisans make a pact among themselves agreeing that none of them will sell for a lower price or work for a lower daily wage than others'.[4] But, in spite of its many critics, the gild system had powerful supporters and in most countries continued to survive. In France Turgot, as Controller General to Louis XVI, abolished the gilds in 1776; but he fell from office a few months later, and the gilds were restored and continued until the Revolution. It was in fact only in Britain that the whole system had fallen into decay or had, in the course of time, been legislated almost out of existence; in London such regulations as remained had been taken over by the City Corporation. But whether the gilds retained their old authority or not, the small workshop continued as a survival from the past; and this was as true of England as it was of Russia, Germany or France. Examples are to be found in the watch-making and clock-making of Geneva and Nuremberg, in southern Germany; in the nail-making and toy-making of Birmingham (which, unlike Manchester, remained for long a centre of artisan production); in chair-making, gold and metal-work, printing and book-binding, and in the multiplicity of crafts and trades plied in every capital city. Typical is the case of Paris, whose *faubourgs* on the eve of revolution were teeming with small workshops of this kind. In the Faubourg Montmartre, for example, there were nine master carpenters employing between them eighty-one journeymen and apprentices, twenty-three blacksmiths employing 146 and twenty-five locksmiths fifty-one; with an overall average of five to six workers for every master craftsman. In other districts, the old regulations limiting the number of apprentices were either more laxly applied, had fallen into disuse or were being more generously interpreted; and, taking the city as a whole, the proportion of workers to employers was a little over sixteen to one.[5] London, like Paris and Birmingham, was still essentially a city of old crafts and small workshops; but the old regulations, as we should expect, tended to be more openly flouted or conveniently ignored. A case in point is that of silk-weaving which was still nominally at least bound by old rules severely limiting the number of apprentices and journeymen a master might employ. Yet, in the days of the 'Forty-Five' when the Young Pretender threatened to march on London, it was found that several of the master weavers who offered to enlist the services of their journeymen to stop him employed as many as sixty or even a hundred in their shops.

In some countries such as Germany where the old customs and regulations tended to be more religiously observed, such examples might be harder to find. Yet here too, as in every country engaged in manufacture, a great many industries had by now moved into the countryside or into the suburbs or 'free' districts of old towns. Sometimes this was imposed on trades that were considered 'offensive' or a public nuisance such as tanning, slaughtering, soap-making, brewing or the like; but more often the move had been made to escape the restrictive regulations of the craft or merchant gild. To quote an example: in the 1720s and 1730s, shoemakers and hosiers were migrating northwards from London, partly in search of cheaper fuel and labour, but also to evade the City's regulations. The case of the hosiers is the more typical of the two: while the shoemakers were seeking freedom by moving to the less restrictive environment of another city, Northampton, the hosiers were leaving the city altogether and setting up shop in the country, in what became the 'hosiery' counties of Nottingham, Derby and Leicester. It is a reminder that, between the decline of the medieval city and the emergence of the industrial revolution, the typical (though not necessarily the most frequent) location of industry was the country and no longer the town. This was particularly the case with the clothing trade, which was generally based on the countryman's cottage. The 'cottage' or 'domestic' system was one in which the weavers and spinners (who were often members of the weavers' family) spun their yarn and wove their cloth under the direction of the clothier, a merchant-capitalist who provided the yarn and the looms and marketed the produce. This village-based domestic system was by now almost universal and was as typical of the woollen and cotton industry in France (centred round Lille, Rheims, Sedan, Elbeuf, Abbeville) as it was of sailcloth making at Kaluga, flax-spinning for linen in Bohemia and Silesia or the cotton-spinning and stocking-making of Glarus and St Gall. It was practised perhaps on the largest scale of all in England; and Daniel Defoe, in his travels round the island in the 1720s, described with enthusiasm the busy scene he found in the country around Halifax, the centre of the woollen trade in Yorkshire, where 'the whole country, however mountainous . . . is yet infinitely full of people' and 'whose people are all full of business'. He noted two things in particular: one was the location in the proximity of coal and water: 'with coal and running water upon the tops of the highest hills'; the other was the way in which the whole village and whole families were involved in producing cloth:

Among the manufacturers' houses are likewise scattered an infinite number of cottages or small dwellings, in which dwell the workmen which are employed, the women and children of whom are always busy carding, spinning, &c. so that no hands being unemployed, all can gain their bread, even from the youngest to the antient, hardly any thing above four years old but its hands are sufficient to it self.[6]

An alternative or extension of the rural domestic system was that carried on in the urban 'manufactory' (to use Marx's term). It was not a factory in the modern sense in that, qualitatively at least, it was no more highly mechanised than the weaver's cottage; but for the hat-maker, lace-maker or wall-paper manufacturer it had the advantage of assembling larger numbers of workers and looms under one roof; and in this limited sense it had some resemblance to the factory of modern times. Thus, in the suburbs of Paris, when the Revolution broke out, there were several manufactories, mainly in lace and gauze and cotton, that employed 200 or 300, or even 500, workers in the same building. In England, there was the silk-mill set up by Thomas Lombe at Derby in 1717–21, which employed over 300 workers handling machinery with more than 26,000 wheels. Something similar was true of the state manufactories established in France in Louis XIV's time by Colbert (porcelain at Sèvres and Gobelins tapestries) and those more recently promoted by Peter the Great in Russia and by Frederick William I and Frederick II in Prussia. Finally, there was the mode of production which was neither based on the small workshop, the cottage or the urban manufactory: the assembling of workers on building sites, and mines and foundries for the extraction of coal or the manufacture of iron. Among the larger undertakings of the kind were the Anzin collieries founded near Valenciennes in 1757; the Le Creuzot arms 'factory' established near Autun in Burgundy; Dietrich's furnaces at Niederbronn in Alsace; the German iron foundries in the Ruhr and Peter I's foundries in the Urals; and the state-owned arsenals and dockyards at Kronstadt, Chatham, Spandau, Liège and St Etienne. Some of these were organised and financed on lines that look forward to the more developed industrial society of the nineteenth century.

It was by means of a combination of these productive systems – and of the domestic system, in particular – that industry expanded in the eighteenth century. Essentially this was as true of Britain and France as it was of Spain, Switzerland and Russia. Yet, within this framework, the expansion was genuine enough. It was the most notable and the most continuously sustained in Britain, where industrial production trebled between 1700 and 1790 and saw the most rapid forward leap in the

1780s. In that decade the production of cloth in Yorkshire, which earlier had so delighted Daniel Defoe, almost doubled where it had barely doubled over the whole half-century before. In France, if anything, it was the other way about. Following a rapid development after the Spanish War, there had been a slackening in the mid-century and something like stagnation after 1770. Yet, taking the century as a whole, there had been a considerable expansion in industry, as there had in trade: in textiles in particular. At Lyons, which had a recession in the 1780s, there were 40,000 silk weavers tending looms whose number nearly trebled between 1720 and 1788. That year, there were 15,000 workers employed in and around the woollen town of Elbeuf where there had been 8,000 employed a little over a century before. The output of woollens doubled at Amiens between 1713 and 1750 and trebled at Beauvais between 1724 and 1755; while, though times were hard in the 1780s, in 1792 Amiens was using between one-half and one-third of all the 'spinning jennies' that had by this time been imported into France. Another thriving centre of woollens was Abbeville, where Van Robais' new mill employed 1,800 workers and 'put out' work to a further 10,000 spinners and weavers in the country round about. Meanwhile, developments in coal and iron were laying some sort of basis for the heavy industry of the future: 3,000 miners were employed in the pits at Littry, while the Anzin Mining Company, which employed 1,000 miners on the eve of its official opening in 1756, employed more than 3,000 in 1783 and 4,000, distributed over thirty-seven pits, in 1789. Moreover, France produced 130,000–140,000 tons of pig-iron at this time, which was more than double that produced in Britain.

Belgium also saw developments in textiles and mining. In Flanders, which combined the two, linen exports to Spain and South America were increasing; Bruges had a cloth manufactory employing 277 workers; and the coal exported down the River Haine rose from 16,000 tons in 1764 to 100,000 tons in 1800. Liège, now in French-speaking Belgium and then a self-governing principality within the Austrian Empire, had two considerable industrial towns: Verviers, a recent creation, and Liège itself, 50,000 of whose population of 83,000 lived in its industrial suburbs, many of them working in the mines, which employed 7,000 miners in 140 pits.

Among other important textile-producing centres were Bohemia, Switzerland and Spain. Switzerland, besides leading the world in its production of clocks and watches at Geneva, was next to England the largest importer of raw cotton from North America. In the 1780s, there were 150,000 Swiss workers employed in cotton, including 34,000 domestic spinners in Canton Glarus alone. Bohemia, which became an important industrial region after 1770, had 200,000 domestic flax-spinners producing yarn for the linen trade. Spain's main centres for

47

silk and linen were Valencia and Barcelona. The number of Valencia's silk looms, according to Joseph Townsend, who visited the country in the 1780s, expanded from 800 in 1718 to 3,195 in 1769 and 5,000 in 1787: the rise may well have been at the expense of Lyons whose industry was going through a crisis at this time. Meanwhile, the cotton city of Barcelona, which was said to be only second to that of the midlands in England, employed 80,000 workers; and such was the spectacular nature of Spain's economic boom (short-lived, it is true) that the directors of the Banco de San Carlos in 1785 spoke rapturously of 'the progress of our industry, the multiplicity of modern factories in Catalonia, the extension of those in Valencia, the growth of agriculture, and the increase in demand for its products'.[7]

Finally, there was Russia. Peter the Great had, like other enlightened despots before and since, established a number of industries, mainly for the purpose of equipping his army and navy. There was the sailcloth industry at Kaluga (employing 9,000 workers by the end of the century) and, most important, there was the metallurgical industry which he founded in the Urals to make that region the main industrial centre in the country. To get labour Peter issued an edict in 1721 enabling merchants to buy serfs, a unique privilege hitherto reserved for the nobility. In 1722 there may have been 5,000 peasant-labourers employed, which later rose to twice or more that number. The number of foundries, most of them transferred to private owners, rose in accordance – there were fifty-four in 1745, a further thirty-four were added by Catherine II, and Coxe, on his travels, gave the figure of 105 in the 1780s (though there appear to have been 140 twenty years before). The peak period of activity was during the Seven Years War when the Urals produced two-thirds of Russian production of copper and iron. This was also the period of triumph of one of the earliest industrial–capitalist families in Europe, the Demidovs. Nikita Demidov, the founder of the dynasty, was a one-time serf who had acquired his first iron foundry in 1702. This had been expanded to twenty-eight, shared equally between three Demidov brothers (who also held other properties and 30,000 serfs) in 1762. Five years later, when Procope Demidov, one of the three, sold out his six foundries and other associated properties, they fetched what was then the very considerable sum of 800,000 roubles.[8]

There were, of course, countries which remained more or less untouched by this industrial expansion or whose industries lagged or stagnated. These probably included the greater part of Germany and Italy, Sweden in the latter part of the century and Holland, whose old industrial cities, Leyden and Haarlem, were, like most of the old German trading cities, in sad decline. But generally, as we have said, industrial production expanded with the expansion of trade and the one reacted

on the other. In most cases this took the form of an arithmetical progression which, with its ups and downs, meant that at the end of the
century there were more goods being produced and more hands,
machines and buildings employed than there were at the beginning;
and alongside this industrial advance, there were expanding markets
(both at home and overseas) to consume the goods produced. Had this
been all, however, we could hardly speak of an industrial 'revolution'.
That revolution, as we know, did more than merely expand production:
it transformed the manufacturing processes in a number of trades, gave
rise to the modern factory system and, eventually, brought into being a
new industrial society as well. These further developments belong essentially to a later period and need not therefore concern us here. But what
does concern us are the actual processes of change, and where and when
the decisive steps were taken (during what Professor Rostow has called
the 'take-off' period) that eventually led from what was basically a
'domestic' system to the factory system of the future. Some historians,
looking particularly at the British coal industry, have traced these
decisive beginnings to the seventeenth century; others have placed them
in the 1740s or 1760s; but it is now more generally accepted that anything like a 'self-sustaining' and continuing process of growth and
change only began about 1780.

Can we find the germs of such a 'take-off' in the picture of industrial
expansion we have presented so far? Contemporaries certainly do not
appear to have found them (and they can hardly be expected to have
looked into the future). What they were impressed by, like the directors
of that Spanish bank in 1785, was the arithmetical progression of trade
and industrial output and not by any radical change of method; even
John Aikin, in the picture he painted of Manchester ten years later,
while filled with awe and admiration for the number of new machines in
use, the vast pace of expansion in the production of cotton goods and
'the prodigious extension of the several branches of the Manchester
manufactures', does not appear to have appreciated their wider implications for industry as a whole. For us, with the wisdom of hindsight, it is
easy to look back and pick out changes whose significance was not evident to those who saw them taking place; and, in order to do better, it
might be tempting to see the beginning of a new type of industrial
organisation in Peter's iron foundries in the Urals, the Bohemian or
Silesian 'putting-out' system, the state manufactures in France or
Russia, in the operation of the Anzin or Liège mines or in the fortunes
accumulated by industrial capitalists like the Demidovs in Russia, de
Wendel in France or Gotzkowsky in Prussia. There was some novelty in
all this – particularly in the emergence of a new type of industrial
capitalist (the banker Périer of Grenoble, for example, combined banking with a direct interest in manufacture, and this was something new);

but to see much more would be an optical illusion. Essentially, there was no great change from the old productive methods of the past. The prevailing mode was still the domestic system, operated in rural cottages; and even a great woollen merchant like Van Robais 'put out' work to five times more domestic workers than the number he employed within his manufactory at Abbeville; and something similar was true at Amiens, Elbeuf, Rheims, Kaluga and elsewhere. Nor had the domestic worker much in common with the industrial proletarian of the future: he was essentially a half-time peasant, and even the 3,000 workers in the Littry mines in France were peasants recruited from the fields who went back to their old occupations at times of harvesting and sowing. Equally, there was nothing new about the peasant-serf labour employed in Peter's and Demidov's foundries: the great enterprises of eastern Europe and the textile industry of Bohemia were manned by the conscripted labour of serfs, or of criminals, vagrants, foundlings and soldiers; and even Van Robais' textile mills and the Royal State 'factories' in France were a kind of industrial Bastille in which the workers were subject to an almost military type of discipline. Moreover, the new industrial technology, which later revolutionised production, was still in its infancy. In the Urals, the foundries, being able to draw on an almost unlimited supply of conscripted labour, had little need for technical innovation; and their equipment, M. Portal tells us, remained virtually unchanged for 150 years. Elsewhere, there were some improvements in mining, and Newcomen's 'fire-engine', which had replaced Savary's earlier model, was in use at Anzin and Liège. During the 1780s, James Watt's steam-engine, which opened up far greater possibilities, began to be manu-factured under licence by Périer in France; and twelve of these engines were in use at Anzin in 1790. But this was quite exceptional, as France, faced with economic crisis and revolution, was slow to apply the new technology. By this time, Périer had sold only forty of the new steam-engines and France had imported only 900 'spinning jennies' (the most primitive of the new English devices in textiles) where there were 20,000 in use in Britain.

In short, there were few signs of any radical break-through on the continent of Europe; these, as our hindsight now tells us, could only be found in Britain. It now also appears that there the crucial preparatory period, after which nothing would ever be quite the same, was during the years 1740 to 1770 when there was a rapid and sustained growth of trade and production, with rising markets and industrial output mutually sustaining and reacting upon one another;[9] Eric Hobsbawm may well be right in saying that 'by 1750 . . . there was not much doubt that if any state was to win the race to be the first industrial power it would be Britain'.[10] But this was still only the promise of what the future might bring. It needed something else for the promise to be translated into performance and for the lead once gained, to be maintained and not relinquished (as it had been earlier by France and Holland). This new element was provided by the technical inventions of Hargreaves, Arkwright, Watt and others that had hardly begun (and had certainly not begun to have any visible effects) by the middle of the century. How one invention led to another, particularly in the new key and rising industry of cotton, needs now to be briefly considered.

It started with Kay's invention of the flying shuttle (1733), which doubled the weaver's output. When it came into general use (in the 1750s and 1760s) it led to a noticeable shortage of yarn. So there came a series of experiments and inventions with the deliberate aim of bridging the gap by improving the production of the ordinary cottage spinning wheel, leading to Hargreaves' spinning jenny (1768) which, by allowing one operator to work several spindles (eventually a hundred), made it possible for the spinners to catch up and for domestic industry to expand all along the line. But Hargreaves' invention was not adaptable to power; it needed Arkwright's water-frame (based on an earlier invention of Lewis Paul's) in 1769 and Compton's 'mule' (1779), which combined the virtues of the two, to bring about the next forward leap by making it possible to harness the new machinery to water, and thus extend domestic manufacture into the power-driven mill. And as demand and production expanded social necessity proved once more to be the mother of invention and when James Watt's improved steam-engine (with its capacity to drive machinery) was ready for use, the mule became adapted to steam-power and by 1800 had become a power-driven factory machine; though it still required the services of a skilled operator to control it. The last step was taken when, between 1805 and 1830, Richard Roberts, an experienced machine-maker (not a carpenter weaver like Hargreaves, a speculating barber like Arkwright or a weaver-cum-farmer like Compton), perfected an automatic power-driven machine and thus completed the cycle from cottage to mechanised factory, a cycle that in sixty years had brought about a hundredfold increase in the production of cotton goods.

Meanwhile, the iron industry had been similarly revolutionised over the same period of time (1718 to 1780) by the successive experiments and inventions of Abraham Darby (who first used coke instead of charcoal to smelt iron) and Henry Cort (with his 'puddling' process and 'reverberatory' furnace), which made it possible to smelt iron by coke on a massive scale. So, in 1780, there were eighty-one coke-fuelled furnaces in Britain compared with twenty-five that were using charcoal. By this time the other technologically-minded nations, which in the mid-century had been using technical processes at much the same level as those being used in Britain, had given up the race; British experts were invited to France, Switzerland and Belgium to instruct them in the use of the

'English machines'; and it was on the basis of the technical knowledge provided by the British that the industrial revolution in these countries proceeded, when conditions became more favourable, in the early decades of the nineteenth century.

But why – an often repeated question – did the industrial revolution first take place in Britain, and not (say) in France, Belgium or Switzerland? An obvious snap answer is that it was England and Scotland that provided the inventors whose skill and ingenuity made such changes possible. But this in turn raises further questions, such as why should such men have appeared in Britain and not elsewhere, and (more important) why were their inventions taken up and put into practice when they were? (None of this is obvious: plenty of inventions, including many of those of the period 1760–1830, get put on the scrap-heap; and even good ones need favourable circumstances to get them off the ground.) To this last point one answer was already suggested when we used the term 'social necessity'. Peter the Great's iron foundries in the Urals, as we saw, did not develop technically because, having a surfeit of serf labour to work them, there was no social necessity to do so. The English inventions, on the other hand, followed one another in a sort of logical sequence, each one stimulated by the social needs created by the one that came before.

But even this is not so obvious as it appears at first sight and prompts other questions. How did the British inventors acquire their skills, and where did the *entrepreneurs* who took the inventions up and invested large sums in the new mills and machines acquire the motives, the flexibility and business acumen, and the labour and money, to do so? And why, once the first phase was over (essentially in cotton, coal and iron) did the 'self-sustaining' process continue and embrace a wide range of other industries as well? The last question, as it applies to later developments, need not concern us here and, for the rest, only the most general answers will be attempted. The first question is perhaps the easiest to answer. Britain had a long technical tradition, which the agricultural revolution had served to enrich; nor was there any real problem about the comparatively simple mechanical adjustments and experiments involved in the inventions, which, given the inducement, could have been carried through as easily in France, Switzerland or Belgium. Where did the money come from? Historians have argued about the finer points, though it appears to be generally agreed that the profits of empire and the long history of commercial expansion spreading over 150 years had provided a source that could be readily tapped. To this Paul Bairoch has added that the agricultural revolution played an important role by supplying both capital and *entrepreneurs*; while Bertrand Gille has stressed the role played by England's provincial banks in providing short-term credits.[11]

Again, Britain's industrial *entrepreneurs* were favoured by expanding markets and a ready supply of labour. Her overseas markets, as we have seen, were constantly expanding; and this continued in spite of the American War in the 1770s and 1780s and the loss of her American colonies. Internally, her market was favoured by a rising population: this was particularly the case in the crucial period after the 1740s. It was further helped by her system of communications. Her roads were poor – certainly far poorer than the French – until engineers like Metcalfe, Telford and Macadam and the turnpikes of the latter part of the century brought improvements; but by this time she also had a network of canals; and above all she had the advantage of having a single internal market, untrammelled by feudal survivals like tolls on roads, rivers and bridges which, in France and other countries, obstructed the free circulation of goods. Moreover, a rising population, the decay of the gild system and the social consequences of the agrarian revolution combined to assure her of an adequate supply of labour that was not firmly rooted to the land. But this is a two-edged argument which should not be pressed too far. In the long run, it certainly required a large surplus of labour, both from England and Ireland, to build the canals and factories and provide migrants for the new factory towns; but had that surplus been too large or too readily available in the crucial period of the 1760s to 1780s, there would have been no more inducement in Britain than in Russia throughout the century, or in France after the 1770s, to embark on a long and costly process of technical innovation.[12]

Finally, to return to our unanswered question: why, even given these other advantages, did the British *entrepreneurs* show such flexibility and daring (rather like the Dutch and Belgian farmers of the seventeenth century) in seizing the opportunities offered and in investing their money in such radically new adventures? David Landes, after raising the question, answers it by pointing to the distinctive qualities of British eighteenth-century society, which, he claims, was far more 'open' and 'mobile' than that of any of her industrial rivals. This openness, he goes on to say, engendered a spirit of enterprise in the business community and a willingness to take risks in pursuit of profit: British commerce was more energetic, forceful and 'open to innovation' than any other; no society, with the possible exception of Holland's, was so 'sophisticated commercially'; and no state was 'more responsive to the desires of its mercantile classes'.[13] But this question of the open society brings us to problems that we shall be discussing at greater length in a later chapter.

CHAPTER 4

CITIES

An aspect of eighteenth-century Europe that astonished and sometimes alarmed contemporaries was the growth in the number and in the size of the cities. Urbanisation was, in fact, as much a feature of the time as the growth of population and the general expansion of industry and trade; indeed they were all connected. In 1800 there were twenty-two cities in Europe with a population of 100,000 or above where there had been no more than thirteen or fourteen a hundred years before. They were spread over a dozen countries: there were five in Italy; three in France, two each in Britain, Russia, Germany and Spain; and one each in Austria, Portugal, Poland, Denmark, Holland and Turkey-in-Europe. The ten largest cities, by this time, were London, with a population between 900,000 and a million; Paris (with 550,000–600,000), Naples (400,000), Lisbon (350,000), Constantinople (over 300,000), Moscow (300,000), St Petersburg (270,000), Vienna (230,000), Amsterdam (220,000) and Berlin (170,000); and these were closely followed by Rome, Dublin and Madrid.

Some of these giants had, of course, expanded far more rapidly than others. St Petersburg, founded by Peter the Great on a swamp in 1702, had already grown to 68,000 in 1730 and into a great city of over a quarter of a million by 1800. Berlin, also virtually a new creation, had more than trebled its population in a hundred years. Moscow had exploded even more vigorously; from a mere 16,000 households in 1700 to 300,000 inhabitants a century later. Naples, with 186,000 inhabitants in 1700, had, with 409,000 in 1800, become the third largest city in Europe. London, which in the course of the century had wrested the first place from Paris, had seen its population grow from 550,000 to 575,000 to nearly a million. Other large cities, while showing an increase in numbers, had relatively declined; among these were Amsterdam, Constantinople, Paris and Madrid, and all the great Italian cities with the exception of Naples and Turin. Only one great city could show no increase at all: perhaps not surprisingly, this was Venice, whose population stood at 138,000 in 1700 and at 137,600 in 1800.[1]

But such figures, of course, give us only a very one-sided picture of urban growth and tell us little about urbanisation as a whole. A dozen countries, as we have seen, had large cities, but comparatively few had a substantial number of middling-sized cities or large market towns as well. Generally speaking, the eastern and northern countries had little urban development on this level outside their principal cities. Russia, apart from Moscow and St Petersburg, had only Astrakhan with a population of over 30,000. In Scandinavia, only Copenhagen and Stockholm had more than 50,000 people. The extreme case was Poland whose towns, once flourishing, had markedly declined since the sixteenth century. The one exception was its capital Warsaw, whose population rose from 35,000 to perhaps three times that number between 1700 and 1800. For the rest, they had become large villages rather than towns. 'The ruin of the cities,' states a Polish manifesto of 1744, 'is so universal and so evident that with the single exception of Warsaw the first ones in the country can well be compared to caves of robbers.'[2]

Once again, there was no hard-and-fast dividing line between East and West. In Germany, whether east or west of the Elbe, provincial capitals and ports, enriched by the Baltic trade, tended to expand: thus Dresden's population grew to 62,000, Breslau's to 60,000, Königsberg's to 55,000, while Danzig's remained around 50,000; and, in the West, it was not only Venice that declined but Holland's urban population as a whole. But, with these exceptions and with the exception of the larger cities, urbanisation was largely confined to the South and West. Among the older urban communities, Italian cities still grew in size and number, particularly where they attracted trade; in 1800 there were nine cities with a population of over 70,000; and Leghorn, while not among them, had increased its numbers from 13,000 to a little under 50,000 in a hundred years. Germany had by this time five cities with a population of over 50,000 and a further eight between 30,000 and 50,000. Spain had (in addition to Madrid) eight cities of over 40,000; among them Barcelona, whose numbers rose from 37,000 in 1714 to 115,000 in 1802. Most marked was the urban expansion in England and France. On the eve of the Revolution, France had seven cities (apart from Paris) with a population of 50,000 and above, where she had had only four a century before; and England, in 1800, had five (or seven if we add Scotland) where she had had none when the century began.

So much for the bare facts concerning the rise in the size and number of cities; but to complete our picture of urban expansion we still need to know not only how many people but what proportion of the population at large came to live in them. Unfortunately, we can only hazard a guess in the case of the greater part of Europe, but we know something about the two countries in which urbanisation appears to have been the most rapid, that is, England and France. It has been estimated that something like one Frenchman in ten lived in towns of 5,000 or over by the time of the Revolution, and of Englishmen one in six by the middle of the century and perhaps one in four by the end. So England, with its small though rapidly expanding population, appears to have become the most urbanised country in Europe in the sense that a larger proportion of its citizens lived in a directly urban environment than anywhere else. Other factors appear to substantiate this point as well. For one thing, as David Landes reminds us, industrialisation in England had the effect of concentrating larger numbers of weavers and spinners in manufacturing districts which, though still rural and not yet urban, became densely packed: 'full of people' as Defoe wrote of the country around Halifax in the West Riding. Thus a kind of semi-urbanisation took place by a 'thickening of the countryside', a process that was far more marked in the case of England than in the case of Belgium or France.[3] Moreover, there was the peculiar phenomenon of London, the 'great Wen', which not only had the largest population of any city in Europe, but drew a far larger proportion of the nation as a whole within its orbit than any other urban community. In fact, as Dr E.A. Wrigley had demonstrated, one Englishman in every ten lived in London, where one Dutchman in eleven lived in Amsterdam and only one Frenchman in forty (or even fifty) lived in Paris.[4] It was, indeed, this picture of London as octopus which excited the astonishment and admiration or alarm of observers. Defoe reflected some of this feeling in his portrait of the city in the 1720s: having described how London would spread further in the immediate years to come, he asked, 'And whither will this monstrous city then extend?' Others like David Hume, writing after the middle of the century when London's population had already reached 700,000, believed it to be 'a kind of impossibility' that any city could expand much further. There were also the pessimists who, seeing its expansion, believed it was sucking in the life-blood of the nation. Among them was Dr Richard Price, who wrote gloomily in 1783 that 'the inhabitants of the cottages thrown down in the country fly to London, there to be corrupted and perish'.[5]

There were both general and particular reasons why the eighteenth century should have been a century of urban growth. Among the general reasons were the rise in national population, the expansion of industry and commerce, and in some countries (though not in all) the displacement of growing numbers of country-dwellers by an agricultural revolution. In addition, in central Europe, the ending of the religious wars of the last century had given a general stimulus to urban building and reconstruction. But cities also grew in response to particular pressures, depending on their situation and the functions they were required to perform. Some grew as centres of government and administration – and this was the case with most capital cities; some around a court, a bishopric or a military establishment; others as ports or as centres of trade or manufacture; and a few cities, the multi-functional cities, in response to a multiplicity of social pressures and demands.

Some motives for developing cities were comparatively new; others were traditional or a hang-over from the past. There was nothing new, for example, in the motives that prompted Peter the Great to found his new city of St Petersburg on the banks of the Neva or the Prussian kings to develop Berlin as the capital of their new Kingdom of Prussia: they were built to the greater glory of the monarch and to give notice that two new great powers had arrived on the European scene. But Frederick I, Berlin's founder, as his grandson the 'great' Frederick sadly relates, was not really cast for the part that the new capital and the new kingdom required him to play. Under him Berlin developed as a centre of the arts and became (in his words) 'the Athens of the North'. It needed the tougher qualities of Frederick William I, the 'Sergeant King', to effect the necessary transformation. So Berlin from being an Athens became a Sparta. 'Berlin,' Frederick wrote, 'was like the magazine of Mars. Every artist that can be employed in the service of an army was sure to thrive, and their ware was sought for all over Germany. At Berlin we set up powder-mills, at Spandau sword-cutlers, at Potsdam gunsmiths; and at Neustadt tradesmen, who worked at copper and iron.'[6] He might have added that another of the principal industries subsidised by the Prussian exchequer was the manufacture of blue cloth for soldiers' uniforms.

But, in this regard, Berlin was an exception, both in Germany and elsewhere. The fortress-city had become something of an anachronism, as it seemed to Daniel Defoe when he visited Edinburgh and bewailed the fact that its 'impregnable castle', which no doubt had had its uses in the past, presented 'infinite disadvantages'[7] for the city of the present. Somewhat different priorities attached to the development of the smaller German capital cities. Outside Prussia and Bavaria, Germany was composed of congeries of petty principalities and states, and this fragmentation of power was reflected in the multiplicity of small cities, each duplicating each other's functions, yet each growing as normal civilian life returned after the upsets and devastation of the civil and religious wars. Some of these small cities were, like Berlin itself, a creation of the recent past. Thus Karlsruhe and Mannheim were built in 1714 and Ludwigsburg between 1704 and 1733; all three reflected the princely whims of their founders in the symmetrical layout of their gardens and streets. But whether of recent growth or of older establishment, all such cities had a similar pattern of semi-rural existence: each had its princely palace and petty court, its bureaucracy and garrison,

57

its theatre, library and picture gallery or zoological garden; with its manufactures (if any) limited to porcelain, ribbons, lace, playing cards and other luxuries for the service of the court. Lady Mary Wortley Montagu, who travelled about Germany early in the century, noted the contrast between life in the free trading cities and these petty capitals as follows:

In the first there appears an air of commerce and plenty. The streets are well built and full of people, neatly and plainly dressed. The shops are loaded with merchandise, and the commonalty clean and cheerful. In the other, a sort of shabby finery, a number of dirty people of quality tawdered out; narrow nasty streets out of repair, wretchedly thin of inhabitants, and above half of the common sort asking for alms.[8]

Such urban survivals from the past were by no means peculiar to Germany; there they were only more frequent because of the peculiarity of her political development. On a more heroic scale, there were large capital cities that could show similar features: Rome and Madrid, for example, where populations were still growing (though slowly) but where social life stagnated and reflected past rather than present glories. On a smaller scale again, there were plenty of French, and even English, provincial cities where tradition lay heavy on the present generation: medieval county seats, for example, like Lancaster, Lincoln, York and Chester in England; or the numerous French provincial towns that had grown up – and often continued to grow – around old markets or cathedral chapters. We may take as an illustration the sleepy old cathedral city of Angers in the west of France. Angers had, on the eve of the Revolution, a population of 34,000. It was a clerical city, in which one resident in every sixty was either in a major order or a member of a religious community. So life revolved around its cathedral close, its abbeys and monastic houses, its fifty-three courts of justice and its parish churches, of which there were no less than seventeen within its walls. It was a city in which, according to a visiting traveller, one might savour 'the grandeur of decay and ruin'. Of trade and industry there was virtually none, much to the despair of forward-looking government officials, who wrote contemptuously in a report of 1783: 'The present generation vegetates, just as that which preceded it vegetated, and as the succeeding one will vegetate.'[9]

Sharply contrasting with this type of sluggish urban development was the vigorous growth of cities that were expanding under the impact of industry and trade. One such city was Glasgow, which combined the two. Defoe, in visiting Glasgow on his travels, described it as 'a city of business; here is the face of trade as well foreign and home trade; and, I may say, 'tis the only city in Scotland, at this time, that apparently encreases and improves in both'. It may interest Glasgow's present-day critics to learn that Defoe wrote of it (in sharp contrast to his opinion of Edinburgh, with its 'stenches and nastiness') as 'the cleanest and beautifullest, and best-built city in Britain, London excepted'.[10] Among ports whose trade and population were both rapidly expanding were Hamburg, Marseilles, Leghorn, Liverpool and the great French west-coast ports of Nantes and Bordeaux. Hamburg's population rose from 60,000 to 85,000 in the course of the century, while Bordeaux's and Bristol's doubled and Nantes', Marseilles' and Leghorn's more than trebled. Liverpool's ascent was the most sensational of all. Defoe saw it as 'a large, handsome, well built and encreasing or thriving town' when he went there first in 1680 and, on his third visit in the 1720s, as 'one of the wonders of Britain'.[11] Its population grew at an enormous pace: from a town of 12,000 people in 1703 it had doubled these numbers by 1760, trebled them by 1773 and reached 78,000 by 1801; and long before this, it had built handsome new docks and eclipsed Bristol as the second port in the kingdom.

Among expanding manufacturing centres there was Barcelona, whose population trebled in seventy-five years while that of the Spanish capital city, Madrid, increased by less than 40,000. On a far more modest plane, there was the small Norman textile town of Elbeuf: small but thriving, it was fast becoming the largest wool-producing centre in Normandy. With the rise in the number of woollen workers employed in the city (from 3,000 to 5,000 in 120 years) went a rise in its population from some 4,000 to 6,000 from the beginning of the century to the outbreak of revolution. But even Barcelona's expansion was modest compared with that of some of the new manufacturing cities in Britain. The process had begun long before there could be any talk of an industrial revolution, though the pace naturally quickened as the new technology took root and the new factory-towns began to emerge. Before the end of the century, Britain's industrialisation had given her an urban pattern that was different from any in Europe. In other countries, while the capital headed the list of large cities, it was followed by others that were either centres of local administration, of commerce or industry, or a combination of the three. Thus in France which next to Britain was the most commercial and industrial of European nations, these 'runner-up' cities (all with a population of 50,000 or more) were by the time of the Revolution: Lyons, Marseilles, Bordeaux, Nantes, Lille, Rouen and Toulouse, of which the last two were provincial capitals, while of the rest the ports outnumbered the manufacturing cities. In England, the pattern was quite different: by the end of the century old cities like York and Norwich had fallen out of the race, and following London came Manchester, Liverpool, Birmingham, Bristol and Leeds, that is two ports and three industrial towns. Manchester, the first of the cotton towns, had the most remarkable expansion of the three and followed a course very similar to Liverpool's. A population of 12,500 in 1717 had risen to 20,000 in 1758, and from there it escalated, with the expansion of the cotton industry (as Liverpool's had with the cotton trade), to 84,000 in 1801, thus becoming the second city of Britain.

While most expanding cities grew predominantly under the stimulus of some single factor such as administration, trade, industry or political prestige, there were a few cities, as we noted above, that were multi-functional and whose growth, therefore, cannot be explained in such elementary terms. To a greater or lesser extent, of course, this was true of all capital cities, all of which combined the presence of a court and bureaucracy with a certain minimum of industry (luxury or other) and cultural activities revolving round a theatre, libraries, schools or a university; and all of these could serve as a spur to immigration. But as multi-purpose cities Paris and London stood out from the rest. In the first place because they were bigger: Paris had been for two hundred years the largest city in Europe until it was overtaken by London. The functions that both cities served in relation to the nation at large were in most respects the same. Both were large markets, consuming great quantities of the produce of the surrounding countryside (Defoe speaks of London as 'sucking the vitals of trade in this island to itself'). Both were centres of government, politics, law, entertainment, intellectual life and the fine arts: here, during this century at least, there was not much to choose between them. Paris, like London, was a centre of industry, with growing manufactories and a multiplicity of crafts; though in London manufactures played the larger role. Paris was also, like London, a centre of banking and trade and, in financial affairs, it certainly had the lead over all other cities in France. But in neither of these activities did it approach the eminence of London. The Bank of England was founded in 1694, the Bank of France not until 1800; London was second only to Amsterdam as a centre of credit and finance. Paris was also a large port: in 1798, we are told, no fewer than 9,700 boats loaded and unloaded at its quays, bringing with them cargoes of 500,000 tons of merchandise.[12] But it was not a great international port like Marseilles, Nantes or Bordeaux, still less was it like London, the largest port of them all. More than half of all the ships coming to English ports unloaded their goods in London; and in one single year, 1794–5, more than 14,500 ships (one-quarter of them from overseas) brought with them cargoes totalling 1,800,000 tons, or nearly four times the tonnage handled by Paris. So it was this peculiar combination of roles – as capital city, producer and distributor, money market and as world centre of shipping and trade – that distinguished London from Paris and from every other city in Europe. It was its role as a great port, in particular, that served as a powerful stimulant to immigration: it has been estimated that something like one-quarter of London's working population in 1700 was employed in one or other of the numerous trades associated with the port of London.[13]

So clearly function is of some importance in explaining why some cities grew more rapidly than others. Yet *how* cities grew is a far wider question which cannot be explained in terms of immigration only. The actual size of cities depends on other factors too, such as birth rate and death rate and the presence or absence of such disasters as famines, plagues or wars. In the previous century it appears that such catastrophes were prevalent enough to have served as a serious check on the growth of both the size and the number of large cities. In the eighteenth century, while occasional catastrophes of the kind continued, they were no longer so frequent and appeared generally in a more muted form. This, as we saw in an earlier chapter, was one reason why in the new century the general population of Europe so rapidly increased. But such disasters as remained – notably disease and famine – were more liable to take a heavy toll in cities than in the countryside. London, for example, during a large part of the century, was exposed not only to the ravages of gin but to such killer diseases as typhus and smallpox; this helps of course to explain the gloomy reflections of Richard Price. In Lancashire in the 1750s the death rate in towns was more than twice that in villages; and in every European city the mortality of infants in particular remained notoriously high. In some cities – in Italy, Spain and the Austrian Empire – famine was still a present reality; in others, as in France, food shortage (even if not actual starvation) reduced the chances of survival: a recent study of Strasbourg, for example, has shown how a combination of diseases and poor harvests slowed down the growth of population for nearly fifty years.[14]

After the mid-century, as has often been noted, there was a general improvement; but the improvement was slow, and while the death rate fell and the birth rate rose, there was still generally what has been called an 'endemic' deficit of births. This was more strikingly so in the case of some cities than of others; it was more true, for instance, of German cities and of those along the Baltic coast; less true of Berlin (where the deficit had its ups and downs) and London (where it began to tail off in the 1780s); and least true of Paris, which was the first major city to reverse the trend. So, with a slight, but constant, margin of births over deaths, Paris was the one great city where such a growth of population as there was can be explained largely in terms of a natural increase, with the net effects of immigration playing a negligible role. In all other cities, it was the other way round, as the birth–death factor served as a check rather than as a stimulus to growth, and growth depended largely on the numbers that could be attracted from outside (balanced in turn of course by the numbers that went out). So the really significant figure becomes the net intake of new arrivals, which naturally varied from one city to the next. In the case of mid-century London, Dr Wrigley has estimated that it amounted to 8,000 persons a year, and other evidence suggests that these numbers were maintained, or expanded, during the second half of the century. And who were these new arrivals? In Dr Wrigley's view, they were mainly young provincials, largely composed of 'household servants of both sexes, apprentices and labourers (who) came to London in large numbers, together with girls in trouble, younger sons without local prospects, fugitives from justice, those unable to find work, the restless, and those attracted by the scale and consequence of city life'.[15] A great many of them, as we have noted, settled in the dockside districts. In Paris, too, the docks and central markets proved a focus of attraction. We know, for example, that many of the numerous seasonal workers in the building trades (called *limousins* because of their origins in the Creuse and around Limoges) came to lodge in the rue Mouffetard or city centre and that a large proportion of the city's porters, carriers and riverside workers were recent immigrants from Picardy, Savoy and Auvergne who came to lodge around the markets or close to the docks and wharves along the Seine.[16]

In general, however, we know little about the sort of people who migrated to cities at this time though we may assume that they were mainly peasants, servants and tradesmen from adjoining country districts or market towns. Yet if we know little about the new people who came to the city, we know more about the population they encountered when they arrived. In all cities the inhabitants might typically be divided into three main groups. At the top of the pyramid was the small minority of aristocrats, gentry, patricians, rich merchants, officials and upper clergy; in the middle a larger group of petty merchants, manufacturers, professional people and what the English called 'people of the middling sort'; and, at its base, there was the large and mixed population of small tradesmen, master craftsmen, journeymen, apprentices, labourers, domestic servants and city poor. While this was the general pattern, there were of course infinite variations depending upon the type and size of city, the functions it performed and the social development of the country it was in. Thus a court or garrison town, or an old-fashioned administrative centre, might have a disproportionate number of courtiers, soldiers or officials, and certain Spanish cities might, like Angers in France, have an unusual number of monks and priests. To take a few examples. In Moscow, according to a census made in 1730, there were over 7,000 officials and 15,000 soldiers in a population of 139,000. In Dresden, in 1791, there were 6,600 officials and soldiers in a population of 58,000 and more than 13,000 others dependent in some capacity on the electoral prince. In Berlin as we might expect the proportion of soldiers was higher and of officials not much less: a count taken in 1783 revealed that in a population of 141,000, the garrison (with families) accounted for 33,000, officials (also with families) for 14,000 and attendants on courtiers and officials for another 10,000; so that rather more than one-third of the inhabitants were dependent on the king. In Vienna, soldiers and officials were not so much in evidence, but courtiers and their attendants were: here, in 1795, there were 3,253 members of the aristocracy, 6,000 lackeys and 34,000 other personal servants in a population of 260,000.[17] In all such cities, whether in eastern or central or southern Europe, there was always a merchant class of some importance; but the industrial bourgeoisie was either non-existent or played a negligible role. In sharp contrast to these, the small industrial town of Elbeuf in Normandy had virtually no aristocracy at all: only one substantial nobleman had an estate there at the time of the Revolution, and of the hundred most highly taxed owners of property nearly all were from the merchant or manufacturing middle class.[18] Elbeuf was, of course, a rare exception and would have been so even in England at this time. Far more typical of France was the situation in cities like Orleans and Toulouse. In both cases, the aristocracy and their families formed a tiny fraction of the urban population: under one and a half per cent at Orleans and a bare one per cent at Toulouse; but they dominated local affairs and owned one-quarter of the properties in the first and forty-four per cent of the land attaching to the second.[19]

More subtle variations were to be found between the social make-up of London and Paris. In both cities, a wealthy nobility lived within easy reach of the court; in both a wealthy upper clergy ranked with the nobility; and in both a lesser provincial nobility (in England, the gentry) paid occasional visits to the capital. Yet the differences were equally apparent. For one thing the English aristocracy (and gentry) played an active part in political affairs, whereas in France they were virtually forbidden to do so. But as a kind of compensation, the Parisian nobility (and not only those at the top) lived in more magnificent style and occupied far more splendid town establishments than their opposite numbers in London: the Georgian terrace house was no match for the aristocratic *hôtel* of the Faubourg St Germain or the Faubourg St Honoré, a difference that did not escape the notice of visitors to London. A more important difference was the part played in Paris by the privileged legal caste known as the *noblesse de robe*; they numbered some 1,500 to 2,000 persons who, through purchase or inheritance, held the main administrative, financial and judicial offices in the capital or at Versailles, and had no equivalent in London. There were equally significant differences among the class that Defoe termed 'the rich', between the tax-farmers, or Farmers-General, and the *gens de finance* in

Paris and the bankers and larger merchants of the City of London; some of these will emerge, no doubt, from our discussion of European society in the coming chapter. Again, there were differences in the wealth and status of the 'middling' group of small merchants, manufacturers and shopkeepers in London; such people were, in general, more numerous, more prosperous, and enjoyed a higher social status than they did in Paris. The shops in London, particularly those in the City of Westminster, were more brightly lit, were better installed and carried more elegant displays. 'The magnificence of the shops,' wrote Archenholtz, an observant German visitor in 1789, 'is the most striking thing in London; they sometimes extend without interruption for an English mile ... The largest shops of the kind [he is speaking of jewellers' and silversmiths' shops] in Paris, in the Rue St Honoré, are mean compared to those in London.'[20]

But at the bottom of the social pyramid differences were not so pronounced; and as between one city and another there appears to have been a greater degree of uniformity among the great mass of the urban population, those whom Englishmen termed the 'lower orders' or 'the Mob', Frenchmen the *menu peuple* and Italians the *populo minuto* or *popolino*. In manufacturing centres, like Elbeuf, Manchester or Liège, the wage-earners were beginning to detach themselves as a separate social group; but these were as yet the exception and in no city at this time – not even in Manchester – can one speak of a distinctive working-class population, in the nineteenth-century sense, with its own distinctive manner of living, dress, entertainments, speech, culture, lodgings or residential districts. The common people of the cities, in fact, were a mixed population, including small workshop masters and shopkeepers as well as employed craftsmen, servants and 'labouring poor'. These groups, though occasionally divided by conflicting interest, lived cheek by jowl in the same districts, used the same speech and wore the same dress, and had most interests in common. In Moscow, Peter the Great's mania for organisation – and for raising taxes – prompted him to make provision, within his *possady* (communities of trades and crafts), for the segregation of master craftsmen from common labourers or workers; but in practice, they all lived together in the same common suburb outside the walls of the Kremlin. In both Paris and London, it was common for small employers and workmen to live on different floors of the same building; while in the workshop, where master and journeyman worked side by side, the journeyman often lived under his master's roof, ate at his table and even married his widow or daughter. Such intimacies, it is true, were dying out in cities like Paris, as the journeyman's chance of ever becoming a master or of setting up his own shop was wearing thin; and a sign of the times was the growing number of journeymen's strikes and 'combinations'. But though the issue of wages might divide them there were still overriding issues that bound the small master and journeyman together. One was a common concern for the 'state of trade': even in London we find master weavers and their journeymen marching together to Parliament, as on a number of occasions in the 1760s and 1770s. A matter of even greater common concern was the need to provide the shops and markets with cheap and adequate supplies of food, particularly of bread, which was the staple diet and the largest item in the poor man's budget. It was this common interest in the price and supply of bread which, more than any other, held the small shopkeepers and employers and their wage-earners together and made them, on occasion, when harvests were bad, markets were poorly stocked and prices rose, unite in common protest against wholesalers, merchants and city authorities. At moments of tension such protest exploded into the food riots that we shall be considering in a later chapter.

In every city, on the fringe of this working or labouring population, there was also a large sub-group whom the more respectable workers and tradesmen tended to despise and reject. These were the destitute, the beggars, the homeless, the vagrants, the *gens sans aveu* and the casually employed, who floated in and out of jobs, *dépôts de mendicité*, *hôpitaux*, doss-houses and prisons – those whom Defoe placed below 'the poor' in his social categories and called 'the miserable' and whom Patrick Colquhoun, with his police magistrate's prejudice, lumped together under the common heading of 'criminal elements'. (Some historians have been equally misguided in closely identifying what they call the 'dangerous classes' with the labouring population as a whole.) In all cities these elements were a matter of constant concern to the police and public authorities, whether they appeared in the guise of the beggars of Naples, Rome and Madrid, of the peasant vagrants and vagabonds who flocked into the Paris *faubourgs* and Belgian cities, or of the more wretched of the denizens of St Giles's, Field Lane or East Smithfield, in London. How many were there? It might be as much as a quarter or a fifth of the urban population. In Belgian cities in the 1770s, it appears that about one-quarter of the inhabitants were on poor relief, and an enquiry of 1790 found that the same was true of Toulouse. In Strasbourg, a census of 1784 counted over 9,000 'poor' in a population of 50,000. In Paris, figures published over a twenty-year period between the 1770s and the 1790s suggest that about one-sixth of the population were constantly in receipt of public charity; and, according to the estimates of Colquhoun, the proportion in London was probably as high.

How were cities governed? Again, there were considerable variations but, broadly, municipal government was of half-a-dozen types. In the first place there was the sort of control-from-above as practised within the Ottoman Empire, where cities were entirely subordinated to the sultan's will and had no separate status or identity at all. At the other extreme were the old German free cities and Italian city-states, which continued to enjoy a large degree of autonomy in their relations with the central authority. Then there were certain emerging industrial cities which had been too small in the past to have been given a charter and had still not been granted municipal status: such as Manchester, for example, which Defoe called 'the greatest meer village in England'. More commonly, cities had had a medieval past from which they had acquired certain charters and 'liberties' which still survived in some form. In some cases, royal absolutism had whittled these down to the point where government rested largely in the hands of the emperor or king. Paris, for instance, was still 'la bonne ville', the brightest jewel of the king of France. He governed it despotically and centrally through his Intendants, lieutenants and officials, either from Versailles or from the Châtelet in Paris; yet the old medieval city authorities still survived in the small oligarchy of wealthy citizens – the self-perpetuating *échevins* and *prévôts* – who continued to exercise a limited authority from their Hôtel de Ville. More often, the ruling oligarchies had a greater degree of freedom and retained some semblance of the old authority of the craft and merchant gilds on which they were commonly based; this was usually the case in France and Germany and nominally at least in Moscow. In Strasbourg, for example, the twenty gilds each elected fifteen members of the Council of Three Hundred and a member of the governing Senate. In Toulouse, where government was predominantly aristocratic, the main levers of control were held by eight ennobled magistrates known as *capitouls*, who were aided by a Political Council of forty-two, equally divided between nobles, former *capitouls* and bourgeois 'notables'. Oligarchies in fact, whether aristocratic or wealthy bourgeois, were the order of the day; and this applied as much to the cities of France and Spain as it did to the Scottish 'royal burghs' and 'burghs of barony', to English 'corporation' boroughs and to the self-appointing or hereditary administrations of Berne and Geneva, Amsterdam, Strasbourg and Frankfurt.

Generally, more democratic forms were reserved for the lower organs of municipal administration, such as the vestries in England and some of the villages and smaller cantons in Switzerland. The City of London (though not London as a whole) was once more the great exception. With their two governing and elective Courts, the Court of Aldermen and the Court of Common Council, and their twenty-six (or twenty-eight) wards, the City's 12,000 freemen formed what has been aptly called a 'ratepayers' democracy'. Assembled within their wards or Common Hall, they returned the City's four Members of Parliament and conducted the bulk of the City's municipal affairs. The majority of Common Councilmen, who shared with the aldermen (generally merchants of substance) the direction of business, were tradesmen and craftsmen, whose influence increased as the century went on; for, with the growing volume and complexity of municipal affairs, the aldermen were compelled to transfer more and more business to the Court of Common Council.

There were three matters that, above all others, concerned the governors of cities in the eighteenth century: the treatment of the poor, the assurance of law and order, and the embellishment and improvement of the city's services and physical appearance. The treatment of the poor was a somewhat summary affair: keeping them off the streets (if beggars) and returning them (if outsiders) to their parishes of birth; seeing that they were supplied with cheap bread; raising rates or taxes for their maintenance; and putting them away when old or feeble or unable to work, in workhouses, *hospices* or *dépôts de mendicité*. The question of law and order was less easy to solve, partly because any extension of authority was bound to encroach on traditional 'liberties'. But all cities were liable to food riots or (worse) the sort of violent disorders that London experienced in the Gordon Riots in 1780. So property-owners, whether aristocratic or bourgeois, were inclined, after some prompting or some experience of rioting, to close their ranks and subscribe to a more effective police system than that so often inherited from a medieval past. London's police system was notoriously defective: it rested largely on the Watch and Ward, a medieval body recruited in the parishes, and the ability (or willingness) of magistrates to summon troops in cases of emergency. In the 1770s, on the eve of the Gordon Riots, the metropolis had a combined force of some 1,000 peace officers and 3,000 watchmen and patrolmen, with about 4,000 troops available at the magistrates' summons. Paris was more liberally provided, having at this time some 7,000 police officers and soldiers, with a reserve force of 5,000 to 6,000 Swiss troops and Gardes-Françaises. Here, unlike London, there was a single central direction vested in the lieutenant of police whose office had been created by a law of 1699. In the course of the century, a similar pattern was to be followed (sometimes in theory rather than in practice) in all other cities in France.

More durable in its results no doubt was the concern of governments and city authorities of the day for urban development and improvement. Despots, whether enlightened or not, were not tight-fisted when it came to erecting for posterity monuments to their glory, their achievements, or to their sense of luxury or good taste. (In this respect, however, Frederick the Great's father, Frederick William I, was a notable exception.) Among the more lavish of these monuments were the Peterhof and Imperial Palace at St Petersburg; the Palace of Schönbrunn at Vienna; Frederick II's palace of *Sans-Souci* at Potsdam (the

67

last two modelled on Louis XIV's palace of Versailles); the Nymphenburg at Schleissheim in Bavaria; and the numerous *places royales* constructed for the rulers of France: as at Nancy, Rennes and Rheims. It was the time of the Royal Arcade at Bath and the Unter den Linden and Charlottenburg at Berlin; the time, too, when the great ports of Nantes, Bordeaux and Liverpool were being developed and embellished with their new broad avenues, gardens and public buildings that so delighted Arthur Young. Paris was a late starter and only matched the incessant activity of Louis XIV's day after the middle of the century. After that, little time was lost; and, in 1788, Sébastien Mercier noted that, in the last thirty years, one-third of Paris had been rebuilt and 10,000 houses had been erected. It was during these years that the Duke of Orleans laid out his magnificent gardens and arcades at the Palais Royal, that the streets about the Champs Elysées were planned and constructed and the Théâtre Italien, the Théâtre Français (later the Odéon) and the Opéra were built, the last in the remarkable time of seventy-five days. In London, building and improvement had gone on intermittently throughout the century, only interrupted by wars. Here it was the age of the Georgian square, the planned parish of St Marylebone and the New Road, and the terrace houses, built in the fashionable neo-classical style by Robert and James Adam. Late-century visitors noted, however, that the main developments had, as in Paris, been in the west and not in the east. Archenholtz, in recording his impressions, observed that 'the contrast between this [the east end] and the west end is astonishing: the houses are mostly new and elegant; the squares are superb, the streets straight and open . . . If all London were as well built, there would be nothing in the world to compare with it.' He also observed that after the Westminster Paving Act of 1762 and other Acts for London's greater improvement the City had finer pavements, street-lighting and sanitation than any other in Europe.[21]

There was of course another side to it; the German visitor had touched on it lightly when he showed how the fashionable west had been developed and the plebeian east neglected; and this was as true of every other city in Europe. With all its improvements, London still retained its verminous 'rookeries', its slums and alleys, its filthy and overcrowded prisons and its barbarous treatment of the poor. Paris, with its insalubrious riverside districts, its overcrowded tenements and *maisons garnies*, was certainly no better; and in Paris, the poor were exposed to lower wages and to more frequent shortage of food. Rome, Madrid, Naples and Moscow had the reputation of being far worse. Whatever image the eighteenth century has projected, it has never been that of an age of the common man.

CHAPTER 5

SOCIETY AND ARISTOCRACY

Eighteenth-century society tended, even more than the city, to be 'aristocratic'. This means that in most countries in Europe an aristocracy of birth, wealth or legal status was able to exercise a disproportionate influence over the lives of their fellow men, either as governors and magistrates, as manorial lords, as monopolists of high office in army, church and state, or merely in their way of life or their opportunities for cultural attainment and foreign travel. This was the class that a French *philosophe*, the Abbé Raynal, had in mind when he wrote in 1770 that 'in all states of Europe, there are a sort of men who assume from their infancy a pre-eminence independent of their moral character'. Broadly, this applied to both East and West, to countries of absolute and limited monarchy, to aristocratic cities like Venice and Berne and even, if we stretch the meaning of the term 'aristocratic' a little, to the merchant-cities of Frankfurt, Zürich and Amsterdam. It is, of course, no paradox to add that it applied less to states in which the ruler's power was absolute or despotic than where it was circumscribed, and least of all to an eastern-style despotism like the Ottoman Empire, where the sultan's word alone was law and where in theory at least there could be no intermediate authority between him and the nation at large and where even the royal favourite, the grand vizier himself, found that such fame and fortune as he possessed were strictly tied to his tenure of office. Elsewhere, what bound this international brotherhood together was the twin exercise of privilege and wealth; but while the degree of privilege varied greatly from one country to the next, it was wealth and style of living that served increasingly as a common denominator and had become the hall-mark that linked the English landed magnate with the French *grand seigneur* and the Spanish grandee. In England the great landlords forming the aristocracy were few in number. There were perhaps 400 of them with noble titles and with incomes of £10,000 and above; while a handful – such as the Dukes of Bedford, Bridgwater and Northumberland and the Marquess of Rockingham – had rent-rolls that ranged from £10,000 to £30,000 a year. For, as with other aristocracies, the prime source of wealth was land; and these families owned between them one-fifth of the cultivable land of England. Some, however, like the Duke of Bedford, drew a large part of their fortune from real estate (in his case, a yearly £8,000 in the 1770s); others from financial speculation or trade: in 1762, the value of a Secretaryship of State was reckoned to be £8,000 or £9,000 a year. The centre of ostentatious living was the aristocrat's county seat. The Duke of Devonshire spent £40,000 on extensions to his property at Chatsworth, and the Marquess of Rockingham spent over £180,000 on his two properties at Wentworth Woodhouse and Audley End, the first of which claimed to be the largest private home in Britain. Another great house was Sir Robert Walpole's at Houghton, of which Lord Hervey wrote in 1731 that 'a little snug party' of thirty would sit down to dinner, including 'Lords Spiritual and Temporal, besides commoners, parsons and freeholders innumerable'.[1]

No other aristocracy was as rich as the English, but aristocratic entertainment was probably more lavish in France. This was particularly true of the capital cities; for even the splendours offered to their guests by the Duke of Richmond at Richmond House and the Prince of Wales at Leicester or Carlton House could not match the magnificence displayed at the princely mansions of the Duke of Orleans at the Palais Royal or by Monsieur (the king's eldest brother) at the Luxembourg Palace. Moreover, to live at the court of Versailles was, for the aristocrat, both an expensive and a lucrative business: a colonelcy in the Dragoons might cost him 120,000 livres (roughly £12,000); but the Duchesse de Polignac, a favourite of the queen, received 800,000 livres in the 1780s as a dowry for her daughter and a further 400,000 livres to pay off her debts. In Spain, a few thousand of the half-million who claimed to own deeds of nobility were men of great wealth. These were the *grandes* and *títulos* who reaped enormous fortunes from their *señorios* and *mayorazgos* – men like the Conde de Altamira, who owned a thriving commercial city in Valencia, and the three dukes who (according to Joseph Townsend) shared between them the greater part of Andalusia and Catalonia. Properties in Hungary were almost as large. Count Louis Batthyány left an estate valued at nine million florins; Prince Esterházy's income was over 700,000 florins, and Count Czobor's a million (yet he landed in debt). In Bohemia, a hundred noble families held between them one-third of all the cultivated land; among them, to own a mere thirty villages was considered a matter of slight account. In Belgium the Duke of Arenberg had an income of 732,000 francs, which was eighteen times that of the richest member of the merchant class. In Poland the Grand-Hetman Branicki had a palace at Byalystock of such splendour that it was called the Polish Versailles, and Prince Karl Radziwill and Prince Felix Potocki kept over 10,000 retainers apiece. A great Russian nobleman, as we have seen, counted his wealth in terms of serfs rather than acres. Among the great Catherine's favourites, Prince Potemkin was rewarded with nine million roubles and 37,000 serfs, and Alexis and Gregory Orlov with seventeen million roubles and 40,000 serfs. No wonder that William Coxe, who dined at Alexis Orlov's table when he came to Moscow, was able to commend his 'true style of Russian hospitality', laced with an abundance of assiduous attendants. He noted too that the great Russian nobles had 'stupendous piles of building' within and out of Moscow and that on their country estates 'they reside as independent princes, like the feudal barons in early times, have their separate courts of justice and govern their vassals with almost unlimited sway'.[2]

But of course such fortunes and style of living were only confined to a few: they were certainly not typical of the mass of the nobility, whose wealth, social status and importance were far inferior to the few hundred grandees or magnates who sat at the top. In Spain, grandees like the Dukes of Osuna, Alba and Medina Coeli, owners of vast *señorios* in Andalusia and Catalonia, towered above the humbler *caballeros*, and all the more above the mass of impoverished rural gentry, or *hidalgos*, who formed by far the greater part of a nobility that, by the end of the century, accounted for one in twenty of the population. The poor *hidalgo*, of whom it was said that he 'ate black bread under the genealogical tree', had a number of privileges that set him aside from the rest of the community: he could not be arrested for debt or be forced to quarter soldiers, he had the right to display his coat of arms and, like Don Quixote, be addressed as 'Don'; but he was debarred from practising trade and generally counted for rather little. Similar differences could be found in France, where the 4,000 court aristocrats, owners of large estates and incumbents of bishoprics and high army posts, looked contemptuously on the far greater number of provincial *hobereaux*, who, bereft of capital and vigorous outlets for their energies, had often little more to cling to than memories of past grandeur, their names, titles and cherished immunity from paying taxes. Having such memories, the small country nobleman was inclined to be the most conservative of the nobility and the most tenacious in clinging to such old ways as still survived: among them the *seigneur*'s duty to stay on his land and look after his tenants instead of seeking the pleasures of the capital. One such country nobleman (though a little more than a mere *hobereau*) was the elder Mirabeau, who laments the fact that 'the seigneur no longer does anything for the inhabitants'; so it follows, he adds, that 'when nobody knows the seigneur of his domain any more, everybody will rob him – and that is as it should be'.[3]

In Poland, a similar chasm divided the rich aristocrats from the small country gentry, who formed the bulk of the *szlachta*, a petty nobility over a million strong, far more numerous even than the *hidalgos* in Spain. The *szlachta* had the right to vote in the local diet, they could claim all the legal privileges of nobility, and they might lord it over what peasants they possessed, exercise their right to wear distinctive clothing and to occupy a reserved seat in the village church; but their poverty exposed them to ignominious dependence on the dozen or so really great magnates who effectively ruled the country – the Radziwills, Czartoryskis or Potockis. The case was similar in Russia and the Austrian dominions. In Bohemia remnants of a once-proud gentry, the knights, had been reduced to a position of subservience to the great ruling families, while their numbers had declined from 1,128 families in 1648 to a mere 238 a hundred years later. Meanwhile in Hungary owners of great estates like the Esterházys and Palffys, and in Russia the Cherkasskiis, Galitzines and Dolgoroukis claimed a social pre-eminence, in fact if not always in name, over a horde of proud, though poor and semiliterate, rural gentry.

In some countries, the distinctions, though genuine enough, were of a somewhat different kind. In Venice, for example, there was the growing contrast, in wealth if not in status, between the impoverished ancient families, or Barnabotti, and the jumped-up men of wealth who had more recently acquired titles of nobility by having their names inscribed in the Golden Book. In Lombardy the division was not between two groups but (as in Spain and France) between three. In the first place, there was an old feudal nobility that prided itself on being a vassal of the Holy Roman Emperor; secondly, there were the more recently ennobled patricians of Milan who counted as their equals; and thirdly, the most recent of all, whose title of nobility went back no further than to the age of Spanish domination of the past two hundred years; these last were considered on an altogether lower plane. And finally, there was the landowning class of Britain, this time divided not only by wealth but by legal distinction as well. For, in Britain, the gentry, who corresponded to the lesser or rural nobility of other countries, were not an aristocracy at all: they were the traditional Knights of the Shire, who since time almost immemorial had sent their representatives to sit in the House of Commons. For practical purposes they may be divided into three: the 700 or 800 wealthy gentry (usually knights or baronets) who carried influence in the county and rubbed shoulders with the aristocracy; the 3,000 or 4,000 squires; and the far more numerous 'gentlemen' whose standards were no higher than those of the middling tenant farmers. According to Dr Mingay's calculations, the top gentry could expect towards the end of the century to earn around £3,000 to £4,000 a year, the squires from £1,000 to £3,000 and the mere gentlemen £300 to £1,000 compared with the £10,000 or more of the heads of noble families.[4]

Britain was also distinctive (a distinction shared, in this case, with the Dutch) in that its aristocracy, having had a revolution, enjoyed no more than the barest remnants of older legal privileges and immunities. A nobleman might still claim to be tried by his 'peers' and (if not an Irish peer or an unfavoured Scottish one) he could sit in the House of Lords; but otherwise peer and commoner were equal before the law and had equal access to public office and an equal right to hold property in land, commerce and manufacture. It was the peer's eldest son who inherited the estate and the title; all other sons were classed as commoners and, in consequence, had no distinctive privileges at all. Thus in England social classification was, more decidedly than elsewhere, becoming increasingly determined by wealth alone and the power and prestige that wealth could bring. In other countries the aristocracy enjoyed legal privileges – rights of jurisdiction, right to extract obligations from their peasants and immunity from varying types of taxation and other burdens that were part of the ordinary citizen's lot. In return for these favours, the aristocracy had originally been called upon to serve on the king's council or to lead his armies in the field; but, with the few exceptions we shall note, these old responsibilities had by now fallen into general disuse.

The status and privileges of the aristocracy naturally varied from state to state; and, once more, the rough dividing line lay between East and West (though Scandinavia proves to be an awkward exception). In France, the *noblesse* formed less of a closed caste than it did in eastern and northern Europe: it was not registered as a corporate body; and while a nobleman could lose his privileges and title (*dérogeance*) if he engaged in 'ignoble' or manual trades, he was not debarred (like Spaniards, Poles and Hungarians) from taking part in more respectable – and lucrative – ventures such as overseas trades or mining, or from membership of the more prestigious of the Paris gilds. Besides, by a reverse process of infiltration, access to the nobility still remained open to wealthy commoners – though to shrinking numbers, as we shall see – by the purchase of expensive hereditary offices. Thus, from the seventeenth century, a new and wealthy administrative nobility, the *noblesse de robe*, had grown up to challenge the social status and pretensions of the old-established *noblesse d'épée* ('nobility of the sword'): by this time, it provided most of the Secretaries of State and Intendants and, even more significant for future developments, it dominated the Parlements – the great hereditary legal corporations that, in times of weak and divided government and idle or incompetent rulers, were able to exercise considerable political authority by refusing to register the government's edicts. Such authority was denied to all but a few of the older nobility, but as owners of estates they still exercised many of the privileges of the old feudal lord of the manor: rights of local justice and

73

village surveillance; rights of monopoly, such as the exclusive right to hunt and to maintain a mill, an oven or a wine-press (*banalités*); and above all the right to exact a wide range of feudal dues, rents and services from their peasants. In addition, members of the French nobility as a whole enjoyed a considerable degree of exemption from direct taxation. They were virtually immune from payment of the principal and most onerous of these taxes, the *taille* (levied on both estimated income and on land); and in large measure too they evaded payment of their proper share of the *vingtième* and *capitation*, introduced to supplement the *taille* at the end of Louis xiv's reign, taxes to which both nobles and commoners were nominally subject. Members of the clergy, whose upper ranks belonged almost without exception to the *noblesse*, enjoyed even greater privileges: in addition to the income derived as landowners from rents and feudal dues, they drew tithe (which might amount to one-twelfth of the yield of land) and discharged their obligations to the exchequer by the payment of a relatively small percentage of their income in the form of a *don gratuit* or voluntary gift.

The pattern in other western continental countries with a hereditary nobility was similar, although not identical. In Spain, the aristocracy enjoyed tax-exemption and, as in France, land-ownership went with a bewildering complexity of feudal dues and obligations. But here seigneurial jurisdiction was far more extensive and oppressive than in France, and landlords dominated the villages and towns as mayors, councillors and judges either in person or through their appointed nominees. In Italy there were sharp contrasts: in Lombardy feudalism on the land had virtually disappeared, whereas in Naples there were landowners who enjoyed an almost medieval independence, and four out of five Neapolitans were said to live under feudal jurisdiction. In Belgium the nobles still retained important privileges and old feudal property rights: they paid only a minimum of taxes, they had special representation on the provincial estates, nominated judges and magistrates in local law courts and levied a wide range of dues and obligations on their tenants. German nobles had these and other privileges besides: they were exempt from billeting troops, had the right of presentment to livings in the church and held a monopoly of all the chief offices of state. Moreover, the German nobility, being scattered over such a confused variety of princely states, came to attach an inordinate importance to precise formula, precedence and ceremonial; Voltaire recorded the fact in a hilarious passage in *Candide*.

Outside western Europe, the exemptions and privileges of aristocracy tended to be more clear-cut and less hedged about with reservations, and the gulf separating nobles and commoners to be more sharply defined. In Poland, the *szlachta* claimed virtual immunity from arrest and, until 1768, retained powers of life and death over their serfs. In Hungary, none but nobles could own land and administer local justice and, after 1741, they enjoyed complete immunity from paying taxes. In Sweden, the great titled magnates (a small minority among a large host of lesser nobility) formed a closed caste, which, for fifty years after the aristocratic constitution of 1720, was able to impose severe restrictions on the king's right to enlarge their ranks by ennobling commoners. In other countries in eastern Europe, while the rights and privileges of the aristocracy were closely defined, they were never in a position to dictate such terms as the Swedes and the Poles. This was the case in Russia and Prussia, countries whose autocratic rulers in the course of the century largely re-cast and re-defined the functions and privileges of their aristocracies. In Prussia, under Frederick William I and his son Frederick II, the nobles were transformed into a class of hereditary state servants, obliged to serve the monarch by holding office in the army or the administration; as compensation they were given, as we noted in an earlier chapter, extended powers of jurisdiction and economic control over their tenants and peasants. In Russia Peter the Great went further and devised a strict Table of Ranks, the higher grades in which were reserved for the landowning class which, in return for a stated period of compulsory service to the tsar, was granted a highly privileged hereditary status and increased authority over their serfs. So here, at least, there was some semblance of a return to the old medieval tradition of an aristocracy with defined duties as well as rights. However, Peter's strict provisions were relaxed by his successors. Under Anna and Elizabeth, the aristocracy was able to regain a degree of its former independence; and, in 1763, Peter III freed the greater nobles from the legal obligation to serve the state. A new compromise was arrived at under Catherine the Great whereby, in return for service, rights and privileges were made more secure; and by the Charter of Nobility of 1785, the Russian *dvoryanstvo* was given the status of a privileged ruling class somewhat similar to that of the French *noblesse*.

In some countries the social pre-eminence of the aristocracy was matched by the authority and responsibility it exercised in the nation's political life; in others this was not the case at all. On the one hand, there were countries like Prussia, where state service by the aristocracy was not only enforced but had come to be considered a mark of distinction; or Russia, where the tradition of state service, though not universally obligatory, lingered on. On the other hand, there were states like France, Spain, The Two Sicilies, Denmark and many of the smaller German principalities, in which the aristocracy, while retaining its privileges and dancing attendance at court, had ceased to play an effective part in political affairs. In Italy, the aristocracy was more generally involved than not: in Lombardy, for example, the Patricians

75

dominated the magistracies and local estates in Milan until Joseph II, the reforming emperor, restricted their activities in 1786. The self-governing city of Berne, in Switzerland, was ruled by a small hereditary aristocracy of 250 families who divided the control of the state between them. In Hungary, the greater nobles filled the highest offices of the church and administration and held control of the national assembly; even the poorer members of the gentry, whose representatives sat in the lower chamber of the assembly, administered justice and raised taxes in their districts. The Polish and Swedish aristocracy enjoyed for a large part of the century something like a golden age. The Polish nobles controlled the diets and the government's policies besides appointing tax-collectors and church dignitaries and running local government. In Sweden, the noble heads of families for fifty years held the whip-hand in the diets and the secret committee of the four estates, and occupied every seat in the Royal Council. As we shall see, there was in both countries a revolution 'from above' and a reassertion of royal authority in 1772; but, in Poland, the diets continued to form a sort of 'democracy' of nobles and country gentlemen and, in Sweden, it was not until 1809 that public office was thrown open to members of the non-privileged estates.

In such matters, the position of the British landowning classes was closer to that of the Swedish than to that of any other continental aristocracy. They certainly enjoyed no legal or prescriptive right to monopolise high office and their victory over monarchy in 1689 had been far less than that of the Swedes in 1720. But, while sharing power with the crown, they continued to exercise a remarkable degree of effective influence, in both Houses of Parliament and in local administration. The House of Lords still retained in its own right, as a legislative and judicial body, a measure of authority that was almost equal to that of the Commons. In addition, it could immeasurably supplement these powers by its near-monopoly of cabinet posts, its family connections and its ownership of 'pocket' and 'rotten' boroughs. As Lords Lieutenant of the counties and justices of the peace, landowners and gentry enjoyed virtually complete authority in local government. It is true that the situation was never quite the same after George III's accession to the throne in 1760. Then, by a strange combination of circumstances which we shall explore more thoroughly in a later chapter, the intervention of the royal authority on the one hand and middle-class radicalism based in the City of London on the other served for a while to weaken the aristocratic element in the constitution; and the return of William Pitt in the election of 1784, with both royal and radical support, was in this sense a defeat for aristocracy. Yet nothing fundamental was changed: in 1783, when Pitt first became Chief Minister, he was still the only member of the Cabinet who did not have a seat in the Lords;

and it was not until after the Reform Act of 1832 that the English aristocracy began to lose its overwhelming ascendancy in both government and Parliament.

But society remained aristocratic in other ways as well. It was not only the direct impact of titled landowning classes that made it so, but its ability during the greater part of the century to absorb and impose its image on other up-and-coming groups. This, in the days before an industrial revolution, meant the class of bankers and merchants who, enriched by trade and financial operations, were a notable feature of the times and, in great trading countries of the West in particular, were rapidly gaining both wealth and social distinction. But far from offering a resolute challenge to aristocratic society, their greatest ambition was to climb into it, or at least to come to terms with it as junior partners in a profitable enterprise. This absorption of the moneyed class might happen in a variety of ways: by merchants marrying their daughters to sons of the nobility, by the purchase of public office or estates, by the acquisition of titles and distinctions or by creating their own exclusive patriciates in municipal government, merchant gilds or administration. In some countries, where towns were few and merchants formed an insignificant minority, the process had not gone very far. Russia was such a case. Here, in spite of Peter's strenuous efforts to increase his revenue by creating a privileged merchant class, little progress had been made, and until Catherine II's day, few of these merchants were to be found outside the great trading cities of Moscow, St Petersburg, Tver and Astrakhan. But even so, there were exceptional cases like the Demidovs who, as we have seen, were not without favour at court. Equally exceptionally, it was possible in a country like Hungary, which was notoriously short of both cities and merchants, for a handful of merchants such as the Henschels and the Hallers to acquire title deeds of nobility. In Prussia, the rising middle class was a far greater social reality than it was in Hungary or Russia; but even though titles could not be so easily acquired, merchants could satisfy their social ambitions by serving the king in a rapidly expanding and privileged state bureaucracy. Other opportunities were available in the more developed commercial communities of western Germany, Switzerland and Holland. The great trading cities of Germany – Hamburg, Leipzig and Frankfurt-am-Main – and Basel and Zürich in Switzerland had long established native patriciates of merchants, which, with growing prosperity, had become more proudly exclusive and more jealous of their social distinctions and inherited privileges. The same was true of the United Provinces, where a wealthy patriciate of merchants (the Regents) governed the great cities of the province of Holland, dominated its provincial estates and sent representatives to the Estates General to sit alongside those of an older, but poorer, aristocracy of the land.

While these Dutch patricians were staunch republicans and would tolerate no encroachments from the Stadholder and his landowning supporters, they were equally unwilling to surrender any of their privileges in favour of a wider urban democracy.

In France and England the merchant class was more developed than anywhere outside Holland, and its social impact took other forms. In France, Louis xiv's wars had created a fertile breeding-ground for contractors, bankers and financiers. As a counter-weight to aristocracy it had been the royal policy to draw into the service of the state the sons of men enriched by trade and finance (Colbert is an obvious example), so much so that Saint-Simon, an aristocratic critic, contemptuously dismissed the period as '*un règne de vile bourgeoisie*'. Monsieur Jourdain, in Molière's *Le bourgeois gentilhomme*, had married his daughter to a marquis; and the practice continued with greater frequency in the century that followed. It was one way for the merchants to climb, if only on unequal terms, into aristocratic society, while for the aristocrat it had the compensation of paying off his debts. In this way, a mid-century observer wrote, 'there are few fortunes that do not find their way into the distinguished families . . . without the commerce which has grown up between pride and necessity most of the noble houses would fall into misery and in consequence into obscurity'.[5] Others, financiers like the four Pâris brothers, Laborde and Samuel Bernard, who were bankers to the court and founders of commercial empires, might take a more independent line by 'living nobly' on their own account and snap their fingers at the common run of courtiers. In the eighteenth century, rich bourgeois built mansions and bought estates (Laborde alone owned a dozen) and, by setting up as lords of the manor, enjoyed the full exercise of seigneurial rights attaching to their properties; and it was Jaurès' view that the feverish re-building of Paris on the eve of the Revolution was due even more to bourgeois than to aristocratic enterprise. A select few became Farmers-General and made great fortunes by 'farming' the royal taxes and administering the internal customs. More commonly, rich bourgeois preferred, rather than plough their profits back into trade and industry, to invest them in the purchase, either for themselves or their heirs, of one of the numerous offices that might fall vacant, or be newly created, in the judiciary, the central administration or the government of a chartered town. In Tocqueville's words, 'no sooner did he [the middle-class Frenchman] find himself in possession of a small capital sum than he expended it in buying an official post instead of investing it in business'.[6] It might be an expensive pastime: towards the end of the *ancien régime*, the office of secretary of the king was rated at 150,000 livres (£15,000) and the office of *président à mortier* of the Parlement of Toulouse at 120,000. But such investments yielded a rich return both in the financial emoluments and in the social distinction, or even the title, that they might bring in their train. It was a good investment for the state as well: not only did it bring in revenue, but it also assured it for many years of the loyalty of the wealthy commercial class. For as long as the state remained solvent enough to pay the interest on its loans and such channels of social advancement remained open, the French merchant and financial class could be relied upon to be among the staunchest defenders of the throne and of the aristocratic society on which it rested. When the state went bankrupt, however, and when such avenues appeared closed, it was a different story, as we shall see in a later chapter.

In England these classes had achieved a greater degree of social independence and authority in their own right. Enriched by the commercial and colonial expansion and wars of the Commonwealth and Restoration, they had been the allies of aristocracy and gentry in carrying through the 'glorious revolution' of 1688. They had founded the Bank of England to identify their own interest more closely with that of the crown and had been the most loyal supporters of war against Louis XIV. Nowhere was aristocracy itself so closely linked with the merchant class: merchants sat in the Commons, alongside the gentry, as Knights of the Shire; dukes and marquises married their sons to daughters and grand-daughters of London merchants and bankers; and the big landowners themselves were deeply engaged in trade and invested their capital in docks, mines and real estate. Defoe spoke no more than the truth when he wrote in 1726 that 'our merchants are princes, greater and richer, and more powerful than some sovereign Princes', and contrasted the 'immense wealth' of men enriched 'behind the counter' with the declining fortunes of the gentry and many 'ancient families'.[7] Walpole could generally count on the support of the great London merchants, sated with trade and honours, in 'letting sleeping dogs lie' in the 1720s and 1730s; and, even when a few years later London turned to opposing the government, the great bankers and directors of insurance offices and trading companies continued to support the policies of court and administration. Here then, as in France, the 'moneyed interest' remained, for the greater part of the century, staunch supporters of the régime. In England, however, the middling and lesser merchants were far more vocal than in France; they were wealthier and more independent; besides, they had, as we have seen, an important base of political, as well as economic, power in the City of London. They had allies too among the new class of 'interloping' merchants, based not only on London, but on Bristol and Liverpool, who were anxious to muscle in on the trade of the older mercantile establishment and to come to grips with the Spaniards and French. In consequence, the clash between merchants and government started far earlier in England than in France; and long before the French bourgeoisie began to challenge the authority of the royal government at Versailles, the English merchants were engaged in serious collisions with Parliament and king.

England, again, was peculiar in that she alone, having embarked on the early stages of an industrial revolution, was creating a new and independent class of manufacturers, who were beginning to grow rich on the proceeds of industrial, rather than largely mercantile, capital. We have already seen that while other countries, like France, Russia, Belgium, Bohemia and Switzerland, saw a remarkable expansion of their industries in the course of the century it was only in England that this expansion was accompanied by a technical revolution in such industries as cotton, iron and coal. While the machine-driven factory had nowhere made its appearance, the industrial north was already emerging in the neighbourhood of rivers and canals and leaving its mark on social development. One of the first of its effects was the arrival on the scene of a distinct class of industrial *entrepreneurs* sprung from farming and commercial stock and who were already beginning to leave their mark on the nation's economy. These new men included Samuel Whitbread, the brewer; Jedediah Strutt, the hosier; John Wilkinson, the iron-master; and Josiah Wedgwood, the potter. It took time, of course, for such men, in spite of their wealth, to be accepted on anything like equal terms by aristocratic society; and James Watt could write with bitterness in 1787 that 'our landed gentlemen reckon us poor mechanics no better than slaves who cultivate their vineyards'. Yet they would soon have their day. It was barely a generation later that court and aristocracy would make their pilgrimage to New Lanark, in Scotland, to view the industrial experiments of 'the remarkable Mr Owen'; and soon after Manchester, with its strictly middle-class commercial values, would appear as a second capital of England.

So England, while remaining aristocratic, was nearer than any other country to the new industrial middle-class society of the century that followed. Does this mean that her society (and here we return to the question briefly posed in an earlier chapter) was more open than any other – that is, that there was, in essence, a greater degree of social mobility (or two-way traffic) between her nobility and commercial classes? Of course, no country however caste-ridden – not even Poland or Hungary – was entirely without it; and we have given examples of merchants climbing into the aristocracy in both Hungary and Russia. Yet such examples were few and, basically, these societies remained closed rather than open. In fact, it has long been held that England was the one exception to the rule; and that even France had an essentially 'corporate' society, in which social classes and groups were largely frozen within their own privileged enclaves; and that it was the virtual absence of these in England which set her apart from the other nation of eighteenth-century Europe.

This traditional view, which was held by Tocqueville and many other writers since his day, has recently been challenged; and it has been argued on both sides of the channel that the great divide, if it existed at all, was not nearly as great as had been believed. On the one hand, it has been shown that in England, while there were no legal obstacles to prevent an aspiring merchant from climbing into the titled landlord class, the practical difficulties were forbidding: these included the small number of new peerages created at this time; the resistance of the old peers to the new; and the great expense involved in acquiring a large estate coupled with the landowners' reluctance to sell. In fact, the only easy path to advancement was through marriage into the class above, which was now more popular and more welcome to both parties than it had ever been before.[8] On the other hand, it has been argued that in France the dilution of the nobility by new arrivals was far greater than had generally been supposed. Pierre Goubert gives the example of the fifty-eight nobles of the Beauvaisis who sent a *cahier* of their grievances to Versailles in 1789: of the fifty-eight, only ten could trace their nobility back to 1604 and sixteen had been ennobled since 1740. Moreover, the confusion of privilege with wealth had, by the last years of the *ancien régime*, reached such a stage that Turgot could write in 1776: 'The cause of privilege is no longer the cause of the distinguished families against the *rôturiers* [commoners], but the cause of the rich against the poor.'[9]

From such evidence, then, it appears that the gap between the two societies was not as great as had previously been supposed and that French society, even before the Revolution, was undergoing an important transformation. Yet the gap, even if narrowed, still remains. In France, there were certainly more opportunities for climbing upwards by acquiring a title than there were in England; but to do so was becoming harder rather than easier as the century went on; and, as Roland Mousnier, Franklin Ford and others have demonstrated, the *privilégiés* of robe and sword were closing their ranks in a common front; after 1770 they were placing obstacles in the path of aspirants to offices and titles of nobility that had not existed before. In both countries, it has been suggested, it took three generations for a merchant's family to become fully assimilated and accepted on equal terms by the social group into which it had climbed. But what about the merchants who did not rise or the friends and relations of those that did? In England, even late in the century, there were frequent complaints by City merchants of their contemptuous treatment at the hands of the aristocracy; none the less, there were ample means of communication between the two: in Parliament, for example, or through business enterprise conducted in common. In France, by the very rules governing the status of nobility, these were bound to be fewer; and even if (as Turgot claimed) wealth rather than privilege was becoming the hall-mark of the *grand seigneur*, the re-investment of that wealth – through purchase of land and real estate – was still very much on the aristocracy's own terms. And what of the more casual day-to-day relationships between the aristocracy and the new arrivals or those left behind? In writing of these 'inter-class alliances', David Landes makes the point: 'The real test is not the union; it is what follows: how many great families in such circumstances are willing to know their relations after the wedding?'[10] In short, it is one thing to marry the girl; it is quite another to ask Dad and Mum to tea. The English appear to have been more willing to do so than the French and to have shown a greater capacity for social mixing in general. We saw how the 'little snug party' at the Walpoles' included commoners and freeholders as well as Lords Spiritual and Temporal. Arthur Young noted the difference when, half a century later, he called in at the Duc de la Rochefoucauld's estate at Barbésieux in the Dordogne.

At an English nobleman's [he wrote] there would have been three or four farmers asked to meet me, who would have dined with the family amongst the ladies of the first rank. I do not exaggerate, when I say, that I have had this at least a hundred times in the first houses of our islands. It is, however, a thing that in the present manners in France would not be met with from Calais to Bayonne, except by chance in the house of some great lord that had been much in England, and then not unless it was asked for.[11]

So English society was without much doubt the more mobile and open of the two, and industrial revolution would hasten the process of dissolving the old aristocratic values and social exclusiveness there more quickly than in any other country in Europe. But though England in this as in other respects was different from the rest, it was not as different as all that. It was only a matter of degree; for even in England it was still the aristocracy, and not the up-and-coming bourgeoisie, that really called the tune.

II

GOVERNMENT AND IDEOLOGY

CHAPTER 6

GOVERNMENT

The French historian Albert Sorel wrote of the political institutions of eighteenth-century Europe: 'Every form of government existed . . . and all were considered equally legitimate.' This hardly accords with the theories of legitimacy of most of the political thinkers of the day; yet ever since the Dutch had overthrown the Spaniards and the English had beheaded 'God's image', Charles I, the older forms of legitimacy had had a savage beating, and practice had tended to outrun theory. So, on the face of it, the statement seems true enough. The prevailing form of government – and here practice conformed to theory – was absolute monarchy; in which the royal authority towered over that of the other estates; yet there were great differences in the way it was exercised; and there were several states in which the monarchy, far from being absolute, had been limited by the encroachment of aristocracy or Parliament, or had been superseded by republican forms. There were, for example, evident differences between the operation of hereditary absolute monarchy in France, Spain, Sweden, Prussia and the Austrian Empire; Britain alone had a limited, or parliamentary, monarchy; Poland's monarchy was in practice what Austria's was in theory – elective; the autocracy of Russia was of a different kind from the absolute monarchy of France or Spain and the oriental despotism of Turkey; and the republics of Switzerland, Geneva, Genoa and Venice were very differently constituted from the near-monarchical republic of the United Provinces (Holland). Yet Sorel undoubtedly exaggerated and pressed his argument too far; particularly when he wrote that 'popular' forms of government were, both in theory and practice, as legitimate as any other. This hardly corresponds to the realities of Europe in the century before the French Revolution: however considerable the differences that distinguished them, all European governments were either 'monarchic' or 'aristocratic': they all had in common that they severely restricted what the political theorists called the democratic or popular element in the constitution. The democratic element was largely a myth; for in no state did democracy extend a voice in government to the common people; as it did briefly in France in 1793 and, later, in western Europe, Australia and North America in the century that followed.

Nor is this surprising, as government was bound to reflect, within fairly narrow limits, the prevailing aristocratic and hierarchic society that has been described in the last chapter. Though the claims of aristocracy were everywhere being pressed, this is not to say that the tendency in all countries was towards an aristocratic form of government: monarchic forms, which balanced competing claims and usually made for a stronger state, might suit the competing claimants better. Of course, where aristocracy was weak or only recently rising to social ascendancy (as in Russia or Prussia), the degree of authority exercised by the monarch would be the greater. In its extreme form, this could be seen in the Ottoman Empire, where the nobility enjoyed only such temporary status as was conferred on its members by the sultan, or Grand Signor, and where the sultan, in consequence, provided he could exercise in practice as well as in theory that 'prodigious power and unlimited authority' that Aaron Hill, an English visitor, described in the early years of the century, had little to fear from an aristocratic challenge from below. But the proviso was an important one, as Turkey was as much a theocratic and a military state as it was the personal province of the ruler; and if the ruler, through personal weakness or military defeat, failed to impose his authority on his partners, he was liable to be torn from his seraglio and flung to the wolves with no more ceremony than the Grand Vizier or any other of his minions. Lady Mary Wortley Montagu saw this side of the picture when she wrote from Adrianople in 1717:

The government here is entirely in the hands of the army. When a minister displeases the people . . . they cut off his head and feet, and throw them before the palace gate, with all the respect in the world; while that Sultan, to whom they profess an unlimited adoration, sits trembling in his apartment, and dare neither defend nor avenge his favourite.[1]

Lady Mary had some justification for writing as she did, as the previous ruler (Mustafa II) and the current ruler (Ahmed III) were both overthrown by an army revolt. Yet the next sultan, Mahmud I (1730–54), imposed a far greater measure of authority and, with the aid of two exceptionally able Grand Viziers, was able to win back from the Austrians their conquests of 1718 (including Belgrade) in a renewal of wars in 1736–9. But this revival of the sultan's authority and fortunes was short-lived; and after being propped up by French diplomatic aid during the middle years of the century, Turkish power and the sultan's authority were further diminished by Russian victories in the wars of 1768–74. So it was probably the theory rather than the practice that

Lord Broughton had in mind when, in discussing the 'transmission of absolute authority' in the state in his *Travels in Albania and other Provinces of Turkey* (1809–10), he wrote that in Turkey, 'there is one master – the rest are slaves without individual or aggregate dignity'.

The nearest approach to this theory and practice of oriental despotism could, in the rest of Europe, be found in the autocratic government of Russia. There, too, there was no undisputed right of succession from father to son, as in the more ancient absolute or limited monarchies of the West. Admittedly, the succession was assured to a member of the house of Romanov; but the Romanov claimant who succeeded to the throne had to win the support of a strong faction of the nobility and Palace Guard. So it was in the case of Peter I who only secured his throne firmly after a couple of *coups* of this kind. Peter went on to disinherit and execute his own son; and the enthronement of the short-lived tsars and longer-lived tsarinas whose reigns spanned the rest of the century was effected by similar means: notoriously so in the case of Catherine the Great, who quite literally mounted the throne over the body of her husband, Peter III, in whose murder she connived. Moreover, the authority of Peter I was both in theory and practice as unlimited as that of the sultan of Turkey; and his autocracy was all the more complete because the Russian aristocracy had up to that time been weak and divided, had accumulated little hereditary landed wealth and enjoyed only limited authority over their peasants. So Peter had a great deal to offer; and we have seen that he quite deliberately, by his Table of Ranks, raised the aristocrats' social status and extended their privileges in return for binding them to the service of the state. Thus on the tsar's own initiative, there appeared on the scene a new intermediate channel of authority that might, if not kept strictly in its place, serve as a counter to his own. Yet the tsar's autocracy remained; and even under Catherine half a century later William Richardson, an English traveller, wrote that 'the sovereign of the Russian Empire is absolute and despotic in the utmost latitude of these words and master of the lives and properties of all his subjects who, though they are the first nobility, . . . may nevertheless for the most trifling offence be seized upon and sent to Siberia'.[2] Yet this was an exaggeration, for great as was the ascendancy established by Catherine after her palace *coup*, there was by now, springing from Peter's reforms, a divergence between the theory and practice of the Russian autocracy. Under Peter, that autocracy had been about as absolute as it could be; but under his successors, owing to the circumstances of their rise to power, the aristocracy had been able to assure itself of a greater measure of wealth and authority. This was patently the case with the Empresses Anna and Elizabeth and the three infant or adolescent Emperors – Peter II and III and Ivan VI – who became, to a greater or lesser degree, prisoners of aristocratic and military factions at

87

court. Elizabeth, for example, was well aware that she owed her throne to the intervention of the Guards. So she bestowed favours on them and gave them new regiments, but she also rewarded the noble landowning classes as a whole. She restored the Senate to its old role as a forum for aristocratic legislation; by a law of 1746 she forbade any persons other than nobles to purchase 'men and peasants without lands or with lands', and in 1758 she refused to allow those who had acquired personal nobility by service in the lower categories of the Table of Ranks to acquire estates, 'since the children are not nobles and cannot have and purchase villages'. And her successor, Peter III, during the single year of his ill-fated rule, carried the process further by abolishing compulsory state service for the greater nobility. Catherine's great service to the autocracy, during her long reign, was to rid it of dependence on changing military and aristocratic factions at court by binding the aristocracy to the throne at every level of government; so, in a sense, there was work provided for all. But even she, as we saw, had to pay a price in the more durable and less 'servile' status she conferred on them through her Charter of Nobility in 1785. Yet from the autocracy's point of view it was a price worth paying as it ended the era of palace *coups* and stabilised the relations between the nobility and the throne.

The Prussian monarchs, too, had the problem of winning the landed classes as a subordinate partner in the conduct of the state. But as long as the Electorate of Brandenburg remained an open-ended frontier state fighting, as a client of the French, for a place in the sun, the process of taming the nobility and the estates had not gone far. A firm foundation, however, had been laid by the founding father of the state, the Great Elector of Brandenburg, who in the previous century fought successful wars, extended the frontiers by gaining East Prussia, created a considerable army (of 27,000 men in a population of 1,700,000) and built the nucleus of a stable centralised government to which the old estates and warring nobles were forced to pay allegiance. But his successor, who as Frederick I became the first ruler of the Kingdom of Prussia, nearly undid his work. He built up Berlin as his capital, favoured the arts and spent money on luxuries; but he let the army run down and allowed the nobility to play a more independent role in the direction of affairs: in short, in the words of his grandson, Frederick II, he was 'great in small things and small in great'. The next ruler of Prussia, Frederick William I, was, as his nickname the 'Sergeant-King' denotes, of a different temper altogether. He reversed Frederick's order of priorities by pruning expenditure on everything but the army, which he built up to a force 80,000 strong and which, as he became involved in no wars, he was able to leave intact to his son, together with a well-stocked treasury that was the envy of every other ruler. Above all, Frederick William reasserted the royal authority and impressed the

Prussian nobility for service to the state in much the same way as Peter did in Russia; thus the provincial nobility were conscripted as *Landräte*, or subprefects, who became paid civil servants with jurisdiction over the local *Kreise*. But the process in Prussia was more thorough and more drastic than it was in Russia: the country was smaller to govern and, until Frederick II's new war of 1740, had longer years of peace and consolidation. Moreover, the Prussian line of succession had become firmly fixed not only within the House of Hohenzollern but from father to son; and the son that succeeded Frederick William, although they had quarrelled bitterly in the old king's life-time, was admirably suited to continue his work. Yet there was an important difference. Unlike his father, Frederick did not keep his powder dry and, with his wars and conquests, he inevitably became more dependent on the aristocracy both to command his troops and to man the more privileged higher posts in his civil service. So, like Catherine II in Russia, he had to make concessions; and the prestige and social status of the Prussian nobility correspondingly increased. Thus the royal despotism of Frederick William was tempered by his son; but the full effects of the surrender, with its eventual weakening of the Prussian state, were not to be realised until the time of his successors.

In France, the monarchy was, in theory, as absolute as in Prussia and in most other German states. Louis XIV, during his long reign in the previous century, had been credited with almost divine powers; and Archbishop Bossuet, a staunch bulwark of absolute monarchy, had written of him: 'This is the image of God who, seated on His throne in the highest heavens, sets the whole of nature in motion.'[3] And with Louis, as with Peter of Russia, theory and practice seemed almost to be as one. He had built up at Versailles a formidable concentration of authority: the old *noblesse* had been stripped of political power and danced decorative (some would say useless) attendance at court, and from the king and his council alone stemmed government, justice and promotion to high office in church and state. Yet even under the *roi soleil* there remained the residual authority of the Parlements and provincial estates, though now emasculated and put into abeyance; and the purchase of hereditary offices which went on apace assured their holders of a limited measure of independence of the crown. So, even in the golden age of the court of Versailles, royal absolutism was never quite as complete as it seemed; and this became more apparent with the first grumblings against Louis's authority that were heard during the wars of his latter years. Under his successors, the royal authority generally retained its form, but its substance became greatly changed. This was blatantly the case in the aristocratic 'reaction' that followed Louis's death when, during the Regency of the Duke of Orleans, there was a deliberate devolution of authority and for a few years Parlements and nobility enjoyed a spell of political licence and independence: it was a kind of aristocratic revenge for Saint-Simon's *'règne de vile bourgeoisie'*. Nominally, the absolute monarchy got back on to course when Louis xv came of age in 1726; but there followed the long *ministériat* of Cardinal Fleury (from 1726 to 1745) during which Louis xv's work was done for him in much the same way as Louis xiii's, early in the previous century, had been done for him by Richelieu. On Fleury's death, however, the king announced that he was returning to his great-grandfather's system in practice as well as in name: there would be no more Chief Ministers of the Richelieu–Mazarin type and authority would once more flow from the King-in-Council at Versailles, with the king attending and directing in person each one of the Council's four constituent parts: the *Conseil d'en Haut*, the *Conseil des Dépêches*, the *Conseil des Finances* and the *Conseil Privé*.

Yet the reality proved to be quite different. The king had excellent qualities: he was intelligent, he was brave (he led his troops in person at Fontenoy in 1745), he had a commanding presence and plenty of charm. He regularly attended the *Conseil d'en Haut*, at least; but without enthusiasm, for he had none of the bureaucratic genius and indefatig-ability that distinguished Louis xiv. He had a different set of priorities: he was far more devoted to the hunt and to the ladies and pleasures of the court than to affairs of state; he allowed government to drift and its direction to be disputed by rival factions, in which a procession of Secretaries of State, pretenders to office, Princes of the Blood and royal mistresses (such as the versatile and highly intelligent Madame de Pompadour) all had a part. The Marquis d'Argenson, having fallen from office in 1747, wrote of the Council at this time as 'a republic . . . of heads of factions: each thinking only of his own concern, one of finance, another of the navy, another of the army, and each achieving his own ends according to his greater or lesser facility in the art of per-suasion'. When every allowance is made for the exaggeration of a dis-gruntled ex-minister, the picture is still damning enough. And when able ministers like Choiseul and Maupeou momentarily restored the government's credit, other more abiding ills (some of them inherent in Louis xiv's whole system) persisted and became magnified. The bureaucracy of office-holders, as it became larger, more firmly en-trenched and more independent, tended to become a law unto itself and a buffer, rather than a link, between government and people. And as government lost its authority, or was brought into contempt, the claims of the aristocracy and privileges became all the more insistent. Louis xv's reign was a long one and when his grandson, Louis xvi, took over in 1774, it would have required a considerable effort and combination of talents to put the whole machinery back into gear, or (better still) adapt it to meet the changing needs of the times. But the new king, while he had a sense of duty which his grandfather had so patently lacked, was weak, shy and unimaginative, and fundamentally a conservative and timorous of change. Yet he had good intentions and reforms were carried through which patched up the government system, extended civil liberties and even opened the door to an elementary form of consultation through local assemblies. But the basic problem remained: how to persuade the privileged classes to make some contribution to the effective running of the state? And this is a question, as we shall see in a later chapter, to which even the best-intentioned of all reforming ministers were quite unable to find an answer.

Spain and the Austrian Empire were also countries of absolute monarchy; in Austria, although the monarchy was nominally elective, the succession had for generations been guaranteed to the eldest in line of the house of Habsburg. In both countries the monarchy was faced with a problem broadly similar to that of the French, the Prussians and Russians: how to retain the authority of the central government against the centrifugal forces from without. But, in their case, these forces were not so much those of a single privileged class as whole regions and provinces that had never been fully assimilated and claimed a degree of regional autonomy. In Spain, the War of Succession of 1702–13 had seen a determined attempt by Catalonia and Aragon to throw off the rule of Castile; the provincial estates (*Cortès*) of Castile and Navarre continued to meet; and the Basque provinces even continued to enjoy the particular privilege of not being taxed without their consent. But the Spanish monarchy had the good fortune, unlike the French, to have a succession of competent rulers or competent ministers (with reasonable tenure of office) to keep the problem in check. In the long reign of Charles III (1759–88), the two were combined and the king and his ministers were able to establish a higher degree of national unity than Spain had known in the past.

In the Austrian dominions the geographical distribution of authority posed problems that were even more complex and intractable. The Empire sprawled southwards to Milan and northwards to the Netherlands and was composed of a patchwork of provinces, whose political traditions, social structure, language and economic development all varied widely and tended both to divide them among themselves and from the court of Vienna. In such circumstances, a certain devolution of authority was bound to persist and the centralising efforts of the Emperor were continually challenged by the provincial estates of the Netherlands, the Patrician magistrature of Milan and the diets of Bohemia and Hungary. Hungary, in particular, retained throughout the eighteenth century its own system of administration based on the county assemblies (*Komitats*), which were dominated by a gentry which claimed almost complete immunity from paying taxes to Vienna. So the problem was one that was bound to command the attention of a succession of rulers. Charles VI had a dual problem: both to keep his dominions together and, having no male heir, to ensure the succession (barring the title of Holy Roman Emperor) to his daughter Maria Theresa. With his Pragmatic Sanction, which he hawked around Europe, he was successful in persuading his provinces to accept the principle of an undivided Empire; but it was at the price of confirming all their privileges and immunities. Maria Theresa proved to be a woman of courage, energy and persistence, who having lost Silesia to Frederick II in 1740 kept the rest of her dominions together during the forty years of her reign with an authority which was probably unmatched by any of her predecessors. After the Empress's death in 1780, her son Joseph II tried to go much further in sweeping provincial claims aside and subjecting the whole Empire to rule from Vienna. But we shall see that he overreached himself and nearly lost his throne in the attempt.

In the Scandinavian countries absolute monarchy had its ups and downs, depending on the balance of power between crown and aristocracy. In Denmark (which at this time included Norway), the crown had, until the middle of the previous century, been elective though assured to the male heir in the Oldenburg line. But, as the price of election, the king's authority was strictly circumscribed: in the first place, he had on his succession to reward his electors by the issue of a charter of privilege; and, secondly, he had to share his sovereignty with the three estates – the nobles, clergy and commoners – which in practice meant the nobility. By this division, the executive power was vested jointly in the king and the Senate (composed of the principal nobles), while the legislative authority resided entirely in the three estates. So the government was overwhelmingly aristocratic. However, in September 1660, what William Coxe called a 'singular revolution' took place, in which Frederick III, with the support of the clergy and commons, carried through a *coup d'état* which overthrew the old 'aristocratic' constitution, reduced the powers of the nobility and vested undivided executive authority in the person of an hereditary king.[4] And this, broadly, remained the pattern in Denmark for the next one hundred and fifty years.

In Sweden there was a similar tug-of-war, but the roles were reversed. After the death of the absolute Charles XII (1718), it was the aristocracy that carried out a *coup* and inaugurated an era that historians have, according to their fancy, called an 'age of freedom' or an 'age of anarchy'. Under a new constitution, the powers of the crown were abridged in much the same way as they had been in Denmark a century before; but with one important exception: the crown remained hereditary, though the Diet had the right to choose between two claimants in the case of a disputed succession. In other respects royal authority was just as rigidly circumscribed, with the king sharing executive power with the Senate, while the Senate derived its authority from the Riksdag composed of the four estates, which was also the sole legislative body and had the power to make war and peace. The aristocratic party, however, divided into two and the governments that followed were shared between two rival groups, the Caps (who ruled till 1738) and the Hats (from 1739 to 1765), with a period of uneasy balance between the two from 1765 to 1772. It was partly as a result of the dissatisfaction and confusion caused by these divisions that the crown was able to reassert its authority by a *coup d'état* of its own in August 1772, when Gustavus III rode through the streets of Stockholm to the cheers of the crowd, dispersed the Hats and Caps and took over the government of the state. Yet, in Sweden, absolutism was tempered by a constitution and did not revert to the despotism of Charles XII. While the king regained overriding authority, his power was not despotic or autocratic, nor as absolute as that of the kings of France and Spain; and William Coxe was most indignant when it was suggested that the Swedish king was 'no less absolute at Stockholm than the French monarch at Versailles, and the Grand Signor at Constantinople'. It was, of course, a matter of degree. The king was absolute enough in the sense that, being the complete master of the Senate, he had in fact the sole executive power which, according to the constitution, was supposed to be shared between them. But the legislative authority was shared with the estates; so he had no right to enact or repeal laws nor to impose taxes without the consent of an elected assembly. There were no such restraints on absolutism in France or Spain, let alone in Prussia or Russia.

Unique among the state-systems of Europe was that of Poland. It was a monarchy, but an elective one; and, in this case, there was no guarantee that the candidate of any royal house would be preferred to that of any other. It was simply a matter of the forces that one faction of the major nobility could muster against its rivals with the aid of one or more of the European powers (generally France, Russia or Austria): the so-called War of the Polish Succession (1733–5), which ranged the Austrians and Russians against the French and ended in the triumph of the Austro-Russian candidate, was merely the most bloody and violent of the succession-struggles of the century. So the victorious candidate was even more dependent on the favours of his electors than the Danish king had been before 1660; and, as the price of his victory, he was obliged to accept the *pacta conventa* (or traditional 'liberties') presented to him by the magnates. Poland was in fact a monarchy in name only and in practice a sort of republic or 'democracy' of nobles, governed by the large landowning families, who controlled the diets, in which a unanimity of votes (the *liberum veto*) was required for any law to be enacted. Meanwhile, the executive authority was further weakened

93

(again, as in early seventeenth-century Denmark) by its division between the king and Senate and by the meagreness of its revenues and
its lack of a standing army. Such a system had the weakness of paralys-
ing both government and legislation at any time; but it might work
without doing irreparable damage to the state as long as Poland's neighbours (Sweden, Austria, Prussia and Russia) were either weak or divided
among themselves. But after the Northern War and the War of the
Austrian Succession, from which first Russia and then Prussia emerged
as major powers in the east and centre of Europe, Poland's situation
became critical indeed as she lay wide open to the predatory ambitions
of powerful neighbours. The outcome, during the latter part of the
eighteenth century, was a series of partitions of her territory between
these countries and Austria which thereby settled their own differences
at Poland's expense. By the first partition (in 1772), she lost nearly one-
third of her territory and over one-third (four millions) of her population in fairly equal portions to the 'enlightened despots' of the three
neighbouring great powers. There followed a remarkable flowering of
Polish arts and culture and, for a while, the truncated state was governed
by Stanislas Poniatowski, a one-time favourite of Catherine turned
Polish patriot, who managed to keep the magnates and *szlachta* under
reasonable control. The revival, however, was short-lived; and when
the Poles attempted to carry through a liberal–aristocratic revolution in
1791, Catherine stepped in again with the support of the two German
powers; and by the further partitions of 1792 and 1795 Poland was
effectively wiped off the map for several years to come.

Unique, too, in its own way was the 'limited' monarchy of Great
Britain. Formally, it was closer to that of Sweden than to that of
France, Prussia or Spain; but in practice it was poles apart from them
all. The essential difference lay of course in the more advanced social
and economic development of the country that we noted in earlier
chapters. Englishmen prided themselves on their 'mixed' or 'balanced'
constitution.

And herein [wrote Sir William Blackstone in 1765] consists the excellence
of the English government, that all parts of it form a mutual check upon
each other. In the legislative, the people are a check upon the nobility, the
nobility a check upon the people, by the mutual privilege of rejecting what
the other has resolved; while the King is a check upon both, which preserves
the executive power from encroachments.

It was these checks and balances that delighted Montesquieu, and both
he and Blackstone were fully justified in noting the considerable powers
that the limited monarchy still left in the hand of the king. He still
retained the power to select his ministers and though he no longer exercised his prerogative right to refuse to sanction bills passed to him by the
Houses of Parliament, he had ample means for influencing legislation

and the outcome of elections, and for promoting the policies of his choice. George II, it is true, left some of these powers in abeyance during the latter part of his reign and entrusted more authority than his father had done before him or his grandson would do after him to a combination of Whig magnates who, with the eclipse of the Tories, enjoyed a political monopoly in Parliament and at court. George may have exaggerated when he said he had become a 'King in the toils' and complained that 'ministers are the Kings in this country'; but so have certain historians exaggerated in claiming that, when George III came to the throne in 1760, there was no 'palace revolution' or determination by the new king to avoid his grandfather's experience and that everything went on much the same as before. Yet George III broke with the old Whig 'undertakers' of the 1740s and 1750s and made efforts, which were largely successful, to restore the authority of the monarch to what it had been in his grandfather's earlier years.

So Blackstone was right to stress the powers of the crown in eighteenth-century England. Yet, like other constitutional lawyers, he exaggerated the role of 'the people' within the system. To him 'the people' were the Commons, as though they were elected by the nation at large. But the Commons were in fact elected on an extremely limited and anomalous franchise, in which landed property-owners held the trump cards, but in which there were still vestigial remnants of a more popular county and borough electorate which had survived from medieval times (London, Westminster, Preston and Middlesex are obvious examples). Moreover, as we have seen, where the Commons were not controlled and manipulated through aristocratic connections and pocket and rotten boroughs by the great landed families, they were largely the preserve of the gentry. Country gentlemen (and their aristocratic relations) decided county elections among themselves, and Sir Lewis Namier believed that 'probably not more than one in every twenty voters at county elections could freely exercise his statutory rights'.[5] So the composition of the British Parliament retained its predominantly landed flavour throughout the eighteenth century: the main change was that the proportion of merchants in the Commons rose from one-ninth to a quarter in the half-century following the 1760s. And as the landed aristocracy and gentry between them also controlled the counties as Lords Lieutenant and justices of the peace, the 'mixture' within the constitution was not quite what Blackstone and the lawyers proclaimed. It was in fact the landed classes, with a growing sprinkling of merchants, that provided within the political system the effective check on the royal authority. But we shall see that in the 1760s and later 'the people', in a broader sense than Blackstone intended, also began to have something to say.

Finally, there were the republics, in which monarchy had been superseded by the authority of noble families or of merchant patriciates, but

95

where (with one notable exception) democracy was no more in evidence than it was in the governments and parliaments of other states. By far the wealthiest and most powerful of the republics was that of the United Provinces; but here the monarchical form had not been fully abandoned. The legislative power was vested in their High Mightinesses the Estates General which were composed of the deputies, both burgher and noble, of the seven provinces; and each of the large towns (there were several in the single province of Holland) was governed in turn by Regents drawn from a small number of local ruling families – the Hasselaers, Bickers, Hoofts and De Witts. So here the wealthy merchant class, rather than the older landed nobility, was predominant; yet the remnants of monarchy survived in the person of the Stadholder whose office, after 1751, became hereditary in the house of Orange. The Stadholder was commander-in-chief of the armed forces as well as formal head of the administration; and, in years of public emergency or when the great merchants of Amsterdam were unable to hold him in check, he might wield an authority that eclipsed that of his rival to executive power, the Grand Pensionary of Holland.

No such dualism existed in the other, smaller republics. Switzerland was a loose federation of a dozen cantons, each of which regarded itself, for most practical purposes, as an independent state and owed only the barest allegiance to the federal diet at Zürich. The rural cantons had retained considerable elements of an earlier primitive democracy and were governed by elective assemblies: William Coxe applauded them, 'notwithstanding the natural defects of a democratical constitution'; but he shared the prevailing opinion that it was only in small communities of this sort 'that this kind of general democracy can have place'.[6] The cities, on the other hand, were oligarchic and ruled by small privileged groups either of aristocrats (as at Bern) or merchants (as at Basel and Zürich). Bern was governed by an hereditary nobility of 250 families who alone were considered *regimentsfähig*, or fit to rule; and seventy of these families (the Wattenwills, Jenners, Steigers, Tscharners, Graffenrieds and others) divided the control of the state between them, filling all the seats in the Council of Two Hundred and the sixteen places of its inner cabinet. Similar was the hold kept on the governments of Basel and Zürich by a self-perpetuating oligarchy of privileged merchant families, who spoke in the name of the merchant gilds. Not yet a part of Switzerland was the small city state of Geneva, the home of Calvin and Rousseau. Geneva was governed by a small group of two hundred citizens (*citoyens*), who jealously upheld their exclusive right to hold office against the claims of the partly disfranchised smaller merchants (*bourgeois*) and the wholly disfranchised artisans (*habitants* and *natifs*), with consequences that we shall note in a later chapter.

To the latter half of the eighteenth century belong a number of rulers who have been given the name of 'enlightened despot'. It has become a fashionable term, and for many years enlightened despotism (or 're-pentant monarchy', as Lord Acton called it) has been given a chapter of its own in nearly every history textbook of the period. Recently, some historians have become less certain and have either reduced these rulers in stature or simply lumped them in with the other rulers of the day. The difficulty has been to decide which of them were worthy of the distinc-tion and which were not and how far their successes or failures were due to the one quality rather than to the other. It would seem, however, that, to qualify, a ruler would have to have some combination of the two. An enlightened monarch might be one who made some attempt to govern according to the 'philosophical' principles of the time or, at least, one who showed a particular concern for the welfare or happiness of his subjects. As for despotism, it must presumably have been used for some particular purpose such as to strengthen the monarchy against disruption from within. So, if the term is to be used at all, it seems reasonable to apply it to those rulers who set out to modernise the administration and to strengthen the monarchy at the expense of such challengers as church, aristocracy or provincial estates, accompanied by a greater or a lesser degree of concern for their subjects' wellbeing.

The monarchs to whom the title of enlightened despot has been most frequently applied were Frederick the Great and Catherine II of Russia; yet, in some respects, they were perhaps the least worthy of the name. Admittedly, they were both enlightened in the sense that they read the works of the French 'philosophical' writers and prided themselves on being their pupils; and Frederick gave hospitality (though with disas-trous results) to Voltaire at Potsdam, while Catherine entertained Diderot and made energetic, though vain, attempts to bring Voltaire to St Petersburg. But did they, in fact, do anything to put their ideas into practice? Or, for that matter, could they, in the circumstances in which they were placed, have done so to any purpose had they wished? Frederick certainly ruled Prussia with an authority that was un-disputed; he saw himself as 'the first servant of the state'; he supervised in person the work of his bureaucracy; he introduced judicial and edu-cational reforms; he built canals and promoted industries and begged his heir to follow his example ('a country without industries is a body without life'); he settled foreign workers; he released a few serfs on the royal domain; and he preached religious toleration and refused to allow the churches to meddle in the affairs of state. But these were nearly all developments that had been begun or had been sketched out for him by his father, Frederick William I. In fact, the only important respect in which he departed from his father's practice was in the more tender regard he showed for the aristocracy. Under him, the army became exclusively officered by nobles, the higher administration was reserved for men of noble birth and the aristocracy was allowed a social importance and a share in government that it had not known before. It may, indeed, be argued that Frederick's reforms served a useful purpose in holding his state together under the shock of the wars of the first half of his reign; but it may equally be argued that he left an unfortunate legacy to his immediate successors.

Catherine's role in Russia was similar to Frederick's and her enlightenment had similar limitations. She talked of agrarian reform, abolished torture, practised religious toleration, secularised church lands and closed down monasteries, extended industry, established colonies of foreign workers, brought state education to the towns, reformed local government and strengthened administration at the centre. It was an impressive body of reform, some of it long-lasting: her new system of local government, for instance (of which more will be said in the next chapter), survived for a hundred years. But, once more, these measures were not innovations but had been inherited from Peter I and the more competent of his successors. Her one departure from precedent and her one great innovation was, like Frederick's, to give greater rope to the nobility by bringing them into closer partnership at every level of administration. While, in the case of Russia, this does not appear to have weakened the operation of the autocratic state, it made it virtually impossible to bring any relief to the long-suffering peasantry of which there had been so much talk, both by the Empress herself and among her intimates, in the early years of her reign. So enlightenment, in whatever sense we choose to use the term, appears to have come off a rather bad loser.

There were other rulers whose reforms, or attempted reforms, were more original or more far-reaching. In Portugal, Joseph I, after the Lisbon earthquake of 1755, entrusted the government of his country to the Marquis of Pombal who ruled it as virtual dictator for the next twenty-two years. Some of Pombal's innovations were startling: he expelled the Jesuits before any other ruler (1759); he cowed, browbeat and tyrannised the nobility (he executed members of one of the oldest noble families, the Tavoras); he abolished slavery and passed laws against anti-semitism, and against the colour-bar in the colonies. All this was carried through with the maximum of ruthlessness and the minimum of 'philosophical' finesse. He naturally made enemies: even the *philosophes* disowned him; and the Austrian envoy wrote, on the eve of his fall, in 1776: 'This nation, crushed by the weight of the despotic government exercised by the Marquis of Pombal, the king's friend, favourite, and Prime Minister, believes that only the death of the monarch can deliver the people from the yoke which they regard as tyrannical and intolerable.' The king died the next year and the prophecy was fulfilled.

Another enlightened despot, whose career, though far shorter, was as dramatic as Pombal's, was Johann Struensee, a Prussian physician, whom Christian VII of Denmark met on his travels, brought back to Copenhagen and, in 1771, made his chief minister. Struensee, like Pombal, became the dictator of the country; and in this role in a remarkably short time he modernised the court, abolished sinecures, did away with the privy council, curtailed the privileges of the nobility, lightened the burdens on the peasants, gave freedom to the press, began to reform the administration and embarked on a large programme of public works. But he had also become the lover of the Queen, Caroline Matilda; so it ended in tragedy. After a palace revolution in 1772, the queen was confined to a fortress and Struensee was executed. Thus, it is interesting to note, the attempt to tighten the screws on the aristocracy in Denmark (for this was the essence of the Struensee interlude) failed in the very year that it proved triumphantly successful in Sweden, and even had a short-lived success in Poland.

Other princely reformers who may lay some claim to enlightenment were Charles III of Spain, the Margrave Charles Frederick of Baden, the Archduke Leopold of Tuscany and his brother Joseph II of Austria. After being King of The Two Sicilies since 1735, Charles ascended to the Spanish throne in 1759 and, with the aid of a succession of able ministers, the Count of Aranda (who corresponded with Voltaire and Diderot), Pedro de Camponanes and Floridablanca, carried through some spirited though limited reforms: these included the modernisation of Madrid; the building of roads and canals; encouragement to industry and the arts; and the founding of the Bank of San Carlos at Barcelona. They also expelled the Jesuits and attempted to end mendicity by establishing workhouses and vocational schools. In Baden, Charles Frederick was far more ambitious: he abolished torture, the death penalty and serfdom; and he even tried (though unsuccessfully) to put into practice the Physiocrats' remedy for social ills, a single tax on land. Even more remarkable in many respects was the rule of the Grand Duke Leopold of Tuscany (1765–90): in him at least there appears to have been a stronger mixture of enlightenment than of despotism. For one thing, he was a pacifist and, far from wishing to build a powerful army or to extend the boundaries of his state, he worked hard to ensure its permanent neutrality. Moreover, unlike other despots, he sought to limit rather than to enlarge the ruler's authority, though not to the advantage of aristocracy. By his Charter of 1782, which remained a paper project, he envisaged a network of elective communal and regional assemblies, sending delegates to an assembly at the centre, which would be armed with consultative rather than legislative powers. It is true that this was only a small step towards democracy but it was the first project of its kind to be put forward on the continent of Europe before the Revolution in France.

But Tuscany, like Baden, was a small province where political experiments might be projected or even carried through without causing any disturbance to the balance of power or affecting the interests of other states. The case of the Austrian Empire itself – and not just one of its numerous components – was, of course, a different problem altogether; and it was here that the most daringly enlightened innovator of them all appeared in the person of the Emperor himself. Joseph II's measures, like those of Frederick and Catherine, were, of course, not entirely new: in some respects, he merely followed in the steps of his mother, the redoubtable Maria Theresa. Her government had already taken firm measures to end the provincial separatism of Bohemia by annulling its charters and by suspending and reducing the powers of its Diet. The Hungarian Diet was forbidden to meet for twenty-five years; torture was abolished in Austria-Bohemia; several monasteries were dissolved; and by an Act of 1755, all the Austrian dominions, with the exception of Hungary, were brought into a single tariff union. So the Austrian Empress herself had as good a claim as many others, including Frederick and Catherine, to be called an enlightened despot. But Joseph, who had ruled jointly with his mother for her last fifteen years, was far more thorough and, alone of the despots, attempted to carry through a consistent and comprehensive policy, combining radical social measures with the assertion of the power of the crown over every imaginable subordinate authority, whether church, nobility, provincial estates or chartered towns. In pursuit of the former aim, he completed the abolition of torture, abolished personal serfdom (though not labour service) by his *Unterthanspatent* of 1781, limited the lord's right to punish his peasants and did away with the *corvée*. In his dealings with the Catholic church, he anticipated much of the work of the French revolutionaries of 1789: he dissolved a further seven hundred monastic houses and used their funds to promote education and poor relief; he abolished the Inquisition; he freely tolerated Protestants and extended the civil rights of Jews; he silenced the clerical opposition and permitted public criticism of the church; he made marriage a civil contract; he undermined the authority of the Pope in his dominions; compelled the bishops to take an oath of allegiance to the Emperor, and turned the clergy into salaried servants of the state. In his war with the nobility he withdrew their right to claim tax-exemption in the various provinces, drastically weakened their authority over their peasants and used his political police to suppress their protests. He was equally ruthless in dealing with provincialism: he imposed the German language on his Hungarian and Bohemian dominions, suppressed the local authorities in Milan and

Lombardy and restricted the operations of the ancient gilds and town assemblies of the Netherlands.

But enlightened despotism, in so far as it was enlightened, was almost universally a failure. It succeeded best where the object was limited administrative reform rather than drastic social experiment. Frederick II made no profession of such intentions and Catherine, for all her earlier talk of lightening the burdens of her peasants, gave up all thought of social reform after the great rebellion headed by the peasant leader Pugachev in the 1770s. Gustavus III (who was himself something of an enlightened despot) tipped the balance significantly in favour of monarchy in Sweden, and Charles III and his ministers did something to reassert the authority of the crown in Spain. But more thoroughgoing reforming ministers like Pombal in Portugal and Struensee in Denmark saw most of their work undone when they fell from office; and even Margrave Frederick William was unable to realise his single-tax project in Baden. Above all, the experience of Joseph II, who was more determined than any other to build for the future and break with the past, illustrates how narrow were the limits within which a reforming despot might successfully operate. For lack of an educated native middle class, Joseph had to depend for the execution of his plans on a small group of enlightened officials in Vienna; but their devotion and the support of a powerful machinery of state – not to mention the goodwill of many peasant families – were quite insufficient to break the resistance of the outraged church, nobility, provincial estates and chartered towns, whom his reforms and his high-handed methods had alienated and antagonised. The result was that the Netherlands revolted and Hungary almost seceded from the Empire. To save his dominions from disintegration, Joseph and his successor, Leopold II, were compelled to make concessions to the church, the nobility, the chartered towns and provincial estates that destroyed a great deal of his handiwork. Yet he left an important legacy: 'Josephism', while anathema to the established church and the privileged classes, had roused a great hope among the enserfed and downtrodden peasantry and the lesser bourgeois and craftsmen of the cities. Many of the 'Josephians' of the 1780s became the 'Jacobins' of the 1790s; and enough of Joseph's land reforms survived to serve as a stepping stone towards the elimination of the last vestiges of feudalism in 1848.

In short, enlightened despotism failed because when it came to the point its two component qualities proved to be irreconcilable. This was not necessarily due to bad will, but in the circumstances of the times the reforming despot found himself in a dilemma. He had either to build up the monarchy with the aid of the privileged classes, which is roughly what happened in Russia and Prussia; or he might look for alternative support among other classes in order to strengthen his authority at the expense of aristocracy or church. Both courses were fraught with problems and difficulties. The first meant a certain surrender to privilege, which might weaken the state (as with Prussia) while enlightened reform would almost certainly go by the board. The second course posed equal, sometimes insoluble, problems: the only possible alternative support would have to come from the middle classes, who were either too weak to help (as in Russia and Austria) or were beginning to think of solutions of their own (as in England and France). Most despots, if they had had to make a choice, would have leaned towards the first course rather than the second, either because they preferred the lesser evil or had no practical alternative (here Joseph and possibly his brother Leopold were notable exceptions). So aristocracy and privilege, so often the proclaimed target of enlightened despotism, emerged out of the whole experience strengthened rather than weakened. And we shall see that it was not only in Russia and Prussia that there was something of an aristocratic resurgence, or a 'feudal reaction', in the latter half of the eighteenth century.

CHAPTER 7

BUREAUCRACY

Every government of the eighteenth century, whether monarchical, republican or aristocratic, had certain general purposes in common: to maintain the boundaries of the state; to extend them, if possible or desirable, by diplomacy or war; to maintain internal justice; and to protect the established church. Naturally on this list of priorities some always stood higher than others and the order in which they appeared varied between one government and the next. The Turks and the Prussians, for example, placed war and territorial aggrandisement at the top or near the top of their list; whereas Britain, while concerned with expansion overseas, could, with her island position and natural frontiers, afford to look on the building of a standing army as an unnecessary luxury or even as a dangerous provocation to the 'liberties' of important persons in the state. Again, to the rulers of Spain and the Habsburg Empire, the defence of the state religion would be a matter of more continuing concern than it would to the rulers of Prussia, Russia or England. But, whatever the priorities, the rulers of all states could only realise their tasks and promote their objectives with the aid of a permanent staff of servants, officials or bureaucrats, on whose loyalty they could depend and whose tenure of office was not cut short by every political commotion. The selection of these servants depended in part on the personal choice of the rulers, who would naturally look to groups of people literate enough and able enough to carry out their wishes. Thus, in the previous century, Louis xiv had quite deliberately selected 'new' men from the merchant bourgeoisie to fill his administrative posts in order, after the civil wars of the Fronde, to make the monarchy less dependent on the nobility. Similarly, at the beginning of the eighteenth century, Peter the Great of Russia had equally deliberately staffed his administration with a mixture of new nobles (newly ennobled for the part), townsmen and old nobility with the common duty of serving the state within a complicated social hierarchy which found expression in his Table of Ranks. Frederick William i of Prussia, who, like Louis xiv and Peter i, had some reservations about the loyalties of the older landowning class, clearly showed his predilection for commoners: in 1730 only three out of eighteen Privy Councillors were of noble birth; and during his reign there was a higher proportion of commoners in the Prussian civil service than there would be until the end of the First World War. The Austrian Emperors preferred to depend on Germans, whether middle-class or aristocratic, whenever they could find them in sufficient numbers to staff their bureaucracy in Vienna. In the Ottoman Empire the most educated among the peoples of the occupied Balkan territories were the Greeks; so it was Greeks trained in the Turkish capital of Constantinople who were generally found as administrators of their provinces in Europe. Again, when the Bourbon King of Spain, Philip v, ascended his new throne as the nominee of the King of France, it was natural that he should bring with him a team of French advisers, as the Emperor Charles v had brought with him Belgians and Burgundians two centuries before, and as Charles III, who had been King of The Two Sicilies, brought with him Italian advisers half a century later.

But the ruler's personal choice was hardly ever unrestricted. It was usually circumscribed by such factors as geography, historical development or political tradition; or simply by the dimensions of a problem that tended to get beyond direct personal control. So it was comparatively rare that the bureaucracy, even if it was originally created at the ruler's whim or in his image, remained so for very long. The Russian and Habsburg Empires, for example, sprawled over hundreds of miles of territory, embracing people with different languages, cultures and traditions whom it was hard to fit into a single uniform administrative pattern cut to measure in St Petersburg or Vienna. This, as we saw, was part of Joseph II's problem in Austria; and whatever the personal wishes of the Emperors concerned, both Maria Theresa and Joseph found that to implement their major reforms they had to rely on administrations headed by members of old landed families, men like Haugwitz, Kolorat, Cotek, Kaunitz and Zinzendorf. There was of course the further reason that even in the middle ranks of administration there were not enough middle-class, or former middle-class, officials to draw on. In fact the absence of a substantial educated middle class in many countries – it applied as much to Spain, Sweden, Russia and Prussia as it did to the Austrian Empire – imposed severe restrictions on rulers looking round for new men who could be entirely beholden to them for their selection and preferment. In France the problem was not so great and it was found possible from the early seventeenth century onwards to create a new administrative class by selling offices, which later became hereditary, among the rich merchant families in the cities and ports. In Prussia, as David Bien has pointed out, there could be no such market for the sale of offices, as the merchant towns were too few and far between to provide a regular source of buyers; and it may be that Frederick

William had this sort of limitation in mind when he chose to follow the Russian pattern rather than the French; and it may be, too, that this sort of necessity played a part, as well as the ruler's particular bias, in shaping the new social composition of the Russian and Prussian administration under Catherine and Frederick the Great.

In addition, historical tradition clearly played a part in the selection of state servants. It was one thing to choose and train bureaucrats in a tightly-knit autocracy like Peter's Russia or Frederick William's Prussia; it was quite another in loosely-knit monarchies like the Spanish or the Austrian, where provincial particularism acted as a constant brake on the imposition of uniform administration from a common centre; and we shall see how this affected the administrative relations between Hungary and Vienna and between the Basque provinces and Madrid. In England, there was a long tradition, going back to medieval and even to Saxon times, which involved the landed gentry in local administration. Cromwell tried to break the habit with the rule of his Major-Generals; but it was not a great success and the experience may have contributed to the tenacious survival in the English counties of rule by the justices of the peace.

A common problem of all governments in search of reliable bureaucrats was how to train them and give them some degree of professional competence in the exercise of public duties, that is, duties that concerned the state as a whole and not some private or particular interest. Some rulers tried to tackle this by the provision of special training schools and examinations for aspiring bureaucrats; as was done by the 'enlightened despots' of Austria and Prussia. In Prussia, Frederick William I founded chairs of 'cameral studies' at two universities, where practical courses were given in various branches of the administration. Frederick II extended the system by making promotion dependent on examinations, while his successor, Frederick William II, went further still by introducing a form of pre-selection whereby students were only admitted to the courses after passing a number of tests. Such measures were indicative of a new and sterner attitude towards professionalism that developed during the century and they may have helped to force the pace; but it was an uphill task as long as the public and private sector in administration continued, particularly in local government, to be inextricably confused. This is hardly surprising in an age when rulers – even despotic rulers – often continued to look on the state as a mere extension of their private domain, in much the same spirit as Louis XIV had conducted his dynastic wars in the preceding century. Moreover, the very nature of society – being both 'corporate' and aristocratic – tended to favour amateurishness and to resist the evolution of a professional government class. Gilds, churches, universities and other corporate bodies prided themselves on their immunity from state interference and their right to run their own affairs. In England Parliament insisted on appointing its own officers for collecting the land tax and in 1698 actually withdrew the right previously granted to the crown to appoint its own officers to do so; and every researcher among eighteenth-century English records will know that many of the most important state papers are to be found among the private papers of individual ministers. Moreover, it was considered a virtue rather than a weakness that administrative duties should be undertaken as an honorary function and remain unpaid. Such a practice often commended itself to governments as it saved them money. Yet it might be at the price of both efficiency and honesty: thus in France tax-farmers and in England Paymasters of the Forces tended to recoup themselves for their exertions by helping themselves liberally out of the public till. In France the selling of public offices also perpetuated the role of the wealthy amateur in administration. It brought the state money, as we have seen, but it also had the effect of creating an official class that in the course of time was bound, by the very circumstances of its attainment of office, to place its own privileges and emoluments above the public interest.

However, against these tendencies that perpetuated the survival of amateurs must be set the very real needs of the ruler, whose interest lay in the creation of a professional public service. These needs were most urgent in the states of the East, with their sprawling empires and exposed land-frontiers, whose survival depended (and Poland's sad fate was there for all to see) on some degree of administrative efficiency in the hands of a central directing authority. The needs were not so pressing perhaps in France and England; but in all the major European states there were important developments, particularly in the central direction of the state, which we must now consider.

To start with Sweden; here the first important steps were taken in the early seventeenth century to build the modern bureaucratic state, with the creation of specialised administrative departments run on lines broadly similar to those of our ministries of today. It began with Gustavus Adolphus, who transformed the old hereditary offices of state into departments organised as 'colleges' or 'boards'. By the mid-1630s, the central administration of Sweden consisted of five boards, whose heads sat in a Council of State and which were variously concerned with finance, correspondence, defence, foreign affairs and justice. This remained the pattern for the century that followed.

The Swedish example served as a model for the Russians. On assuming power, Peter I had found a bewildering maze of overlapping authorities: at the centre was the old Council of Boyars (staffed by the old landowning nobility) supported by two-score or so *prikazi* (departments) with varying, often undefined and unco-ordinated responsibilities. In the course of the next quarter-century, Peter reformed the system by putting in its place a Senate (based on his new state-serving nobility) and nine specialised colleges on the Swedish model, each one with strictly apportioned functions such as foreign affairs, war, admiralty, justice and finance (of which the last had no less than three departments of its own). Meanwhile local government was brought into line, the country being divided into fifty provinces each with its own officials, locally appointed but subject to the control of, at first, the Senate, and, later, the colleges. Peter's death, as we have seen, was followed by an aristocratic reaction, which kept the elements of his system in being, though weakening its efficiency and experimenting with a number of new policy-making bodies at the centre: thus the Senate became at various times a Privy Council, a *Kabinet* and a *Konferentsiya*. In 1730 when Peter II died, the Supreme Privy Council tried to impose on the Empress Anna, as the price of her accession to the throne, a number of conditions which would have placed the autocracy at the mercy of the great landowning families. The move, however, was defeated with the aid of the lesser nobility who would have been the victims of the deal; and the system that Catherine II inherited in 1762 was basically that created by Peter half a century before. Catherine, too, maintained the system while modifying its form and changing its content. She made two important innovations. One, as we have seen, was to integrate the landowning classes as a whole – and not only the oldest noble families – more closely within the whole administrative apparatus. The other was her local government reform of 1775, which divided Russia into fifty-one *gubernii* (provinces). These were further divided into ten times as many districts, each with defined responsibilities and controlled from a common centre, but whose officials were elected by the local nobility. Thus two purposes were achieved: on the one hand, the autocracy built up what, on the face of it, was a more highly centralised system at both levels of administration; and, on the other, it was one in which a large part of the authority was in the hands of the landowning classes.

It was widely held in Frederick II's time – and the view was no doubt supported by the glamour of his military victories – that Prussia was the most efficient and best-governed state in Europe. The tribute was partly undeserved; but when account is taken of the unpromising situation that Prussia's founders encountered at the beginning of the century it is remarkable that it could have ever been paid at all. Admittedly the Great Elector of Brandenburg had, as we noted, taken some steps to set up a strong centralised government and reduced the powers of the nobility and provincial estates, but the machinery of administration remained largely traditional and chaotic. In no country in Europe, at the time that Frederick William I took over, were the public and private sectors so inextricably confused. The ruler's domain lands alone accounted for between one-third and one-quarter of the peasants in the kingdom; in consequence, there was a natural urge to administer the whole territory as an extension of a private estate. In fact two systems of management existed side by side: the one based on the domain lands consisted of 'finance' committees; while the other was responsible for collecting the war tax through 'war' committees in the rest of the country. Frederick William merged the two, unifying the two committees in every province and subjecting them to the control of a *General-Ober-Finanz-Kriegs-und-Domänen Direktorium* (in short, a General Directory) at Berlin. Thus a central direction was given, in name at least, to the administration of the state. But there followed a curious addition of new departments, some of which were related to the General Directory while others were not and of which some at least exercised functions that duplicated those already exercised by the Directory. It was a highly personal arrangement, as was the king's relationship with his servants of whom he expected the most complete and unqualified obedience. 'One must serve the King' [he wrote a year after his succession] 'with life and limb, with goods and chattels, with honour and conscience, and surrender everything except salvation. The latter is reserved for God. But everything else is mine.'[1] The tradition, once established, was passed on to his successor, who in this matter as in so many others trod faithfully in his father's steps. Though Frederick was often critical of the amateurish procedures of the General Directory, he kept it on and created further specialised departments in its orbit, such, for example, as the new ministries he added for commerce, the army and Silesia, in the 1740s, during the first of his wars. Some of these additions, like his father's, bore no relationship to the General Directory, and there continued to be no formal link between them or any overriding authority to give them direction, except that given in the person of the imperious monarch himself. This personal touch was as much a part of Frederick's practice as of Frederick William's. It gave the whole system unity as long as they both survived; but once the guiding hand of father and son had been withdrawn, the weaknesses became all too apparent and left problems to be sorted out by their less fortunate and less gifted successors.

The Habsburg rulers of the Austrian Empire had problems similar to those of their neighbours. They also had an imperative need to build up a strong central administration in order to hold their scattered dominions together, a need that was all the greater because their authority was more liable to be challenged by long-established landowning families and regional separatism. The first of the eighteenth-century Habsburgs, the Emperor Charles VI, was in no strong position to do much about it as he had his hands full with another more immediate problem: how to assure the succession to his daughter, Maria Theresa. This, as we have seen, he was able to do; but at the price of making concessions to aristocratic and provincial claims. So the matter was left for his daughter to tackle. It was the war with Frederick of Prussia that acted as a spur. In the attempt to hold on to Silesia, the Empress carried through a number of military reforms which brought in a regular income to her exchequer at the expense of the privileged church and provincial estates. New agencies were created at Vienna that overrode and permanently weakened the control of the estates over their own finances. Once the war was over Haugwitz followed up these exceptional measures by introducing in 1748 a general tax law that put the government's finances on a more permanent footing. Meanwhile, other institutions had begun to appear, such as the State Chancery for Foreign Affairs in 1742; the two separate Chanceries of Austria and Bohemia were merged under the presidency of Haugwitz in 1749; the *Staatskanzlei*, or Foreign Office, was reformed in 1753; and a new overriding authority, the *Staatsrat*, or Council of State, was created in 1760. Some of these measures, such as the merger of the Chanceries of Austria and Bohemia, were copied from the Prussians, but the eventual system that emerged was entirely different from theirs, as responsibility was vested in ministers acting under the Emperor's direction in the Council of State. Thus, formally at least, the Habsburgs had developed, by the time Joseph II joined his mother as co-ruler in 1765, the most systematically structured bureaucracy and the most specialised system of administration in Europe, and not one which, as in Frederick's Prussia, depended on the temporary whim of the ruler. But, as we shall see, the centrifugal forces within the Empire continued to pose problems which the system was not fully equipped to solve.

The Spanish Bourbons, again, had problems not unlike those of the Austrian Habsburgs; they also had similar aims, but the degree of centralisation they achieved in the course of the century was far more limited than theirs. When Philip V acceded to the throne of Spain, he found a jungle of competing authorities not unlike that found by Peter I in the *prikazi* in Russia. In Spain, the prevailing system was based on the Great Councils largely composed of grandees which between them handled every imaginable item of public business. The most important was the Council of State which advised the king on foreign affairs. In addition there were Councils of War, Inquisition and the Military Orders and other Councils with more specific regional jurisdiction, such as the Councils of Aragon, Italy, Flanders, the Indies and Castile. The Council of Castile, in particular, handled a vast range of business: justice, church affairs, hospitals, universities, industry and trade, corn supplies, law and order, mines and municipal finance all fell within its competence. But the functions of all these bodies overlapped both geographically and administratively; they had their finger in every pie, but without discrimination or co-ordination; their procedures were slow and cumbersome, and they were incurably inefficient. Coming as he did from France with French advisers, Philip naturally attempted to remodel his administration in imitation of the French as Peter had done in imitation of the Swedish. So he appointed ministers, corresponding to the Secretaries of State in France, to each of whom was entrusted a particular sphere of business. Philip added three more ministers of this kind to the only one he found on his accession: one to deal with war and finance, a second with church affairs and a third with the Indies and the navy; while a further minister (making five in all), whose sole responsibility was finance, was appointed by his successor in the 1750s. Philip also managed to dismantle the political institutions which had given a virtually independent status to his provinces of Catalonia, Valencia and Aragon, though he failed to do so in the case of the Basque provinces and Navarre. So something at least was done to build up a central administration with the responsible ministers at Madrid. But to abolish the Grand Councils altogether proved an insuperable task, and they remained an awkward legacy to Philip's successors. Among his successors the most determined to impose a more uniform system of government was Charles III, who surrounded himself with a team of specialists to carry out further reforms. Their intentions were good, but the obstructions proved too great; and the administrative reforms that the king, his ministers and bureaucrats projected had, for their implementation, to be left over to the more favourable opportunities arising after the Napoleonic wars.

In many respects the building of a specialised bureaucratic machine had gone further in France than in any other country in Europe. The first steps went back even earlier than they did in Sweden. This was the creation of the Secretary of State, whose functions were broadly ministerial. The office had appeared in Henry II's time in the middle of the sixteenth century and went through various stages of specialisation, which continued during the highly personal though essentially 'bureaucratic' rule of Louis XIV a hundred years later. In Louis XV's day, the Secretary's office was closely defined, the four Secretaries being variously responsible for foreign affairs, war, navy and colonies, and the *maison du roi* (roughly corresponding to a modern Ministry of the Interior crossed with a department for religious affairs). A fifth ministerial post, though not a Secretaryship of State, was that of Controller General of Finance who in addition to his duties as a Finance Minister appointed Intendants to the provinces, supervised communications and a great deal of the nation's economy, and was usually in a stronger position to influence the king than anyone else. These, then, though they did not formally constitute a ministry and were individually appointed and dismissed at the royal pleasure, formed with the Chancellor and Keeper of the Seals

2 France and its provinces in 1789

a government élite whose advice and guidance the king might or might not accept. But the king's authority was exercised through other channels as well: in particular through Louis xiv's old system of councils, of which earlier mention has been made – the *Conseil d'état* or *Conseil d'en haut* at the summit and the other subordinate councils, the *Conseil des dépêches*, the *Conseil des finances* and the *Conseil privé* (a sort of high court of justice). But these, through the long reign of the indolent Louis xv, tended to lose a great deal of their former importance. One other channel of authority, however, continued through all the vicissitudes of royal indolence and ministerial crisis to maintain its importance: this was the rule of the Intendant. The Intendant had become in fact a sheet-anchor of royal absolutism in France. Holding a temporary roving commission in Richelieu's day, the Intendants had become the king's permanent representatives in the provinces early in Louis xiv's reign, and continued to levy taxes, maintain law and order, build roads, control grain supplies and administer royal justice in the thirty-one *généralités* into which the country was divided. The Scots financier, John Law, was so impressed by the authority they exercised even at the time of the Regency that he is reported to have told the Marquis d'Argenson: 'This kingdom of France is ruled by thirty Intendants. You have neither Parlements . . . nor Estates nor Governors . . . but thirty [men] . . . on whom depends the welfare or the misery of the provinces.'[2] It was a slight exaggeration, even as regards the Estates and the Governors, at the time it was said; but it would prove a far greater one when applied to the conditions of France in the later eighteenth century. The Intendants' role, it is true, remained relatively undiminished; but the Parlements, far from being non-existent, had by 1760 begun, as we shall see, to question the authority of every aspect of the royal administration. Thus in France, as in Austria and Prussia, the bureaucratic machine proved less strong and impregnable than it seemed.

Once more the British system was different from that of any other major state. Superficially it resembled most the systems that had developed in France and Sweden. Nominally, as in those countries, the administration was in the hands of the crown; and it was the king who appointed to the chief Cabinet and ministerial posts – both to the older offices of Lord Chancellor, Lord Treasurer, Lord Privy Seal and Lord High Admiral, and to those more recently evolved, like the two Secretaries of State, the Secretary at War, the Postmaster General and the Paymaster of the Forces. Some of these offices were assigned to boards, others to individuals; and some senior officers, though not others, sat in the policy-making committee or Cabinet over which the king ceased to preside after the reign of George I. But the Cabinet still remained a somewhat amorphous body, being sometimes attended by non-ministerial Household officers and such dignitaries as the Lord Chief Justice and the Archbishop of Canterbury; ministers were still individually appointed and were liable (though more in theory than in practice) to individual dismissal. It was only on rare occasions (as under Walpole in the 1730s, the Pelhams in the 1750s and the younger Pitt in the 1780s) that they could speak with a single voice and exercise a degree of collective responsibility. So, formally, eighteenth-century ministers in England looked much like the Secretaries of State in France, and English ministries and Cabinet more closely resembled the colleges and Council of State in contemporary Sweden than they resembled the political institutions of Britain today. Yet there was an important difference: the role of Parliament, though it had a certain parallel in the Swedish Riksdag, had no equivalent at all in France. The British Parliament was able to ensure that the great offices of state were nearly always held by men prominent in the Lords or Commons; and since Sir Robert

Walpole's accession to high office in 1722, it became more or less established that while the king had the right of appointment, he could not retain in office men who did not enjoy the confidence of Parliament, nor could such men be dismissed unless they lost favour with both Parliament and king. So, in sharp contrast with the practice in France, the court favourite had little hope of ministerial survival unless he had other connections to offer; and even George III, who expected great things from his ministerial re-shuffle of 1761, was compelled to dismiss his favourite, the Earl of Bute, only two years later.

So in all countries the eighteenth century saw steps taken towards more efficient methods of administration and towards a greater degree of specialisation whether in colleges, ministries, boards or departments. But apart from the particular weaknesses that have already been mentioned there were others that were of a more general application. For instance, there was the evident difficulty of collecting taxes and duties to finance wars or conduct the day-to-day affairs of government, or of raising revenue from customs or the royal domains. In the first place, it was difficult to make regular and equitable assessments of citizens' resources, particularly of movable wealth, at a time when banks were few and far between and when assessments, even if equitably made, tended to be years out of date. Moreover, privileged persons, estates and institutions claimed a variety of immunities. The Prussian king had the reputation of being the only ruler on the continent who could balance his budget; but even in Prussia (outside East Prussia) nobles claimed exemption from the direct tax known as 'the contribution'. In France the clergy and nobility were exempt from paying the *taille*, the direct tax on land, while the more privileged *pays d'états* paid at a lower rate than the *pays d'élection*. In Hungary and Poland the privileged classes were even more notoriously immune from paying taxes than they were in France; while in Spain on the contrary both nobility and clergy were taxed, the clergy being compelled to pay a proportion of their tithes into the national exchequer. In some countries, for example France and Lombardy, the towns tended to be favoured at the expense of the countryside; and even in England, which like Prussia had an enviable reputation for raising revenue, the land tax tended to be under-assessed in the western counties, probably because they had a disproportionately large representation in Parliament. Raising revenue from customs was another intractable problem, as Sir Robert Walpole discovered when he introduced an Excise Bill in 1733 and was compelled to withdraw it soon after. If England had her problems, France's were certainly greater. Here, a succession of public-spirited ministers and officials from Colbert onwards tried for over a century to make some sense of the bewildering complexity of *péages*, *octrois*, *aides*, *traités* and *gabelles* whereby privileged interests levied a wide variety of tolls on the circulation of goods and persons throughout the length and breadth of the country. Colbert had tried to rationalise the system in the interests of the crown by creating a single customs union and levying a single uniform tariff at the national frontiers alone. He failed dismally and only succeeded in dividing the country into three separate regions for customs-levying purposes. His efforts were renewed by a succession of officials in the eighteenth century, but their attempts were continuously obstructed by the vested interests of nobles, tax-exempt provinces, tax-farmers and Parlements. The matter was eventually solved, along lines broadly similar to Colbert's, by the Constituent Assembly of the Revolution in 1791.[3]

Another evil which also caused considerable resentment was the practice of farming out the collection of taxes to wealthy individuals. The practice was not universal: it was unknown or hardly existed in Britain, Russia and Prussia; but it was prevalent in parts of Italy (in Lombardy until 1770) and in France. In such countries the tax-farmer (or Farmer General, as he was known in France) was empowered to levy certain specified taxes in return for a lump-sum payment. The system lent itself to obvious abuses as the tax-farmer had an interest in making as large a profit as possible, which he could do either by squeezing his customers beyond the specified limit or by giving the government short change. Moreover, the greater the state's need for a rapid return, the less favourable were the terms it was able to negotiate with the tax-farmer; but the practice, even after its dishonesties became apparent, continued as it saved the government the need (even if it had had the means) of devising a more efficient and professional means of collection. In addition, there were countries where tradition imposed other, non-professional, methods of collection. In Russia, for example, the government leaned heavily on the aristocracy to collect its local revenues; and in England, the collection of the land tax in the counties was in the hands of receivers-general, usually country gentlemen, who were paid a commission on the money collected.

A further weak spot was the administration of justice. The problem did not really apply to England (though the case of Ireland and Scotland was somewhat different), as the English through their battles with the crown in the seventeenth century had created a judicial system that in most important respects was independent of the administration. Judges, for example, from 1700 onwards held office while 'of good behaviour' and could not be dismissed as they had been under the early Stuart kings on purely political grounds. Moreover, the courts, far from taking their cue from administration, were able when they felt so disposed to act as a check on the exercise by government of practices that were considered illegal or had become an abuse: an example here was the initiative taken by the judges, following the *North Briton* affair of

1763 (see page 187), in declaring the illegality of arrests by general warrant. In France too, the Parlements could by virtue of their judicial powers and their right to 'remonstrate' against royal decrees act as a brake on ministerial 'despotism'. But in France the exercise of justice was inextricably confused. Roman law prevailed in the south and customary or common law in the centre and north; and the exercise by the provincial Parlements of their rights of jurisdiction trespassed on that of the royal courts while offering their clients no saving in money or time; nor for that matter any prospect of a more enlightened justice. Besides in France, as in several continental countries, nobles still exercised their old feudal rights of seigneurial justice, often with results that were detrimental to their tenants' interests. In eastern and central Europe, there was a further problem as well. As there were no parliaments or constitutions there was no fundamental charter of liberties or Bill of Rights to which the citizen might appeal against the tyranny of government or administration. In fact, the judiciary often served as a branch of government or a department of state. This was true of Russia and Prussia as it was of the Habsburg dominions. Yet some progress was made to distinguish between the exercise of justice and the interests of state. Frederick II, for example, in 1748 forbade administrative bodies to interfere with the proceedings of the courts.

In every country, however efficient its central administration, there was bound to be a certain devolution of authority. Whether this was a sign of health or a sign of weakness naturally depended on the circumstances in which the country and its ruler found themselves; and overall judgements on the vices or virtues of decentralisation are obviously out of place. It is a matter of opinion, for example, how far Britain was strengthened or weakened by the tenacious survival of the justices of the peace, who continued to exercise their remarkably wide range of activities until late in the nineteenth century. The part they played in the English counties has in fact been compared to that played by the French Intendants in their *généralités*: they acted as courts of law, they maintained law and order, they recruited men for the armed forces, they fixed wages and prices, they built roads and bridges, they administered the poor law and they even established precedents for other justices to follow. But there were important differences between the two: unlike the Intendants, the justices acted collectively as well as individually; they were not centrally appointed but local men; they were not directly answerable to any central authority; and (with the exception of a few 'stipendiaries' in large cities) they were unpaid. And being mainly country gentlemen or Church of England parsons their jurisdiction tended to be conservative and highly responsive to local property interests. This class-nature of local administration was equally evident in Russia, particularly after Catherine's local government edict of 1775 left its operation in the *gubernii* almost exclusively to committees elected by the landowning class; yet it does not appear to have followed that the Russian autocracy, by sharing power with the nobility, thereby weakened its own hold on the administration.

In Prussia the case was different. There was no devolution of authority as there was in Russia and England between the centre and the provinces; such devolution as there was developed within the central machinery of government itself. Frederick II, as we have said more than once already, favoured the aristocracy at the expense of commoners and gave the plums of administrative office to a combination of nobility by descent and the more recently created nobility of service. In the course of his reign this noble bureaucracy tended to close its ranks, first against penetration of newcomers from without, later (though more discreetly) against the absolute monarch himself. Thus the bureaucracy, conscious of its class origins and interests, began to assume the guise of an almost independent force, which, as Hans Rosenberg has argued, began even before Frederick's death to weaken the authority of Prussian Cabinet government.[4] In France this process of dissolution from within had gone much further by the late eighteenth century than it had in Prussia and its consequences were far more injurious to the interests of the absolute-monarchical state. Here too there was a consolidation within the ranks of the administrators, though not within the administration as a whole. The Intendants, for example, though increasingly drawn from the aristocracy of the Robe, retained their functions as individual servants of the crown, whom the king continued to appoint and dismiss at will. There were certainly cases of Intendants who were won over to the new 'enlightened' ideas and tended to go their own way; but in no sense can they be said to have acted as a challenge to the authority of the king. This challenge came from another quarter. In France, with its largely unpaid civil service, a large part of the effective administration was conducted by men who had risen into the higher ranks of the bureaucracy by the purchase of hereditary office. These included both *parlementaires* and *maîtres de requêtes, secrétaires du roi* and a host of other noble or quasi-noble *officiers*, whose property-rights protected them against dismissal and assured them of a permanent tenure of office. As such men began not only to close ranks among themselves, but to identify their interests with other privileged groups – the older *noblesse*, the high clergy, gilds, chartered cities and provincial estates – they became a serious danger to the monarchy itself. Thus the royal bureaucracy, for all its long traditions and its apparent vigour, became progressively disrupted from within and without.

While in England, France, Russia and Prussia the devolution of authority had developed with the active or tacit support of the rulers, this was certainly not the case in Spain or the Habsburg dominions. Here devolution came from necessity: it was not a matter of the personal choice of the rulers but of a pistol pointed at their heads. In fact, provincial separatism sometimes imposed a pattern of local government on the rulers of Spain and the Austrian Empire that was by no means of their choosing but one that they had to put up with. We have seen that in Spain Philip v succeeded in integrating Catalonia, Valencia and Aragon within his national system, but that the Basque provinces and Navarre eluded him. These provinces continued to be largely self-governing with their own General Assemblies and Provincial Deputations. Royal agents were subject to rigorous control, and these border provinces (or *fueros*) were exempt from Spanish conscription, taxes and customs duties: in fact, as has been said, 'the national customs frontier ran along the Ebro'.[5] The problem was a similar one in the Habsburg dominions. Here too, integration met with a greater or lesser degree of resistance, for every one of the dominions clung in one form or another to its own customs, traditions and institutions and the privileges and immunities that went with them. Maria Theresa's reforms, however, were adequate to keep such forces in check in the Austrian and Bohemian provinces. These were divided into forty-seven districts, each of which was put in charge of a district officer or *Kreishauptmann*, a factotum whose responsibilities became by stages as all-embracing as those of the Intendant in France: in 1770 they were described as being 'to fulfil her Majesty's orders reliably, to keep good order and to look after everything concerning the public welfare'. Accordingly, the authority of the provincial estates declined, and these parts of the Habsburg dominions became progressively incorporated within an imperial system. The case of Hungary was a very different one, and here centrifugal forces persisted which defeated all attempts made by Vienna to bring them to heel. Where the Bohemians and Austrians had their district officer trained in Vienna, the Hungarians had their *foispan*, or high sheriff, a local magnate who looked on the Emperor and his officials as intruders and treated their directives with little or no respect. So, in spite of Haugwitz's financial reforms, the Hungarians continued to pay a lower proportion of taxes than any other imperial province; they remained outside Maria Theresa's customs union of 1755, and they retained their own diets and county assemblies. In short, they continued to be a disintegrating factor within the Empire for which even Joseph ii's zeal for uniformity proved to be no match.

By and large then, the aims and ambitions of the rulers and administrators of the eighteenth century were never fully realised. These limitations were imposed, as we have seen, by a combination of factors: by geography, tradition, regionalism; and even more by the nature of society itself, with its pockets of privileges, immunities and liberties, which served as so many obstructions to the realisation of the despot's or bureaucrat's dream of an omnicompetent state, as they so often did to the more modest aims of humanitarian reformers. Yet nothing stood still and reforms were made, particularly during the latter half of the century, which even if they found no adequate solution to the problems of the time, left a certain legacy for later state-builders and bureaucrats to build on. Let us consider some of these briefly before concluding this chapter.

In Spain reform remained largely on paper. Charles III's team of advisers were well aware of the difficulties of their task: one of them wrote of his country as 'a body without energy, a monstrous Republic formed of little republics which confront each other because the particular interest of each is in contradiction with the general interest'. For him and his colleagues the obstacles proved too great to resolve; but the centralising plans of the Caroline bureaucrats reappeared in the radical–liberal programme of the Cortès of Cadiz in Napoleon's day, and they were implemented by the liberals of the 1830s and after.[6] In both Austria and Prussia there were important reforms in the administration of justice. In Austria a unified code of laws was issued in 1769; judicial torture was abolished in 1774; and the death penalty was abolished, except in cases of armed rebellion, three years later. In Prussia the number of executions for capital crimes was among the lowest in Europe (notoriously lower, for example, than it was in Britain); and the laws were codified in a great statute of 1791. In England and France a more general administrative revolution was taking place in the latter half of the century. In both countries more and more public servants were being paid, higher professional standards were being exacted, public records were being more systematically kept and the surviving confusions between the public and private sector in the conduct of the nation's affairs were being progressively ironed out. A part of this process was the transformation in the handling and auditing of public funds. Early in the century such funds had been handled by a variety of agencies and individuals without any form of public accounting or central control; so that the Treasury in England or the Minister of Finance in France acted as a paymaster who, to discharge his obligations, had to dip into a number of separate tills without powers to inspect their contents or to control the activities of those who filled them. In England government departments tended to raise and control their own finances and made their own estimates of receipts and expenses; while in France public funds were privately managed by a host of accountants, or 'capitalists', who kept their own separate chests or *caisses* which were entirely immune to any form of public accounting or inspection. In England, by the mid-century, the Treasury had already established its controls over the spending of most government departments, though for long the Admiralty held out as a lone bastion of private enterprise. The process was virtually completed by the time the younger Pitt, on taking office in 1784, announced that as First Minister of the Crown he should be 'the person at the head of the finances'. So all was set for firm Treasury control under the Prime Minister's direction and for the modern budget and public accounting as well. In France vested interests were more firmly entrenched and the nut proved harder to crack. Reform took place in three main stages. First, three reforming Finance Ministers (Terray, Turgot and Necker) in the decade 1771–81 reduced the number of collecting agencies to four and subjected the accountants to some degree of government control. In the next phase, a fourth minister, Loménie de Brienne (in 1788), created the modern French Treasury on lines roughly corresponding to the English. At the third stage, which had to await the Revolution, Brienne's further plans were carried out by extending Treasury control over all government funds and subjecting all the *caisses* to its direction and inspection. Thus, over a period of thirty years, the old French financial system was converted (to use John Bosher's term) 'from a capitalism into a bureaucracy'.[7]

In France, there had been many other important reforms besides; in fact, she probably produced, in the course of the century, the finest body of administrators in Europe. In Louis xv's time, Controller General Orry had launched a great plan for road-building through the department of the *Ponts et Chaussées*, which gave France by the end of the century a system of first-class roads and well-paved causeways that were the envy of every traveller from abroad. Arthur Young noted the fact 'with admiration' when he travelled through Languedoc in 1787. After the Seven Years War the Duc de Choiseul, supported by a team of able government servants, began to overhaul the French army and navy, and by the end of the *ancien régime* France had a lead over every other European power in the use of modern weapons and in the strategy and tactics of warfare. Under Louis xvi, important reforms were made in the administration and exercise of justice. As in Prussia and Austria torture was abolished; the Bastille was emptied of its prisoners (so that there only remained seven for Parisians to release in July 1789); and *lettres de cachet*, which ordered detention without trial, were, under Louis xvi, only being issued at one-third the rate at which they had been issued under Louis xv. So reform was in the air, and it was not for lack of good intentions or of reforming ministers or enlightened bureaucrats that France was standing on the brink of revolution. Tocqueville, reviewing the situation sixty years after the event, arrived at the paradoxical conclusion that 'the social order overthrown by a revolution is almost always better than the one immediately preceding it' and that 'generally speaking, the most perilous moment for a bad government is one when it seeks to mend its ways'. If true, the statement is a sad reflection on the poorly rewarded efforts of Turgot, Brienne and other reforming ministers. But why it might be true, and why it had a particular relevance for France, is a question we must refer, like so many others, to a later chapter in the book.

CHAPTER 8

CHURCH, STATE AND SOCIETY

After the turmoils and battles of the century before, the religious pattern of the eighteenth century was relatively peaceful and undisturbed. The previous century had seen the religious wars in Germany and the 'Puritan' revolution in England; and at its close there had been the bitter struggle of Old and New Believers for control of the Greek Orthodox Church in Russia and the battles between Ultramontanes and Jansenists in France; England under Anne had seen a renewal of the savage infighting between Anglicans and Nonconformists, ranged behind the rival banners of Tories and Whigs. Compared with all this turmoil the new century was an age of calm in which governments and established churches settled down to consolidate their gains, and during which even the polemics of theological dispute were relatively muted. In England the religious 'enthusiasm' which was so fashionable in the century before was frowned upon by the upper classes; the polite disputations of Unitarians, Trinitarians and Deists took the place of the savage rhetoric of Dr Henry Sacheverell who, in denouncing Nonconformity at the time of Anne, had stirred riots and set all London by the ears. Horace Walpole, who had an unrivalled sense for the social proprieties, said that the only reason he went to church was to set his servants a good example. This English 'latitudinarianism', or easy conformity, had its parallel in other countries too, though nowhere among the industrious and the poor. Even in Spain the Inquisition was losing its grip and burned its last victim at the stake in 1781. In France, it is true, the battle over Jansenism continued beyond Louis xiv's death; but it changed its form, lost its theological sting and after a last flare-up over *billets de confession* in the early 1750s became a spent force (see page 128).

Moreover, the international centres of organised religion had received heavy blows from the peace settlements that ended the wars at the turn of the century. The Ottoman Empire, the most militant of the theocracies with a stake in Europe, had lost much of its Balkan possessions to Austria. In Rome the papacy had suffered even more, both as a spiritual and a temporal power. The treaty of Utrecht had tipped the balance of world power sharply in favour of Britain, the richest and most populous of the Protestant states; and the advance into Europe of Orthodox Russia and Lutheran Prussia had chipped further pieces off the province of the Roman church, now reduced to the Iberian peninsula, Italy, France, Ireland and the greater part of south Germany, Poland and the Habsburg Empire. Moreover, the Catholic princes themselves were showing an increasingly scant regard for the papal authority, and least of all for the Pope's temporal claims. His emissaries had been virtually ignored at the treaties of Utrecht and Rastadt in 1713–14, as they were later at Aix-la-Chapelle in 1748; and Austrians and Spaniards, during their Italian wars of the 1730s and 1740s, invaded his territories and all but robbed him of his overlordship in Parma and Piacenza. So the Popes, seeing their dominions shrink and their authority decline, and realising their powerlessness to offer any effective resistance, were inclined to accept the *fait accompli* with good grace. Among the Popes who did so was Benedict XIV (1740–58), who announced: 'I prefer to let the thunders of the Vatican rest . . . Let us take care not to mistake passion for zeal, for this mistake has caused the greatest evils to religion.'[1] But nothing was so indicative of papal decline as the humiliation suffered by Clement XIV when he disbanded the Society of Jesus (Jesuits) in 1773 at the request of the Bourbon kings. Thus, under pressure from the Catholic rulers of Europe, the papacy surrendered one of its principal bastions in the Catholic states.

Yet within all countries whether Catholic or other the churches continued to be well entrenched and to lead a vigorous existence. In the larger Catholic states, the number of 'religious' – priests, nuns and monks – were often striking and showed no signs of any immediate decline. In France, there were some 130,000 of both 'regular' and 'secular' clergy in a population of twenty-five million; in Austria there were (until the 1780s) about 65,000 'regulars' alone; and in Spain a combined clergy of over 20,000, or of at least one in fifty of the population. The number of churches and religious houses was more remarkable still: towards the end of the century, there were 3,000 religious houses in Spain, 2,500 in France and 2,000 in the Austrian dominions. In Spain, Valladolid, with a population of 21,000, had forty-six monasteries with 1,258 inmates, while Burgos (population of 9,000) had fourteen parish churches and forty-two monasteries and convents. Paris, with its fifty parishes, had in relation to population four times the number of parish churches she had in 1900. Gray, in France, had fourteen churches for 4,000 people; and Tréguier, an episcopal seat, had almost as many monasteries and seminaries as private houses (a figure that puts the one-in-six proportion we noted earlier for Angers well in the shade). In Moscow, William Coxe observed that there were '484 public churches, of which 199 are of brick and the others of wood'.[2] In comparison,

London's 186 Anglican churches and chapels (recorded in 1812) seems almost insignificant; yet Paris, in relation to population, probably had no more. And with all these churches and institutions, the churches continued to perform their multiform activities. They conducted religious worship, heard confession and granted absolution; they baptised, married and buried; distributed alms, and provided hospitals and homes for the poor and such popular education as there was. In Russia Coxe, who as a future Anglican Archdeacon was not impressed by a great deal of what he saw, confessed that the abolition of monasteries under Catherine might create a greater evil than it cured, as they were 'the only seminaries of education for those persons designed for the sacred functions'. Yet he consoled himself with the thought that other and better substitutes might eventually be found.[3] In Spain, the distribution of alms to the countless beggars and the organisation of bread and soup kitchens were major operations: 30,000 bowls of soup were given out daily in Madrid alone. Such a situation gave the Spanish church enormous power, and reforming ministers like Aranda, who feared it, tried to reduce it by clearing the streets of beggars and providing an alternative state system of public relief. The Duke of Wellington was also to note the church's hold on the common people, though with greater appreciation in his case. 'The real power in Spain,' he wrote after his peninsular campaign, 'is in the clergy. They kept the people right against France.'[4]

While the churches continued to exercise their traditional functions, it was increasingly as an arm of the secular state. Everywhere, whether in Catholic, Protestant or Greek Orthodox lands, kings and rulers were asserting and extending their authority over their churches and prelates and becoming more intolerant of interference from any outside quarter. The submission of church to state was of course nothing new in the countries of Protestantism: since the Reformation, the supremacy of the secular state had been maintained in Britain, the majority of the north German states and (intermittently) in Scandinavia over the national churches, whether they were Anglican, Calvinist, Lutheran or Calvinist-Arminian. France though Roman Catholic had enjoyed since the Concordat of Bologna of 1516 a large measure of independence of the papal authority, as in the appointment of bishops, the harvesting of revenue from vacant sees and benefices and the independent promulgation of papal bulls. These 'Gallican' liberties had been jealously upheld by a long succession of rulers, and by the majority of bishops and the Parlements as well. And now, in the eighteenth century, as the papal authority weakened, other Catholic rulers were pressing claims similar to those long enjoyed by the French. Not least in Italy, where anti-papal theologians like Giannone of Naples had long campaigned against the pretensions of Rome, while the Archbishop of Taranto even went so far as to speak (in 1788) of 'Papalism as the perpetual enemy of this kingdom'. Venice had for more than a century been at loggerheads with the Curia at Rome; and in 1741 the Pope signed concordats with Naples and Sardinia, largely surrendering his rights over episcopal appointments. Other concordats of the kind were signed with Portugal in 1740 and with Spain in 1737 and 1753. The concessions made to Spain were even more sweeping than those made earlier to the Gallican church in France. By the agreement signed between Ferdinand VI and Benedict XIV in 1753, ecclesiastical appointments were declared to be the sole province of the king of Spain, while the Pope lost even the right to confirm such appointments as were made. Ferdinand's successor, Charles III, went further: he forbade papal bulls to be published in his dominions without the prior consent of his Council; and even the Inquisition was altogether removed from the jurisdiction of Rome.

Outside the Catholic countries, the churches were being bound even more closely to the secular state. In Russia, Peter I had assumed a supremacy over the Orthodox Church which, in all but name, was similar to that assumed over the church in England by Henry VIII two centuries before. He found the church weakened by the dispute between New and Old Believers which had been provoked by the Patriarch Nikon during the previous reign, and he took full advantage of its predicament. In 1700 when Patriarch Adrian died Peter refused to nominate a successor; and twenty years later he created the Holy Synod over which he presided in person. The Synod thus received its instructions direct from the ruler himself; it directed the church's spiritual affairs, appointed to all high offices and became a powerful instrument of state. In Hanoverian England, the role of the church was no less blatantly political. Twenty-six of its bishops sat in the House of Lords as representatives of the established church and attuned their political beliefs to the needs of the court and government of the day. Having been solidly Tory under Anne, they became solidly Whig and 'Hanoverian' after 1714. During the twenty-year administration of Sir Robert Walpole, the compliancy of the bishops even became something of a national scandal. With the Duke of Newcastle as his political manager, Walpole could always count on the twenty-six episcopal votes in the Lords to support his policies; in fact, in the Excise crisis of 1733, they twice saved him from defeat. Perhaps it was with such facts as these in mind that William Blake, in his poem *Jerusalem*, asked the question, 'Are not religion and politics the same thing?'

As the church was a pillar of the political establishment, it was a pillar of aristocratic society as well. In England where the majority of bishops sat in the Lords this was clear for all to see. In other countries, appointments to bishoprics were increasingly being made from aristocratic families. In Rome the aristocracy, both ecclesiastical and secular, was consolidated into a closed caste of 187 families by Benedict XIV in 1746; and in France, under Louis XVI, only one of the 139 bishops holding office was at any time of anything but noble birth; the exception held only the squalid little see of Senez, in the present department of the Basses-Alpes. (This was a further contrast with Louis XIV's day when many appointments, including that of Bossuet himself, had been made from the middle class.) Spain, however, was different. Here bishops continued to be largely recruited among men of relatively humble birth. Spain was also an exception in that high offices in the church were relatively poorly paid, though strangely enough the Archbishop of Toledo, with an income of 85,000 ducats a year, had the reputation of being the wealthiest prelate in Christendom. Elsewhere the churches were often immensely wealthy, and their bishops and dignitaries enjoyed wealth and privileges befitting members of an aristocratic order. In France, the church's properties yielded an annual income of between fifty and a hundred million livres, which represented something between one-twelfth and one-quarter of the landed wealth in every province in the kingdom; while from tithes it drew a further hundred to a hundred and twenty million livres a year; and a remarkably small proportion of all this (perhaps two per cent at this time) was paid in the form of a so-called *don gratuit*, or voluntary gift, into the national exchequer. Among the wealthiest prelates in France were the Archbishop of Strasbourg, with an episcopal income of 400,000 livres, and a further 800,000 livres from his feudal domains in Alsace; and the Archbishop of Paris, with 200,000 livres; while the Archbishops of Albi and Narbonne drew episcopal incomes of respectively 120,000 and 160,000 livres, further supplemented by the 100,000 and 120,000 livres they drew from the abbeys under their jurisdiction. In the Catholic provinces of the Habsburg Empire the church was the owner of vast estates, extending over three-eighths of all the lands in private occupation. The Belgian share was even greater; one-half, it was said, in Flanders, and two-thirds in Brabant. In England bishops might be elevated for services rendered from a poor see like Bristol (with an income of no more than £450) to an important and wealthy see like Winchester, Durham or Canterbury, where incomes rose to £5,000, £6,000 and £7,000 a year. In Russia the monasteries were, until Catherine took most of them over, the main depositories of ecclesiastical wealth. According to Coxe, their estates had previously yielded an annual income of £400,000. After 1764 Catherine annexed these church lands to the crown, drew their revenues herself and paid an annual salary to the monks and clergy. Under this new arrangement bishops and archbishops were paid (Coxe tells us) between £1,000 and £1,200 per annum, which was a considerable sum in Russia but was a modest income compared with that of the wealthy prelates in England, Austria and France.

With wealth, privilege and defined political commitment went a considerable amount of laxity and abuse in the exercise of ecclesiastical duties. Some high prelates were frank disbelievers: it is said that Louis XVI, when Loménie de Brienne was recommended to him for the see of Paris, objected that 'at least the Archbishop of Paris should believe in God'.[5] In England Bishop Watson of Llandaff, having been persuaded to become a political pamphleteer, claimed that for twenty years he supported 'the religion and constitution of the country by seasonable publications'. In France sons of noble families tended to become bishops earlier than others: Talleyrand became a bishop at thirty-five years of age and the Cardinal de Rohan at twenty-six. The princely bishops of west Germany, the Abbé Latreille tells us, neglected their spiritual charges more shamefully than any other prelates in Christendom; and when Pacca, the Apostolic Nuncio, arrived at the small town of Arenberg in the principality of Cologne, he found no fewer than 16,000 persons waiting to be confirmed.[6] Pluralism and absenteeism were the main causes of neglect, as they often were also in England and France. In France it was discovered in 1764 that no less than forty bishops were living in Paris, and the scandal became so great that Louis XVI, some years later, felt obliged to order his bishops not to leave their diocese without his permission. In England Hoadley, Bishop of Bangor in the reign of George I, never once visited his see. Nor were such extravagances confined to bishops: in London at the close of the seventeenth century forty-three incumbents of City churches had country livings which they rarely visited; a century later, 6,000 out of 10,000 country parsons were said to be non-resident; and Arthur Young had previously recorded that 'country towns abound with curates who never see the parishes they serve, but when they are absolutely forced to it by duty'.[7] But, of course, this is not the whole story. There were churchmen who, whatever the pressures to conform to an easier way of life, were zealous in the discharge of their pastoral obligations. In England there were Bishops Wake and Gibson who succeeded one another at Lincoln, and Ross and Keppel at Exeter: in 1764 Keppel confirmed more than 40,000 persons in the course of a confirmation tour. Among such men in France there was Boisgelin, Archbishop of Aix, who had the reputation of being an excellent administrator as well as a man of saintly virtue; as there was Jean-François de la Marche, Bishop of St Pol de Léon, who resided continuously in his diocese for twenty years, tending to his episcopal duties and watching zealously over the education of his clergy; and Arthur Young, in his travels in France, found that the French clergy, unlike so many in his own country, had 'an exterior decency of behaviour'.

But whether the upper clergy were zealous or lax in the discharge of their duties, there was generally a social gulf separating them from the lower clergy or the common run of monks or parish priests. In France the *bas clergé* were, almost by definition, of commoner, or *rôturier*, stock. A curé in a fashionable Parisian parish might earn as much as 10,000 livres a year. But this was altogether exceptional and it was far more common for a country priest (and he was in the great majority) to subsist on an income from tithe or the yearly stipend known as the *portion congrue* of 1,000 or 700 livres. In Spain the country priests were even poorer, and often as poor and as ignorant as the peasants they were called upon to serve. In Russia the parochial clergy were probably poorer and more ignorant still: Coxe described them as 'the refuse of the people', many of them illiterate and living on an income that might rise (in the case of the 'proto-pope' of a cathedral) to £20, but was more often £4 a year; he adds that generally they were 'too low and ignorant to be qualified for admission into genteel societies';[8] while townsmen wrote of them derisively as 'ploughmen in cassocks'. The role and status of the English country vicar or curate were quite different. They too were notoriously underpaid: in George 1's reign, one benefice in eight carried an annual stipend of £20 or less, and over half the benefices were of under £50 a year; curates' fees were much the same. But the English country parson enjoyed a status that the Spanish parish priest, the French curé or the Russian *papa* so conspicuously lacked: he might eat at the squire's or the rich man's table; he might even share, in a latitudinarian, non-ascetic age, in the conventional sports of the countryside: Arthur Young quotes a contemporary advertisement: 'Wanted a curacy in a good sporting country, where the duty is light, and the neighbourhood convivial.'[9] Though Young deplored them, such outlets may have served as a bond of common interest within the English clergy and to have mitigated the social results of the cleavage between rich and poor. There were divisions it is true: for the first part of the century, the parish clergy were generally Tory and suspicious of court and administration, where the bishops were Whig and latitudinarian almost to a man. But these divisions were not fundamental, and they certainly never reached the bitterness of feeling that divided the *bas clergé* from the *haut clergé* in France and contributed without much doubt to the important part played by the French parish priests on the popular side in the early stages of the Revolution.

Meanwhile the churches, however strong and secure their outward appearance, were being challenged by opposing forces from within and without. From within came the challenge of minority religious groups who in every country were asserting their own rights of belief against the privileged position of the established church. In the European territories of the Ottoman Empire, the great majority were Orthodox Greeks, while a minority – mainly in Bosnia and Albania – subscribed to the ruling Muslim faith. In France there were close on one and a half million Calvinists, mainly in the south and south-west; but these were among the most loyal of the French king's subjects and offered no challenge other than to demand their civil rights and freedom of worship. There were also the Jansenists, originally the followers of Bishop Jansénius of Ypres, whose Augustinian, neo-Calvinist teachings within the Catholic church, with their emphasis on salvation by grace and denial of freedom of will and suspicion of 'good works', had been condemned in a roundabout manner by the bull Unigenitus in 1713. In the half-century that followed, the issue was no longer one of support or rejection of the views of Jansénius, but acceptance or rejection of Unigenitus, to which Louis xiv had given support in the last years of his reign and which the majority of French bishops – here at variance with their Gallican principles – continued to uphold. By now, however, the Jansenists were protected by the Cardinal de Noailles, the Archbishop of Paris; but when he withdrew his support in 1728, they were left without any influential protection within the church and had to seek it outside: from the Parlement of Paris, in particular, which defended their right to publish a clandestine journal, the *Nouvelles ecclésiastiques*, against the censorship of Cardinal Fleury. Jansenism at this time, from being merely a minority movement within the church, went down to street level; and in the 1730s the diarist Barbier wrote that two out of every three Parisians held Jansenist sympathies. Matters came to a head in the years following 1749 when Christophe de Beaumont, Archbishop of Paris, introduced the notorious *billets de confession*, whereby dying persons suspected of Jansenism were refused the final absolution unless they could produce a signed certificate to vouch for their submission to Unigenitus. The move was condemned by the Paris Parlement and led to riots outside the Archbishop's palace. After this, Jansenism lost its vitality and tended to merge with Richerism, a rank-and-file movement of the parish clergy which claimed that the church should be governed, not only by its bishops and canons but by the whole community of its pastors; and the 'Jansenism' that played a part in the opening years of the Revolution was really a mixture of the two.

Jansenism also played a certain divisive role within the Catholic church in Spain and Portugal, the Habsburg Empire, Italy and the southern German states. But in Germany, as in Switzerland, Scandinavia and Bohemia, a far more significant challenge to the churches was made by Pietism. Pietism had begun as a revivalist revolt against the cold conformism of the official Lutheran church in Germany. Its first manifesto was P.J.Spener's *Pià Desiderata* of 1675, which (like the Lutherans) stressed the personal element in faith but also insisted that faith must be accompanied by good works. It found protectors among the rulers of some of the German states, as in Baden and Württemberg; but its main appeal was to the moral earnestness of the industrious middle class among whom it won converts in the merchant cities. It spread northwards to Scandinavia after 1728 and had its most notable successes in Denmark, where it won the enthusiastic support of the King, Christian VI, himself. As an offshoot of German Pietism sprang the Moravian community (so-called from its Bohemian origins), which was founded by Count Ludwig von Zinzendorf, a godson of Spener, on his estate at Bertholdsdorf in Saxony in 1722. The Moravian Brothers at first intended to remain a small discussion circle within the Lutheran church based on their settlement of Herrnhut (the Lord's Hill); but with repression they gradually developed a liturgy of their own, and Zinzendorf became the first Moravian bishop in 1737. They went on to become the greatest Protestant missionaries of the age, founding overseas settlements in Greenland and Labrador which may be compared with those founded by the Jesuits in Paraguay.

But the most remarkable and eventually the most influential of all the 'vital religions' of the time was Methodism, which was jointly created by John and Charles Wesley and George Whitefield in England in the late 1730s. Methodism began as a 'Holy Club' of Oxford students in 1729, and went through a series of transformations and conversions before the Wesleys set up their official headquarters at a disused foundry in Moorfields, London, in 1740. One of the elements that went into Methodist teaching was the piety and moral earnestness that John Wesley learned from the Moravians whom he visited at Herrnhut in 1738. The Wesleys insisted, like the Moravians and Pietists, on the necessities of faith, prayer and self-examination, but they added to them their own particular concern for the means of grace and the search for salvation. John Wesley was an indefatigable preacher and organiser. During more than half a century of pastoral activity he travelled 224,000 miles through England and Wales and preached 40,000 sermons, most of them in the open air. Before he died in 1791 the Wesleyan Methodists (from whom Whitefield had parted fifty years before) had in Britain 70,000 members and 350 chapels, which at that time were still within the Anglican church. Wesley's attitude to the established Church of England was similar to Zinzendorf's in Germany: he wanted to remain within it. But after his death the Wesleyan Methodists broke with the Church of England and set up a church of their own.

In England there were also other minority groups. There were the old Protestant dissenting groups – Presbyterians, Independents, Baptists and Quakers – who had known persecution in the past, but after the 'High Church' riots of 1716 had settled down, like their Anglican brethren, to a life of relatively placid and easy conformity. Like the Anglicans, they built few churches in the eighteenth century and until late in the 1790s they suffered a serious decline. Moreover they were riddled with dissension; and from this Old Dissent there sprang, partly under the impact of Methodism, a whole number of new sects and revivalist groups: Unitarians, Muggletonians, Sandemanians, Socinians, Universalists, Swedenborgians, Huntingdonians and many others. By the end of the century they formed an impressive body of Protestant dissent; and an enquiry of 1812 revealed that the number of places of worship of Old and New Dissent combined was 265 (compared with the Anglicans' 186) in the metropolitan parishes of the diocese of London. Meanwhile, English Roman Catholics had led a more precarious existence. Their numbers, until the mass influx from Ireland after the Napoleonic wars, were few, partly as the result of persecution and discrimination. The old 'recusancy' laws, compelling Catholic to attend Anglican places of worship were, although seldom evoked, still on the Statute Book; the Test and Corporation Acts of Charles II's time were more vigorously enforced against them than against the Protestant nonconformists to whom they equally applied; and an Act of 1699 condemned Catholics keeping schools to perpetual imprisonment and disabled them from inheriting or purchasing land. Moreover Catholics were under constant observation and became natural targets of both official and popular animosity on occasions like the Jacobite rebellions of 1715 and 1745. Yet once the 'Forty-Five' was over, there was little open persecution of the Catholic community; juries became more tolerant and denunciations fewer; and in 1778, a Catholic Relief Bill, designed to repeal the more barbarous of the provisions of the Act of 1699, passed unopposed through Parliament. (Yet, as we shall see, this was not the end of the affair.) By this time there were 14,000 Catholic families in London and maybe four times that number in the country as a whole.

The most widely dispersed and the most consistent targets of discrimination among all the European religious minorities were the Jews. There were two main Jewish communities: the Sephardim of Mediterranean origin, who spoke Ladino; and the Ashkenazim of eastern European origin, who spoke Yiddish. The Sephardic Jews, who were the more exclusive and the more prosperous of the two, were to be found in Spain and Portugal (though only in small numbers after the expulsions of the fifteenth century); at Bayonne, Bordeaux and Avignon, in the south of France; at Leghorn and Florence in Italy; at Amsterdam in Holland, where their first synagogue was built in the early seventeenth century; and in England, where they began to settle in Cromwell's time and numbered 6,000 to 7,000 persons before 1800. The Ashkenazim were the poorer and the more numerous; 800,000 of them were living in the small towns and cities of Lithuania and the eastern part of the old Kingdom of Poland before they were transferred, almost *en bloc*, to Russia with the first Polish partition of 1772. The next largest group were in Germany, where they were scattered over all the larger states: in Prussia (1,000 families in 1700), Saxony, Bavaria and Hanover; in the Hanse trading towns and large commercial free cities like Frankfurt and Würzburg. In France their main concentration was in Alsace, where there were 20,000, and in Metz (420 families) and Paris (500). In Holland they formed a majority among the combined Jewish community of 50,000; and in England, where the first Ashkenazi synagogue was built in 1722, they numbered perhaps 10,000 to 12,000 by the end of the century.

The rich Jews were nearly all found at this time among the Sephardic families of Madrid, Amsterdam, Bordeaux, Hamburg, Frankfurt, Berlin and London. Among Jewish bankers and merchants were the Suassos of Madrid; the Pintos, Belmontes and Da Costas of Amsterdam; the Pereiras of Bordeaux; the Texeiras of Hamburg; the Bethmanns (and later the Rothschilds) of Frankfurt; the Itzigs and Friedländers of Berlin; and, in London, Joseph Salvador and Samson Gideon, who were among the wealthiest of the City's financiers. Where the two Jewish communities existed side by side, as they did in England, the Sephardim had become westernised, spoke English and were well established brokers, financiers and merchants in the Turkey trade. They were becoming socially (if not yet politically) assimilated into English national life. The Ashkenazim, on the other hand, were still strongly marked by their east European origins: as recent immigrants from the ghettoes of eastern and central Europe, they wore beards, spoke a German–Polish dialect and engaged in a multiplicity of mainly humble trades. And at the bottom of the poverty scale, and outside all the areas of immigration, were the impoverished Jews of the ghettoes of eastern Poland.

What then was the response of the established churches and of the state that gave them protection to this challenge from within, whether it came from Wesleyans, Pietists, Jansenists, Jews or the Protestant and Catholic minority groups? Briefly, the challenge was met with varying degrees of hostility, active repression or uneasy toleration. Among the more gruesome of the responses was the continuation of the Inquisition in Spain: the *auto-da-fé*, or public burning of heretics, continued, though at a diminishing rate, until 1781; and there were 700 such spectacles in the reign of Philip v (1700–46) alone. Another savage response was the continued burning of so-called witches in Switzerland. Witch-burning came to an end in Zürich in 1701 and in the Catholic cantons in 1752; but, in Protestant Glarus in 1782, a servant girl was racked and decapitated for 'bewitching' a child. Thirty-five years earlier Jacob Schmid had been racked and strangled at the stake in Catholic Lucerne for diffusing Pietist tracts. In 1719, the town council of Torun in Poland sentenced Calvinists to death for riotous behaviour. Throughout the century Protestants were persecuted in Hungary and the Rhenish

Palatinate of Germany; and in 1728 the Bishop of Salzburg expelled 20,000 of his Protestant subjects at three days' notice. Under Louis xv there was a renewal of persecution of Protestants in France. By a royal declaration of May 1724 Protestants attending religious assemblies might be sent to the galleys for life and all their possessions be confiscated, while their preacher might be punished with death; there followed a new round of forcible conversions reminiscent of Louis xiv's notorious *dragonnades*. In 1761, Jean Calas, a Protestant textile merchant of Toulouse, was broken at the wheel and hanged, by order of the Parlement, for the alleged strangulation of his son, a recent convert to the Catholic faith – a crime of which Calas was later proved to have been quite innocent. In 1766, the Chevalier La Barre suffered a similar fate at Abbeville for publishing 'impious' tracts and insulting a religious procession. Even in Catherine's Russia, where toleration was preached, Novikov, a Freemason and critic of the régime, was locked up in the Schlüsselburg fortress. Zinzendorf and his Moravian brothers were expelled from Saxony. In England Methodists had their chapels destroyed and their meetings broken up, often with the connivance of ministers of the Anglican church. Catholics suffered more: after the Jacobite rebellion of 1715, their community was expelled from London and the old recusancy laws were re-invoked to convict 350 Catholics in north Yorkshire alone; and in London the Catholic Relief Act of 1778 was followed by riots that destroyed a hundred houses and schools either belonging to Roman Catholics or to people believed to be in league with them.

But almost everywhere those who suffered from the most persistent disabilities – though rarely from the most savage form of repression – were the Jews. With minor exceptions, all the institutions of aristocratic and corporate society – the Christian churches, the gilds, Parlements, feudal nobility, merchant oligarchies, chartered towns and provincial estates – were marshalled against them: most vigorously in central and eastern Europe, more sedately in the great commercial cities of the West. In some places they were refused the right to worship, as in Vienna and Strasbourg. In many more they were segregated, either by residential exclusion, as at Vienna, Augsburg, Zürich, in most of Russia and in the chartered towns of Prussia; or by the designation of prescribed areas of residence, such as the Jewish Pale in Russia (after 1791) and the urban ghettoes of Lithuania, western Russia, Rome, Vienna, Bonn and the *Judengasse* of Frankfurt. Sometimes their numbers were limited by law: to 450 families at Metz, to 180 in the rest of Lorraine and to one single family at Ulm. In the Austrian Empire, until the time of the Emperor Joseph, they had to wear beards; in Berlin, Jewish doctors appeared on a separate register; and – most prejudicial of all – they were excluded, in eastern and central Europe, from agriculture and all established trades and confined to such occupations as banking, commerce, money-lending, peddling and trading in gold and silver. In addition, Jews paid special taxes to inherit properties, to cross frontiers (as in Germany) or to enter forbidden cities (as in Alsace and Lorraine). A Jewish poll-tax was levied in Germany, Austria and Poland, and in France until 1784. At Amsterdam they paid double fees at weddings. In Alsace they paid protection-money to the king, the bishop and the lords of the manor; and in Bohemia Maria Theresa made them pay a tribute of three million florins to save their community from expulsion. Moreover Jews were without exception excluded from public office; and rights of citizenship were only allowed them where they could establish a claim to naturalisation through native birth; but this was fraught with obstacles; and even in London in 1753 a Bill to extend the naturalisation of 'alien' Jews had to be withdrawn after a violent public outcry that only just stopped short of riots. And in this respect several of the enlightened despots were as discriminating as any others: Frederick II, for example, considered that Jews 'injure the business of Christians and are useless to the State'; and Catherine II, in admitting foreigners to Russia by an edict of 1762, specifically excluded Jews from its operation. Occasionally, too, such hostility exploded in violence: as in the pogrom at Uman, near Kiev, in 1762, when 20,000 Poles and Jews were slaughtered by peasants and rebellious Cossack tribes.

Yet by and large intolerance and repression were not as savage as they had been in the age before; moreover repression was not so much in evidence at the end of the century as it had been in its earlier decades. There were no more *autos-da-fé* after 1781 and no more witch-burnings after 1782. In England, Methodism had become socially acceptable by the mid-1760s, and there were no more large-scale anti-Papist riots after 1780. The first lawful Roman Catholic chapel was opened in Westminster in 1792; and by 1814 there were twelve such chapels in London, with thirty-one priests administering to a community of nearly 50,000. The Orthodox Christian communities in the Balkan lands continued to enjoy a remarkably high degree of toleration by their Turkish masters though any suspected political intrigue with their Orthodox or Catholic neighbours was severely repressed. In France there was no repetition of the savageries exercised against Calas and La Barre after the 1760s; and Protestants were allowed to worship freely and given a large measure of civil rights by the edict of 1787. In the Austrian Empire Joseph II's Edict of Toleration of 1781 allowed Calvinists, Lutherans and Orthodox Greeks to build churches, to claim rights of citizenship and even, by special dispensation, to hold public offices; only Unitarians and Deists were given no relief at all. Even the Jews benefited from the growing spirit of toleration. John Locke had asked many years before: 'If we allow the Jews to have private houses . . . amongst us, why should we not allow them to have synagogues?'; and Montesquieu had argued later: 'You Christians complain that the Emperor of China roasts all Christians in his dominions on a slow fire. You behave much worse towards the Jews, because they do not believe as you do.' Such propaganda was not without its effects. Pombal, as we saw, combated anti-semitism in Portugal. In Berlin Moses Mendelssohn, the hero of Lessing's *Nathan the Wise* (1779), was a highly respected citizen and even won the Academy's Philosophical Prize, in preference to Kant, in 1763. The poll-tax was remitted in France in 1784, and in Prussia under Frederick William II in 1787; similar reforms were adopted in Baden, Mecklenburg and Brunswick. Most remarkable of all were the measures taken by Joseph II to relieve the disabilities of Jews in the Austrian Empire and to integrate them within the community at large. He abolished all passports and special taxes; he permitted Jews to learn handicrafts and to engage in agriculture; and he encouraged them to build their own schools (though teaching must be in German) and to enrol at academies and universities. Yet certain restrictions remained: public worship was discouraged; some cities were still closed to them; and only limited entry was allowed to Vienna. Moreover, in view of the crisis at the end of Joseph's reign, much of this remained on paper.

Such toleration was in itself an affront to established religion and tended to undermine its authority all over Europe. But the challenge from without was conducted on a broader front by the 'philosophical' writers, the Freemasons and enlightened despots. Besides preaching toleration (in some cases but not in others), the *philosophes* carried on a protracted duel with the established churches. It took a number of forms, some of which will be discussed more fully in a later chapter. There was the war waged on the broadest possible front by Voltaire with his slogan '*Ecrasez l'Infâme!*' and by the contributors to Diderot's and d'Alembert's *Encyclopédie* (first published in 1751), with Diderot's mock-respectful article on 'Christianity' and the sustained sniping at 'fanaticism'. There was the propagation, as an antidote to Christianity, of new 'natural religions' such as Deism, deriving from Locke's rationalism and Bayle's *Historical Dictionary* of 1697; such views were put forward in Germany by Christian Wolff, in England by Matthew Tindal and many others and in France by Voltaire in and out of season, but most explicitly in his *Dictionnaire philosophique portatif* of 1764. From 'natural religion' and Deism, it was a short step to Rousseau's claim that religion should be a civic cult dedicated to a Supreme Being, whom it was the citizen's bounden duty to venerate. A more permissive form of civic religion was that preached by the Abbé Raynal in his *Histoire philosophique des deux Indes* (1770), where he argued that it should be left to the state to decide the type of religion that was best suited to the community's interest. Atheism found few supporters: among French writers of note there were Delisle de Sales, the Marquis de Sade, Helvétius and Holbach, and Sylvain Maréchal, whose *L'Homme sans Dieu* would enjoy a certain vogue among the Revolutionary 'de-christianisers' of 1793.

Among the secular cults that prided themselves on their rationalism and civic virtues was that of the Freemasons. Freemasons bound their members together by secret oaths; they preached human brotherhood and closer co-operation between classes; and they denounced the traditionalism and dogmatism of the established churches: all reasons why they should rapidly attract adherents and be viewed by the churches with the greatest suspicion. The masons founded their first Grand Lodge in England in 1717; they set up lodges in France and Italy in 1726, and in Prussia in 1740; and they won a notable convert when Frederick II consented to become Grand Master of a Berlin lodge in 1744. However, as Freemasonry spread eastwards to Russia and Poland, to Bohemia and Bavaria, it assumed more mystical forms under the guise of Rosicrucians, Illuminists and Knights Templar and other quasi-religious sects. That the masons, whether of one kind or the other, had some influence on people's attitudes towards the churches seems scarcely to be in doubt; yet it is hard to take seriously the extravagant claims made for them as general agents of revolution or social disintegration by contemporary propagandists like the Abbé Barruel, or by later writers such as J.B.Fay and Auguste Cochin in France.

An equally radical challenge to the authority of the churches was that made by the rulers themselves – and particularly, though by no means exclusively, by the practitioners of enlightened despotism. Both Frederick and Catherine as we have seen brought large numbers of foreign workers of other religious denominations into their dominions; they even gave refuge to Jesuits expelled from other countries: and although they discriminated against Jews they extended as large a degree of toleration to these new arrivals as they did to their subjects as a whole. This toleration was prompted partly by reasons of state, and partly, too, because these rulers regarded religious practice, except in so far as it could benefit the state, with almost complete indifference: Frederick in particular was noted for his undisguised impiety. Frederick also kept a watchful eye over his churches and refused to allow them any part in political affairs. Catherine went further and following Peter's precedent secularised church lands and closed down over 400 religious houses. It was enlightened despotism, too, that set the pace in driving out the Jesuits and destroying their influence within the Catholic communities. Here, as we saw, it was Pombal that took the first steps. He accused the Society of complicity in attempted regicide; and, on this pretext, closed it down and, in September 1759, expelled the Jesuits from Portugal. Louis xv, though reluctantly, came next: prodded by the Parlements, he closed down the order in France in 1764. Spain followed suit under Charles III; after riots in Madrid and Barcelona (1766), which Aranda attributed to Jesuit intrigue, Jesuits were arrested and deported in bulk in 1767. The same year, Jesuits were expelled from Naples and Parma, and even the Knights of St John – hardly to be considered as the enemies of Rome – followed the general example. And, as we have seen, the whole process of expulsion and dissolution was rounded off in 1773 when Clement XIV, under pressure from the Catholic princes, disbanded the Society of Jesus in every Catholic country in Europe.

Joseph II had been a junior co-ruler with his mother when these events took place in Rome, so he had no part in them at all. But in every other move to harry the church and place religion at the service of the state he was more thorough and more consistent than any of his fellow despots. Maria Theresa had already closed down monasteries within the Habsburg Empire; but she was a devout daughter of the church and anxiously wrote to her son in her closing years: 'Will you allow people to act as they please? If there were no state religion and submission to the church, where should we be?' Although Joseph (unlike Frederick and Catherine) was a devout believer himself, he thought otherwise; and 'Josephism' proceeded to deal a number of hard blows at both the papacy and the church within the Austrian dominions. These included, as we noted in an earlier chapter, the closing down of a further 700 religious houses (reducing the number of 'religious' from 65,000 to 27,000); and the abolition of the Inquisition; the toleration of Protestants and Jews; the promulgation of bulls only with the Emperor's consent; and the transformation of the clergy into salaried officers of state, obliged to take an oath of allegiance to the Emperor – thus greatly increasing the authority of the state at the expense of both church and pope. Naturally the Imperial Edict filled the Curia with alarm; and in 1782 Pius VI travelled to Vienna to persuade the Emperor to change his mind, but he achieved no immediate success. Meanwhile Joseph's brother, Leopold, had projected, and partly carried through, similar reforms in the Duchy of Tuscany. Yet in the event none of this came to very much in either Florence or Vienna; for the reaction that followed the outbreak of revolution in France swept most of the reforming schemes of both brothers away.

Yet even if the most advanced reforms failed in their objectives there can be little doubt that the state emerged strengthened and the church and papacy weakened as the result of these encounters. We have seen, too, that the age was one of relatively easy conformity for the upper classes, for whom 'enthusiasm' had lost its appeal; and it has often in consequence been called an age of reason or enlightenment. Even if these epithets are well deserved, can we add that it was also an age of religious indifference or even disbelief? This seems a highly doubtful proposition unless we are to limit the picture to the rulers and polite society alone. In fact, if we take account of the people as a whole, it might as appropriately be termed an age of faith or of religious revival; and this is as true of the latter part of the century as it is of its beginning. Perhaps the grosser forms of fanaticism belong to the earlier rather than to the middle or later years. By the end of Peter's reign in Russia the self-immolating activities of the Old Believers, who set fire to themselves in barns and sheds rather than surrender their souls to 'Anti-Christ' or the New Belief, had been exhausted. The extraordinary scenes enacted outside St Médard's church in Paris, when crowds of believers engaged in mass-convulsions at the tomb of the saintly Jansenist deacon Pâris, belong to the 1720s and early 1730s. Similarly, the great turn-out of *madrileños* to see heretics burned at the stake, as they would to see a *corrida* today, belong essentially to the earlier half of the century; and 'touching for the King's evil' in England went out with Queen Anne. But popular religious revivalism was quite another matter, and this belongs mainly to the period after 1730. It was in the 1730s that Moravians and Pietists ceased to be small exclusive sects and began to attract a mass-following in Germany, Switzerland and the Scandinavian countries. In England John Wesley, following George Whitefield's example, began to preach in the open in 1739, and the Wesleys' first mass-conversions of Kingwood miners, London craftsmen and north-country shopkeepers and tradesmen date from the 1740s. Forty years later, partly as an offshoot of Wesleyan teaching, came the 'enthusiasm' displayed, much to Horace Walpole's disgust, in the 'No Popery' riots in London. Meanwhile, the proliferation of other revivalist groups, such as the Swedenborgians and Socinians, had begun in England and these were soon to be followed by the disciples of Joanna Southcott, the 'Mother of God'. Meanwhile, too, Rosicrucians and Illuminati found adherents for their mystical cults in Bavaria and Russia and Jewry had a mystical pietism of its own in the Hassidim sect. It was noted too that when Pius vi made his visit to Joseph ii in 1782, while he received a cool welcome from the Emperor and his ministers, he was greeted with enthusiasm by the faithful in the streets of Vienna.

So in viewing the picture as a whole we see that it was not so much an age of 'reason' or of religious toleration or indifference as one of sharp contrasts. The established churches, the papacy and clericalism took some hard knocks; and under the impact of latitudinarian and 'enlightened' ideas the upper classes, while not neglecting their devotions altogether, tended to take them less seriously or (like Horace Walpole) merely wished to set their servants a good example. This was one side of the picture. The other was the continuing hold of the Catholic church on the poorer classes, and in Protestant countries the mass-conversions of the revivalist groups. So the age was very much a mixture of the two. It was not quite what the philosophical writers or enlightened despots like Joseph II had hoped for. Voltaire, viewing the situation towards the end of his long career, commented sadly: '[We] live in curious times and amid astonishing contrasts: reason on the one hand, the most absurd fanaticism on the other . . . a civil war in every soul.'[10]

CHAPTER 9

THE ARTS

The eighteenth century was not a 'golden age' of the arts or an age of literary giants like the century before. There were no dominating cultural centres like Louis XIV's court of Versailles; there was no Milton nor Calderón, no sculptor with the powers of Bernini, no architect with the vision of Christopher Wren. Yet it was an age of extraordinarily fertile artistic and literary activity of which the second half is perhaps more remarkable than the first. (The 1760s serve once again as a significant turning-point or parting of the ways.) Throughout it was an age of great public building, of churches, squares and colonnades and of city *hôtels* and country houses for the aristocracy and rich. From the earlier period date the French-classical palaces of Sans Souci at Potsdam and the Zwinger at Dresden; the great *places royales* of Bordeaux, Rheims and Nancy; the Palais de Soubise in Paris; the Royal Crescent at Bath; Wren's last Roman baroque churches, and those of his followers Archer and Gibbs in London; and the florid baroque churches of Vienna, Prague, Bavaria, Italy and Spain. In the later period came the elegant houses built in the neo-classical style by the brothers Adam in London and the French counterpart, the '*style Louis Seize*', of the late eighteenth-century French *hôtels*, of Soufflot's church of Sainte-Geneviève and the colonnade of the Palais Royal in Paris. Among sculptors there were the Frenchmen Houdon and Roubiliac, of whom the former left a memorable bust of Voltaire and the latter one of Handel. Among painters of the earlier years were Tiepolo in Venice, Watteau, Lancret and Chardin in France and Hogarth in England; and these were followed by Boucher, Greuze and David in France, by Reynolds and Gainsborough in England and by the most illustrious of them all, Goya, in Spain. In music at least, there was no lack of giants in a century that produced Bach, Handel, Mozart, Haydn and Gluck. Drama on the other hand found few outstanding talents: from Voltaire's adaptations of the classical drama of the past, through the social comedies of Beaumarchais in France and Sheridan in England, to Lessing's 'bourgeois' drama and the blood-and-thunder of *Sturm und Drang* in Germany. In poetry the

139

great talents came mainly at the end: while the earlier, the classical or Augustan, age had Pope, the later, the lyrical or pre-Romantic age, had Hölderlin and Goethe in Germany, Chénier in France and, in Britain, Cowper, Burns and Blake; though Byron, Shelley and Keats were yet to come.

It was an age of innovation, too. No other age was so rich in social and political satire: from Fénelon's *Télémaque*, Swift's *The Tale of a Tub* and *Gulliver's Travels*, Voltaire's *Henriade* and *La Pucelle* and Montesquieu's *Lettres persanes* (all belonging to the years up to 1730); through Voltaire's *Candide* and Hogarth's *Marriage à la Mode* and *Gin Lane* (of the 1740s and 50s); to Novikov's *Kóselek* in Russia (1774), Goya's savage indictment of war in *Los Caprichos* and the political caricatures of Gillray, Cruikshank and Rowlandson which began with the American War. An even more fruitful innovation was the rise of the novel, with its turning-point in Richardson's *Pamela* (1740), but with earlier models in Defoe's *Moll Flanders* (1722) and Prévost's *Manon Lescaut* (1731). It was an age of self-conscious criticism of the arts as well. It began with the great debate in France between the Ancients and Moderns. Pope, in his *Essay on Criticism* (1709), took the side of the Ancients ('Moderns beware!') which won him Voltaire's praise as 'the Boileau of England'. But the Moderns soon found ready defenders: at first in the Abbé du Bos' *Réflexions critiques* (1719); later throughout Europe in the critical writings of Samuel Johnson, Diderot, Lessing, Herder, Goethe and Schlegel. And finally, as an accompaniment to 'modernity' and the rejection of old models, came the beginnings of new national literatures in Russia, Poland, Bohemia and Scandinavia and the emergence of a school of national painting in Britain. These, in turn, were reflected in the appearance of a large number of new academies for the promotion of the arts: among them the Academy of the Fine Arts of St Petersburg (1758), the Royal Academy in Britain (1768), the Royal Uppsala Literary and Scientific Society in Sweden (1740), the Royal Society for the Improvement of Northern History and Languages in Copenhagen (1746) and the Trondheim Scientific Society in Norway (1760).

Being an age of innovation and variety, it was also an age of experiment in artistic and literary styles and genres. Architecture, in particular, had a bewildering complexity of styles, some existing side by side, others following one another in rapid succession. The prevalent style at the beginning of the century was 'baroque'. Baroque was of two main types: the exuberant, but near-classical, baroque of Bernini's monumental sculpture and of the Gesù Church built by the Jesuits in Rome (1660); and the more florid, decorated baroque that had its original home in Spain and soon migrated to the Austrian Netherlands, Switzerland, Austria, Bohemia and southern Germany. The first baroque continued to enjoy favour in the north of Italy; but in France it was

generally crossed with 'palladian' – a more elegant, regular and classic-
ally more symmetrical style deriving from the Italian artist Palladio
(1508–80); this French-classical mixture was that generally found in
French monuments and *places royales* (both in France and abroad)
during the first half of the century. In England pure baroque never
caught on at all; but Palladian did, and is to be found in early
eighteenth-century London churches, in Vanbrugh's Blenheim Palace
and Castle Howard and most characteristically in Earl Temple's Stowe
House at Buckingham. (Sometimes, it even became mixed with gothic,
as in Hawksmoor's London churches of the 1720s.) The other baroque,
in its southern and eastern migrations, developed a more ornate and
elaborate form in rococo, as seen in Swiss churches like that at Einsiedeln, near Lake Lucerne, and at the Prinzregententheater at Munich.
In Spain, it assumed the brightly coloured *bric-à-brac* patterns of the
Spaniard José de Churriguerra; and, later still, in both France and
England it developed further, under the impact of the new interest in
the Far East, into the *chinoiseries* associated with Horace Walpole's
mansion at Strawberry Hill (where it was also crossed with gothic) and,
in a purer form, with Frederick II's Dragon Cottage at Potsdam and his
Japanese pavilion at Sans Souci. But these exotic diversions did not last
long; for in the meantime a fresh turn had been made to the Greek
originals of the whole classical tradition; and from this had arisen a
'neo-classical' style, which in England found expression in the Adam
terraced house, and in France in the *'style Louis XVI'* of Soufflot's Pan-
théon and the Palais Royal Colonnade. And neo-classicism, with its
variations, remained in vogue until well into the nineteenth century.

Music, having a shorter history, was even more susceptible to change.
Early in the century, music had two main forms: one was in the Italian
opera, which had its origins in Naples the century before; the other was
in the cantatas and oratorios of religious music, in which all the great
masters of the age – Bach, Handel, Haydn, Mozart – had their earliest
training. The opera branched off, at an early stage, into the *opera buffa*,
or *opéra comique*, which enjoyed its greatest vogue in France but probably
had its greatest single triumph in John Gay's *Beggar's Opera* in London.
But, more generally, new musical forms followed in the wake of the
advance in techniques. Thus the older viola was soon supplemented by
the violin and violoncello; the piano emerged from the harpsichord in
about 1709; and the flute (beloved of Frederick II) became fashionable
in 1750, while the clarinet had its beginnings soon after. A Frenchman,
Rameau, evolved the principles of harmony; and this was soon followed
by a musical 'revolution' in the course of which the small selective concertos of the past gave way to subscription concerts, sonatas and sym-
phonies, played by larger, professional orchestras and attended by
audiences drawn from both the upper and middle classes.

In painting and literature there was also a succession of new genres and forms. Early in the century the large-scale decorative ceiling, such as that painted by Lebrun for Louis XIV at Versailles, still enjoyed a certain vogue: it was continued by Tiepolo at Venice and moved from there with him and his pupils to Würzburg, Milan and Madrid. In France, however, it had ceased to be fashionable with the Regency, which saw the emergence of a new, more light-hearted genre in the *fêtes galantes*, or fantasies of court life, as painted by Watteau and later by his pupil Lancret. There were also the still-life interiors of Chardin in France and the pictorial social commentaries of Hogarth, whose popularity reached far beyond the aristocracy and court; there was, further, the new passion in England for historical pictures with ennobling themes. But no genre could match the continuing favour enjoyed by the portrait, which outlasted all others and survived from the portraits of Rigaud, Nattier and Kneller at the beginning of the century to those by David, Gainsborough, Romney and Vigée-Lebrun at the end. Poetry too had its succession of forms: the epic died out temporarily with Pope, but revived, half a century after and in new forms, with Hölderlin and Goethe in Germany; the ode remained in vogue in England with Edward Young, William Collins and Thomas Gray and in Russia with Derzavin and Lomonosov; but each of these was eclipsed by the lyric and folk-ballad which, in the hands of the English, Scottish and German poets from the 1780s onwards, won a popularity never enjoyed by any type of poetry before. Meanwhile the novel too had been through a series of developments: from the *picaresque* novel of the Spaniards and Le Sage, through Defoe's novel of adventure in *Robinson Crusoe*, to the sentimental novel of Prévost and Richardson and the novel of realism of Fielding and Sterne; with, as an offshoot, the gothic novel, as in Horace Walpole's *Castle of Otranto* (1764).

So it was a century of variety and experiment in artistic forms. But why did the eighteenth century produce these forms; and what were the influences behind the art? If the artists' and writers' own talents and predilections are not taken into consideration, these influences can be seen to be both national and social, and most often the two in combination. They were national not only for the evident reason that every artist or writer is a product of the nation from which he springs, but because certain nations in the eighteenth century were able to impose their literature and arts on others, particularly on those countries that were only in the process of developing a native art or culture of their own. During this period these 'exporting' countries were Italy and France in the first part of the century and England and Germany (and more briefly Austria) in the second. Up to the mid-century there was even a cultural rivalry between Italy and France, though with Italy playing the minor role. Italy was, as we have seen, the progenitor of the baroque and Palladian in architecture, as she was of church music and the opera. In architecture that influence was seldom decisive: baroque assumed other forms as it moved into Spain, the Habsburg Empire and southern Germany; France merged baroque with her own classical tradition; and England, while rejecting baroque, drew on palladian for a couple of generations at the most. The Italian opera had a longer life. In Italy itself vast audiences of every social class filled the opera houses of Naples and Venice; and from Italy the opera radiated outwards to Madrid, Paris, London and the courts of the German princes; Handel alone wrote twenty-six operas after he came to London in 1715. But outside Italy the opera was mainly confined to courtly and aristocratic audiences, and it had its ups and downs. In London, for example, the Italian opera, which was played at the Haymarket Theatre, almost lost its 'genteel' patrons overnight when John Gay's *Beggar's Opera* opened at the Covent Garden Playhouse in 1727. It had a brief revival in the 1730s; but when opera returned a quarter of a century later, it was no longer the Italian but the new dramatic and more 'natural' opera of Gluck and Calzabigi, whose *Orfeo ed Euridice* was played in 1762. Meanwhile, an operatic revolution had taken place in Paris too. The joint production of Pergolesi's light-hearted *La serva padrona* and Rousseau's *Le devin du village* in 1752 had divided the critics into two camps, the '*coin du roi*' and the '*coin de la reine*', the former favouring the traditional Italian and the latter the newly emerging *opera buffa* or *opéra comique*. It was the latter that won; and from now on French composers began to squeeze out the Italian, and in Europe generally the lead in music passed from Naples to Vienna.

French cultural domination was more persistent and spread more widely than the Italian. This is hardly surprising as it had a more recent tradition to fall back on and, above all, it was supported by a political authority that the Italians so conspicuously lacked. In the late seventeenth century the models set by the court of Versailles in both literature and the arts had been imitated in every capital in Europe. French became the accepted language not only of diplomacy, but also scholarship, letters and polite society. In 1697 it was claimed that 'the French language has succeeded the Latin and Greek language . . . it has become so general that it is spoken today throughout almost the whole of Europe, and those who frequent society feel a kind of shame when they do not know it'.[1] It was an influence that continued into the eighteenth century and was particularly strong in Poland, Russia, Sweden and the German states. In these countries, whose national literature was only just emerging, French translations and French imitations held the stage for many years. Thus in the 1720s and 1730s Fénelon's *Télémaque* appeared in Polish and also in German alongside Boileau's *Satires* and Prévost's *Manon Lescaut*; while imitations of Boileau's *Art poétique*,

Voltaire's dramas and Molière's comedies abounded in Germany, Denmark, Poland and Russia. Even Englishmen were affected: Gibbon's *Essay on the Study of Literature* and William Beckford's *Vathek* were originally published in French. At a more exalted level, Gustavus III of Sweden, the Empress Maria Theresa and Catherine the Great all wrote a large part of their correspondence in French. Frederick II was an even more extreme example. Despising his own language as a barbaric dialect, he only spoke and wrote it when he had to and even ordered that the papers read to the Academy of Sciences in Berlin should be published in French. It was only after his death that they began to appear in German as well.

French cultural domination was, however, not confined to letters. The architectural splendours of Versailles had already in Louis XIV's day found imitators at foreign courts; this influence became strengthened at closer quarters in the early years of the eighteenth century when French Bourbon rulers established themselves at Madrid (1701), Naples (1731) and Parma (1748). Philip V built himself a French-classical palace at La Granja; he was followed by John V of Portugal at Queluz and the rulers of Naples at Caserta and Parma at Colorno; and Frederick II, when he built his own palace of Sans Souci in the French style, was following the example of his grandfather, Frederick I, who had built Charlottenburg according to French design half a century before. Meanwhile French architects, town planners, painters and monumental sculptors were bringing their models and their talents to almost every European capital. One result of this cultural invasion was that baroque was being gradually edged out by French classic not only in southern Germany, but even from the countries of its birth, as in parts of Italy and Spain. So it was perhaps with pardonable pride – and pardonable exaggeration – that Patte, a French court architect, wrote in 1765: 'Travel through Russia, Prussia, Denmark, Württemberg, the Palatinate, Bavaria, Spain, Portugal and Italy, and everywhere you will find French architects . . . Our sculptors, too, are spread all over Europe . . . Le Lorrain, Tocque, Lagrenée, painters of our Academy, have been summoned in turn to Russia. Paris is to Europe what Greece was at the time of its artistic glory: it provides the whole world with artists.'[2]

By this time, however, French cultural hegemony was already past its prime. Other national influences were beginning to assert themselves and would gradually corrode it. In the first place, there was the growing influence of England, which began around the 1720s but only became considerable, as an antidote to the French, in the latter half of the century. It began with the novel. Defoe's *Robinson Crusoe* was translated into French and German in 1720 and in Swedish in 1734; and numerous adaptations followed in these and other countries. Swift's, Richardson's and Fielding's novels had an enormous success: Richardson's *Pamela* probably more than any other; and translations of these books appeared in French, German, Swedish and Russian from the early 1740s onwards. It was through England too that the new vogue in antiquity and 'neo-classical' themes percolated into the various countries of Europe, and even (with suitable adaptations) into France herself. It began with the Greco-Roman excavations at Herculaneum in 1738 and at Pompeii in 1748. Painters and architects flocked to Italy – Robert Adam, for example, travelled to Spalato (now Split, in Yugoslavia) and Reynolds and Richard Wilson to Rome – to derive their inspiration at first hand; and J.J. Winckelmann, whose claim it was that 'nature' must be studied in the ancients, wrote the first of two great treatises on the art of the ancients in 1755. Among the first effects of this return to the ancient past was the evolution of the neo-classical style in architecture and interior decoration which the brothers Adam began to apply to their Georgian terraced houses in London a few years later. In France, as we have seen, it took the more elaborate form of the *'style Louis Seize'*, which dates from the early 1770s; elsewhere, it appeared (on the French model rather than on the English) in the Brandenburger Tor in Berlin and in Catherine's summer residence of Tsarskoe Selo near St Petersburg. Another result of the new turn to antiquity was to introduce new historical themes into portraiture and painting. This tendency, too, was most marked in England, where Reynolds emerged as the leader of a new school and became president of the Royal Academy at its inception in 1768. The fashion passed to France, where Jacques-Louis David, the future artist of the Revolution and Empire, painted his *Oath of the Horatii* for the Paris salon of 1785.

But the challenge to French supremacy in literature and the arts came from another quarter too, and by means that were in the long run to be more significant for the future than the substitution of one dominant national culture by another. This was through the gradual evolution among northern and eastern nations of native literatures and cultures of their own. It was most striking in Germany, which had since the Thirty Years War relied almost entirely on foreign models for her artistic and literary products, a situation of course that Frederick II did nothing to relieve by his slavish devotion to the French. The turn came in the 1750s when Lessing wrote his first plays with German social themes; these were followed by Lessing's and Herder's literary criticism and evocation of Germany's cultural and historical traditions; by the German historical drama of *Sturm und Drang* and Goethe's folksongs and his harrowing tale of the sorrows of young Werther. And such was their success that, before the end of the century, the Germans had the satisfaction of turning the tables on the French by invading Paris with modes and themes of their own. Meanwhile a similar literary evolution had been taking place among the Scandinavians, Poles, Russians and Czechs, who all began to replace the borrowed French models (sometimes as in Sweden, Poland and Hungary, dressed up in Latin) with models of their own design. In Norway and Iceland, it began with sagas and heroic exploits: Snorri's *Edda* appeared in Iceland in 1746 and was translated into Norwegian soon after. The Swedes and Danes produced tragedies, a national opera, history and literary criticism; and Ludvig Holberg, a Norwegian, wrote his *History of the Kingdom of Denmark*, the first history of Scandinavia. In Bohemia, the Czech national theatre was opened at Prague in 1737. The Latvians had their first national dictionary in 1772 and the Romanians their first national grammar in 1787. Russia produced her first national playwrights and poets, among them Michael Lomonosov who wrote a patriotic ode to celebrate the capture of Khotin from the Turks in 1739. Poland had a thriving new literature in the 1750s and 1760s and opened her first national theatre in 1765. There was also a literary awakening among other national and ethnic groups: among the Celts of Scotland, Ireland and Wales, the Slavs of the Austrian and Ottoman Empires and the Flemings and Walloons of Belgium.[3]

But if artists and writers responded to the call of nationality they were equally responsive to the pressure of society. It was almost an axiomatic truth that every artist, writer or composer had to find himself a patron and that he wrote, composed or painted for a market that was reasonably well defined – either for the court or aristocracy or, later, for the bourgeoisie. As it was an age of monarchy, it was natural that patronage should, in the first place, emanate from the monarch or the prince's court. Thus, among musicians, J.S.Bach was successively choir-master to Duke William at Weimar and Prince William of Anhalt Köthen; Stamitz belonged to the court orchestra of the Elector Palatine at Mannheim; Haydn worked for over thirty years for the Princes Esterházy and Mozart was attached to the imperial court at Vienna; and when Handel came to England, having first served with the Duke of Chandos and the Earl of Burlington, he was appointed court composer to George i and tutor to the daughter of the Prince of Wales. Bach's son, Carl Philipp Emanuel, became harpsichordist to Frederick the Great in 1740: it was probably no sinecure, as Frederick himself played the flute and had a passion for flute concertos. Similarly among artists Watteau was court painter to the Regency, as Lancret, Boucher and Fragonard were painters to the court of Louis xv and Goya, on occasion, to the court of Charles iv of Spain; and among the many Swiss artists, architects and city planners who were employed by foreign courts were Anton Graf of Wintertur, who was court-painter in Dresden, and Luigi Rusca, a Ticinese of Agno, who was summoned to build cathedrals and palaces for Catherine the Great in Russia. Among writers Voltaire, who rode many horses in a long and adventurous career, had a succession of princely patrons or would-be patrons: he spent some tempestuous years at Potsdam in the service of Frederick of Prussia; in France, in spite of his numerous enemies at court, he enjoyed royal patronage for a while through the graces of Madame de Pompadour; but he refused Catherine's invitation to come to Russia. And in England John Gay held the post of Gentleman Usher to the Princess Louisa (aged two); and Johnson, Hogarth and Smollett, though not literally in the pay of the court, became government men as pensioners of the favourite, the Earl of Bute.

As the court provided patronage, it also provided the artists and writers with a ready market and it was of course not necessary for an artist to be in the king's or prince's direct employ for him to reap its benefits. In fact, in most countries, in the first part of the century at least, the arts tended to be 'monarchic' rather than 'aristocratic' in the sense that they catered for the needs of the ruler and his court rather than for the town *hôtels* and country mansions of a patriciate or aristocracy. Some art was 'princely' almost by definition: the Italian opera, for example; most baroque building (where it was not, as so often, commissioned by the church); and the great murals that Tiepolo, in the tradition of the previous century, painted for the Doge of Venice. Painting tended to be no longer on this grandiose scale, while remaining 'princely' none the less. In Spain, for example, there is an early Goya portrait of Charles IV and his family which looks more like an exercise in satire than a work commissioned by the king (whom it reduced to less than life size): yet it is court art and it was painted by royal command. In France too, fashions had changed, yet the arts remained attuned to the needs of the court. Painting again is a case in point. Watteau's great fantasy, *L'Embarquement pour Cythère*, is as far removed in form and feeling from the stately ceilings that Le Brun painted for Louis XIV as chalk is from cheese; yet it was a work done for the court of the Regency, a court whose needs were vastly different from those of the stately court of the *roi soleil*. After the Regency, there was a return to the more formal type of court painting as seen in Nattier's portraits of the Marquise d'Antin and Louis XV's wife, Marie Leczinska. But styles changed again while patronage remained constant; and Boucher's salacious canvases of *Venus* and *Diana and the Nymph* were as well attuned to the sophisticated tastes of Madame de Pompadour as Vigée-Lebrun's sentimental family portraits were to those of the more ingenuous Louis XVI and Marie-Antoinette. French architecture bears even more clearly the stamp of royal patronage; as in the numerous *places royales*, both the French and those built for foreign rulers; the endless monuments erected to the glory of the monarchy (note the title of Patte's treatise of 1765: *Monuments élevés à la gloire de Louis XIV*); and the more elegant extensions to Versailles in the later years, such as the Salle de l'Opéra (opened to celebrate the Dauphin's marriage in 1770) and the Petit Trianon built by A.J. Gabriel for Marie-Antoinette between 1762 and 1768.

Official art included of course that sponsored by the church. In the eighteenth century, this was mainly in architecture and music, with painting playing a minor role compared with the past. Baroque had, as we have noted, its origins in the Gesù church in Rome; and the patronage of the churches continued to be in evidence in much of the rococo and Churriguerist adaptations from the baroque in Switzerland, Belgium, southern Italy and Spain. Notable examples are Fischer von Erlach's churches at Salzburg and Vienna, the monasteries of Melk and Altenburg in Austria, the Swiss churches of Sankt-Gallen and Einsiedeln, and many churches, chapels and oratories in Dresden, Prague, Munich, Lemberg (Lwow), Warsaw, Salamanca and Madrid. Similarly with music (though here the patronage was often shared between church and court). As the opera was the favourite form of music for the court, so for the church (though it might be for the princely patron as well) it was the oratorio, or the mass, the 'passion', the choral and the cantata. Handel, Bach, Haydn and Mozart were all, as we saw, masters of the cantata and oratorio; one of the greatest of Mozart's works was his *Requiem*; and Bach alone composed five masses, two oratorios, 150 cantatas, a large number of chorals, besides his two famous Passions of St Mark and St John.

Aristocratic art is not so easy to distinguish. Court painters like Nattier, Goya and Boucher might as readily paint for the aristocracy, both in and out of court, as they did for royalty or the court itself; in England, Reynolds' portrait of *Lord Heathfield* is as famous as any he did for the royal family at Windsor. Indeed in some countries – as in England, and perhaps in Poland and Sweden too – the aristocracy provided a market and a patronage that were even more important than those provided by the court. We have noted already how Handel, when he came to England, had two aristocratic patrons before he transferred to St James's Palace: the Duke of Chandos at his country seat of Canons and the Earl of Burlington at Burlington House in Piccadilly. Similarly, Alexander Pope was a regular guest at the Dover Street house of Edward, Earl of Oxford; John Gay found a patron in the Duke of Eglington in Queen Street, Mayfair; and even the redoubtable and highly independent Samuel Johnson, some time before he became a pensioner of the Earl of Bute, made an unsuccessful attempt to woo the patronage of the Earl of Chesterfield in Grosvenor Square. Some aristocrats in England were munificent patrons of the arts, in much the same way as the Duke of Orleans and the kings of France, Frederick and Catherine and Maria Theresa were on the continent of Europe. Among them were the Earl of Burlington and the Dukes of Portland and

Bedford, whose ambitious building schemes are commemorated in a long list of London squares and streets. Again, many of England's architects devoted a great deal of their time to planning and building for the English aristocracy. The Adam brothers are the outstanding example; but there were many others: among them Sir John Vanbrugh, who built Blenheim Palace for the Duke of Marlborough and Castle Howard for the Earl of Carlisle; William Kent, who designed Chiswick Villa for the Earl of Burlington and Strawberry Hill for Horace Walpole; and James Gibbs, who (with others) designed Canons for the Duke of Chandos at Stanmore. There were also the English landscape gardens, which Bridgeman, Kent and Chambers designed for the English aristocracy and whose natural exuberance contrasted with the stylised elegance of those designed by the Italians and French. Moreover, there were painters like Gainsborough, Romney, Raeburn, Zoffany and Reynolds who specialised in painting portraits of the aristocracy and gentry; and cabinet-makers like Chippendale and Sheraton who catered essentially for aristocratic tastes. France, too, made use of equal talents, though they came later, as in the *hôtels* and interiors designed for the nobility and *haute bourgeoisie* in the Louis XVI style of the 1770s and 1780s.

While the arts tended, therefore, throughout the century to cater for the social needs of monarchy and aristocracy, there was also a point at which they began to reflect more directly the values and social aspirations of the bourgeoisie as well. This turn to what we may call a 'bourgeois' form of art, in which bourgeois tastes began to impose a distinctive pattern of their own, began to appear, like so much else, around the middle years of the century. In one sense of course the needs of the bourgeoisie had long been catered for as offshoots of those of the court and aristocracy: so long as the rising mercantile classes adapted themselves to an aristocratic society and an aristocratic way of life, they adapted themselves equally to aristocratic (or courtly) tastes in literature and the arts. So we find rich bourgeois families applauding Italian opera all over Europe and sitting for portraits by Largillierre, Reynolds and Gainsborough, as we find them moving into Cavendish Square and St James's Square in London and building themselves fashionable *hôtels* in the Faubourg St Germain; but this no more entitles us to call the Adam house in London or the Louis XVI-style *hôtel* in Paris a bourgeois art form than a portrait by Zoffany or a still-life by Chardin; nor can any one of the nine old-style tragedies that Voltaire wrote for the Paris salons and the court and nobility between 1730 and 1760 be properly so called.

But meanwhile there were bourgeois that were not merely living nobly and aping the manners of their 'betters' but were beginning to devise a manner of living and to make social demands of their own. This growth of an independent middle-class way of life and outlook was nowhere as marked as it was in England; and Voltaire, while a stranger to it himself, noted it with admiration when he came to London in the 1720s and commended it to his countrymen in his *Letters concerning the English Nation*. It was natural that this middle-class outlook should express itself not only in political institutions (like those of the City of London) or in the coffee-house or daily press, but in middle-class forms of art as well. This first happened with the novel, which as we saw, developed between the 1720s and 1740s. There is a world of difference in the various moods (quite apart from the plots) in such books as Defoe's *Moll Flanders* (1722), Richardson's *Pamela* (1740), Fielding's *Joseph Andrews* (1742) and Smollett's *Roderick Random* (1748). But all have in common, in addition to their literary innovations, a new realism and the assertion of a new middle-class morality as an antidote or challenge to the aristocratic traditions and assumptions, and what their authors and readers saw as the anomalies, hypocrisies, insensibility and amorality of the society of their day. Similar qualities are expressed in the pictorial art of Hogarth, whose realistic social commentary and refusal to come to terms with fashionable trends marked him off from all other artists of the time. So it is no coincidence that while Horace Walpole dismissed him as a painter of 'slender merit', his engravings should have hung on thousands of middle-class walls. A generation later, the same public flocked to exhibitions of modern historical themes by artists like William Woollett and Jonathan Copley: Copley's 'Death of Chatham' (1780) drew over 20,000 spectators when he displayed it in his gallery at a charge of a shilling per head. So it was in the first place through the novel and the painting that something of a middle-class cultural revolution took place in England between the 1720s and 1780s. 'With Hogarth, as with the great novelists,' writes Christopher Hill, 'English middle-class art came of age in the eighteenth century.'[4]

But the 'revolution' was not limited to England, and other art-forms came into play as well. All over western Europe – in France and Germany as well as in England – actors, dramatists and theatre managers were finding it necessary to attune their plays and productions to the standards of a new middle-class morality, in which homely virtues like pride in work and conjugal fidelity should be rewarded and crime, sloth and moral laxity be punished. David Garrick found this in London, and it was his willingness to 'doctor' the old plays – including Shakespeare's – to accommodate these new moral imperatives that accounts, in part at least, for his enormous popularity. But it was soon a matter of not simply doctoring the old but of writing new plays that accorded more directly with middle-class tastes. This was first done in Germany in Lessing's *Miss Sara Sampson* (1755) and, in France, in Diderot's *Le Père de famille* (1758); and these were followed by Lessing's *Minna von Barnhelm* (1764), by the sentimental drama of

Hannah More, a high priestess of the fashionable cult of 'sensibility' in England and, in France, after Diderot, by the writers of the 'comédie larmoyante'. The same school in France had its equivalent in the sentimental, morally didactic paintings of Greuze, which were admired by Diderot and patronised by the court banker Laborde, and in which, as in Hogarth's saga of the Industrious and Idle Apprentice, crime always leads to disaster and virtue always pays. Meanwhile, the novel of sentiment had really come into its own with the great success enjoyed by Goethe's *Sorrows of Young Werther* (1774) and Bernardin de Saint-Pierre's *Paul et Virginie* (1789). So it was a revolution that, if it can be said to have been launched by the English, was consolidated by the Germans and French and, if we take account of the new 'natural' opera coming from Vienna, by the Austrians as well. But taking the movement as a whole, the biggest single individual role was without much doubt that played by Rousseau. By his *Confessions*, his *Émile*, his *Nouvelle Héloïse*, his musical writings and his constant complaint of the corrupting influence of society, he contributed more than any other writer to the new cults of 'sensibility' and 'nature', which, together with middle-class common sense and respectability, were the basic ingredients in this cultural revolution of the middle class.

But during this period there were also the elements of a distinctive popular culture besides. Some of this was traditional and by no means peculiar to the eighteenth century, like the folksongs and folklore, which had deep roots in the past and were carried by word of mouth and only appeared as literature when recorded by professionals like Snorri and Grimm. There were also the folk-festivals, like May Day in England, and the great fêtes and processions of the *confréries* of the arts and crafts in France. Moreover, the arias of Italian opera were sung by Neapolitan boatmen and Venetian gondoliers, as the tunes of the *opéra comique* were adapted and relayed in the *chansons populaires* of the Parisian *menu peuple*. But was there a popular music or a popular literature that was not merely handed down by tradition or borrowed from the repertory of other social groups? Robert Mandrou, in a recent study of French popular culture of the seventeenth and eighteenth centuries, insists that there was. This was the literature sold, often clandestinely, on the streets of cities by book-selling pedlars, or *colporteurs*. In one single city collection, that housed by the library of Troyes, are listed 450 titles of contemporary books and pamphlets meant solely for popular consumption. They include, the original collector noted in 1783, 'novels that the smallest bourgeois would not dare to boast of having read, not because of their style or language, but because they contribute to the amusement of the lowest classes of the people'; and he records the case of an aristocratic lady who, anxious to read 'the history of Pierre de Provence', was only able to satisfy her curiosity by the grace and favour of her *femme de chambre.*[5] Halfdan Koht, in his account of Norwegian peasant movements of the period, gives us further examples. The eighteenth century, he writes, was not merely a period of a general national cultural revival, but of peasant handicrafts and painting; and when the peasants painted, they adapted the prevailing baroque and rococo forms and infused them with a new content and spirit of their own. It was also a great century for popular poetry and folksong; and the first collection of Norwegian melodies – many of them of peasant origin – was published in Paris in 1786. Moreover, he adds, the peasants often imposed their own idiom and dialect on the professional song-writers; so that now, 'for the first time, it was peasant culture that provided the upper classes with their models'.[6]

Presumably, France and Norway were not unique in this regard; but from the slender information available we can only guess that similar movements were afoot in other urban and rural communities of the time.

CHAPTER 10

ENLIGHTENMENT

If some doubt remains about the artistic and literary achievements of the eighteenth century, there can be none whatever about its importance in the history of ideas. It was, in fact, an age of outstanding intellectual vigour, which extended over the greater part of Europe – an age of Enlightenment, that the French have called '*le siècle des lumières*', the Germans '*die Aufklärung*', the Italians '*i lumi*' and the Spanish '*el siglo de las lucas*'. In its wider context, the Enlightenment reached into almost every brand of knowledge: into philosophy, and the natural, physical and social sciences, and into their application in technology, education, penology, government and international law. In the physical sciences it was the age of Euler in Switzerland, of Lomonosov (also a poet) in Russia, of Franklin's lightning conductor in America, of Lagrange's *Mécanique analytique*, a work second only to Newton's *Principia* in the history of mechanics; and of Galvani's and Volta's experiments (1783), that led, a dozen years later, to the discovery of current electricity. In chemistry Joseph Black discovered 'latent heat' (and later 'fixed air') which helped James Watt to make his separate condenser; while Cavendish discovered hydrogen (1760) and Priestley oxygen (1774), and Lavoisier combined the two by revealing the properties of air and water and, in his *Traité élémentaire de chimie* (1789), for the first time expounded the law of the conservation of matter. In botany Linnaeus, a Swede, made his great collection of plants and wrote his *Systema naturae* (1735); while Réaumur wrote his *Histoire naturelle des insectes* (1732–42); and Buffon, director of the Jardin des Plantes, wrote his best-selling *Histoire naturelle* (1778), which exploded old myths and anticipated modern theories of the history of the earth. In sensational psychology, Diderot wrote his *Lettres sur les aveugles* (1749), Condillac his *Traité des sensations* in 1754 and Helvétius his *De l'esprit* in 1758. In philosophy, Hume wrote the *Treatise on Human Nature* (1739–40); Voltaire issued his *Dictionnaire philosophique* in 1764; and, at Königsberg in Prussia, Kant wrote in succession the *Metaphysics of Morals* in 1775, the *Critique of Pure Reason* in 1781, the *Critique of Practical Reason* in 1788 and the *Critique of Judgement* in 1790.

Even more it was an age rich in speculation in the social sciences. It began with Vico's great treatise on the philosophy of history, *Scienza nuova*, in 1725, which was followed by the historical writings of Voltaire in France, Hume and Robertson in Scotland and Gibbon in England. In penology there was Beccaria's *Of Crimes and Punishments* (1764). In the new science of economics, Quesnay wrote his *Tableau économique*, the bible of the Physiocrats with its plea for a single tax on land, in 1758; and in 1776 Adam Smith preached free trade and an end to mercantilism in his *The Wealth of Nations*. In education there was Rousseau's *Émile* (1762) and La Chalotais' *Essai d'éducation nationale* (1763); in literary criticism Lessing's *Laocoon* (1766) and Herder's *Philosophy of History and Culture* (1775); and, in government and political ideas, Montesquieu's *De l'esprit des lois* (1748) and Rousseau's *Discours sur l'inégalité* (1755) and *Du contrat social* (1762).

Among these writers and thinkers, there were many – though by no means all appearing on this list – who have been given the name of *philosophe*, or 'philosopher'. The term, of course, originated in France; and among the *philosophes* the most active and, in many respects, the most influential were Frenchmen: men like Montesquieu, Voltaire, Rousseau, Diderot, d'Alembert, Holbach, Buffon, Helvétius, Condillac, Raynal, Turgot and Condorcet (to cite the dozen or so best-known names among them). But there were others in other countries who acquired the title as well, though several were at a somewhat junior level: such as Beccaria in Italy; Robertson, Hume and Adam Smith in Scotland; Gibbon and Bentham in England; Franklin and Jefferson in America; Kant, Lessing, Grimm, Mendelssohn, Goethe (and possibly Herder and Wieland) in Germany; Vattel in Switzerland; Kollataj in Poland; and Lomonosov in Russia; while others professed to be of their company and through courtesy were sometimes accepted; such were Frederick of Prussia and Catherine of Russia. The *philosophes* had no common programme, or manifesto. The nearest they had to one was the *Encyclopédie, ou Dictionnaire raisonné des arts*, which Diderot and d'Alembert published, in seventeen volumes, between 1751 and 1772, and to which many of the leading *philosophes* contributed: Montesquieu on 'taste', Voltaire on 'esprit' and literature, Helvétius on religion and Rousseau on music. Moreover, there were important differences between them. Vico and Montesquieu, for example, held gradualist, evolutionary views of history which most of the later *philosophes* did not. Neither Voltaire nor Hume – nor, for that matter, Gibbon or Kant – shared Rousseau's or Turgot's or Condorcet's views on human progress and the perfectibility of man: Voltaire, in particular, was shaken in his belief in progress by the disastrous Lisbon earthquake of 1755 and in *Candide*, which he wrote a few years later, he made a special point of assailing the optimism of Leibnizian philosophy. Diderot, Holbach and

Helvétius were materialists, or atheists, whereas Voltaire, for all the bitter shafts he directed against *l'Infâme*, remained a deist throughout, and Rousseau, as we shall see, even threatened with death any dissenters from the civil religion he expounds in the *Contrat social*. The quarrel between Voltaire and Diderot took other forms as well: where Voltaire was a devoted adherent to Newton's mechanical view of the universe, Diderot, like Buffon, favoured the life-sciences and saw motion as 'the essence of matter' and world and society in a continuous state of flux. Yet Voltaire and Diderot joined forces against Rousseau, whom they both considered a lost soul: Voltaire in disparaging the *Contrat social* and Diderot in deriding *Émile*. In fact Rousseau, in France at least, was very much the odd man out. Where the *philosophes* in general chose reason as their guide, Rousseau countered with natural instinct, 'sensibility' and the virtues of primitive man; and where the others were urbane, cosmopolitan and *habitués* of the salons and fashionable society, Rousseau remained always the *promeneur solitaire*, who considered society a corrupting influence and, after a brief incursion into the salons, avoided them like the plague.

Yet, even with these differences, the *philosophes* had certain distinctive qualities of thought in common. They all questioned the basic assumptions which their contemporaries had inherited from the past, whether these were philosophical, theological or political. They were generally hostile to organised or revealed religion, and they all rejected the churches' barbarous dogma of original sin. They gave a rational, non-mystical, non-theological explanation of the world and of man's existence and place in society; for (to quote Ernest Cassirer) they were convinced that 'human understanding is capable by its own power, and without recourse to supernatural assistance, of comprehending the system of the world'.[1] Such being their basic optimism with regard to man's capacity to master nature and to comprehend the world and the society in which he lived, they tended to be optimistic too – though this was not, as we have seen, a quality shared by all – about man's future, his perfectibility and possibility of happiness. Moreover, while not practising politicians (Turgot was an exception), they were not armchair philosophers who engaged in abstract or metaphysical explanations: their 'philosophy' was practical and empirical and they used it as a weapon of social and political criticism and tried to persuade others, whether governors or governed, to think and act the same. The *philosophes* themselves were well aware of this empirical, didactic and crusading element in their thinking and behaviour and took pride in it. At Königsberg in 1784 Kant defined the *Aufklärung* as a 'revolt against superstition' and put forward the slogan, *Sapere aude*, 'Dare to know'. Turgot wrote to Hume that '*les lumières*' meant the capacity to know 'true causes'. Diderot believed that *philosophes* must be united by a common 'love of truth, a passion to do good to others, and a taste for truth, goodness and beauty'. To Condorcet, the *philosophes* were men 'less concerned with discovering truth than with propagating it', who 'find their glory rather in destroying popular error than in pushing back the frontiers of knowledge'; and their battle-cry must be 'reason, toleration, humanity'.

So the *philosophes* were a self-conscious élite, a small band of enlightened and dedicated men, who set out to convert others of their kind both by their ideas and the force of their example. But being an élite, their philosophy had its social limitations: they had little message or comfort for the poor and, as Robespierre later complained, they showed little concern for 'the right of the people'. 'It is not the labourers one should educate,' wrote Voltaire, 'but the good bourgeois, the tradesmen'; and Holbach and Diderot, too, admitted that they wrote only for an educated public. And, in a later chapter, we shall see that Turgot (with Voltaire's support) put loyalty to Physiocratic principles before the provision of cheap bread for the poor.

Like all thinkers, the *philosophes* had their intellectual forbears: their ideas, whether in philosophy, or in the physical or social sciences, derived in great measure from the writers and thinkers of the century before. A few of these were Frenchmen. Descartes in his *Discours de la méthode* (1651) had taught, through his maxim *Cogito ergo sum*, that truth is attainable by logical reasoning; but he had drawn a sharp division between intellect and faith; faith lay outside the realm of reason; so, to appease the Church, he had left religion and the Bible untouched. Pierre Bayle, however, a Frenchman living in Rotterdam, had taken up the argument where Descartes had left it off; and in his *Dictionnaire historique et critique* (1697) he had applied Cartesian scepticism and scientific method to a study of history and the Bible. So now the field lay wide open for further exploration, and with no holds barred. But it was their English forbears rather than the French who provided the *philosophes* with their major shot and shell. 'Without the English,' wrote Grimm, 'reason and philosophy would still be in the most despicable infancy in France'; and he added that Montesquieu and Voltaire 'were the pupils and followers of England's philosophers and great men'.[2] In the first place there was Francis Bacon, the great protagonist of inductive reasoning, experimental science and empirical research. 'The true and lawful goal of the sciences,' Bacon had written in words that might have been the *philosophes'* own manifesto, 'is none other than this: that human life be endowed with new discoveries and powers.'[3] Equally important in this ancestry was Sir Isaac Newton, the mathematician and astronomer and author of the *Principia*, or *Mathematical Principles of Natural Philosophy* (1687), and the *Optics* (1704). In the *Principia*, Newton had propounded the laws governing the motions of the earth and heavenly bodies; in his law of gravitation, he showed that gravity was directly related to the density of matter and that bodies attracted one another in proportion to the quantity of the matter they contained. Thus the phenomena of nature and the mysteries of the universe were reduced to simple, universal principles of mathematics. The third great influence – this time, in the social sciences – was Locke. Locke had published his two *Treatises on Civil Government* and his *Essay Concerning Human Understanding* in 1690. In his *Treatises* Locke took over from Hobbes the 'social contract' theory, whereby civil government was presumed to have evolved from a contract between the ruler and his subjects. But whereas Hobbes had argued that the contract implied the complete surrender of the subjects' rights to the ruler's undisputed sovereignty, to Locke the contract was a bargain with obligations on both sides: the subjects must respect the ruler's sovereignty, but he in turn must respect their liberties and rights of property; failing which, the contract might be dissolved. (Thus Locke justified, *post facto*, the 'glorious revolution' of 1688.) Locke went on in his *Essay* to lay the foundations of modern sensational psychology. The mind, he taught, was a *tabula rasa*, on which all impressions and experiences were grafted by the senses, not by innate or inherited qualities or by the accidents of birth. Thus, it might be inferred, all men came into the world as potential equals, all equally subject to the formative influence of the environment in which they lived.

It was Voltaire who first popularised these works in France. Having been exiled from Paris in 1726, he returned two years later from a long stay in England and fed back to his countrymen, in his *Lettres philosophiques* (1734), what he had learned from Bacon, Newton, Locke and the English deists. Having meanwhile become a deist and a Newtonian himself, it was these ideas that he was most eager to propound. At first it was an uphill struggle, as the French Academy was deeply committed to the Cartesian physics that Newton, in his *Principia* and *Optics*, had sought to dethrone. So it was only twenty years later that 'la fureur de l'attraction' won the day in Paris, from where it spread all over Europe. It spread the more quickly because the *philosophes* and their associates, even if not scientists themselves, argued that if the mysteries and chaos of the universe were subject to the harmony of natural law, why then not man's social relations and his political institutions? Meanwhile, the case had been strengthened further by the simultaneous invasion of the continent, in a great wave of anglomania, by the works of Bacon and Locke.

The *philosophes* were not slow to learn their lessons. In 1738, Voltaire wrote the *Éléments de la philosophie de Newton*, which was followed five years later by Maupertuis' more professionally Newtonian *Théorie de la figure de la terre*. In 1749 Diderot, following up Locke's teachings on the relativity of knowledge, argued, in his *Lettre sur les aveugles*, that morality was equally a factor of environment and in consequence was relative as well. Five years later the Abbé Condillac took up the argument in his *Traité des sensations*. 'Ideas,' he wrote, 'in no way allow us to know things as they actually are; they merely depict them in terms of their relationship with us'; and further: 'the good and the beautiful are by no means absolutes; they are relative to the character of the man who judges and to the way in which he is organised'. It was now only a short step to apply the relativity argument to education; and this is what Rousseau did, though in a style entirely his own, in *Émile* (1762), which in his lifetime was the most widely read of all his works. While borrowing from Locke and Condillac, Rousseau really turned their arguments inside out; for, characteristically, he substitutes nature and sentiment for reason; and it is on the basis of Émile's natural instincts and his contact with nature, rather than by any conscious rational direction, that his tutor gradually feeds him knowledge and develops his mind. It is perhaps not surprising that *Émile* became a text book for the 'learning-by-doing' and 'education-through-nature' schools of the future.

More immediate in its impact, in its country of origin at least, was Adam Smith's *Inquiry into the Nature and Causes of the Wealth of Nations* (1776); this, in its own way, was also a typical product of the Enlightenment. Smith was a friend of Turgot and Hume; he was familiar with the work of Quesnay and the Physiocrats in France, and he had, no doubt, also read the earlier free-trade arguments advanced by Boisguilbert in Louis xiv's day. But he cast his net far wider and he broadened the whole debate. He demonstrated that the real producer of wealth was labour, and his thorough analysis of prices, capital and labour and of the laws of supply and demand became a model for all later economists of expanding industrial society to build on. Above all, he drew the conclusion that mercantilism, or the 'merchant system', far from expanding the store of the nation's trade, restricted it by promoting monopoly, thus failing to benefit the nation at large as it favoured the producer at the expense of the consumer:

At first sight the monopoly of the great commerce of America naturally seems to be an acquisition of the highest value . . . The dazzling splendour of the object, however, the immense greatness of the commerce, is the very quality which renders the monopoly of it hurtful, or which makes one employment, in its own nature necessarily less advantageous to the country than the greater part of other employments, absorb a much greater proportion of the capital of the country than what would otherwise have gone into it.[4]

Smith's work was a time-bomb which had a shattering effect on the economic thinking of the early nineteenth century. More immediately explosive in their impact, however, were the developments made by the *philosophes* to Locke's ideas on the 'social contract', property, society and the state. Among the minor writers were Morellet, with his *Code de la nature* (1775), and Mably, with his *De la législation* (1776), both of whom advanced daring theories of social equality and the common ownership of property ('*la loi agraire*'); but these remained abstract speculations to which perhaps rather more weight has been given by some later writers than they deserve. Far more important was the work of Montesquieu and Rousseau (and to a lesser degree of Voltaire), whose conflicting views on state and society have not ceased to command the attention of historians and political theorists and practitioners ever since. Montesquieu's first political treatise was his *Lettres persanes* (1721), which, disguised as a visiting Persian's musings on Paris society and manners, was a critical commentary on the political institutions of contemporary France. His greatest work, *De l'esprit des lois*, appeared almost a generation later (1748). It is remarkable in more than one respect. In the first place, like Vico but unlike many of his fellow *philosophes*, Montesquieu's approach to history and politics was relativist: there was no perfect system of government suited to every country irrespective of time and place. On the contrary, government and institutions, laws and customs sprang from a nation's history, its geography and climate. Thus, of three types of government put forward, despotism (though undesirable, and this was an inconsistency in his argument) was only suited to the enervating climates of the east and south. In Europe, there were the alternatives of monarchy or republic, but the republic (though in theory desirable for all) was in practice only suited to small states, like the city-states of Greece and Rome or their modern equivalents, Venice and Geneva. But Montesquieu's relativism was shot through with absolute moral judgements that, far from condoning existing constitutions, made him reject the existing absolute monarchy in France as being too liable to slip into despotism. So the solution was a compromise: a monarchy whose despotic tendencies must be held in check by a balanced constitution. And here the model was the British, where he thought he saw a perfect 'separation of powers' between the executive, legislature and judiciary. Applying this model to France, he called for greater authority to be given to the 'intermediate' bodies – the aristocracy and Parlements – as a counter to the despotism of the crown. So, in spite of much that is radical in Montesquieu's thinking (he first coined terms like *patrie* and 'the will of the people'), he emerges as the conservative upholder of aristocracy against the despotism of monarchy.

Voltaire was not an original thinker and wrote no political treatise; but in his numerous tracts, philosophical tales (*Zadig, Candide*), dramas (*La Henriade, La Pucelle*), and his voluminous correspondence, he came to represent a political attitude quite distinct from that of Montesquieu. Where Montesquieu promoted the claims of aristocracy, Voltaire was throughout his career a consistent opponent of 'privilege', particularly that vested in the Parlements, whose influence he would gladly have destroyed. So, not being a democrat or a republican, he sought a solution in enlightened monarchy. Hence his support for French ministers like Maupeou and Turgot, who tried to assert the authority of the crown over the privileged orders; hence, too, his long flirtations with Frederick and Catherine the Great, of whom he expected far more than they were ever willing or able to give. So Voltaire, although indebted, like so many others, to Montesquieu, came to counter his *thèse nobiliaire* with a *thèse monarchique* of his own.

Rousseau's problem was a far more intractable one and the solution he found, though highly original, was shot through with contradictions. How reconcile the natural goodness of man, in which he implicitly believed, with community-living in the modern state? The question was first put to him by the Dijon Academy in offering a prize for the best essay on the subject: what is the origin of inequality among men, and is it permitted by the law of nature? Rousseau's answer, in the *Discours sur l'inégalité* (1755), was that equality was only to be found in the primitive state of nature and that inequality, like the loss of man's primitive innocence, arose from the corrupting influence of society. The same thought is repeated a few years later in *Émile*: 'Men are not made to be crowded together in ant-hills . . . The more they congregate, the more they corrupt each other.' The remarkable thing is that the *Contrat social* (1762) appeared in the same year; yet now the whole emphasis has changed. The famous opening sentence, it is true, is entirely in keeping with the negative view of society expressed in the *Discours* and *Émile*: 'Man is born free, and everywhere he is in chains.' But now he goes on to argue that the natural freedom of primitive man has grave limitations and that it is only through the 'social contract', whereby men bind themselves together for living in society, that a higher freedom, security, culture and human dignity may be attained. So the social contract, while destroying man's primitive innocence and freedom, offers him something better in exchange. But how can these gains be assured and maintained? Only, Rousseau answers, through the operation of the 'general will' and the formulation of good laws. But the general will, which is infallible, is not simply the sum total of fallible individual wills: it is the distilled essence of the community's will at large. How can it be tested and translated into laws? Possibly by a majority decision of the assembled people; but as the majority is liable to be corrupted by ill-intentioned propaganda, he tends to favour the alternative of the intervention of a Solon-like law-giver who will act on the community's behalf. Yet, whichever way they come to be enacted, the laws now represent the general will, and as such, they have to be obeyed by all. So there can be no place for dissenters, for the individual having surrendered his rights to the community or sovereign people must now respect its laws. Indeed he may be 'forced to be free'; and, in an extreme case, such as the rejection of the civil cult which Rousseau proposed as a substitute for Christianity, he may even be put to death.

Thus in Rousseau's system individual freedoms and state rights, the rival claims of nature and society co-exist in uneasy association; and plenty of doubts remain as to the method of recognition and operation of the general will and the nature and functions of the legendary 'lawgiver'. Did Rousseau ever intend it for a country as large as France or only for a small state like his own native Geneva? In practice at least he proved to be less than consistent: the subsequent constitutions he devised for Corsican patriots and Polish noblemen (in 1765 and 1772) reverted to the relativism of Montesquieu and made no provision for popular consultation; and, unlike Voltaire, he turned a deaf ear to the appeal of the under-privileged *natifs* of Geneva when they sought his aid to win their electoral rights. And it seems more than likely that, had he lived, he would have condemned the Parisian *sans-culottes* of 1793 for the uses they made of his teachings, much as Luther had condemned the rebellious German peasants who invoked his name 270 years before. Yet, with all the confusion and inconsistencies, the solid fact remains: it was Rousseau's *Contrat social* that first expounded the basic principles of popular sovereignty; so it is not surprising that whatever his own intentions this is the face of Rousseau that, among so many others, has most persistently endured.

We have seen that these writers were anxious to find converts to influence men's minds and to bring about reforms. How successful were they? In the first place, they found converts among professional writers and thinkers similar to themselves; there was, in fact, a sort of international and temporal chain linking the *philosophes* of different countries and different generations. Thus Montesquieu became a kind of father-figure or patriarch of Enlightenment, whose influence was acknowledged by the legal reformers Filangeri and Beccaria in Italy, by Hume, Ferguson and Gibbon in Britain and Rousseau in France, in much the same way as Locke and Newton had inspired Voltaire a generation before. Similarly, Helvétius served as a model for Bentham's utilitarianism in England and Adam Smith derived his ideas, in part at least, from the Physiocrats in France. In Germany Kant, Herder and Goethe all acknowledged a debt to Rousseau, as Lessing did to Diderot and Kant to Hume; while Voltaire's anti-clerical tirades evoked a response from critics of the churches all over Europe. Broadly too, while Montesquieu could, like Locke, claim an ascendancy among letters in every country, there was a kind of territorial division of influence between Voltaire and Rousseau. Thus Rousseau had a noticeably greater following in Spain and Voltaire in Italy. In Germany, Voltaire's impact was greatest among the francophiles at court and, in Prussia at least, among men of science; while Rousseau's was more pronounced among writers like Lessing and Herder and others who were trying to counter French influence with a language and culture of their own. In Hungary and Poland, where the honours were fairly evenly divided, it was partly a question of generation: in both countries the Enlightenment began in the 1760s with a cult of Voltaire; but as the political issues sharpened in the 1770s, Rousseau's influence became the greater. In England, Voltaire was without doubt the greater favourite among men of letters; but then England was probably less influenced by the French *philosophes* than any other country we have mentioned.

In their day the *philosophes* met with a remarkably sympathetic reception from Europe's rulers; it was only after the French Revolution that they and their works came under almost universal suspicion. This response was probably warmest in Germany. In Prussia Frederick II not only welcomed Voltaire to Potsdam, but he also made Maupertuis president of his new Academy at Berlin and, on his death, offered the succession to d'Alembert (who, however, refused but agreed to become Frederick's adviser on scientific affairs instead). In Ansbach Margrave Charles Frederick William had a bust of Voltaire on his desk. At Salzburg the Archbishop-Elector, Hyeronymus Count Colloredo, did even better: he had a bust of Rousseau as well and appointed a pupil of Kant's to be director of his seminary for priests. In Baden Margrave Charles Frederick, as we saw, attempted to put Physiocratic ideas, in the form of a single tax on land, into practice. In Bavaria Elector Maximilian III Joseph was inspired by the teachings of the 'enlightened' jurist, Christian Wolff, to carry out far-reaching legal reforms; while Frederick II of Hesse-Cassel was highly commended by Voltaire for his *Catechism for Princes*. In Austria, Joseph II, while deploring 'philosophical' attacks on religion, borrowed from Montesquieu and Rousseau in conducting his experiments in 'scientific' government; in Tuscany (and later in Belgium) his brother Leopold stood even more heavily in the *philosophes*' debt. In the Duchy of Parma Don Philip of Bourbon appointed Condillac to be tutor to young Duke Ferdinand, his heir. In Poland King Stanislas Poniatowski, a francophile and patron of the arts, gave the direction of the Education Commission he set up in 1773 to Kollataj, his country's leading *philosophe*. In Russia we have already noted Catherine's warm regard for Voltaire and Diderot. She was also a keen student of Montesquieu and, before embarking on her educational reforms of the 1760s, she sought the advice of Beckij, who was an admirer of Rousseau and Locke. In England William Pitt, Prime Minister to George III, was an early convert to the ideas of Adam Smith and gave expression to them in the free-trade treaty he signed with France (the Eden–Vergennes Treaty) in 1786. In Spain even after Voltaire's works had been banned by the Inquisition (in 1762) Aranda,

the 'enlightened' minister of Charles III, allowed his plays to be performed provided the author's name did not appear on the text. In
France, too, where official hostility was almost as intransigent as in
Spain, the *philosophes* were not without supporters in the ministry or at
court. Malesherbes, who shared their views when government censor
between 1750 and 1763, usually allowed a limited number of copies of
their new books to be sold and only brought the hammer down if they
provoked an outcry or aroused complaint. Turgot was the only *philosophe*
to attain high office in France; and when he became Controller General
to Louis XVI in 1774 he attempted (like Charles Frederick of Baden) to
put Physiocratic ideas into practice – but with unfortunate consequences, as we shall see.

If rulers were often sympathetic, the churches generally were not. The
first phase of 'philosophy' in France tended to be sceptical and irreligious; in consequence, all *philosophes*, whether they deserved it or
not, became tarred with the same sceptical brush. So it was generally
the Catholic church which – in France, Italy and Spain – took the
initiative in condemning or proscribing their writings, as happened in
succession to the *Encyclopédie*, and the works of Voltaire, Helvétius and
Rousseau. (Rousseau's *Émile* had the particular distinction of being
placed on the Index and simultaneously condemned by the Sorbonne,
the General Assembly of the Clergy and the Parlement of Paris.) Religious minorities were often no more sympathetic: 'philosophic' views
commended themselves little more to French and Italian Jansenists,
German and Danish Pietists, or Wesleyan Methodists in England. The
exception were the Protestant churches in the north of Germany; for
north German Protestants had emerged from the savagery of the Thirty
Years War with a deep desire for religious peace and toleration. They
found a welcome message in Locke's *Treatises* and this, in turn, made
them amenable to 'philosophy' in general, which in any case was rarely
directed against themselves. The same is probably true of the Protestant
clergy in Hungary who, until Joseph's reforms of 1789, had their own
battle to fight for toleration and civil rights.

But even if the churches were generally hostile, the clergy – both
secular and regular – frequently were not. In France, there were four
abbés among the best-known *philosophes*: Condillac, Raynal, Mably and
Morellet; and their immediate predecessors included the radical parish
priest, Jean Meslier, of Louis XIV's day. At all times, there were
numerous abbés who frequented the Paris salons and provincial
Academies; among the members of the Academies of Bordeaux, Dijon
and Châlons-sur-Marne, the proportion of clergy varied between one in
five and one in eight; and of the forty copies of the *Encyclopédie* sold in
Périgord, twenty-four belonged to parish priests. An archbishop, as we
saw, had busts of Voltaire and Rousseau in his study at Salzburg; the

same was true of a Benedictine Abbot at Angers in France; and, similarly, their works were to be found in monastic libraries in Spain. In Italy a French visitor found in 1739 that the best-stocked libraries were kept by the priests; it was among them, too, that he found the most competent students of Newtonian physics.[5]

As the ideas of the Enlightenment in many countries radiated outwards from the court, so, socially, they generally percolated downwards from the aristocracy or gentry. If High Churchmen found a certain embarrassment in identifying themselves too openly with 'philosophic' views, this presented no problem at all for laymen of the upper classes. It was fashionable enough, as we have seen, to take religion with a pinch of salt; and in France Louis XVI's own brother, the Comte d'Artois, was notorious for totally disregarding fast-days. (There is perhaps some piquancy in the fact that, half a century later, when fashions had changed, the same prince should become the last king of France to be anointed with oil at his coronation ceremony at Rheims.) Philosophical works lined aristocratic shelves; many of the royal Intendants – like Turgot at Limoges – were won over by the new ideas; and some of the highest nobility of France – the Dukes of Orleans, Chartres and Liancourt among them – entertained the leading *philosophes* at their table or rubbed shoulders with them in the literary salons and masonic lodges. As the Vicomtesse de Noailles later lamented, and without too much exaggeration, 'Philosophy had no apostles more well disposed than the *grands seigneurs* . . . the most active and enthusiastic pupils of Rousseau and Voltaire were courtiers, even more than men of letters.'[6] If at Berlin, Vienna, St Petersburg, Munich and Salzburg it was the rulers themselves who took the lead, in other capital cities – at Warsaw and Budapest, as at Versailles or Paris itself – that task fell to the aristocracy. In Hungary, Montesquieu's *De l'esprit des lois* and Rousseau's *Contrat social* both provided the nobility with shot and shell in their duels with Vienna. Some of the best libraries in Hungary were aristocratic: that of the Czáky family had, in the last two decades of the century, 5,160 volumes, of which 3,600 were French, including first editions of the complete works of Voltaire and Rousseau. Admittedly, when the issues sharpened with Joseph II and the French Revolution, the higher aristocracy tended to pull in their horns, and the initiative passed to the lesser nobility and gentry who dominated the Lower Chamber and county assemblies. In Poland, even when Enlightenment was encouraged by the court, as it was under Stanislas Poniatowski, it was always the lesser rather than the higher nobility that joined with the professional bourgeoisie in promoting its aims. In Germany, Italy and Russia the aristocracy followed the court in espousing the Enlightenment as they tended to espouse French literature and language in general; but in Prussia where Voltairianism was courtly and aristocratic, the cult of Rousseau – as with Lessing (whose election to the Berlin Academy Frederick refused to endorse) – was more evidently plebeian and middle-class. In Spain, again, the situation was different. Though the Enlightenment found few adherents, these few included a fair proportion of the higher nobility; and it appears from counts made of the subscribers to the four leading journals spreading 'enlightened' ideas that one in ten or one in twelve were titled noblemen, representing a similar proportion of all the *títulos* and *señores* in the country.[7]

There was, however (with the possible exception of Germany), no clear dividing line between enlightened aristocrats and enlightened men of wealth. Wealth was certainly a consideration, as a large new volume, such as Rousseau's *Émile* or Holbach's *Système de la nature*, might cost the equivalent of fifteen shillings – or considerably more if the work was banned. So patronage went with wealth as much as with aristocracy. In France we hear of financiers, Farmers General and their wives either running salons themselves or attending them, alongside the *noblesse*, to hear the latest books discussed. The great commercial ports and cities too were centres of cultural activity; and at Bordeaux and Marseilles, as at Liverpool, London, Bristol, Hamburg and Frankfurt-am-Main, rich merchants endowed Academies and subscribed to learned journals. Apart from the rich, the Enlightenment made its most direct appeal of all to the professional middle class, who, whether as government officials, lawyers, doctors, agronomists, journalists, writers or university professors, found the new ideas stimulating, congenial or convincing: this would appear, from all that has been written on the subject, to have been the case in every country. Small merchants and businessmen had also a certain interest, to say the least, in what the Physiocrats and economists were writing; but they seem generally to have received these ideas at a later stage, or at second rather than first hand. (It is significant that, in France, Turgot's proposals to abolish the gilds met with little enthusiasm in such circles and that, even in the *cahiers de doléances* of the Third Estate in 1789, opinion was still evenly divided.) The exceptions were Scotland and the north of England; where scientists and businessmen in Glasgow, Manchester and Birmingham met to discuss the pros and cons of the new ideas of Adam Smith and the pioneers of the industrial revolution.

Others who, in every country, received these ideas at a later remove were the small craftsmen and *menu peuple* of the cities and industrial towns. The Enlightenment was always a largely urban phenomenon (even in France, villages were only marginally affected); but there were important deterrents preventing ideas from reaching the urban poor: among them the cost of books, illiteracy, the hostility of the church and the reluctance of aristocrats and men of wealth to allow the common people to share the luxury of impiety, or even to acquire any degree of instruction not deriving from the Bible. This applied of course to Paris almost as much as to any other major city. Yet a contrary view was expressed by a contemporary observer, Restif de la Bretonne, who wrote in 1785 that 'in recent times the working people of the capital have become impossible to deal with, because they have read in our books truths too potent for them'.[8] But Restif is not a reliable witness: he disliked the *philosophes* and he had little regard for Parisians, and for *la population ouvrière* least of all. In fact, a study of the police records for the last dozen years of the *ancien régime* suggests that in Paris there were very few signs indeed of any popular awareness of the new ideas until the very eve of the Revolution. In England, this 'grass-roots' impact came both earlier and later than in France. On the one hand, England's industrial revolution could never have got off the ground as it did in the early 1780s without a considerable involvement in the discussion of the new economic ideas by thousands of skilled craftsmen in the industrial areas of the north. On the other hand, the political ideas coming from across the channel took longer to percolate; and here the great turning-point was the publication of Tom Paine's *The Rights of Man* in 1792.

How, and through what channels of communication, were the ideas passed on? In the first place of course through the direct contact of author and reader. Montesquieu's *De l'esprit des lois* appeared in twenty-two French editions by 1751, had ten English editions by 1773, appeared in Dutch, Polish and Italian in the 1770s, in German in 1789 and in Russian in 1801. In Hungary, it was published in Latin as early as 1751. The *Encyclopédie* drew 4,000 subscribers. Voltaire's *Candide* went through eight editions in 1759 alone. The Abbé Raynal's *Histoire philosophique des deux Indes* (popular then, though little known today) was first published in 1770 and had thirty-five editions in five or six languages in thirty years. Rousseau's *Contrat social* appeared in thirteen French editions in 1762 and 1763 and three English editions, one German and one Russian by 1764; after which there was a lull, and its first Hungarian edition appeared in Latin in 1792. But Rousseau's other works – his *Émile* and *Nouvelle Héloïse* in particular – had, before the Revolution, a far wider distribution than the *Contrat social*; and this applied as much to France as to Poland, Germany, Russia, Hungary and Spain. Meanwhile Voltaire's political, satirical and anti-clerical pieces – and above all his plays – poured out in translation in these and other countries from the 1730s to his death in 1778 and beyond.

The press provided another more indirect means of communication of the new ideas. Indeed, the works of the *philosophes* were attended at every stage by a veritable explosion of new journals and periodicals, particularly in Germany, France and England. The first monthly journal had been founded in Holland in 1686, and the earliest English daily newspaper in 1702. At this time there were in England twenty-five papers and periodicals of every kind; by 1750 they had risen to ninety (half of them in the provinces); by 1780 to 158, and by 1800 to 278. France had been a late starter and had its first national daily paper, the *Journal de Paris*, in 1777. Two years later there were thirty-five papers and periodicals in France and there were 169 in 1789; but the provincial press (as Arthur Young discovered) had only recently begun. Germany, with its proliferation of states and principalities, did better: by 1790 there were said to be 247 periodicals in circulation; but many of them, due to censorship and repression, had short lives and few readers. The German press, like the French, had a late start but made rapid progress, and there were twenty-four political journals in the 1790s where there had been only seven in the 1770s. In other countries – Italy, Spain, Poland, Austria and Russia – the age of journalism was yet to come: the appearance of half-a-dozen periodicals at any time was still considered something of a triumph. Yet certain of these journals, while their coverage of news was limited, were deliberately designed to serve as channels for the new ideas. Such were *Il Caffè*, edited by Pietro Verri, a Physiocrat, at Milan in 1764–6; the *Monitor* of Warsaw (1763–85); and the *Espíritu de los mejores diarios* of Madrid (founded in 1788). But the number of their readers was still almost ludicrously small. Where in the early 1780s the London *Spectator* might count on selling 20,000 copies and the *Post van der Neder Rhijn* in Holland even more, the *Espíritu*, which had the largest circulation of any periodical in Spain, had a mere 765 subscribers in 1788 and 630 in 1789.

Other channels of communication were the academies, universities, literary societies, salons and masonic lodges. In France, as in England, the universities were generally at a low ebb. Not one of France's twenty-two universities – least of all the Sorbonne in Paris – can in fact be said to have been a contemporary centre of Enlightenment. So other means had to be found for its propagation. Most fashionable, and perhaps most fruitful, were the Paris salons, which were presided over by ladies of fashion like Madame Geoffrin, Mademoiselle de Lespinasse and Madame Necker, who were of a literary and 'philosophical' disposition and brought the *philosophes* together with the most influential of their readers and patrons. A similar role was played by certain *seigneurs* in their châteaux and by certain Farmers General and financiers in their city hôtels, as also by the more splendid of the masonic lodges which, after the early 1770s, were patronised by the nobility and became fashionable forums for discussion. (Voltaire, Franklin and Helvétius were all connected with the Nine Sisters Lodge in Paris.) There were also the provincial academies like those in Toulouse, Bordeaux and Marseilles, where educated clergy, nobility and merchants emulated the practice of the Paris salons: where there had been fifty such bodies in 1750, there were twice that number in 1770. Again, there were the Paris cafés which, the police claimed, numbered 380 in 1723 and 1,800 in 1788; the clubs which had by this time become centres for political discussion; and the far greater number of literary and 'philanthropic' societies, which, like the clubs and cafés, began to proliferate after 1770 and by the late 1780s were to be found in every moderately-sized town in France.[9]

In other countries this word-of-mouth diffusion might take different forms. In London there were probably as many coffee-houses as there were in Paris: there were already 550 at the end of Walpole's time, in 1739. The British universities, unlike the French, were not universally moribund: in fact, in Scotland the universities of Edinburgh, Glasgow and St Andrews – with their close association with Black, Ferguson, Hume and Adam Smith – were going through a cultural revolution quite unknown in the south, least of all at Oxford and Cambridge. The new urban centres of Enlightenment lay in the north: at Glasgow and Edinburgh, Manchester, Birmingham and Leeds. The 'dissenters', excluded from the older universities, founded their own Dissenting Academies in industrial towns like Warrington and Daventry. Above all, there was the Lunar Society of Birmingham which counted among its members some of the leading scientists and industrialists of the day – men like Erasmus Darwin, Joseph Priestley, Josiah Wedgwood the potter, John Wilkinson the ironmaster, and James Watt and his business partner, Matthew Boulton. Here then was that union between science and industry – so prophetic for the future – which no other country was able to realise in the eighteenth century.

In countries where the Enlightenment received royal or ducal patronage, as important a part was probably played by officially sponsored societies, academies and universities as by local initiative of this kind. In Hungary it appears that the new ideas first filtered through from the court of Vienna; and that Voltaire's writings, for example, were brought back to their homeland by young guardsmen of the Noble Hungarian Royal Bodyguard, which Maria Theresa had formed to appease the Hungarian nobility in the course of the Seven Years War.[10] In Poland, in Stanislas Poniatowski's day, scientific societies were set up at Warsaw, Cracow, Gdansk (Danzig) and Wroclaw (Breslau); and the ancient University of Cracow was reformed by Kollataj and supplied with 'philosophical' courses of instruction. In Tuscany, the Archduke Leopold similarly reformed the Universities of Pisa and Siena. The Archbishop of Salzburg, besides admiring Voltaire and Rousseau, made his University of Bonn a centre of the new learning; and Hanover's University of Göttingen was probably, with Edinburgh, Leyden and the Academy of Geneva, among the most enlightened of the universities of Europe at this time. But Germany, like France, also saw a blossoming of literary or reading societies and masonic lodges, which brought the

Aufklärung to mixed groups of bourgeois and nobles throughout the country. In the 1770s the Lüneburg and Erlangen societies had a hundred members each, while the Mainz society had 300 members who had at their regular disposal forty-seven newspapers (half of them political) and forty-one French and German periodicals. Even as late as 1797, long after reaction had set in, the Prussian censor complained to a colleague of 'the mania for reading' and of the great number of these societies that continued to increase.[11]

From all this welter of publication and discussion, what practically resulted? Some political historians and historians of political ideas have written as though the ideas of the 'philosophers' became translated into fact by a kind of process of spontaneous combustion. Thus Rousseau's and Mably's views on society and the state may be traced in a closely woven pattern of cause and effect to the 'totalitarian democracy' of Robespierre and Saint Just; or the scepticism of Holbach, Helvétius or Sade to the social nihilism of the hippies of San Francisco. Such a presentation has an attractive simplicity; but it ignores the social climate in which ideas germinate, become adopted and take root as well as the stage reached in a nation's history which causes one nation or class to embrace a new idea and another to reject it. Broadly, it may be true to say that, in eighteenth-century Europe, only those countries with a substantial educated middle class able and willing to adapt the ideas of the Enlightenment to its own use could really absorb them: the preliminary enthusiasm of rulers or nobility, of which we have given numerous illustrations, was clearly not enough. Admittedly this is an oversimplification; yet it may help to explain why Spain remained largely impervious to the new ideas until the 1830s, why in Hungary and Poland the new ideas wilted after the nobility found them too strong a medicine to swallow; why Germany and France both provided a favourable soil, but Germany being (like Italy) politically fragmented, dropped them where France did not; and why in Catherine's Russia 'enlightened' ideas could be switched on and off, almost overnight, by royal command. Moreover we have already suggested that it was largely for lack of an educated middle class in Austria that Joseph's reforms, inspired in part at least by the writings of the *philosophes*, ended in defeat. But why then should England, where the middle classes were so clearly more advanced than in any other major country, have proved comparatively resistant to 'philosophical' ideas? Presumably because a nation only adopts ideas that she can find use for; and this again depends on the stage reached in her historical evolution. England had already had her liberal revolution a century before and England's manners and institutions, based on her 'Revolution principles', were by and large what Voltaire was commending to his countrymen in his *Lettres* of 1734. But England was also in the eighteenth century on the eve of an industrial revolution; and such ideas as Adam Smith's and those of scientists like Priestley, Cavendish and Black were extremely useful to the up-and-coming manufacturing and entrepreneurial classes, to help them through the revolution.

The last point should be a reminder that it is not only a question of *nation*, but also one of *class*. Montesquieu, as we saw, was the spokesman for aristocracy while Rousseau spoke, in so far as he had a clear message, for *la souveraineté du peuple*. Yet the Hungarian and Polish nobility and the French *Parlementaires* of the 1770s and 1780s found it suited them to harness both to their cause, and in their battles with royal governments quoted from each without much discrimination. And a few years later the Paris *sans-culottes*, who were by now as devoted as Robespierre was to Rousseau, read into his teaching a conception of popular democracy that was quite different from that of the Jacobins or the revolutionary middle class.

These are of course longer-term considerations whose ultimate results cannot really be measured. But the Enlightenment, even in the social sciences, had certain short-term, more easily measurable, achievements to its credit. Thus it seems reasonable to suppose that the arguments advanced by Beccaria in his *Of Crimes and Punishments* had some responsibility for the penal reforms (abolition of torture and of the death penalty for various offences) carried out in Poland, Austria, Italy and Prussia shortly afterwards. They undoubtedly influenced Catherine in the Instructions she drew up for the great national assembly she convened in Moscow in 1767. Rousseau's and Condillac's ideas on education reappeared in the plans of the Polish Education Commission of 1773, as they did in Kollataj's programme for the University of Cracow; yet they were probably short-lived. Even more short-lived were Catherine's original plans for education in Russia. We saw that she solicited the advice of Beckij, who had been strongly influenced by Rousseau; but a few years later she abandoned Beckij and based her new state system of education on that devised in Austria under Maria Theresa in 1774. Yet the Russian statute of 1786 had an advantage over Rousseau's system in *Émile*, in that, in place of education-in-isolation, it attempted, following the Prussian and Austrian example, to introduce the compulsory primary school for all. Rousseau had more practical success in Switzerland, where he found an enthusiastic follower in Pestalozzi of Zürich, who expounded his ideas in *Leinhard und Gertrud* (1781) and went on to create his own private schools, with further plans for public education. In France Rousseau had to wait a little longer for official recognition; but his ideas, together with Condorcet's, played a considerable part in the various plans for a national system of education that the National Convention of the Revolution debated in 1792 and 1793.

So far, it does not seem a particularly impressive record, and both Voltaire and Rousseau at the end of their lives (they both died in 1778) were not altogether happy with the results. Kant, writing in 1784, while conceding that he was living in an Age of Enlightenment, denied that the age itself was enlightened.[12] At the time, they seemed to have justification enough; for none of the larger issues they had raised had been resolved, the process of conversion to their views had been slower and more uncertain than they had hoped and the patches of enlightened reforms still lay thinly spread over the European map. Yet, meanwhile, old attitudes were being slowly undermined and changes were brewing which, in the next generation, would create a more favourable climate for another, more impressive, forward leap. So, in the event, they proved to be rather more pessimistic than they need have been. But the great changes, to which they undoubtedly made a contribution, lay in the future; and even *philosophes* could hardly be expected to see that far ahead of their noses.

III

CONFLICT

CHAPTER 11

THE STRUGGLE FOR CONTROL
OF THE STATE

So far we have considered the eighteenth century in terms of its society, its ideas and its institutions, and have therefore tended to bring into relief those aspects making for continuity, gradual evolution or even stability and repose. But the eighteenth century, like all others, was also an age of conflict: of external conflicts between contending states and internal conflicts between opposing classes, factions and political groups. The first type of conflict will be considered in later chapters; the second will be the subject of the present chapter and the next.

As we have seen, in eighteenth-century Europe political power was largely distributed between monarchy and aristocracy: sometimes it rested almost exclusively in the hands of monarchy; at other times the balance was tilted firmly – as in the case of Poland and Sweden and the urban patriciates – towards aristocracy; and sometimes it lay in uneasy balance between the two. It was inevitable in such a situation that tensions should arise and demands be voiced for an extension of authority by one or other of the principal contenders and for a share in government by those who had been hitherto excluded. Whichever forms they took, such demands raised the whole problem of the redistribution of authority, as the solutions offered tended to be mutually exclusive and that advanced by one party rarely commended itself to others. Broadly, these solutions were of three kinds and posed three sets of questions. Should the way to reform, or to achieve a more satisfactory balance, be sought by enlarging the authority of an enlightened monarch at the expense of the aristocracy, the church or the estates; should aristocracy or other 'intermediate bodies' be strengthened as a check on the power of the crown; or should the power of both be balanced, or eclipsed, by vesting greater responsibility in the hands of the people themselves? In short, should the remedy for existing ills be found in strengthening the 'monarchic', the 'aristocratic' or the 'popular' element in the constitution? The answers given naturally varied from country to country and from class to class; they could all, in one form or another, be conveniently justified in terms of 'natural law'; and they could all invoke the authority of one or other of the great political thinkers of the day. (There was also a fourth question and a fourth source of internal tension, but these would arise far more sharply in the next century and they will not be treated separately here. Should the state, whether monarchic, aristocratic or democratic, give greater satisfaction to the claims of internal national groups? The problem presented itself most evidently in the case of multi-national states like Spain and the Habsburg Empire, but it also impinged on England's relations with the Scots and the Irish, and played a major part in Paoli's rebellion in Corsica and a minor one in the internal conflicts in Holland, Norway and Geneva.)

The strengthening of monarchy is of course related to a question discussed in an earlier chapter, that of 'enlightened despotism'. At times, as we then saw, there was a close concordance between the two. Pombal in Portugal, for example, used his authority to strike at both the church and the ancient nobility; and had his reforms been further pursued or merely survived his tenure of office, they would no doubt have tipped the balance significantly in favour of the Portuguese crown. The same may be said of the meteoric career of Struensee, whose work was essentially directed towards strengthening the monarchic element in the Danish constitution. It was true also of Gustavus III of Sweden, of Duke Leopold of Tuscany and, most evidently of all, of the Emperor Joseph II; but here there is clearly no need to recapitulate what has already been said before.

But the relationship between enlightened despotism and resurgent monarchy was not always so close: we saw this particularly in the case of Frederick the Great and Catherine of Russia who, far from being primarily concerned to limit the authority of the aristocracy, welcomed them as closer partners in the government of their states. In their case in fact it was not they but their predecessors – Frederick William I in the one case and Peter the Great in the other – who, while not usually termed enlightened, used their despotism to enhance the royal authority and to force the nobility to play a subservient role. But this, too, has already been said and the point need not be laboured further.

Before we leave the matter altogether, however, we must note that where monarchy took the offensive – as in most of the cases cited above – it was almost always the loser: in this sense absolute monarchy, in the latter half of the century at least, was already, in its relations with aristocracy, a declining force. This was not true early in the century of Peter the Great and Frederick William of Prussia; but it was notably so in the age of enlightened despotism in the case of Portugal, Spain, Denmark and the Austrian Empire, as it was also in that of the more strictly *defensive* operations of the kings of France that we shall consider later. There was, however, one important exception in this later period – Sweden – to which we must now briefly return.

Sweden, as we saw, was for sixty years ruled by the rival aristocratic factions of Hats and Caps, who divided political control between them during the period commonly known as 'the age of freedom'. It was an age, too, of interesting constitutional experiment (the peasants, for example, had their own elected representatives in the Riksdag, a privilege they enjoyed in no other country); but meanwhile the state was being torn apart by the rivalry of the two contending parties, who were subsidised and kept in office by the Russians, Prussians and French. So there was a real danger that Sweden might go the same way as Poland. In 1771, when Gustavus III came to the throne, the French, who had been supporting the Hats, decided to put their money on another horse and, through the Comte de Vergennes, their ambassador to Stockholm, entered into a conspiracy with the Swedish King and a group of noble army officers and government officials to restore the authority of the crown. The plan was to stage a three-pronged attack: in Finland, at Kristianstad in the south and at Stockholm at the centre. It was carried through in a bloodless *coup* in mid-August of the following year, when garrisons in Finland and Kristianstad rose on the King's behalf and Gustavus himself used the Guards regiments in Stockholm to arrest his political opponents. Two days later the King, having assured himself of the support of the citizens of the capital who flocked into the streets wearing the royal insignia on their arms, persuaded the Diet to accept a new monarchical constitution; after which the estates meekly dispersed with the promise that they would be summoned again in six years' time. It was a severe defeat for aristocracy and a decisive victory for the King, who retained his ascendancy until his death (by assassination) twenty years later. It was a victory, too, for the French and a defeat for the Prussians and Russians who had entertained other hopes for Sweden's future; but they were both engaged in the partition of Poland and found it an inappropriate moment for intervention.[1]

Sweden in fact provides the classic example of an offensive operation by the monarchy that succeeded in tipping the balance of power in its favour. Another though minor example was that of Poland, where, after the partition of 1772, Stanislas Poniatowski established an ascendancy over the *szlachta* and nobility in his truncated dominions that for twenty years reversed the pattern of aristocratic 'anarchy' which had previously prevailed. Elsewhere, the trend was rather the other way and monarchy, where it attempted to assert itself against aristocracy, was fighting rearguard and defensive actions against its encroachments in what has often been termed an age of 'feudal' or 'aristocratic' reaction. This aristocratic resurgence of the eighteenth century, which was characteristic of a number of countries, might take any one of a number of forms. Sometimes it took the form of a collusive deal between monarchy and nobility in which the first partner found it to be in its temporary interest at least to promote the other's ambitions. This, as we have said often enough, was what happened under Frederick and Catherine in Prussia and Russia: with more dramatic, and probably more harmful, consequences for monarchy in the first case than in the second. Alternatively, the aristocracy might extend its influence in society and the state by a process of gradual and peaceful infiltration. Such was the case with England and France, and with Sweden before Gustavus III took over. In England, it is true that an attempt made by the Lords in 1719 to promote a Peerage Bill that would prevent further additions to their ranks failed after energetic resistance by Sir Robert Walpole and others; but the trend towards a greater degree of aristocratic exclusiveness in society and administration was clear enough for all to see: from the time of Queen Anne, a seat in Parliament could only be held by those owning considerable property in land; peerages, though they continued to be conferred, tended, until a minor 'revolution' was carried out by the younger Pitt in the 1780s, to be conferred on members of the landed class alone; and the office of justice of the peace became increasingly the preserve of the country gentry, socially acceptable Church of England parsons or even of the aristocracy itself. In Sweden, where one army officer in three had been noble in 1719 (on the eve of the age of freedom), two in three were so in 1760. In France Louis xiv's old system of promotion to high office of a 'vile bourgeoisie' (so much deplored by Saint-Simon) was gradually abandoned in his later years and by his successors, notably so after the 1760s. In 1789 not one bishop and not one Intendant was a former commoner; all but three of the King's ministers appointed since 1718 (with Necker as the most notable example) had been noble; several of the Parlements had for long been refusing to admit commoners to their ranks; and Chancellor Ségur's decree of 1781 made it virtually impossible henceforth for a bourgeois, or even an *anobli* of recent vintage (he had to prove four generations of nobility), to qualify as an officer-candidate in the army unless actually rising from the ranks. Moreover the landowners in France whether noble or bourgeois had some years before the Revolution begun to look more closely into their records to seek out and revive old manorial rights, long since fallen into disuse, or to devise new ones when they could not find them. Thus the peasants, the principal victims of the exercise, came to suffer more than ever from seigneurial exactions.

More spectacular, of course, were the open collisions between aristocracy and monarchy, often fought out in the name of traditional 'liberties' or accompanied by appeals to 'natural law' or to the precepts of Montesquieu and Rousseau. There was an element of such an aristocratic challenge (though admittedly it was mixed up with other national and dynastic issues as well) in the Jacobite rebellions of 1715 and 1745 in Britain. The accession of the Hanoverian dynasty to the throne of England aroused intense hostility, particularly among the defeated minority of Tory peers, the country gentry and clergy in the northern counties and in Scotland the chiefs of the highland clans, who had sworn allegiance to the Stuarts and had a long-standing score to settle with their old enemies, the lowland chiefs along the Border. It was of these elements that Jacobitism was compounded and among them that the Old and the Young Pretenders sought recruits when they landed in Scotland, with French support, in the two successive rebellions of the 'Fifteen' and the 'Forty-Five'. The 'Fifteen' was a short-lived affair which took the form of a Scottish rising in September, led by the Earl of Mar, who assembled an army of 10,000 clansmen, while small-scale supporting operations were conducted in England by the Duke of Ormonde in the west and Earls Forster and Derwentwater in the north. But the rebels lacked both numbers and co-ordination, so that the government forces were able to isolate and destroy one movement after the other; and when James Edward, the Old Pretender, at long last landed in Scotland, the rebellion was all but over and he had to return to France almost as soon as he arrived. The 'Forty-Five' proved a more serious danger: it took place at a time when English forces were already engaged on the continent and overseas; moreover, it had in the Young Pretender a leader of considerably more dash and greater ability to command allegiance than his father. So when Charles Edward landed in the north of Scotland in July 1745, he was well received by the highland clans; he was declared Regent by the Duke of Athol; and, six weeks later, he had his father proclaimed King as James VIII at the Market Cross in Edinburgh and set up court at Holyrood Palace. Soon after, he defeated an English force at Prestonpans, pushed south and reached Derby in December, causing a panic and a run on the banks in London. But the highlanders refused to go further and the Jacobite army returned to Scotland, where the rebels were trapped and cut off from supplies, as the navy blockaded the coast and an English army under the Duke of Cumberland marched north to engage them. In April 1746, Cumberland caught, massacred and routed them at Culloden, near Inverness. This time, the repression was bloody and thorough; the Jacobite districts were systematically laid waste; thousands migrated overseas; and those of the highland chiefs – the Macleans, Camerons, Maclachlans, Frasers, Mackenzies and the rest – that survived were forcibly silenced and compelled to pay allegiance to the Hanoverian crown.

Compared with the violence of the Jacobite challenge, that of the aristocratic Whig leaders in the British Parliament was very subdued indeed. There was no question of overthrowing a dynasty to whose survival all the parliamentary groups were deeply committed, but merely one of tipping the balance of government in favour of the great Whig landowning families. The particular issue was: who should determine the appointment and survival in office of the King's ministers: the King himself, the parliamentary leaders or a combination (and what *sort* of combination?) of the two? Walpole, as we have seen, held office for over twenty years by retaining the confidence of both; whereas his successor, Carteret (the later Earl of Granville), fell from office in 1744 two years after his appointment because, while still enjoying the favour of the King, he had lost his support in Parliament. There followed a tussle over the succession between George II and the aristocratic parliamentary leaders, which resulted in the balance of power being tipped significantly in favour of the latter. For when, in 1746, the King proposed a ministry composed of his own nominees, the Earls of Bath and Granville, and the current leaders of Parliament (the Pelham faction grouped around Henry Pelham and his brother, the Duke of Newcastle) the Pelhams refused to serve on such terms and offered their collective resignation to bring the King to heel. The King had no choice but to submit and so, most unwillingly, accepted a precedent that became established for the next fifteen years.[2] It was these 'toils' imposed on his grandfather by the old Whig 'undertakers' that George III, on his accession, was determined to be rid of, and his efforts to do so constituted what Horace Walpole called the 'palace revolution' of 1761. The Dukes of Newcastle and Devonshire – remnants of the Whig 'old corps' – and their allies, the Earl Temple and William Pitt, were prised from office; and George III attempted for the next twenty years to govern with the aid of new men more committed to king and country than to faction or party. The experiment was on the whole a failure, as for the first ten years one short-lived ministry followed another. And the failure was due, in large part at least, to the determined opposition of the old guard of aristocratic leaders, who believed (in the Duke of Newcastle's words) that they were living under a new 'tyranny' as 'at the end of King Charles II's reign' and were determined to reduce 'the increasing influence' of the crown, and even joined in a movement for the reform of Parliament to do so. However, the aristocratic challenge failed in the end and the balance was firmly redressed when the younger William Pitt and his 'new' Tories won the general election of 1784 with the support of the King, the City of London, the new 'interloping' India merchants and the freeholders of Yorkshire against the 'old' Whig aristocratic combination of Lord North and Charles James Fox. That this was a defeat for aristocracy was certainly the view of some of the victors at least; for as Christopher Wyvill, the Yorkshire freeholders' leader, wrote after the event – possibly with the example of Poland in mind – a victory for the Fox–North coalition would 'have changed our limited Monarchy into a mere Aristocratical Republic'.[3] Yet for the King the victory was somewhat double-edged; it certainly meant no return to the system he had wished to see established in 1761. The price he had to pay for defeating the old Whigs was to allow greater authority and responsibility to Pitt and the new men who had taken their place. Moreover, the Whigs, under Fox and the Duke of Portland, regrouped their 'factions' into a national party organisation. So the election of 1784, as well as routing the Whig old guard, proved to be a landmark in the evolution of the Prime Minister's office and of the British system of party and Cabinet government.

In France the growth of the absolute monarchy from Henri II's time had been attended by a long tradition of aristocratic protest against the gradual encroachment of the crown on what the old landed nobility and the new magisterial *noblesse de robe* considered to be their rightful preserve and hard-won immunities. This protest had exploded into violence in the religious wars of the late sixteenth century and again in the Frondes during the infancy of Louis XIV and the *ministériat* of Cardinal Mazarin. During the greater part of Louis XIV's majority the aristocratic challenge had been effectively held in check: the old nobility and the princes of the blood had been stripped of their governorships and high offices of state and been brought to Versailles to dance attendance on the King, while the Parlements had been forbidden to publish Remonstrances or protest against royal decrees of which they disapproved. The last years of the reign, however, had seen the beginnings of an aristocratic reaction, in which Fénelen, Saint-Simon, Boulainvilliers and others had urged that the nobility be restored to a position of partnership in government. With Louis's death, it was the Parlements that began to take the lead, while the aspirations of the older nobility now tended to be voiced, in a more muted form, through such works as Montesquieu's *De l'esprit des lois*, which was the last great exposition of the *thèse nobiliaire* before the Revolution. The Parlements, however, spoke with a more strident voice and assumed the role of spokesmen for the privileged classes as a whole. Under the Regency, they resumed the old practice of publishing Remonstrances and continued to do so until the end of the *ancien régime*. It was the Paris Parlement that in 1720 led the movement of protest against Law's financial schemes; it opposed the bull Unigenitus and protected Jansenism, fought the Jesuits, protested against the *billets de confession* and generally acted as the mouthpiece of 'Gallican principles' in the relations of church and state. But above all the Parlements obstructed the attempts, made by successive governments from 1750 onwards, to solve the financial difficulties by reforming the fiscal system in such a way as to compel the privileged classes to make a token surrender, at least, of their immunity from paying taxes.

It was this issue above all others that brought the Parlements, as the self-styled champions of aristocracy and traditional liberties, into a series of violent conflicts with the King and his ministers. Between 1749 and 1751, Machault d'Arnouville, when Controller General, attempted to impose a new *vingtième*, or one-twentieth tax on incomes; but he failed to carry it through against the combined resistance of the Parlements and clergy and their supporters at court. A later Controller, Bertin, made similar proposals in 1763 and met with a similar response: this time, the Parlement of Paris borrowed from the newly fashionable 'philosophical' language of the day in accusing the ministers of offending against 'the Sovereign, the law and the Nation'; once more, the Parlements won the contest and Bertin was dismissed from office. In 1770–1, it was the Chancellor, Maupeou, who took the initiative and mounted a determined offensive against the Parlements that won a measure of success. When the Paris Parlement protested against the King's protection of a discredited favourite, the Duc d'Aiguillon, and refused to be silenced, Maupeou exiled the rebellious magistrates, abolished their offices without compensation, closed down the Parlements of Rouen and Douai in addition and set up new law courts in the place of the old; while Terray, the Controller General, proceeded to reform the taxes. These measures received warm support in some quarters and provoked violent hostility in others. Among Maupeou's defenders were the King himself, Madame du Barry (the new reigning mistress), the Archbishop of Paris, the *philosophes* (notably Voltaire) and middle-class lawyers anxious to step into the magistrates' shoes. But in the long run it was the opponents that proved to be the more effective: they included the old nobility, a large part of the clergy and the provincial Parlements in general; moreover the issue stirred up a hornet's nest of provincial separatism within the *pays d'états*.* Indeed, the outcry was such that Louis XVI, on his accession in 1774, felt compelled to dismiss Maupeou and Terray, the villains of the piece, to recall the Parlements and reinstate the magistrates in office.

Terray's successor, Turgot, was, as we have seen, a Physiocrat and a *philosophe* and was therefore even more inclined than Machault or Maupeou to carry out far-reaching reforms. He had agreed to the recall of the Parlements, but the clash between them was not delayed for long; his attempts to abolish the gilds and the *corvée* (rather than his more modest attempt to reform the taxes) aroused such a storm of disapproval from the Parlements and their allies – in this case, the clergy, financiers and disappointed ministers both past and present – that Louis, for the

---

* So called because they still retained their old local assemblies, or Estates, composed of the three 'orders': *clergé, noblesse* and *tiers état*.

sake of peace, withdrew his support and Turgot went the way of Bertin, Maupeou, Machault and Terray.

The next great encounter between monarchy and aristocracy in France was on an even greater scale than that of 1771; this was the so-called *révolte nobiliaire*, or 'aristocratic revolt', of 1787–8 that served as a curtain-raiser to the Revolution. When France found herself facing state bankruptcy at the end of the American War of Independence, Calonne, the Controller General, proposed that the deficit be filled by cutting government expenditure, extending the operation of the stamp duty on papers and documents and replacing the *vingtième* (which many landowners evaded) by a land tax on the annual production of the soil, to be paid by all landowners and collected by local assemblies of owners representing all three estates. Both Louis XVI and his minister realised that to place such proposals before the Parlement of Paris, which had been the usual procedure, would have been to provoke a head-on collision in view of the innovations they entailed. So it was decided to submit them to a specially convened assembly of *notables* – a mixed body of all the estates that had not met for 160 years. The hope that this assembly would prove more amenable proved, however, to be ill-founded. Within the assembly, liberal and die-hard nobles, *parlementaires* and bourgeois *notables* combined to oppose the minister. So Calonne was dismissed and replaced by one of his principal critics, Loménie de Brienne, Archbishop of Toulouse. Brienne modified some of Calonne's proposals, particularly those relating to the land tax, which had encountered the greatest opposition; but the *notables* were not appeased and, having voiced further protest, were dismissed and Brienne had to face the Paris Parlement after all. Here again, liberals and die-hards combined against ministerial 'despotism' and, for quite opposing reasons, demanded that the States General – which had not met since 1614 – should be convened to settle the affair. Brienne refused, promulgated the taxation decrees and exiled the recalcitrant Paris magistrates to Troyes.

So the *révolte nobiliaire* began, in which the provincial Parlements, the orders of the nobility and clergy and the estates of the *pays d'états* all joined forces to oppose the crown. It took place in two stages. First, the provincial Parlements followed the Parisians' lead by refusing to endorse the ministerial decrees; and Brienne was compelled to withdraw both stamp duty and land tax in return for an extension of the *vingtième* and a further loan, and to reinstate the Paris Parlement; it was even promised that the States General should meet in 1792. But negotiations soon broke down again; the Duke of Orleans and two other magistrates were exiled; and when the Parlement resisted, the law courts were ringed with troops and Lamoignon, the Keeper of the Seals, suspended all the Parlements (as Maupeou had wished to do in

1771) and planned for new courts of justice to take their place. This touched off the second stage of the revolt in 1788. It developed into a nation-wide rebellion in which clergy, nobility and provincial estates, and even peasants and townsmen and bourgeois spokesmen for the *tiers état* (like Barnave, the future revolutionary leader, in Dauphiné), joined in a common hue and cry against the 'despotism' of ministers. Riots broke out at Bordeaux, Dijon, Grenoble, Paris, Rennes, Rouen and Toulouse; in some, the troops, incited by their aristocratic officers, refused to fire and fraternised with the rebellious townsmen. The outcome, once more, was a victory for aristocracy and an ignominious defeat for their ministerial opponents. The States General were promised for May 1789; Brienne was replaced by Necker; Lamoignon's judicial reforms were withdrawn; and the Parlements were recalled soon after. So France, as some of Arthur Young's informants had already predicted in the previous October, stood 'on the verge of some great revolution in the government'; but the 'revolution' thus foreseen was likely (in Young's words) to 'add to the scale' of the nobility and clergy. Yet, as we know, the revolution that emerged did nothing of the kind. Why this was so, and why there was a revolution at all, we shall consider in a later chapter.

Meanwhile Joseph II's innovations had stirred feelings of intense resentment within the Austrian dominions, particularly in Hungary and Belgium. In Hungary, as in Transylvania, the aristocracy sent protesting petitions in the name of the 'freedom' and 'equality' of men; but Joseph's successor Leopold made timely concessions in order to hold his empire together, and it never came to an armed rebellion. In Belgium, however, Joseph's measures provoked something like a national revolution; and, like the aristocratic prelude to revolution in France in the same year, it was led by the privileged classes and was concerned to restore the old order rather than to re-build the state on new foundations. Here too, in resisting Joseph, the Belgian aristocrats and patricians, like their fellows in France and Hungary, based their arguments not only on historical precedent but on the writings of the *philosophes* and the experience of the Americans. In the Belgian provinces all three estates – representing the clergy, the nobility and the gildsmen of the ancient cities – held cherished privileges and 'liberties'. The nobility and clergy, who owned most of the land between them, enjoyed more exalted privileges than the humbler Third Estate; but they too, having become virtually an hereditary caste, clung as tenaciously as the higher orders to their old traditions. So when in 1787 Joseph reorganised the whole administration and judicial system of the provinces, abolished manorial courts, estates assemblies and town councils, and relaxed the trading monopolies of the gilds, he met with the combined opposition and rebellion of all three estates. Led by the largely patrician 'Estates party' of the lawyer Van der Noot, the Belgians drove out the Austrians in 1789 and proclaimed a United States of Belgium, closely modelled on the American Articles of Confederation. Meanwhile, a 'democratic' party, formed from middle-class elements – lawyers and businessmen – had come into being under another lawyer, J.F.Vonck (lawyers were plentiful in Belgium), and played some part in the revolution. As 'new' men, the Vonckists were critical of the old privileged orders and the systems they upheld, and advanced moderate proposals for constitutional reform. But these were too advanced for the taste of the aristocratic party and, once the Austrians had been expelled, they were blackened by their rivals as desiring to destroy the church and to subvert the ancient liberties of Belgium; they were arrested in hundreds or driven into exile, many to France. It is significant that they were able to return only with the aid of the Austrians, who regained control in December 1790. They were also able to play a larger part in the second, more democratic, revolution that followed, two years later, in the wake of the French.[4]

It is of course no coincidence that it was only in Belgium, among the Austrian dominions, that a middle-class party was in a position to play any sort of independent political role. In eighteenth-century Europe, it was only there and in Holland, France, Britain and certain of the self-governing cities of Germany and Switzerland that anything of the kind could have happened; for even in France the middle class – in so far as it was actively engaged at all – merely played second fiddle to one or other of the main contending parties in the aristocratic revolt. (This would no longer be the case in 1789; but that is another story.) Elsewhere, the middle classes, having no independent political existence, had the choice, in the encounter between monarchy and aristocracy, either of throwing in their lot with one side or the other, or of keeping quiet and waiting for better times to come.

During the eighteenth century, the states where (in addition to Belgium) the middle classes made some bid for a share of political control were England, Ireland, Holland, Geneva and a number of the adjoining city-states of Switzerland. It was a challenge which, like that of the aristocracy, became more vocal and insistent as the century advanced. In Switzerland there were significant encounters between bourgeoisie and patriciates or clerical autocracy at Neuchâtel and Bern and in the Bishopric of Basel. But the earliest, the most violent and the most protracted of them all were those that took place at Geneva – a fact that may help to explain the development of Rousseau's political ideas. Geneva, as briefly mentioned before, was divided into three main groups of inhabitants with varying rights of citizenship. At the top were the two hundred established and wealthy families (the *citoyens*) who held all the civic offices and all the seats in the Great and Small Councils that governed the city. In the middle were the new burghers or foreign-born (the *bourgeois*), who had the right to vote in the general assembly of citizens but were excluded from holding office; while at the base were the great mass of newer arrivals and more lowly-born citizens – the *habitants* and *natifs* – who were denied entry to the liberal professions and enjoyed no political rights at all. Broadly, the three groups represented three distinct social classes: patricians, bourgeois and artisans; and it was the demand of the two lower groups to share some degree of authority with the group at the top – either by holding office or simply by acquiring the right to vote – that split Geneva into warring political factions contending for power. The challenge to aristocracy developed in four main stages. It began in 1707 when Fatio, a member of the Council of Two Hundred, voiced the *bourgeois* demand that the general assembly be more frequently convened, that voting be by secret ballot and that fewer members of the same family be allowed to sit in the Councils. The *citoyens* made minor concessions; but when Fatio, abandoned by his *bourgeois* allies, refused to accept them, he was shot and things remained much as they had been before. A second *bourgeois* challenge in 1734 was more successful and ended in the Mediation of 1738 (underwritten by France and the Swiss cities of Zürich and Bern), which gave the *bourgeois* the final say in determining war and peace, the rights of petition and remonstrance and access to the city's Great Council; while the *natifs* were permitted to enter the liberal professions. The third challenge began in 1762. It had its origin in the ruling party's decision to follow the French Parlements' example by burning Rousseau's *Émile* and *Contrat social*, which was resented by the citizens at large; it culminated in an armed rebellion with wider objectives that brought the *citoyens* to heel. By an edict of 1768, the *bourgeois* were empowered to elect one-half of the new members to the Great Council and, on the Small Council, to appoint four new members a year. But the patricians refused to abide by its terms and, in league with the French, planned to revert to the Mediation of 1738. This led to two further armed rebellions in 1781 and 1782. In the first, the *bourgeois* seized the city's gates, convened a general assembly and won the support of the *natifs* by conceding their right to vote. When the Council, urged by the French, rejected the assembly's demands, it was the *natifs* that took up arms and, with the Burghers as their allies, besieged the City Hall, locked up the patrician leaders and forced the government to resign. But the French (patrons of revolution in America, but not in Switzerland) now intervened and, with supporting contingents from Sardinia and Bern, ringed Geneva with a force of 10,000 troops, arrested or drove the leaders into exile, and crushed the rebellion. So the clock was turned back again, and by the 'black code' of August 1782 the old aristocratic constitution was restored to what it had been before the Mediation of

1738. The French action created another dangerous precedent: it was the first time in the century that a popular insurrection had been crushed by foreign arms.[5]

In England the middle-class challenge took a less violent and dramatic form; but it was also concerned with an extension of the franchise and with a greater measure of popular control of Parliament. It began in the 1730s when the parliamentary opposition, with support in the City of London, tried to compel Sir Robert Walpole to hold more frequent elections by repealing the Septennial Act. The attempt failed, but it was revived in the mid-1750s by the 'patriots' or radicals of the City of London who, as the allies of the elder William Pitt, added to the demand for shorter parliaments demands for an end of rotten boroughs and for a more equal representation of the people; they also began to appeal to a far wider body of public opinion among the unenfranchised citizens 'without-doors'. But, at this stage, the reform movement was solidly middle-class, with little active support from the 'lower orders', and it was largely confined to the City of London. It was the entry on to the scene of John Wilkes in the early 1760s that gave it a new dimension, both by extending its frontiers into Middlesex and several cities and counties in the north and west, and by enlisting in his cause the small Middlesex freeholders and the poorer citizens of London. Wilkes was expelled from Parliament where he represented Aylesbury at this time, and exiled in 1763 – mainly because he had insulted the King in No. 45 of his paper, the *North Briton*. On his return to England in 1768, he was elected Member for Middlesex and, though confined to the King's Bench prison, was continually re-elected by the freeholders in spite of the bitter hostility of George III and Parliament's refusal to allow him to take his seat. When the Commons, on the third occasion, not only refused to accept Wilkes but allowed his defeated opponent, Luttrell, to take his place, the City radicals and the aristocratic opposition in Parliament (headed by Pitt – now Earl of Chatham – and the Marquess of Rockingham) organised a national petition of protest, which was signed by 38,000 county freeholders and 17,000 citizens, or a little over a quarter of all the voters in England. Though Parliament refused to accept the verdict, it was successful in the long run; for not only was Wilkes returned and seated in Parliament in the general election of 1774, but he was also able to persuade the Commons eight years later to expunge from their Journals a resolution of 1769 that had declared his 'incapacity' to take his seat among them.

Meanwhile a new movement for parliamentary reform had begun under the leadership of Christopher Wyvill, an Anglican clergyman, in Yorkshire; and in 1780 the Yorkshire freeholders (or 'associators') placed another massive petition before the Commons demanding an 'economical' reform by abolishing sinecures and 'unmerited' pensions;

later the Yorkshiremen, in association with other counties and with the radicals of Westminster and Middlesex, extended these proposals to include shorter parliaments and additional county seats. This second movement, like the first, ran for a while in harness with the aristocratic opposition in Parliament, represented by men like Rockingham and Burke, who had their own reasons for wishing to curb the influence of the crown; and Charles James Fox, one of the Whig leaders, even joined a sub-committee in Westminster that called for male adult suffrage and anticipated each one of the Six Points of the People's Charter of half a century later. But the alliance was short-lived, as the opposition Whigs, while eager to carry a limited measure of 'economical' reform, were quite unwilling to support demands for shorter parliaments, to abolish rotten boroughs or substantially to enlarge the electorate. So the partners fell out and when Fox joined Lord North in their ill-fated coalition of 1783 the middle-class reformers preferred to pin their hopes on the new opposition leader, the younger William Pitt, who at least gave some promise of support for a programme that Fox, as the price of his alliance with North, had now patently abandoned. So the Yorkshire 'associators' and most of the London radicals helped Pitt into office in the election of 1784. It proved to be a forlorn hope for the cause of reform, as Pitt followed Fox in abandoning it soon after. It was a serious setback; but the movement revived a decade later with a more radical programme and with a stronger base of popular support under the impact of the revolutionary events in France.

The English reform movement had not been untouched by that of their fellow-countrymen and co-religionists in America. In fact, there was a close reciprocal relationship between the two. When a prisoner in the King's Bench, Wilkes received gifts and messages of support from the Sons of Liberty at Boston and House of Assembly of South Carolina; and his release, in April 1770, was acclaimed at a public meeting at Boston with toasts to 'the illustrious martyr to Liberty'. Conversely, American 'liberties' were championed by merchants in London, Bristol and Liverpool, while English Nonconformists openly sympathised with their Calvinist brethren in New England. In other parts of Europe too, the American experience served as a catalyst which stimulated both noble and middle-class 'patriots' – as in Poland, Belgium, Holland and Ireland – to challenge their native rulers; while in Germany, Italy and France the response, though evident enough, was relatively muted. In Ireland public meetings began to be held in 1775 at which resolutions were passed in support of the colonists; speakers in Parliament objected to Irish troops being sent 'to cut the throats of their American brethren'; and several argued that if Britain subdued the Americans, 'the next step would be to tax Ireland in the British parliament'.[6] So to Irish Protestants, as to English Nonconformists, an early American peace, if not an American victory by arms, appeared a desirable goal. And from the petitions and toasts to the colonists that accompanied these sentiments, and even more from the difficulties England was encountering, there sprang the Irish volunteer army (the Volunteers) which, it has been said, 'in four short years . . . altered the balance of power in Irish politics'.[7] For through the Volunteers and the national movement that developed around them came the peaceful 'revolution' of 1782, when the Parliament at Dublin, led by Henry Grattan, was able to persuade Westminster to release it from the legislative subservience to the British Parliament and Privy Council that had survived since Poyning's Law in Henry VII's time, three hundred years before. Yet this was a comparatively modest step, as the laws that it passed might still be overruled by the British Cabinet. Moreover the Irish Parliament only represented a small minority of Protestant Irishmen; the Catholic majority were excluded altogether. So the reform of the Dublin Parliament became a burning issue which both Grattan and the Volunteers took up. But it encountered stiff opposition in both England and Ireland and hung fire; and with the French Revolution and the rebellion of the United Irishmen that it brought in its train, it was swept aside by the political reaction and religious divisions that followed.

Even more directly related to the events in America was the middle-class Patriot movement that developed in the United Provinces in the early 1780s. The Dutch had been the first nation in Europe to welcome the revolution in America; and in 1778 the city of Amsterdam made a secret treaty with the United States and floated a loan on their behalf. Dutch sympathies for the Americans were all the greater owing to the humiliations Dutch merchants had suffered at the hands of the British and to long-standing grievances and wounded pride which a British defeat might serve to redress. So, in 1780, in spite of the opposition of the Orange party (the pro-British party of the Stadholder, William V), the Dutch went to war on the side of the Americans and French. The Patriot party which emerged from these events under its leader, Capellen de Marsch, was a predominantly middle-class group; and, having democratic tendencies, it challenged simultaneously the authority of the house of Orange and that of the Regent families that controlled the great cities of Holland. This double challenge proved to be a source of both strength and weakness: on the one hand, it won the Patriots popular support; but on the other, it made it easier for its monarchic and aristocratic opponents, normally at loggerheads, to bury their differences and unite against them. The French now threatened to intervene on behalf of the Patriots and the English on behalf of the Orangists. The English had more money, were well advised by their minister at The Hague, Sir James Harris, and persuaded their ally, Frederick William II, the new King of Prussia, to send in 20,000 troops;

while the French, being divided and faced with bankruptcy and hesitant to promote a democrats' *coup*, backed out and left the Patriots to their fate. The Dutch army, under the Prince of Orange, co-operated with the invaders; and Amsterdam alone offered a brief resistance. So the movement collapsed and Dutch Patriots, like Belgian democrats half a dozen years later, flocked in their hundreds into France. But these Patriots had another weakness which would have disqualified them from leading a democratic movement through to a successful conclusion. It was the one picked on by the American, John Adams, who knew the Dutch well and was certainly no democrat himself, when he wrote that they had been 'too inattentive to the sense of the common people of their country' and too dependent on the French.

The movements of these west European 'patriots' and democrats won some immediate successes; yet, in the final outcome, they did not amount to much. The Genevans, having made important gains in 1738 and 1768, lost all they had won in the final disaster of 1782. The English reformers made some solid achievements in the Wilkes affair of the 1760s and 1770s, but Parliament remained substantially untouched by reform when the movement collapsed in the 1780s. Grattan and the Volunteers made only a small breach in the old constitution of Ireland; and the Belgian democrats were driven out by their 'aristocratic' rivals as the Dutch Patriots succumbed to the combined opposition of the Prussians, Orangists and urban patricians. This was partly due to the intense hostility that the middle-class reformers aroused among their aristocratic or monarchic opponents, which proved all the more fatal when, as in the case of Holland and Geneva, it was allied with a military intervention from outside. But it was also due on more than one occasion to that lack of attention 'to the sense of the common people' that John Adams had noted in the case of the Dutch. Whether to call in the aid of the common people or not was a problem that faced many a well-intentioned middle-class reformer or would-be democrat with an awkward dilemma. 'Are my apprehensions,' wrote a correspondent to the *Gloucester Journal* in September 1769, 'are my apprehensions of Tyranny of Government equal to those I have from the Licentiousness of the People?' On the answer, if enough people asked the question, might depend the success or failure of the operation. In this respect we may contrast the failure of the English reform movement in the 1780s with the successes gained in its Wilkite stage in the 1760s and 1770s. In the earlier stage, there was collusion between the middle-class radicals and the small freeholders and craftsmen; in the second, developing as it did in the wake of the 'No Popery' riots in London, Wilkes's successors, having had their fingers burned, avoided such contacts like the plague. Even more spectacular of course was the ability of the Genevan *bourgeois* and *natifs*, when they combined in 1781, to stage a popular revolution

that was unique in Europe until the Parisian events of 1789; so successful was it in fact in its inception that it required a full-scale military
operation by the Sardinians and French to stop it in its tracks.

These lessons were evidently not lost on the French Third Estate when
they were compelled to take on the combined forces of the absolute
monarchy and privileged classes in the summer of 1789. For though
their longer-term interests divided them from the peasants and the
urban lower classes, they decided to throw caution to the winds and
turned to the people for support.

CHAPTER 12

THE POPULAR CHALLENGE

There was a further type of conflict within the state, which also assumed a greater momentum in the latter part of the century. This was the challenge to authority by peasants, industrial workers and the urban and rural poor, struggling for an element of social justice or a place in the sun. There were occasions when such movements became harnessed to those of the aristocracy or middle class, such as in the movements around Wilkes in London and the Parlements in France, and thus contributed to the struggle for the control of the state. Such occasions became more frequent as the century went on; but, on the whole, they were few and far between and popular protests tended to have an identity of their own and to be concerned with more limited objectives. It is partly no doubt for this reason that historians have largely ignored them or treated them with mild disdain or condescension. (G. M. Trevelyan, for example, decided that English eighteenth-century riots, though frequent, were merely blind explosions of anger behind which there lay 'little or no social discontent'.[1])

Popular protests assumed a wide variety of forms, depending on the classes engaged in them and the regions or countries in which they took place. They varied between the peasant rebellions, or *jacqueries*, in eastern Europe and the food riots in the West; between wages' movements and consumers' movements, and city riots from which a political element was never entirely absent. Yet for all their variety they had a certain unifying pattern which broadly distinguished them from popular disturbance in the century that followed. For one thing, they tended to take the form of direct action and destruction to property rather than of petitions or peaceful marches and demonstrations; and this was as true of peasant rebellion as it was of industrial machine-breaking, the imposition of a 'just' price in food-rioting or the 'pulling-down' of houses or the burning of their victims in effigy in city disturbances. Yet such targets were generally carefully selected and destruction was rarely wanton or indiscriminate. Such movements tended to be spontaneous, to grow from small beginnings and to have a minimum of organisation; they tended, too, to be led by leaders from 'outside' or, if from 'inside', by men whose authority was short-lived or merely limited to the occasion. They were generally defensive, socially conservative and backward-looking, more concerned to restore what they had lost of a 'golden' past than to blaze a trail for something new; and, accordingly, such political ideas as they expressed were more often conservative than radical and they tended (with some notable though rare exceptions) to be borrowed from conservative rather than from radical groups. Theirs, in short, was the typical pattern of protest of a pre-industrial age.

Now let us look more closely at the various forms they took. The old-style peasant rebellion was now – for the time being, at least – largely confined to countries in eastern and south-eastern Europe, where feudal tenures and obligations were still firmly entrenched, where agricultural 'improvement' had made little or no mark, and where the taxes levied by the bureaucratic state were an ever-increasing burden on the land. Russia was such a country and since Peter's time, and above all in the reign of Elizabeth and the first dozen years of Catherine the Great, peasant risings were almost endemic. There were seventy-three risings in 1762–9 alone; and these take no account of the innumerable disputes of the indentured peasant-workers engaged in the Urals foundries and mines.[2] Risings were generally directed against officials and landlords – over taxes, land, feudal obligations, army recruiting, or simply poverty and the price of food – but rarely (if ever) against the tsar or the Empress herself. They culminated in the greatest peasant rebellion of the century, that of Emelian Pugachev, from September 1773 to December 1774. Pugachev, an illiterate Don Cossack soldier, arrived in September in the district of Yaik in the south Urals, where the Cossacks were already in open revolt against St Petersburg over the loss of traditional rights. He claimed to be the murdered Peter III, 'the protector of the people',* and promised to restore their lost liberties to the Cossacks and independence to the Bashkir people to the east. So with a mixed Cossack and Bashkir army, swelling to 20,000 men, he marched north and west to the Volga, recruiting peasant-soldiers (and killing their officers) on the way, and urging the serfs on the nobles' domains and the peasant-workers in the Urals foundries to revolt against their masters. He captured Kazan; a serf revolt followed at Nijni; and such of the Urals foundries as were not burned to the ground by the Bashkirs went on strike. Pugachev was now expected to march on Moscow and there was considerable alarm at St Petersburg; so the government, reacting somewhat belatedly to these events, ordered their best generals, including Panin and Suvorov, to the Volga to head him

* Peter's decrees of February–March 1762, easing the burden on monastic serfs and freeing the nobility from service to the state, had raised hopes of a general peasant reform.

off. Pugachev, however, fearing a frontal assault, turned south, capturing Saratov and besieging Tsaritsin; but he was already losing support, as the Cossacks refused to engage in a general peasant uprising, and was defeated at Sarepta in August. Soon after, he was handed over to the army by his lieutenants, brought to Moscow in a cage, broken on the wheel, beheaded and dismembered before the Kremlin on 1 January 1775. The rebellion had been crushed with comparative ease and, in a sense, it was only the culminating episode in a long series of peasant disturbances that had gone on for the past twenty years. Yet it had distinguishing features that set it apart and caused a panic among the governing classes. It had spread over a vast region, enclosing the middle Volga valley and the plains lying between the southern slopes of the Urals and the Caspian Sea. It had won support among such disparate elements as Cossacks, Old Believers, Urals foundry-workers and the serfs of the Volga domains; and it had shaken the throne itself with its widely believed imposture of a 'people's Tsar'. So it stirred up a violent backlash and undoubtedly contributed to the speed with which Catherine abandoned all further thoughts of a general peasant reform.

Outside Russia, the most sustained of the peasant rebellions in the East were those in the Austrian dominions. Broadly, they fall into two main periods: those preceding (or anticipating) Joseph's agrarian reforms, and those following in their wake. Among the first was a peasant rebellion in Silesia, directed against the *Robot*, or compulsory labour service, in 1767. Four years later, the first of the *Robot* Patents, imposing a standard form of service, was applied to Silesia. But it was not yet applied elsewhere though rumours were rife that Joseph, who had been co-ruler with his mother since 1765, was already planning a general charter of peasant 'liberties'. Fed by this rumour, an uprising took place in Bohemia in 1775 when 15,000 peasants marched on Prague; they were led by a young man who looked remarkably like the Emperor himself and they demanded that the landlords should immediately put into effect the charter which they mistakenly believed had already been proclaimed at Vienna. So the demonstration was one of support for, rather than of hostility to, the imperial government; and to justify the peasants' confidence the standard *corvée* was now applied in Bohemia as it had been in Silesia before, while Maria Theresa ordered that the old manual *Robot* be commuted to a monetary payment on her private estates. Joseph's reforms of the 1780s, as we noted in an earlier chapter, went considerably further. The Emancipation Patent of 1781 ended personal bondage by giving the peasant freedom to leave his village and to marry without his lord's consent; and the Taxation Patent of 1789 extended Maria Theresa's earlier and more limited reform by allowing the peasants throughout the Austrian dominions to discharge their labour-service obligations by making a payment in money instead of in kind. But there were two important reservations: the reform applied only to peasants on 'rustical' (that is, non-domain) lands and to those paying a land tax of at least two florins a year. In this way half the peasants were excluded. Moreover there was the usual delay in carrying out the law. So there were rebellions both by peasants excluded by the law and by those impatient to enjoy its provisions. In 1784 there was a revolt of excluded peasants in Transylvania (though this, in addition, had religious and ethnic undertones), and in 1786 in Moravia; and in 1789 by Austrian peasants grown impatient with the long delays. A more despairing outcry was caused by the repeal of Joseph's law of 1789 a year after it had been passed: many peasants had, meanwhile, in anticipation of enjoying its benefits, sold their teams of oxen and naturally felt that they had been badly let down. There was a widespread refusal to render *Robot* at all; but peasant spirits, elated by the hope of a better life to come, had been crushed and no overt rebellion followed.

In other countries the eastern style of peasant rebellion appeared to be a thing of the past; yet in those countries where feudal, or seigneurial, relations still survived – as in France, Spain and Germany – it only needed a new general convulsion, like the revolution in France, to stir it back into life. France herself was in this respect an interesting case. The peasant *jacquerie*, or direct confrontation with the landlord or government (though the latter more commonly than the former), had been a frequent occurrence in the century before. In Richelieu's time, in the 1620s to 1640s, there had been the rebellions of the *croquants* (or 'poor countrymen') and the anti-taxation riots of the *Jean-va-nu-pieds* in Normandy. Under Louis XIV peasant rebellion had flared up again in the great rising over the salt tax around Bordeaux in the 1670s, which had extended over ten provinces in the south and the west. In the 1680s and 1690s, there had been the revolt of the *Camisards* in Calvinist Languedoc and other revolts in Catholic Quercy and Périgord over *corvée*, taxes and tithes. The reign ended in a final outburst of peasant riots over the disastrous harvest and famine of 1709 and the exactions of the tax collectors for the War of the Spanish Succession. After which (if we except a widespread outbreak of rural hunger-rioting during the Regency in the 1720s), peasant rebellion came to a stop and only revived in anything like its earlier form on the eve of the Revolution, in the early months of 1789; while in the intervening sixty-five years such peasant protest as occurred took the form of intermittent food-rioting which, as we shall presently see, involved not only peasants but other small consumers as well. It was a strange phenomenon because the more fundamental peasant grievances over tithe, taxes and seigneurial obligations had by no means been solved, and this would become amply evident when the Revolution broke out. The explanation must lie in the evidence brought forward by Professor Labrousse's researches; they convincingly show that a great part of these intervening years (more particularly those of 1733 to 1778) were years of steadily advancing prices and prosperity for rural proprietors and tenant farmers, or for anyone else in the countryside whose holding was large enough for him to bring his produce to market.[3] So the rest – the strip-farmers, the *métayers* and small consumers – vented their anger in food riots when occasion demanded; while the underlying grievances of the peasant community as a whole lay dormant and would only explode again, with dramatic suddenness, in the economic catastrophe that faced them all in the crisis of 1787–9.

England's case was quite different. Here there was virtually no trace of that feudal or semi-feudal system of landlord–tenant relationships that still existed in France; and here the agricultural revolution effected a more thorough transformation than in any other country in Europe. One of its characteristic forms, as we have seen, was the enclosure of the old open field, the displacement of the small peasant freeholder (or his conversion into an agricultural labourer) and the growth in the size of properties and farms; while, as a further sign of the times, turnpikes were set up to levy tolls on the new roads that brought the growing loads of grain to market. So the destruction of turnpikes and enclosures became a frequent occurrence in the English countryside. There were riots against turnpikes around Hereford and Worcester in 1735–6; around Bristol in 1727 and again in 1753; and, in June of that year, every turnpike was pulled down near Leeds, Wakefield and Beeston in the West Riding of Yorkshire. Enclosure riots, though most frequent after the first General Enclosure Act was passed in 1760, were scattered throughout the century: in Northampton in 1710, in Wiltshire and Norwich in 1758, Northampton and Oxfordshire in 1765, Boston in 1771, Worcester in 1772, Sheffield in 1791 and in the Northampton district in 1798.

The Scandinavian experience was a different one again. Sweden and Norway (though not Denmark) were countries of small peasant proprietors enjoying a relatively dignified and independent status: in Sweden, as we have seen, the peasants even had their own parliamentary representation. Moreover, as in France, the greater part of the century was a period of rural prosperity; nor had the small peasants, as in England, been dispossessed by enclosures or an agricultural revolution. After 1760, however, the peasants began to face a double threat: first, the tax collector; and second, an acute economic depression in the 1780s. They reacted to both in turn. In 1762, there began the 'war of the Strilars' in the south of Norway (and marginally in Denmark), in which the peasants for three years resisted the levying of higher taxes for war.* In Sweden too, in the 1770s the peasants fought tax collectors – in Finland, Halland and Skåne – and royal officials attempting to enforce a government monopoly of brandy. More serious disturbances followed the economic depression of the 1780s: first in Sweden and later in Norway. The most protracted and the most significant of these was the Lofthuus affair that spread through the south-eastern districts of Norway in 1786 and 1787. As in all the Scandinavian countries, it was a period of crop failures and shortage that threatened the peasants and small consumers as a whole. But the Norwegian rural population – cultivators, fishermen and foresters – had other grievances besides: the Danes held a monopoly in the sale of grain (revived after the fall of Struensee in 1772); the high prices of imported wheat were a boon to merchants but a threat to farmers; and rich merchants were buying up the forests at knock-down prices. So a movement developed, involving fishermen, foresters and farmers; its targets were government officials and the wealthy bourgeoisie – but not the King, whom the peasants saw, as they did in Russia and Austria, as 'the father of his people'. The movement found a spokesman in Christian Lofthuus, a one-time prosperous farmer who had been ruined by business failures during the American war. In June 1786, Lofthuus took what was at first a purely private petition, addressed to the King, to Copenhagen. He was received by the Crown Prince who asked him if he spoke for others. Thus encouraged, Lofthuus returned to Norway and began to round up the peasants to support a collective petition to the King. Its terms were: an end of the Danish monopoly; a reduction in the large number of taxes the peasants had to pay; stricter control over the fees and fines being exacted by bailiffs; and, most radical and novel of them all, 'that the King shall give us as our superiors natives of Norway who understand our needs'. The peasants responded with enthusiasm; and when local officials attempted to arrest Lofthuus (collective petitions had been made illegal in 1765), they prevented it; the Intendant was forced to grant him and thirty others a permit to travel to Copenhagen to lay their petition before the King. However, on landing in Denmark, they found that their permit had been countermanded and returned to their homeland to muster further support. Meanwhile, a commission had been set up in Copenhagen to consider the peasants' grievances, which eventually found that most of them were justified; redress was ordered and over-zealous officials were punished. Lofthuus, however, was not spared. A warrant was issued for his arrest; he was hunted down, condemned to a life sentence, and locked up in Akershus fortress, where he died ten years later in 1797. Yet the affair was an important one and, like Pugachev's very different style of revolt in Russia, had considerable

* A Russo-Danish war seemed imminent at this time over Tsar Peter III's dynastic claims in Schleswig-Holstein.

repercussions. It had actively involved two provinces and touched seven others. It had a remarkable success: most of the grievances had been redressed by 1795; and though Lofthuus died, the legend of the great peasant leader lingered on for generations. Moreover, it was an unusual movement of its kind which in its type of leadership, its precise demands and its organisation and peaceful petitioning, looked forward to the movements of the century that followed.

Meanwhile as industrialisation proceeded there developed in several European countries a growing rift between the masters and their employees. As the gild system disintegrated and as the gild became more and more the sole preserve of the master craftsmen, the wage-earners and journeymen found themselves increasingly thrown on their own devices and turned for protection to organisations or 'combinations' of their own. In England, trade unions of hatters, tailors and wool-combers, though strictly illegal, were already in evidence in the early years of the century; in London, strikes were conducted by com-mittees of tailors from 1719 on and there were committees of sailors and weavers in the great wave of industrial disputes in the 1760s. In France, organisation (though never quite as sophisticated as in England) took two main forms. There were the (legal) *confréries* of the trades which, although ostensibly benevolent societies – like the Box and Goose Clubs in England – also raised money for the conduct of industrial disputes. There were, besides, the more exclusive, illegal and secret journeymen's associations, or *compagnonnages*, organised on masonic lines, which in addition to lodging apprentices at ports of call during the 'Tour de France' set standards of work and rates of pay, and organised strikes. There were two main confederations among the *compagnonnages*: the *Enfants de Solomon* and the *Compagnons de Devoir*; and these, in turn, were further divided into *gavots* and *dévorants*, who were often at daggers drawn.

Strikes then as now were generally fought over workers' wages and conditions: to increase or maintain wages, and to shorten hours which were inordinately long (the Paris bookbinders struck in 1776 for a fourteen-hour day!). Or they might, as increasingly after the 1770s, be directed against the use of machinery; or again, against the employ-ment of wage-cutting or unwelcome intruders: in London, weavers and building workers rioted against cheap Irish labour in 1736 and the 'single-handed' weavers fought it out with the 'engine-loom' weavers in 1768; while, in France, *gavots* and *dévorants* were continually at each others' throats. In both countries, there were three main waves of strikes in the period covered by this book. In France, up to the late 1720s, it was the paper workers, the most highly organised of all French industrial workers at this time, who appear to have been most fre-quently engaged. A lull followed in the 1730s up to the 1760s, though it was broken by a great strike of Lyons silk-weavers in 1744. After 1770, strikes become generally more frequent: with the paper workers involved again in 1772 and 1780, Paris bookbinders and printers in 1776 and Beauvais textile workers in 1778. The biggest wave of all was in the years of economic crisis leading up to revolution: Lyons silk-weavers again in 1786, miners in 1788, and a simultaneous movement of trades in Paris, Nîmes and St Etienne between 1786 and 1789. In England it was not paper workers but miners, woolcombers, tailors and London's Spitalfields weavers who were most frequently engaged. Early in the century there were the weavers' 'calico' riots and tailors' strikes in London between 1719 and 1722. In 1768–9, there was a great wave of strikes of London weavers and coalheavers and half a dozen other trades, similar to that in Paris twenty years later; while, in the 1780s, with the advent of an industrial revolution, disputes tended to become more frequent and to spread more widely over the industrial centres of the Midlands and the north.

While the purposes of strikes were often similar to those today, their timing and the forms they took were different. As trade unions were illegal, short-lived and local, or few and far between, disputes tended to take place when labour was scarce rather than in plentiful supply, that is, on the crest of a boom rather than in the trough of a slump. Their methods were sometimes peaceful, taking the form of raising money, marches and petitions: there were a number of this kind in the London strikes of 1768. But these were more often the exception than the rule, particularly in English provincial disputes. More typically, strikes developed into riots and attacks on property, attended by the destruction of the employer's house, machinery or mill. This machine-breaking (or 'Luddism'), as Dr Hobsbawm has pointed out, was of two kinds. On the one hand, it might be a form of 'collective bargaining by riot', whose intention was purely to bring an unco-operative employer to heel; this was the more typical and traditional of the two, reaching back in both France and England to the sixteenth century at least. The other – the more recent kind – was directed against machines that were believed to be putting men out of work.[4] This was seen already in a sawyers' riot in London in 1768, but it became more frequent as the industrial revolution gathered momentum in the 1780s. In France, it was first seen on a large scale in the machine-breaking that took place in the northern textile mills as a protest against the importation of the new 'English machines' in the early months of 1789.

But strikes, whether violent or peaceful, were until the last two decades of the century a comparatively rare occurrence even in the West. Far more frequent and more typical of the age, and embracing far larger numbers, were the movements of small consumers of town and countryside that generally took the form of food riots. Of 275 disturbances that I have noted in England between 1735 and 1800, 175 were of this kind; and Daniel Mornet records a hundred food riots occurring in France between 1724 and 1789, of which more than half took place in the twenty-five years preceding the Revolution.[5] They were frequent both because bread (which was generally concerned) was the staple diet of the poor, accounting for the greater part of the poor man's weekly budget; and because its price was subject to frequent and violent fluctuations. M. Labrousse has estimated that in France, between the 1720s and 1780s, the average wage-earner would spend, even in times of relative plenty, about half his income on bread;[6] in England the proportion was probably not quite so high. These proportions would of course rise significantly in times of shortage and rising prices, which, in both France and England, became more frequent after the early 1760s. This was due to a number of factors, including the subsidies paid to exporters (thus depleting stocks available for home consumption); speculation and the cornering of supplies by dealers; the poorness of communications, which hindered a more effective distribution from producing to consuming districts; the progressive abandonment of government sponsored controls and regulations; and a series of bad harvests which, irrespective of all other considerations, depleted stocks, forced up prices and provoked waves of panic buying. And it was in such years of shortage and the fear of famine (rather than famine itself) that food rioting most characteristically developed. In England, there were provincial riots in 1727, sporadically in the 1730s, in 1740, 1756–7, 1766 (the worst of all), 1772–3, 1783, 1790 and 1795. For France, Mornet has recorded them in forty separate years between 1724 and 1789 and in all but three years of the twenty-five following 1763.[7] In both countries rioting mainly occurred in country districts and market and provincial towns. The capital cities went relatively unscathed, though this was more true of London than of Paris. In Paris serious bread rioting before 1789 occurred only in 1725, 1740, 1752 and 1777, with minor outbreaks in 1771 and 1778; while in London, if we except a few handbills and slogans in 1768, no single food riot took place until the lean war years of 1795 and 1800. This relative immunity was probably due to the special measures taken by governments, for sound political reasons, to provision and police the largest centres of population. In addition, London was less touched than any other major city by the fear of famine. It possessed besides a protective shield that other cities lacked: the shield of the near-urban county of Middlesex, which, to the north and west, could serve as a shock-absorber to riot on its most vulnerable flank. (Paris, on the other hand, lay dangerously exposed to 'contagion' from the villages round about.)[8]

Food riots drew in a variety of participants and assumed a variety of forms. In towns, the small consumers taking part in them were a cross-section of the urban *menu peuple*; in villages, they were typically peasants, cottagers, rural craftsmen and industrial workers: miners, tinners, woodcutters, weavers, spinners and the like. Their object might be to stop grain being shipped overseas or from being taken from a producing to a non-producing district; or, in both types of district, to force the merchants, millers or bakers to reduce their prices. In the first case, they might loot the stocks of grain or prevent the departure of the ships, barges or waggons transporting them; in the second, they might invade the market, flour-mill, barn or baker's shop and loot or destroy stocks or demand that the prices come down. In the latter (more frequent) case, it was generally a mixture of all three; but the most characteristic form of protest and that reflecting most closely what Edward Thompson has called 'the moral economy of the poor'[9], was, having demanded that prices be reduced and having usually received an unsatisfactory response, to impose a reduction of their own (the French *taxation populaire*). This is what frequently happened in two of the largest outbreaks of food-rioting in the century: that of July–October 1766 in England and of April–May 1775 in France.

In the first, riots broke out at intervals in four or five separate regions of the Midlands and west, beginning in Devon and spreading, in a series of disconnected leaps, to Gloucester and Wolverhampton in the west, to Norwich in the east, to Derby and Nottingham in the north and Leicester in the centre. Those taking part in them were, according to newspaper reports, most commonly weavers, tinners, colliers, bargemen, disbanded servicemen, or merely 'poor' – in short, the typical participants in English rural riots of the day; and in nearly every district they invaded markets, flour-mills and bakers' and enforced the sale of wheat and flour at 5s a bushel, bread at 1d or 2d, butter at 6d or 7d, meat at $2\frac{1}{2}$d or 3d a pound. The French riots – the famous *guerre des farines* of Turgot's day – were somewhat different. They were a single snowball movement, starting at Beaumont-sur-Oise, to the north of Paris, on 27 April and, fed by rumour and example, spreading eastwards, northwards and westwards in a series of consecutive and related eruptions from one market or village to the next, and petering out near Fontainebleau a fortnight later. In this time, they had gripped the Île de France, the capital itself and four of its bordering provinces. The rioters (except in Paris, and at Beaumont) were predominantly peasants: wine-growers, farm labourers, small farmers and village craftsmen but with a sprinkling of more well-to-do citizens; and everywhere they imposed a similar pattern of prices, with wheat most commonly fixed at $2\frac{1}{2}$ francs a bushel, flour at twenty sous and bread at two sous a pound. So there were significant variations between the two movements: they followed a different pattern of progression; they involved different sets of people; and in England their targets were not only grain and bread but butter, meat and cheese besides. But the similarities were more striking. In both, the riots were provoked by a sharp rise in prices following bad harvests and shortage. In both, an appeal was made to authority to revive the old custom of 'setting the price' at a just or traditional level; and when authority (in most though not in all cases) refused to intervene, the people stepped in and set it themselves. In neither case was there any serious political intrusion from outside: even Turgot's numerous enemies at court have been exonerated from the charge.[10] In short, in both countries, this was the rural riot in its predominantly spontaneous and undiluted form, as it existed before the events of 1789.[11]

Urban riots, on the other hand, were not so simple and were frequently touched by political ideas. They arose over a variety of issues. It might be the price of bread or shortage of food: rarely in Paris and London (as we saw), but more often perhaps in Naples, Vienna, Palermo or Constantinople.[12] At Edinburgh in 1736 the riots that led to the lynching of Captain Porteous arose from two smugglers having been sentenced to death. At Oporto, there were riots in 1757 against the government's enforcement of a liquor monopoly. In Madrid the riots of 1766 were directed against an Italian, Squillace, who as Minister of Finance had banned the wearing of wide hats and long capes. Parisians rioted against John Law in 1720, against the militia-ballot in 1743 and 1752, against the suspected abduction of children to the colonies in 1720 and 1750, against the *billets de confession* in 1752 and, from 1753 onwards, on behalf of the Parlement in its numerous contests with the ministers of the crown. Londoners meanwhile rioted against Noncomformists in 1709 and 1715, against Walpole's Excise in 1733, and against the Gin Bill and against the Irish in 1736. In 1753, there were commotions (though hardly riots) against the proposal to grant easier naturalisation to alien Jews. On a larger scale altogether were the riots on behalf of John Wilkes in the 1760s and 1770s (see page 187) and against Roman Catholics and their supporters in the summer of 1780. The last of these were the wildest and the most destructive and extensive in the whole of London's history. They lasted for a week, during which £100,000 of damage was done, thirty-two private houses were destroyed, and Newgate and other prisons went up in flames: on the night of 7 June Horace Walpole counted thirty-six fires raging on both sides of the Thames. Nearly 300 people were shot dead in the streets or died of wounds and, of more than 450 persons arrested, twenty-five were hanged and fifty others sent to prison. The destruction of property, writes M. Godechot, was ten times that done in Paris during the whole period of the Revolution.[13] While the violence to property was exceptional, the methods used were not. Both on this and on other occasions – and this was as true of other cities as of London – houses marked for destruction were 'pulled down' and their contents flung into the streets and burned. Yet targets were carefully selected and not left to chance or momentary excitement. Moreover the violence to property was not matched by a similar violence to persons. In the London riots of 1780 not one of the 275 people killed in the streets was a victim of the crowd; and the murder of Captain Porteous in the Grassmarket at Edinburgh was a quite exceptional case.

Apart from the ostensible issues, why did such rioting take place? It may be argued that the very structure of old cities – with their winding lanes and alleys or closely packed and overhanging buildings – was in itself a standing invitation to disturbance. Others have argued that 'urbanisation' or the rapid growth of cities inevitably entailed not only crime and destitution but periodic social protest.[14] Such explanations, however, tend to beg all sorts of other questions and even where they are not entirely misleading do not take us far. Among such other questions, the economic factor clearly played a part. Wages, taxes and food prices were matters of constant popular concern; and these often obtruded even where other issues were more obviously apparent. Food prices, for example, were high at the time of the London anti-Irish riots and the Porteous riots of 1736, as they were in the Wilkite disturbance of 1768–9 and 1771–2 and the Paris riots accompanying the *révolte nobiliaire* of 1788; they were even more obtrusive in the Madrid riots of 1766. Yet there were other riotous occasions – as in London in 1763, 1774 and 1780 – when prices were stable or comparatively low; so this, too, cannot serve as a universal explanation. In some disturbances, a religious element played a part: notably so in the *billets de confession* agitation in Paris and the London outbreaks against Nonconformists in 1709 and 1715 and against Catholics in 1780. In others, there were evident signs of national prejudice or of hostility to foreigners. Thus there were considerable anti-English feelings expressed in the Edinburgh riots of 1736, while the Wilkite movement, conversely, was in part directed against the Scots, as the Madrid riots in 1766 were directed against Italians and the Gordon Riots in London found targets among a variety of foreigners, including Irishmen, Italians, Frenchmen and Spaniards.

But a more distinctive feature of the eighteenth-century urban riot was that it was frequently marked by political undertones: this sets it apart from the other kinds of disturbance we considered before. This political intrusion generally came from outside and from above. Thus in Paris, as we have seen, it was the Parlement that served as the initiator, if not actually the instigator, of the riots over John Law in 1720, over the *billets de confession* in 1752 and in practically every disturbance that was not directly concerned with wages or food or the abduction of

children between 1753 and 1788. In London a similar impetus was given
by the City's Court of Common Council to the disturbances that broke
out over Excise in 1733, gin in 1736 and the ill-fated 'Jew Bill' of 1753;
and, again, over Wilkes on various occasions between 1763 and 1774
and over the Catholics in 1780. (On the latter occasion, the Common
Council protested against the relief being granted to Catholics on the
eve of the riots and repeated their protest when the riots were at their
height.) This is not to say that in either city the crowds had no interest
of their own and were merely carrying out the orders given them by
others; but it does suggest that there was in both a certain collusion
between the rioters and the city authorities in which the Parlement in
the one case and the Common Council in the other served as a kind of
political mentor to the people in the streets. Yet there was a significant
distinction between the two: in Paris the mentor was an aristocratic
or near-aristocratic group; in London it was what we have already
(following the Webbs) called a 'rate-payers' democracy'. The distinction, as we shall see shortly, was to be of some importance.

For the politics of urban riots – where such issues intruded – tended
to be conservative rather than radical; that is, they reflected causes that
were aristocratic, clerical or monarchic rather than those promoting
middle-class liberal or democratic reform. In Madrid the riots of 1766,
while concerned with food-prices, Italians and broad-brimmed hats,
were strongly suspected of having been provoked by the Jesuits to
unseat the reforming anti-clerical ministers of Charles III. In Naples the
lazzeroni, like the *popolino* in Rome and Palermo, were, in spite of their
frequent riots, staunch supporters of church and king.[15] In 1772 the
Stockholm crowd switched its old allegiance from aristocracy to the
'enlightened-monarchic' cause of Gustavus III. In Tuscan cities in 1790
crowds rioted against Duke Leopold's measures to curb the influence
of the church. In Brussels they attacked the houses of Vonckist democrats in March 1789, disarmed them, beat them up and drove them out
of town. In Vienna they welcomed Pope Pius when he came to remonstrate with Joseph II over his church reforms, as they would later
demonstrate against the Republican General Bernadotte when he
hoisted the tricolour over the French Embassy in 1798. Parisians, as we
have seen, were rioting on behalf of the aristocratic Parlement up to the
very eve of the Revolution. In London too, the crowds' allies in the
Common Council were Tories and church and king men until the 1750s;
but when William Pitt, the Great Commoner, arrived on the scene the
Common Council changed its colours and became radical, and the
crowd followed suit. This new political complexion was clear enough
for all to see in the Wilkite riots of the 1760s and 1770s, although it was
not quite so obvious in the 'No Popery' riots of 1780. On the one hand,
they showed no regard for religious toleration and their outcome

strengthened the court party and Lord North at the expense of the old Whig opposition; to that extent they clearly served the established order. On the other hand, hostility to popery was part of a long-standing Whig and radical tradition; and it was City radicals like Wilkes's friend Frederick Bull (and at first they included Wilkes himself) who had protested most vigorously against Catholic relief. So it was not simply a return to the old-style church and king movements of the early years of George I. Moreover when English city crowds turned right again – as they did in the Birmingham and Manchester riots of 1791 and 1792 – it was not for long; and popular radicalism, nourished by the writings of Tom Paine, returned soon after to London and the north.

So the lower orders of London, partly because they had middle-class and not aristocratic mentors, were the first to make a decisive turn to the left; they were followed in the early and mid-1780s by those of Geneva and of certain large cities in Holland like Amsterdam and Utrecht. Elsewhere the turning-point came with the French Revolution. In Paris, the crowd switched sharply to the bourgeois–radical cause after September 1788, when the Parlement, by insisting that the Estates General should be constituted as it had been early in the century before, disappointed all hopes that it might serve as an instrument of radical or popular reform. So the crowd, having abandoned one ally and attached itself to another, moved left. Other cities followed after a shorter or longer lapse of time, depending on what their bourgeoisie had to offer or on their proximity to France; the lapse was shorter in Belgium, Switzerland, the German Rhineland and the north of Italy, and longer (as we should expect) in central and southern Italy, most of Germany, Scandinavia, Austria and Spain.

One further question remains to be considered. We have seen that popular movements, like those of the aristocracy and bourgeoisie, assumed a greater frequency and intensity after the 1760s: the Pugachev rebellion in Russia, the peasant revolts in Austria, the Lofthuus affair in Norway, the Wilkite and No Popery riots in London, the *guerre des farines* in France, the popular uprising in Geneva, all took place in the last twenty or thirty years before the French Revolution. M. Godechot, the French historian, has argued that all of them – with the exception of the Wilkite and Lofthuus movements, with which he is not concerned – should be treated in a common context of industrial and agrarian change, of rising prices and falling wages and of a rapid growth in population; moreover (he adds) they all reflect the consequent development of a common 'revolutionary mentality'.[16] So there are (in his view) substantial connecting links between these riots and the rebellions which broke out from the early 1770s onwards 'from the Urals to the Alleghanies'.[17]

A part of this 'common-context' argument seems sensible enough.

We have already noted that the great changes in population, in industrialisation, the growing exactions of the bureaucratic state, the spread
of the Enlightenment and the lag of wages behind prices were features
of the later rather than of the earlier half of the century. Thus the 1760s
may, as we have suggested more than once before, be seen as a kind
of watershed of social and political change; and this in turn helps to
explain why so many riots and disturbances of every kind occurred in
the last decades of the *ancien régime*. In this sense, even if we insist that
in some countries these factors were far more potent than in others, we
may agree that there is a broad common context in which they may all
be placed and it is perhaps more than a coincidence that the peasant
rising in Bohemia, the French grain riots, the tail-end of the Pugachev
rebellion and the opening of the American Revolution all belong to
1775. But to argue further (as M. Godechot does) that they were all
expressions of a generally developing revolution of the West is surely
to distort the picture and to overstate the case. For even if the Genevan
events of 1781–2 and the Dutch events of 1783–7 may be seen as a
prelude to later revolution, the same can hardly, without outrageously
stretching the limits of credulity, be said of the Gordon Riots, the
Pugachev rebellion or even of the grain riots of 1775 in France.[18] The
distortion perhaps arises from a failure to look through the telescope
at both ends; for each one of these events can only be brought into
proper historical focus by seeing it in its national as well as in its
international context. Moreover, a highly pertinent question arises:
why, if all these other explosions were so radical, was it France, with
her comparatively minor outbreak in 1775, that was the first, indeed
the only, country to have a major revolution in 1789? But this question,
too, has to be deferred until our final chapter.

CHAPTER 13

DIPLOMACY AND WARFARE

Internal conflicts, however, were eclipsed, both as to their frequency and intensity, if not always as to the importance of their results, by the conflicts between states. Wars remained the normal arbiters of international disputes: they were almost continuous from 1715 to 1721; from 1733 to 1748; from 1755 to 1763; and again, between 1775 and 1792; so that, taking the century as a whole, two years in every three were given up to war. On occasion, wars continued to be fought with the old ferocity of the past. The Austrians, when they occupied Lorraine in 1748, gave its inhabitants the choice between surrender or hanging; Frederick II massacred prisoners or forcibly enrolled them in his armies; and the Russians, at Memel in 1757 and at Oczakov in 1788, went on a rampage of mutilation and slaughter. Yet this was no longer typical and by the standards of the century before war was becoming more decorous and restrained. There is a grain of truth in the contemporary belief (reported by James Boswell in 1764) that 'wars were going out nowadays, from their mildness'.[1]

Wars were generally preceded by a fever of diplomatic activity; this was, in the eighteenth century, the last stage but one in Clausewitz's later picture of war as being 'a continuation of politics by other means'. Every major state had its Foreign Office, its *Staatskanzlei* or Ministry or College of Foreign Affairs, and its network of diplomatic agents who specialised in nosing out the secrets of a rival or opponent and, if need be, in weakening his defences by paying subsidies or intercepting correspondence. (The French minister Dubois, under the Regency, is said to have received £600,000 from England; and the French, in turn, paid £1,400,000 to the Swedes in 1763 and £1,830,000 to the Poles in 1766.)[2] Such matters were, of course, discussed behind closed doors and kept secret from the wider public. In absolute monarchies, in fact, all issues of war and peace, as all matters relating to the higher policies of state, were the sole province of the ruler and a small circle of his intimates. Discussions were conducted and decisions taken behind the doors of the royal closet, the cabinet or chancellery, and the outcome was a tightly guarded secret. In France, under Louis xv, secrecy reached almost ludicrous proportions: as government became more faction-ridden, the King adopted the habit of private consultation within an inner cabal of advisers (the *secret du roi*) to promote his own private dynastic policies that were often at variance with those practised and proclaimed by his ambassadors and Secretaries of State. This was notoriously the case in the prelude to the Polish Succession war of 1733 and to the 'reversal of alliances' of 1755 that preceded the outbreak of the Seven Years War. Even in England, with its parliamentary institutions, George III was strongly suspected of carrying on similar back-stairs intrigues with a small group of 'King's Friends'; though such a practice, whether it was contemplated or not, could hardly hope to stand up for long against the blast of parliamentary question and debate. Yet, even there, Parliament had never claimed full control of the conduct of foreign affairs; and in the debate on the Treaty of Aix-la-Chapelle in 1748 (when George II was already complaining of being 'in the toils') Henry Pelham reminded the Commons that 'the power of making peace and war is by our constitution most wisely lodged in the crown, because in both it is absolutely necessary to keep our design secret till the moment of their execution'. Nevertheless, England differed from other countries in that Parliament, by debating and seeking information on foreign policy, in effect determined its outcome and direction; and no minister, however stubbornly supported by the crown, could long survive its active displeasure. Thus Walpole, for long an advocate of European peace, was forced into war against Spain against his wishes; his successor Carteret was driven from office a few years later, owing to the failure of his anti-Bourbon policy; and above all, Lord North, though promoting a policy in the American War that accorded with the wishes of the great majority in Parliament, was hustled out of office in 1782 when the policy proved to be an inglorious failure. In all this, what was new was not so much the assertion of Parliament's views against the King's as the growth of an informed middle-class public opinion outside Parliament itself that compelled the House of Commons to take notice of its wishes. It was the pressure 'without-doors' of the rising class of 'interloping' merchants of London and the great ports and commercial towns, eager to settle accounts with France and Spain, that made Walpole change his policies before re-signing office. By a reverse process, William Pitt was carried into office in 1757, not by the wishes of George II or the parliamentary leaders but by the influence of the powerful merchant interest outside. A similar body of opinion supported Pitt when he resigned office in 1761 and considerably embarrassed George III's government in its conduct of the peace preliminaries, believed to be too generous to France and Spain, that culminated in the Paris treaty of 1763. In the concluding stages of the American War it was the peace party rather than the war party that received the support of the outside public; and it was with its blessing that the Rockingham–Shelburne Ministry took office after the resignation of North in 1783.

Such pressure from outside had of course become the more effective with the growth of that independent political press we considered in an earlier chapter. By the end of the American War, London's eighteen newspapers were devoting considerable space to 'foreign intelligence'; and the *Annual Register*, for one, had for years been instructing its readers in the complexities of European politics. Other countries too had their newspapers, as we have seen: notably the Dutch among whom the readers of the daily press were, relative to the size of population, probably more numerous than they were in England. But wherever the conduct of foreign affairs was a closely guarded secret, the reading public could not hope to be so well informed; and, wherever parliamentary institutions were lacking, middle-class opinion had little opportunity of influencing the policies of government. In France, a powerful financier like Pâris-Duverney might, early in the century, persuade Cardinal Fleury to heed his warnings against costly military adventures. But at this stage such interventions were rare; and in France it was not until the American War that the veils of secrecy in diplomatic and military affairs began to be pierced by the insistent intervention of a wider reading and thinking public. One reason, no doubt, why the French government was willing to engage its forces in America was the enthusiasm that the American cause had aroused among politically-minded Frenchmen; and there were similar responses, as we have seen, in Germany, Italy, Holland and other countries. So, in this respect, the American War may be said to mark a minor turning-point in the history of diplomatic relations.

Such developments towards a more 'public' form of diplomacy, however, were as yet in their infancy; and they certainly had no effect in delaying the transition from diplomacy to war. For once the niceties of diplomacy had been exhausted, war followed almost as a matter of course. It was usual, and considered proper, to precede hostilities by a formal declaration of war; yet there were times when such refinements were dispensed with altogether. Frederick II did not waste much time on them before marching his troops into Silesia in December 1740; and, in August 1756, he repeated the performance by invading Saxony without revealing his intentions, in order to forestall an anticipated attack by the Austrians. The same year England followed his example by opening her hostilities against France with the seizure of several hundreds of her vessels before making any declaration. Such irregularities were frowned on and no doubt contributed to the long-held view among the French of the peculiar 'perfidiousness' of Albion; but they did little to alter the generally accepted view that war was a necessary and fruitful instrument of national policy. Where denunciations of war itself were voiced, they were dismissed as Utopian by nearly all who read them and aroused little sympathy among governments or peoples. The Enlightenment, it is true, did a little to tip the balance of opinion. The notion of a 'social contract' between states and of an underlying 'law of nations' that should govern relations between them was beginning to be discussed in a small circle of international jurists and 'philosophical' thinkers. Among the earliest of these was the Abbé de Saint-Pierre, whose *Project for settling an Everlasting Peace in Europe* (1713) by means of an international authority was later commended by Rousseau; Kant, too, considered war to be a useless waste of life and time and energy and issued a call for a 'perpetual peace'. There was also Richard Price, the English radical, who in 1776 proposed the creation of a Senate, representing all the states of Europe and armed with powers to intervene in and settle their disputes. The Swiss jurist, Emmerich Vattel, while not subscribing to these visionary designs, condemned war as a scourge that was unjustifiable 'on any other ground than that of avenging an injury received, or preserving ourselves from one with which we are threatened'. French Physiocrats and English economists, who were beginning to link peace with free trade, saw the problem in different terms. 'Nothing is so evident,' wrote Sir James Steuart in 1767, 'as that war is inconsistent with the prosperity of a modern state.' Writers as varied as Pope, Hume, Voltaire and Herder ridiculed the military virtues and (here at variance with the *philosophes*' idol, Frederick the Great) were contemptuous of conventional notions of heroism and honour.

But such views went largely unheeded. A few statesmen it is true – among them Turgot, Vergennes and the Marquis d'Argenson in France, and even the younger Pitt in England – responded with a greater or lesser degree of enthusiasm to their arguments; but for the absolute rulers of Prussia and Russia and the more enlightened Joseph II of Austria, all of whom were busily enlarging their dominions, they had no message whatsoever. Some, like the Venetian Paolo Renier, in order to refute them, repeated arguments used in Louis XIV's day in France that 'tranquillity outside', far from ensuring a nation's prosperity, caused stagnation and instability at home.[3] The Prussian Bielfeld, in his *Institutions politiques* of 1760, considered it a 'law of nature' that a large state should be continuously organised for war. His master, Frederick II, was more precise: 'one takes what one can,' he advised his heir in 1766, 'and one is in the wrong only when one is obliged to cede'. Philosophical sceptics were equally unimpressed by the pacifist case. 'The times,' wrote Voltaire (who was certainly no friend of militarism), 'the occasion, custom, prescription and force . . . it is from these that the rights (of nations) derive'; and Guibert, the prophet of the citizen-army of the future, thought that 'to declaim against war . . . is to beat the air with vain sounds'. Gentry and merchants, over-taxed or sated with earlier spoils, might momentarily protest against the mounting cost of a protracted war (this was certainly so in England towards the end of the Spanish War of Succession as it was later during the war with the Americans); but more typical of the prevailing spirit of the British commercial class was the declaration made to a hesitant Parliament in 1742 that they (the merchants) were 'proud to be esteemed the authors of a just and necessary war' against the Spaniards and French. Public opinion at large tended also, as far as it can be gauged, to be unimpressed by pleas for the pacific settlement of disputes. Nor need this surprise us at a time when war, in many countries, touched only a small minority of the population and when the profits that it brought to some might easily outweigh the hardships that it brought to others. Even Adam Smith, who condemned the wastefulness of war, argued in 1763 that 'war is so far from being a disadvantage in a well-cultivated country that many get rich by it. When the Nether-lands is the seat of war, all the peasants grow rich, for they pay no rent when the enemy is in the country, and provisions sell at a high rate.'[4] In France and England, peasants and townsmen rioted against press-gangs and Militia Acts – like the 5,000 Hexham colliers in the north of England who, in March 1761, lost forty-two dead and forty-eight wounded in a bloody encounter with the militia. But in England at least there was little popular opposition to war as such. Indeed the opposite might be the case: the jingoism of William Pitt, when war-minister in the 1750s and 1760s, was matched by that of his supporters of both the 'middling' and 'inferior' sort; and, in 1780, after five years of the disastrous American War, there were ample signs of hostility to Catholics, Frenchmen and Spaniards – the traditional national enemies – but there appeared to be little revulsion against the war itself. The same mood, however, might not prevail in countries like Prussia, Austria, Russia or Scandinavia, where war imposed heavier burdens in terms of peasant-conscripts, taxes and rising prices. We have seen how Danish and Norwegian peasants protested against the higher taxes levied at the end of the Seven Years War; in Austria, Joseph II's war against Turkey in 1788 was universally unpopular, while the conclusion of peace a year later was met with demonstrations of relief and joy.[5]

While then the belief of rulers in the efficacy of war remained con-stant (and was generally shared by the peoples), the objects that they sought to attain by its prosecution were gradually changing. In the first place, as befitted an age of toleration and enlightenment, little remained of the more strictly ideological preoccupations of earlier centuries. For Cardinal Richelieu and even for Cromwell, the narrower considerations of religious orthodoxy had, when it came to war-time alliances, tended to be overshadowed by the more pressing motive of 'reasons of state'. To the rulers of the eighteenth century, they were things of the past and the state, or national, interest had taken over entirely. Exceptionally, such slogans as the defence of 'the Protestant interest' might be invoked to justify England's alliance with Frederick of Prussia in 1756, but they served a merely propagandist aim and were not considered seriously as guides to conduct by kings, ministers or military commanders. 'Holy Alliances', crusades or 'concerts' of Europe were, in fact, to remain in cold storage until Europe's old rulers began, after the 1790s, to see their collective interests threatened by the progress of the revolution in France. On the other hand, as long as absolute monarchy remained the typical pattern of government, wars would continue to be fought over the old dynastic issues; and as long as feudal notions of land-tenure persisted, rulers would tend to see the extension of their territories, as they had in earlier centuries, in terms of a fresh acquisition of landed estates. In the new century we see the survival of such concepts in the series of Wars of Succession – over the Spanish dominions, Poland, Silesia and Bavaria; in the French monarchy's preoccupations (underlying the *secret du roi*) with its Family Compact with the Spanish Bourbons and in the lingering hostility of Bourbons and Habsburgs. This could prove to be a serious diversion; and it may be argued that it was France's long reluctance to abandon such aims that put her for so many years at a grave disadvantage in her contest with Britain for colonial possessions.

Linked with this concept, but more universal and persistent, was that of the balance of power. It was moreover a flexible concept that could be attuned to serve a variety of needs: in fact a French envoy of the mid-eighteenth century was instructed, 'it is purely a matter of opinion, which everyone interprets according to his own views or his special interests'. So the balance might be invoked to justify the numerous transfers of territory that took place without any thought for the national interest of the peoples concerned, or merely to insist on the maintenance of an 'equal balance' or *status quo*. Thus in the seventeenth century other states had sought to achieve the balance by forming successive coalitions to restrain the ambitions of the largest continental powers, France and Spain. England had fought against Louis xiv, as she had earlier against Philip ii, to prevent the occupation of the Low Countries facing her own south-eastern coastline by a hostile, or potentially hostile, great power. After France's defeat in 1713, no single state was powerful enough to dominate western Europe once the Austrian Habsburg claim to Spain had been brushed aside, and the pattern had become more flexible. In the first half of the century, the continental balance was generally achieved by ranging France with Spain, Prussia and Bavaria on the one side against the Austrian Habsburgs, usually supported by Great Britain and the United Provinces, on the other; other states, in the East, in Italy and Germany fitted in as the occasion demanded. But during these years the pattern was rudely disturbed by the emergence of Russia as a great power dominating the East and the Baltic and, after 1740, by the meteoric rise of Prussia as a powerful counterweight to the Austrian Empire in the centre. Meanwhile, Sweden had ceased to be a power of military importance, Poland was virtually eclipsed and the Ottoman Empire was being thrown on the defensive by the expansionist aims of Russia and Austria. The result was to shift the centre of the European balance away from the West, where it had remained so long, to bring to the fore such issues as Polish Partition and the 'eastern question', and to drive the western powers – notably France and England – into new alignments.

But there was another factor, and one of increasing importance, that both altered the balance among the powers and provided new scope for conflicts between them. This was the growth of trade that we noted in an earlier chapter and the growth of colonial empires that went with it. That trade which was organised on aggressive mercantilist lines was conducive to war and had been evident since early in the century before, when Thomas Mun, an Englishman, proclaimed (in 1622) that 'we must ever observe this rule: to sell more to strangers yearly than we consume of theirs in value'. Thus one nation's prosperity meant its neighbour's loss; and it was in accordance with this principle that Louis XIV, who had no lack of mercantilist theorists of his own, had made war on the Dutch after Colbert's restrictive commercial regulations of the 1660s, and that wars between England and Holland followed England's Navigation Acts (also directed against the Dutch) in 1651 and 1660. And, even with the Dutch out of the race, the possibilities for conflict became more pronounced and explosive in the century that followed. By the treaty of Utrecht England won the precious *asiento*, opening the door to South American trade, extended her possessions in America and the West Indies and emerged as the dominant commercial and colonial power. Her subsequent wars, fought against France and Spain in 1739–63 (of which more will be said in the next chapter), tipped the balance further by extending her conquests in India and North America. In these, England had the advantage of naval ascendancy and the ability to concentrate her energies on overseas engagements, while subsidising her European allies from a well-filled Treasury. France enjoyed a more developed machinery for war and diplomacy, but she was for long diverted from the colonial contest by her out-dated preoccupations with dynastic ambitions in Europe and the mirage of

P

her Family Compact with the Bourbons of Spain. One result of England's colonial gains was the re-appraisal of their value, not only in trade and treasure but in terms of foreign policy and the balance of power; and not only by herself but by others. Early in the century, Defoe had proclaimed that 'to be Masters of the Marine Power is to be Masters of all the Power and all the Commerce in Europe'; and John Campbell, in *The Present State of Europe*, argued in 1750 that 'the Interest and Commerce of the British Empire are so inseparably united that they may be very well considered as one and the same'. In the scale of colonial values, it should be noted that contemporary opinion ascribed the place of first importance to the possession of the slave and sugar islands of the West Indies – and not without good reason, as the value of Britain's annual trade with her Caribbean possessions in 1783 amounted to no less than £4,240,000 (over half of this with Jamaica alone) compared with a little over £2 million with India and £882,000 with Canada and Newfoundland.

Nor is it surprising that this shift in the balance of colonial power should impress opinion in other countries as well, especially in those whose merchants had lost wealth and dominion through Britain's increasing ascendancy. And so in the middle years of the century we find a French pamphleteer arguing that 'dominance of the sea would give a nation universal monarchy'; and the French minister Choiseul claimed that the English, 'while pretending to protect the balance on land which no one threatens . . . are entirely destroying the balance at sea which no one defends'. Such considerations played a part in bringing about a change in France's foreign policy: she began to abandon her dynastic ambitions (she even held aloof from the problems of Poland and Bavaria in the latter part of the century), 'reversed' her traditional alliance against the Habsburgs and kept her hands freer for settling her overseas account with England. In this she had the advantage too that other European countries, whose merchant shipping had been searched at sea by the English for contraband, were easily persuaded that both the freedom of the seas and the balance of trade were being endangered by Britain's high-handed methods and increasing domination. So Britain, from 1763 onwards, found herself virtually isolated in Europe, and France, Spain, the United Provinces and the neutral Northern Powers combined with the Americans, in the war of 1775–83, to strip her of her American colonies. Yet this turn in the direction of France's policies came too late, and in her case at least the final outcome of the affair was not, as we shall see, quite what her merchants and rulers had hoped.

Other factors that, in the course of the century, were influencing the nature, scope and conduct of wars were the development in military techniques and organisation and the growth in some countries (though strikingly not in others) of a middle-class public opinion. The typical army of the eighteenth century was officered by noblemen and manned by foreigners, criminals and down-and-outs. The first fact, if not the second, was a direct reflection of aristocratic society itself and responded to the widely-held view that among the military virtues honour was that to be most highly esteemed and was the hardest to find among men other than those of noble or gentle birth. It was a view that prevailed among the Russians, Prussians, Swedes, English and French, though curiously enough less importance was attached to it in Spain. In Prussia Frederick William I, although he gave ample scope for middle-class talents within his administration, was less inclined to do so in his army and became the creator of the Junker officer class. Frederick II was more obdurate still and believed that to admit commoners to commissioned ranks would be 'the first step toward the decline and fall of the army'. In France too, as we have already seen, there was an increasing tendency to deny commissions not only to bourgeois but to recent *anoblis*; and even in England, where military virtues and honour were not held in such high esteem, 'officers' and 'gentlemen' had become almost synonymous terms. Moreover this social exclusiveness, far from being on the decline, tended to increase and to become more firmly entrenched as the century went on. In part, this responded to the general 'aristocratic reaction' of which mention has already been made; but it was perhaps also due to the sort of armies that officers were called upon to command. A few voices were already being raised – such as Möser's in Germany and Guibert's in France – in favour of 'national' armies in which all citizens might enlist; but these were generally ignored and the notion persisted that the productive classes, so essential to the nation's economic health, must be used only sparingly in warfare. Frederick II, the greatest army-recruiter of the age before Napoleon, argued that 'useful hardworking people should be guarded as the apple of one's eye, and in wartime recruits should be levied in one's own country only when the bitterest necessity compels'; while in France the Comte de Saint-Germain, while stressing the desirability of creating 'an army of dependable and specially-selected men of the best type', insisted that 'it would be destruction to a nation if it were deprived of its best elements'. In consequence, the choice was between foreign mercenaries, deserters from other armies and a nation's own jail-birds and misfits; and England was certainly no exception in recruiting the bulk of her 'other ranks' from vagrants and criminals, the latter often faced with the choice of enlistment or transportation overseas. Meanwhile, France, Spain, England and the United Provinces regularly employed many thousands of foreigners in their armies, and Switzerland and small German states like Hesse-Cassel conducted a thriving trade in the export of mercenaries.

Certain consequences followed from the constitution of armies of this type. One was the exaction of blind obedience. 'For the officers,' ran the Saxon-Polish Field Service regulations of 1752, 'honour is reserved, for the common man obedience and loyalty.'[6] And as loyalty and pride in service could hardly be natural qualities in armies so composed, they had to be imposed by fear; and Frederick's belief that the soldier should fear his officers even more than the enemy led inevitably to savage punishments, including flogging and mutilation. Such repression led in turn to desertion on a massive scale, which often depleted the ranks more effectively than the enemy's fire. In Frederick William's reign the Prussian army lost over 30,000 men in this way, at a time when it was hardly ever engaged in military operations. The Seven Years War took a particularly heavy toll in the numbers of deserters: over 62,000 among the Austrians, 70,000 among the French and 80,000 among the Russians; while in the War of the Bavarian Succession (1778–9) the Prussian army lost five times as many men through desertion as it did in combat.

Such considerations played a part in shaping tactics and in keeping armies small. It was believed that an army should keep together and not become dispersed; so it was not fashionable either to drive the enemy far from the field of battle or to live off the land. (Hence the importance of the cumbrous baggage-train and the comparative immunity from looting of the local population.) Thus tactics tended to be simple: to march a line or column of infantry towards the enemy and only to halt and fire and charge with the bayonet when he was well within range. (So the famous French cry at the battle of Fontenoy, 'Tirez les premiers, Messieurs les Anglais!', was less a chivalrous gesture than the expression of a desire to survive.) Such tactics tended to be costly in manpower of all ranks: thirty-one Prussian generals were killed in the Seven Years War. They tended also to make for comparatively small armies as it was widely believed that large armies would be hard to supply and manoeuvre. France's armies were generally little larger than they had been during Louis xiv's wars; and the Maréchal de Saxe, one of her foremost military thinkers, held the opinion that no army should engage more than 46,000 men in battle at one time, for 'multitudes serve only to perplex and embarrass'. Yet while the numbers in most armies, in response to such views, tended only to rise slowly in the course of the century, this was not the case with the rising great powers, Russia and Prussia. Russia's military strength rose from 132,000 men in 1731 to 458,000 in 1796 and Prussia's from 38,000 in 1714 to 80,000 in 1740; and at one stage of the Seven Years War Prussia's forces accounted for 4·4 per cent of her population, which was a far higher proportion than was considered desirable, or even practicable, elsewhere.

Yet inevitably, though progress was slow, tactics, techniques and the use of weapons changed and never remained stable for long. In an age of 'philosophy' and industrial development, traditional methods were constantly being questioned and there was no lack of critics, both bourgeois and aristocratic, who demanded that armies should be attuned to meet new needs. To some it seemed that the standing army itself, with its roots in the feudal and 'absolutist' past, was already an anachronism and should be superseded by the nation at arms. In France the Maréchal de Saxe, in his *Rêveries*, called for the institution of universal military service; he also recommended the use of mobile units of infantry and cavalry to act as auxiliaries to the columns advancing in close formation. In Prussia Justus Möser, a civil servant, urged the creation of a national militia so that Germans might recover their old pride in the bearing of arms; while the Comte de Guibert in his *Essai général de tactique* of 1772 carried the whole argument further. He stressed the virtues of the simple battalion column against the prevailing line of battle; he urged that an army must live on the country within its field of operations, thus dispensing with the costly and cumbrous baggage-train; and, like Möser and Saxe, and being also a companion of *philosophes*, he advised that armies be recruited from citizens, devoted to their country and capable of initiative, rather than mercenaries, vagrants or criminals, forced into service by hunger, press-gang or fear of the gallows.

The more radical of these proposals had to await another generation before they began to be adopted, while others accorded well enough with more immediate needs. For rulers, though not prepared to look too far into the future, were responsive to the need for gradual change and were taking a more personal interest in the equipment, direction and deployment of their armies. The military exploits of Frederick II have become legendary and his presence on the battlefield was reckoned the equivalent of 30,000 men (a modest figure, it is true, compared with the half-million later ascribed to Napoleon!); and even George II of England and Hanover, though not a particularly soldierly figure, led his troops into action at the battle of Dettingen in 1743. This personal concern was also reflected in the founding of schools and academies of military education, which was a notable feature of the age. It was during this period that the Russians established their noble cadet corps at St Petersburg (1731), the French their Royal Military School in Paris (1751) and the Austrians their military academy at Wiener-Neustadt (1752); while schools for engineers appeared at Woolwich in 1741, at Mézières (in France) in 1748 and in Russia in 1756. And it was from these schools and academies – from the French ones, in particular – that there flowed a stream of manuals on military problems, leading to the development of new techniques, not startling in themselves but stepping-stones to the more important innovations of the future.

The most important single achievement was perhaps the increase in fire-power. Where the average soldier in an efficient European army could, early in the century, fire little more than a round a minute, the introduction of cartridges and iron ramrods had, fifty years later, increased this rate to three. Another innovation which accorded with some of Saxe's and Guibert's views was to make artillery lighter and more mobile. This was above all the case in France, where an Inspector General of genius, Gribeauval, introduced an improved flintlock musket and lighter and more efficient field-guns in the 1770s; thus a twelve-pounder gun could now be drawn by six horses and an eight-pounder by four where it had required three times that number to do so two centuries before. Moreover, the bayonet, an invention of the seventeenth century, now came into general use; and shrapnel, a new invention, was first demonstrated by the French at Gibraltar in 1787.

The increase in fire-power reacted in turn on developments in tactics. It led to experiments with irregular and more mobile units in place of, or as a supplement to, the parade-ground precision of the old ordered line, undue reliance on which perpetuated deadlock and indecisive encounters. So mobile and lightly-armed troops came into fashion: first used on a major scale by the Austrians in the 1740s, they were used for scouting duties by the British in North America in the 1750s and for field combat in the later American War; by which time they had also been adopted, from the 1760s onwards, by the Prussians, the Russians and French. But until fire-power improved further they could only play a strictly subordinate role, and Guibert, among others, argued that the real problem was to find a way of giving more flexibility to the main forces at the centre of the battle. So further discussion raged over the relative merits of the traditional *ordre mince*, or thin battle line, and the more recent *ordre profond*, reminiscent of the old classical phalanx, in which a dense mass of troops used additional weight and speed to gain the momentum required to break through the enemy's ranks. The new school found considerable support among the French, but its critics were able to point to the evident disadvantage of exposing closely-packed columns of men to withering enemy fire. So the argument continued, and new solutions were found by subtly combining the two and switching from line to column, and back from column to line, in the course of an engagement. But this was at best an uneasy compromise which left the main problem untouched; and nothing fundamental was achieved until the old rigid parade-ground methods were abandoned altogether by the armies of the Revolution and Empire, and the greater fire-power, mobility and use of artillery inherited from Guibert, Gribeauval and their contemporaries were adopted in their place.

Navies and naval warfare tended to be equally traditional and as slowly susceptible to social change. Yet in one respect at least navies responded more quickly than armies to contemporary needs. As colonial expansion and conflict laid greater emphasis on the war at sea, there was a natural tendency for fleets to grow in size. Since the closing years of Louis XIV, Britain had been the largest of the naval powers; and she remained so. By an almost continuous progression, a fleet of 124 ships of the line and 105 smaller ships in 1721 had grown to one of 174 and 294 by the end of the American War. France's fleet had been heavily depleted during the War of the Spanish Succession; but by 1739 when she was involved in war with Britain again, she had, with fifty ships of the line, the second largest fleet in Europe; and she maintained this position with fifty-seven ships in 1754, sixty ships in 1773 and eighty-one in 1780. Spain's expansion was similar to the French: starting with an almost non-existent force in 1713, she had thirty-three ships of the line in 1739, fifty-eight in 1774 and (perhaps) seventy-two in 1789. Russia's naval expansion, like her record of government, had its ups and downs. Under Peter she had become a major naval power; she lost her position under Anna and Elizabeth and recovered it again under Catherine. By 1788–91, her fleet was divided between a Baltic squadron of thirty-seven ships of the line and a Black Sea squadron of twenty-two, thus giving her a position little inferior to that of France and Spain. Compared with these four, the fleets of other naval powers were small or insignificant. The United Provinces had shrunk from a first-rate to a second-rate power during the Spanish War, and were never again able at any time to put more than fifty ships into active service. The fleets of Tuscany, Portugal and Naples were of little account; and the Turkish fleet, though large, was badly manned and armed and, having remained inactive for the half-century before, was almost annihilated by the Russians off the coast of Asia Minor in 1770.

In navies, as in armies, officers were largely (if not overwhelmingly) drawn from the nobility and gentry. In France the older-established aristocratic officer-corps (the *rouges*) were, until the Revolution, generally successful in keeping their middle-class rivals (the *bleus*) out of anything above junior officer rank. In England promotion from the lower deck, though not common, was easier: there were even cases of pressed men becoming admirals and James Cook, for one, rose from warrant-officer to ship's commander. Recruitment below decks was, as with armies, compounded of a mixture of cajolery and compulsion; but, with the possible exception of Britain, sailors were a more faithful reflection of the nation's working population. In Russia they were mainly conscripted peasants, while in France and Spain (which followed the French example after 1737) they were generally recruited from a pool made up of the seafaring inhabitants of coastal districts. In Britain the net was flung wider by offering bounties, letting the press-gangs loose in ports and cities and scouring off a part of the prison population. Thus the British warship was, socially, almost a replica of the army barracks. 'In a man-of-war,' wrote an officer in 1756, 'you have the collected filth of jails. There's not a vice committed on shore but is practised here.'[7] Disease – typhus, yellow fever, scurvy – was rampant. Wages were appallingly low: in France they remained the same for a hundred years, and in Britain the ordinary seaman's wage of 19s a month had, by the time of the naval mutinies of 1797, remained unchanged for a century and a half. Punishments were cut to measure; and Admiral Vernon told the British Parliament in 1749 that 'our fleets, which are defrauded by injustice, are first manned by violence and maintained by cruelty'. In consequence, as with armies, desertions were frequent; and of 176,000 men raised by the British navy between 1776 and 1780, 1,200 were killed in action, 18,500 died of disease and 42,000 deserted.

Technical progress was slow and not particularly impressive. The most striking change from the seventeenth century was the virtual disappearance of the once-familiar galley, which by the time of the Revolution only lingered on as an occasional and outmoded relic from the past in the fleets of Spain and some of the Italian states. Naval engineering and ship-building reached a higher degree of excellence in France than anywhere else, and a French ship, the *Etats de Bourgogne*, carrying 118 guns and launched in 1782, was considered a model of its kind and was still sailing as a flag-ship in 1848. British men-of-war, on the other hand, had the reputation of being too small, badly designed and too heavily encumbered with guns; so that ship for ship the British navy lagged far behind the French. Yet the British introduced some of the most significant technical innovations of the day. One was the use of copper to protect the ship's hull, a technique only later adopted by the French. Another was the short-barrelled large-calibre gun known as the carronade, first used by Britain in the 1770s and copied soon after by France and other naval powers. A third innovation – and perhaps the most impressive of all – was the simple device of using lemon juice to combat scurvy. It had sensational results when it was tried out by Cook and other captains, and whereas Anson had lost three-quarters of his men from scurvy on his round-the-world trip in 1740–4, Cook did not lose a man on his second voyage in 1772.

If battles on land were often indecisive, at sea they were rarely anything else. Such victories as were won depended, for most of the century, on an overwhelming superiority in fire-power or numbers; otherwise fleets, if they engaged at all, exchanged a few volleys and steamed off.

'Do you know what a naval battle is?' Maurepas, the French minister, once asked. 'I will tell you: the fleets manoeuvre, come to grips, fire a few shots, and then each retreats . . . and the sea remains as salt as it was before.'[8] Such an outcome was due to the obstinate rigidity of naval tactics, which were based on the notion that the main purpose of a nation's fleet was to protect its colonies and sea-borne trade and to harass those of the enemy rather than to seek out his ships and destroy them. So the line of battle must be preserved at all costs and dispersion (if not battle itself) avoided like the plague. In consequence, commanders were encouraged to be cautious and take no chances, all the more so as signalling systems were primitive and made it difficult for orders given at sea to be understood and obeyed. The break-through came late in the 1770s – soon after Maurepas asked and answered his question – when signalling methods were improved in the British navy; and this innovation contributed as much as anything else to the outcome of Admiral Rodney's encounter with the French at The Saints in 1782, which was the first time for nearly a hundred years that one of two major fleets of almost identical strength won a decisive victory over its opponent.

CHAPTER 14

WARS AND THE EXPANSION OF EUROPE

The wars of the eighteenth century may for convenience be divided into seven. First, there was the Spanish attempt to undo the Utrecht settlement by asserting new claims on Italy (1717–31). Second, there followed the recovery of France and the War of the Polish Succession during the greater part of the 1730s. Third, there was the renewal of the colonial struggle between England, France and Spain and the War of the Austrian Succession (1739–48). Fourth, after a dramatic reversal of old alignments, the Seven Years War (1755–63). Fifth, the Russo-Turkish War of the 1760s and the first partition of Poland (1767–72). Sixth, the isolation of Britain in Europe and the American War of Independence (1775–83). And, finally, the renewal of 'the eastern question' in Russia's and Austria's war with the Turks in the 1780s.

Three immediate consequences flowed from the post-war settlement in the West effected by the treaties of Rastadt and Utrecht (see Chapter 1). One was that Britain temporarily enjoyed a dominant role in Europe, making it possible for her to intervene actively to maintain the new settlement and balance of power. A second was that France was temporarily weakened, both by the war and by Law's financial crisis that followed soon after, and needed time to recover. Moreover the Regent, Philip Duke of Orleans, had hopes, should the sickly young Louis xv die, of the French succession; this estranged him from his rival, Philip v, the new Bourbon ruler of Spain, and threw him into the arms of England. A third consequence of the treaties was that Spain, who had been stripped of her Italian possessions, sought to recover them, a prospect that seemed all the easier to realise when Philip took as his second wife Elizabeth Farnese, the niece of the Duke of Parma. So Philip v, prodded by his wife and her confidant, Spain's new Italian minister, Giulio Alberoni, declared war on the Austrian Emperor in July 1717 and quickly overran Sicily and Sardinia. But Spain lacked a fleet to consolidate her gains and when France, as England's ally, declared war and invaded the Basque provinces and Catalonia, Philip was compelled to acknowledge defeat, dismissed Alberoni (1719), renounced his claims to Sicily and Sardinia and (repeating an undertaking already given at Utrecht) his claim to the throne of France as well. This, however, was only the first round in a long succession of alliances, counter-alliances and wars on the Italian peninsula, at the end of which the Austrians surrendered Naples and Sicily by the treaty of Vienna in 1738 to Don Carlos, the son of Philip and Elizabeth Farnese. Ten years later Don Carlos's younger brother, Don Philip, acquired the Duchies of Parma and Piacenza. So the Spanish Bourbons became firmly established in the southern part of Italy and remained there, with a long intermission under Napoleon, for the next hundred years.

Meanwhile, France had long recovered from her wartime and financial crisis, and from 1731 onwards began to resume her old active role in Europe; it was a role that was all the easier for her to fill as England, during the long ascendancy of Walpole (1722–42), was pinning her hopes on peace and consolidation and had virtually ceased to interest herself in continental-European affairs. France's first attempt, however, to assume her old role was only a partial success. In 1733 Augustus II, the Saxon King of Poland, died, leaving, as the custom was, a contested succession. Two candidates entered the lists: Augustus III, Elector of Saxony, a nephew of the Emperor Charles VI, and Stanislas Leszcinski, father-in-law of Louis XV of France. So the contest immediately stirred up the old traditional enmity between the Bourbons and Habsburgs, which Chauvelin, the French Secretary of State for Foreign Affairs, was (unlike the chief minister, Cardinal Fleury) eager to revive. Stanislas was elected but soon afterwards was expelled by the Russians and Austrians who staged a new election and had their own candidate, Augustus, enthroned in his place. The so-called War of the Polish Succession inevitably followed; but it was fought over Italy rather than Poland. Here the French allied themselves with the Spaniards and the Sardinians, undertaking to help the former to acquire The Two Sicilies for Don Carlos and the latter to take over the Duchy of Milan – both at Austria's expense; while France, for her part, was to receive the Duchy of Savoy from Sardinia. Milan was soon occupied (1734); but the final outcome was not quite what the partners had hoped for, with the exception of Spain. By the treaty of Vienna (1738), Austria, as we saw, gave up The Two Sicilies to Don Carlos, but she retained most of the Milanese and, for a while, was compensated with the Duchies of Parma and Piacenza. Moreover, the Duchy of Tuscany (whose ruler had died in 1737) passed to Francis Stephen, Duke of Lorraine, and, soon after, through his marriage to Maria Theresa, became a part of the Austrian dominions. Sardinia acquired no more than a small corner of Milan. Although denied Savoy, France did somewhat better, as she was assured of the reversion of the Duchy of Lorraine on the death of Stanislas, who received it as compensation for his lost Polish throne.

3 Italy on the eve of the French Revolution

France was granted further concessions in the Balkans; for, in accordance with her traditional alliance with the Turks, she gave diplomatic support to the Sultan when the Austrians, with Russian support, invaded the Balkans in 1737. By the treaty of Belgrade (1739), the Turks recovered Serbia and Wallachia from the Emperor; and they rewarded the French by renewing the Capitulations, the commercial and religious privileges that they had previously enjoyed within the Ottoman Empire (1740).

Meanwhile, the old colonial struggle had opened up again when England, after her long neutrality and peace under Walpole, declared war on Spain in October 1739; France entered the war as the ally of Spain in the following year. But shortly afterwards events in Europe converted these preliminary exchanges between the great maritime powers into a more general conflagration on both land and sea that extended over widely scattered regions of the globe. In October 1740 Charles VI died, leaving his daughter, Maria Theresa, in uncertain possession of the Austrian dominions. The Elector of Bavaria and the Kings of Spain, Sardinia and Prussia all staked claims with varying degrees of validity; but Frederick of Prussia acted more promptly than the rest, marched his army into Silesia and thus precipitated the War of the Austrian Succession (December 1740). The late Emperor had persuaded France to sign the Pragmatic Sanction to assure the integrity of his daughter's inheritance; so she had no compelling motive for intervention. But the Comte de Belle-Isle, who had the King's ear in foreign affairs at this time, was, like Chauvelin before him, an anti-Habsburg traditionalist who thought the moment a propitious one for bringing the Empire to its knees. Moreover, the French nobility, unlike the English, was as yet comparatively little involved in colonial affairs. Fleury, who once again held other views, was old and was easily overridden; and only the French East India Company made a show of resistance, even proposing to the English Company, as late as 1743, to continue trading and to leave the war to their respective governments – an offer, however, that was not accepted. So France directed her main effort to the war in Europe, formed a coalition with the Electors of Saxony and Bavaria and the kings of Spain and Prussia and prepared to defeat and dismember the Habsburg dominions. The allies won early victories: Frederick occupied Silesia and French Bohemia, while the Elector of Bavaria was elected Emperor as Charles VII in January 1742. But soon afterwards their fortunes turned. Saxony, seduced by a higher bid, dropped out; England intervened with subsidies for Maria Theresa and enlisted mercenaries for George II to command in Germany; Frederick himself, when promised possession of Silesia, abandoned the contest; and in 1745 Charles VII died and Maria Theresa's husband, Francis Stephen, was elected Emperor in his place. So Austria, taking her

BESSARABIA

TRANSYLVANIA

MOLDAVIA

HUNGARY

BOSNIA

WALLACHIA

Kutchuk-
Kainardji

REPUBLIC
OF RAGUSA

MONTENEGRO

BULGARIA

*BLACK
SEA*

ADRIATIC SEA

ALBANIA

RUMELIA

Constantinople

MACEDONIA

Salonika

EUBOEA

Smyrna

Chesme

*Acquired by Austria
1718, recovered by the
Ottoman Empire 1739*

Acquired by Austria 1718

Acquired by Austria 1775

*Acquired by Venice
1699, recovered by the
Ottoman Empire 1718*

Venetian possessions

CRETE

RHODES

MEDITERRANEAN SEA

4 The Balkans in the eighteenth century

revenge, formed a new coalition against the French; and France was only saved from disaster by the brilliant victories of the Maréchal de Saxe in the Netherlands. Meanwhile, diverted by her dynastic pretensions, she had left the British a comparatively free hand in Canada and India: they captured Louisbourg, though they lost Madras. So the war ended inconclusively and the treaty of Aix-la-Chapelle (1748) gave no rewards, except, of course, to Don Philip in Italy and to the Prussians in Silesia. Maria Theresa had lost a province; but at least the imperial crown had, through her husband, reverted to the Habsburgs and it seemed best to cut her losses until another day. France and England exchanged their respective conquests in Canada and India and returned to the positions they had held before.

So nothing being resolved, except in Italy, the main issues that had arisen – the integrity of the Austrian Empire and the division of colonies and trade – remained to be fought over once again. Thus the principal confrontation – that of Austria and Prussia over Silesia and of France and England over their colonial possessions – continued and was resumed where it had been broken off in 1748. But the partners that attached themselves to one or other of the principal disputants changed as the result of the complicated series of diplomatic manoeuvres and conventions that have been called the 'diplomatic revolution' or the 'reversal of alliances' of 1756. This 'revolution' began with the Austrian government which from 1749 onwards aimed to break Prussia's alliance with France, to isolate Frederick and to defeat him with the aid of Russia and (hopefully) of France. France, however, showed little inclination to receive these advances until Frederick, fearing an Austro-Russian coalition, signed an agreement with Britain to neutralise Germany in the event of a general war (Convention of Westminster, January 1756). This led France to abandon old policies and conclude a defensive alliance – the first treaty of Versailles – with Austria, to which Russia adhered soon after (May–December 1756). The treaty, though defensive in form, could hardly be so interpreted by Frederick; and, in August 1756, anticipating an attack by the Austrians and Russians with support by the French, he invaded Saxony, thus precipitating the Seven Years War in Europe. And so began what an American historian, with a certain taste for hyperbole, has called 'the most terrible conflict of the eighteenth century, one that convulsed Europe and shook America, India, the coasts of Africa, and the islands of the sea'.[1]

Frederick had subdued the Saxons by October, but his enemies had had time to marshal their resources and his next attack, on Bohemia, was beaten back with heavy loss (June 1757). Moreover the French had meanwhile signed an offensive alliance with Austria and Russia, and Frederick's new ally, Britain, was overrun in Hanover, while the Russians invaded East Prussia and the Austrians threatened (and even briefly occupied) Berlin. So the year 1757 was for the Prussians a year of disaster, only partially retrieved by the victories Frederick won over his enemies at Rossbach and Leuthen in November and December. There followed, on the credit side, a British subsidy of £670,000 a year and a massive – and bloody – victory over the Russians at Zorndorf in August 1758; but while such victories served as a holding operation and helped to inflate Frederick's reputation as a brilliant military commander, their effects were soon negated by equally sensational defeats (as at Kunersdorf by the Russians in August 1759). So, on the whole, Prussia's position became steadily worse and was perhaps only saved from utter disaster – and certainly from the loss of her conquered province of Silesia – by the death of Frederick's old enemy, the Empress Elizabeth of Russia, in January 1762 and the succession (brief though it was) of an equally fanatical admirer, Tsar Peter III, who made peace, withdrew his troops from Germany and was only prevented from concluding an alliance with the Prussians against the Austrians and Danes by his own murder and the accession of Catherine the Great. Meanwhile the French, with their attention increasingly diverted towards their colonial struggle with the British, had reduced their commitments – and subsidies – in Germany; and Maria Theresa, faced with the loss of her allies and the impossibility of recovering Silesia, signed the Peace of Hubertusburg with Frederick in February 1763. He, too, had been weakened by the desertion of an ally, for Britain had cut off her subsidies a year before. So the war in Europe ended with a return to the *status quo ante* (with Prussia retaining Silesia but surrendering Saxony) and with mutual recriminations between the partners on both sides. Yet Prussia, though surviving, had been bled almost white; and the only victor proved to be the new ruler of Russia, Catherine the Great.

Meanwhile, the colonial war had brought substantial victories to the English and little comfort to the French. England, like Frederick in Europe, had stolen a march on her opponents (in June 1756) by seizing 300 French merchant vessels, with their 8,000 sailors, lying at anchor in her ports, without declaring war. The French never recovered from this initial disadvantage, partly because of their European entanglements and partly because of the mistaken belief that the war in Europe would soon be concluded. As the continental war dragged on, France neglected her Indian and Canadian possessions, only sending pitifully inadequate reinforcements, while the British, stimulated by their war-minister William Pitt, built up their fleets and increased their armies in North America by nearly 60,000 men. By 1761, when France had virtually disengaged herself from Europe and Spain had entered the colonial war on her side, it was already far too late. In Canada, Louisbourg had fallen in 1758, Quebec in 1759 and Montreal in 1760; while, in India, Pondichéry fell in 1761; and, after Spain's entry, Britain occupied

Florida as well. So the war, concluded by the Peace of Paris in February 1763, ended with heavy losses for the French: the surrender of Canada, the whole Ohio valley, the left bank of the Mississippi, the West Indies islands of Grenada, St Vincent and Tobago and most of the trading posts in Senegal and all but five in India. They lost even more; for the Spaniards, having given up Florida to the English, won compensation from the French in Louisiana. Yet the war-party in England – including Pitt and the merchants of the great ports – were less than satisfied, as the French retained the Newfoundland fisheries and the much coveted sugar islands of Martinique, Guadaloupe and San Domingo. So the Peace of Paris, like the Peace of Hubertusburg in Europe, left, even among the victors, bitter resentments and shattered hopes.

One result of the Seven Years War was to shift the European balance eastwards towards Turkey and Poland. During Choiseul's ministry, the French at last made a determined effort to build up their navy and repair their fortunes overseas; England had, following her victory, a number of North American problems on her hands; and Prussia, having lost 300,000 men, was now far more interested in peace than war. So the Russians – and, to a lesser degree, the Austrians – were left free to pursue their territorial ambitions in the East. The victims were the Poles and Turks. Augustus III of Poland died in October 1763 and Russia and Prussia combined to have Catherine's lover, Stanislas Poniatowski, elected to succeed him, while a Russian protectorate was installed to ensure his subjects' 'liberties'. In 1768 the French, as traditional allies of the Turks and Poles, provoked the Turks into war with Russia. It proved disastrous for the Turks: they lost the Romanian provinces of Moldavia and Wallachia and the port of Azov on the Black Sea, and their fleet was destroyed at Chesmé, off the coast of Asia Minor (1770). Russia's easy successes caused anxiety to Frederick, as they did to the Austrians; and, fearing a war in which Prussia might become involved, he now proposed to Maria Theresa and Catherine that they compose their differences by partitioning the Kingdom of Poland. The First Partition followed in July 1772. Maria Theresa, who (in Frederick's words) 'wept and yet took her share', acquired Galicia and 2,600,000 new subjects; Catherine took most of Lithuania, with 1,600,000; while Frederick settled for Prussian Poland (less Danzig and Thorn), with only 700,000 new subjects, but the addition sealed the gap between East Prussia and Brandenburg. The unhappy Poles were further forbidden to change their constitution without their despoilers' consent; and the three partners, to enforce their conquests, bound themselves by a Triple Alliance which was as much directed against the French as it was against the Poles.

Meanwhile, the conclusion of the Seven Years War faced Britain, as we noted, with new problems in North America. In the first place, the

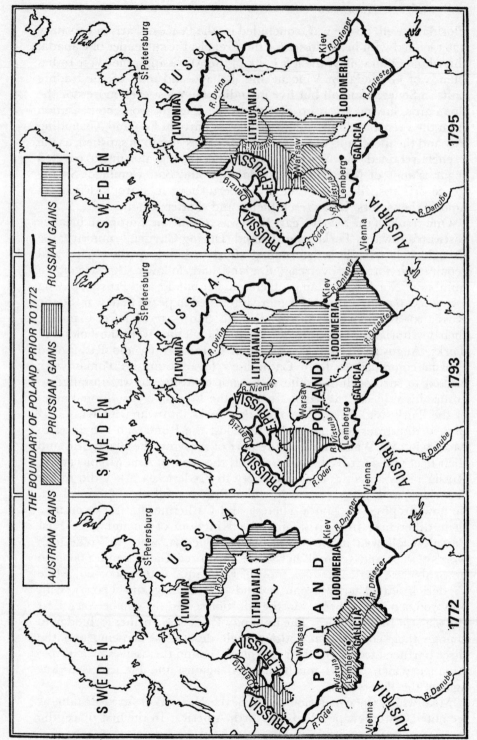

5 The partitions of Poland

defeat of the French in Canada brought to a head the long-standing grievances, both political and economic, of her subjects in the thirteen colonies. With the French danger removed, the colonists felt encouraged to assert a greater degree of independence of the Westminster Parliament, while Parliament, in turn, felt the need to tighten its imperial controls and to impose on the colonists the obligation to contribute to a military establishment. These two tendencies, so obviously at variance, proved in the next dozen years to be utterly irreconcilable; and, after a long succession of bitter exchanges over taxation, 'coercion' and retaliation, war broke out in April 1775 and the Americans declared their independence in July 1776. Now the chickens of wartime victories, and the high-handed methods she had used to ensure them, came home to roost; and Britain found herself without a friend in Europe. For reasons that we briefly touched on in our previous chapter, the maritime powers – and not only the Spaniards and French – harboured resentments that made this appear an admirable opportunity for joining Britain's enemies and settling old scores. So the French joined the Americans in 1778, the Spaniards in 1779 and the Dutch in 1780; while the northern Powers (Russia, Sweden, Denmark, Prussia and even Portugal) formed, on Russia's initiative, an armed neutrality to assert their claim to the freedom of the seas. And it was this isolation in Europe and the antagonisms her earlier policies had aroused that were as much responsible for Britain's defeat in America as the obduracy of George III and the Westminster Parliament, the bungling of incompetent ministers and the difficulties of supplying her armies over 3,000 miles of sea. The outcome was a total victory for the Americans and a partial victory for the Spaniards and French. Under the terms of the treaty of Versailles (3 September 1783), Britain accepted the *fait accompli* of the new United States and ceded her citizens further territories between the Alleghanies and the Mississippi; while Spain recovered Minorca and Florida and France Tobago and Senegal and the long-disputed right to fortify Dunkirk.

Yet while losing her colonies, Britain could at least draw some comfort from her defeat. The Americans, having gained their independence, were well enough disposed to trade, though on new terms that should be of advantage to both sides. The French, for their part, had won comparatively little: the return of Tobago and Senegal was a poor substitute for India and the West Indies, the hoped-for prizes for which she had entered the war. Moreover, France was fast approaching a state of national bankruptcy to which her recent engagement had dangerously contributed, and was in no position to renew her challenge; so there was a grain of truth in the clause of the Versailles treaty which solemnly proclaimed between 'the Britannic and most Christian Majesties' of England and France 'a Christian, universal, and perpetual peace'.

231

Thus France, though a victor, had the problem not only of restoring her finances but of embroiling herself as little as possible in the wider affairs of Europe. Britain's problems were not the same. She shared with France the need to restore her financial situation; but she also required to end her twenty-year-old isolation in Europe, the main cause of her American defeat, by re-forming old friendships, as with the Dutch, and entering into new alliances. Pitt, her new Prime Minister, who had read Adam Smith and been convinced by many of the arguments of the new school of political economy, set about the work of peaceful reconstruction in vigorous style: he increased the annual revenue, reduced the national debt, kept public expenditure on a tight string and even signed a 'free trade' agreement (the Eden–Vergennes Treaty of 1786) with the French, which, given her technical lead over other countries, proved highly advantageous: so manufactures and commerce prospered. But Pitt's financial system could only work and bring further benefits to the business and trading community as long as the peace was kept and rumours of war remained in abeyance. His good fortune here was the enforced passivity of France and the increasing difficulties of Austria; and as long as he could restrict his active interventions to the West, while keeping a watchful eye on the East, he might weather the dangers and keep his powder dry.

Though Pitt's chances of finding an ally in Europe seemed at first to be slim, he was favoured by the restless activity and thwarted ambitions of the Austrian Emperor. Among Joseph's plans was that of exchanging his Belgian provinces for Bavaria. This roused against him the hostility of the German princes, who found a champion in Frederick the Great. The League of German Princes that now emerged under Frederick's direction compelled Joseph to abandon Bavaria and prompted him to put into operation his alternative plan for the economic development of Belgium. With this end in view, he tried to force the Dutch to open the River Scheldt for free transit to Antwerp. Though England was alarmed by this challenge to her trading interest, she was still on bad terms with the Dutch; and it was the French who, called upon for assistance, were able to persuade Joseph to give up his plan for the Scheldt, and signed a treaty of alliance with the United Provinces (1785). This was a temporary set-back to England's diplomacy; but Joseph's mounting difficulties in Belgium, the financial problems of France and the internal conflicts within the United Provinces combined to promote her advantage. The French alliance had strengthened the Dutch urban patriciates and the rising Patriot groups in the provinces in their opposition to the pro-English party of the Stadholder, William v. The Stadholder was suspended from his offices by the Estates of Holland; but the radical agitation of the Patriots alarmed the patricians who, to defend their threatened privileges, turned to the house of Orange for protection.

Prussia too was an interested party as the Princess of Orange, the Stadholder's wife, was the sister of the new Prussian King, Frederick William II. While Sir James Harris intrigued at The Hague in England's interest, the Prussians intervened actively with an army of 20,000 men after the Princess of Orange had been publicly humiliated by the Patriots of Utrecht. By October 1787, Amsterdam had been taken and the Stadholder was fully restored to his offices. France, being bankrupt and threatened by an 'aristocratic' rebellion, was unable to support her Patriot allies; and Joseph II had, as we have seen, a revolution in Belgium on his hands. The outcome was a Triple Alliance between the English, the Prussians and the Dutch for common defence and the maintenance of the *status quo*. So, after twenty years of isolation, England had regained a foothold in Europe.

But the main focus of diplomatic interest, as of great power expansion, still lay in the East. After the first partition of Poland, Russia had, as part of her bargain with the Austrians and Prussians, returned the Crimea and Moldavia and Wallachia to the Turks; though by the treaty of Kutchuk-Kainardji (1774) she retained, with the acquisition of Azov, a foothold on the Black Sea. Soon after, as the cautious policies of Maria Theresa gave way to the more adventurist policies of Joseph, the Austrians were able to be persuaded that they might also, by a deal with the Russians, win substantial pickings at Turkey's expense; and by 1780 negotiations were already on foot for an Austro-Russian alliance whose main purpose was to divide up the Ottoman Empire in Europe. Meanwhile Sweden had her eyes on Finland and Carelia, Denmark on Swedish Gothenburg and Prussia on Polish Thorn and Danzig. In 1783, Catherine annexed the Crimea and compelled Turkey, a year later, to recognise the fact. In 1787, hostilities broke out again in the Caucasus and the Crimea; and, as a Russian army under Potemkin laid siege to Oczakov, near Odessa, Joseph II, summoned to Catherine's aid, engaged the Turks along the Danube. The war looked like becoming another general conflagration when Sweden, taking advantage of Russian preoccupation in the south, opened an offensive against her in the north by marching into Finland, while Denmark joined the Russians and invaded Sweden. At this point, the Triple Alliance, being anxious to limit the scope of the conflict, intervened on Pitt's initiative and forced an armistice on Denmark. A year later, the Swedes, weakened by mutiny and defeated in Finland, made peace with Russia and accepted the *status quo*.

Austria's intervention, too, was short-lived. Joseph died in February 1790; and his brother, Leopold II, concerned to recover Belgium and to restore his authority in his disintegrating dominions, accepted the mediation of the Triple Alliance and, by the treaty of Reichenbach with Prussia (October 1790), agreed to withdraw from the Turkish war. But the Russians had no such compelling reasons for responding to the

233

wishes of the Anglo-Prussian alliance; so Catherine, having disposed of the Swedes in the north, concentrated her efforts more fully against the Turks. Potemkin had (by means we have noted before) reduced Oczakov; then the fortress of Ismail on the Danube fell to Suvorov, and his armies occupied all the territory between the rivers Bug and Dniester. The Russian drive towards Constantinople and the Mediterranean had by this time thoroughly alarmed the English, who demanded that Catherine make peace with the Turks and restore her conquests. When Catherine refused to restore Oczakov, which she valued as a Black Sea base, England was for a month on the brink of war with Russia (March 1791). But the Triple Alliance was already breaking up; and while England had nothing to fear from France, she knew she could achieve no result in the East without Prussian support. Poland proved to be the stumbling-block. In 1790–1, while Russia's attention was otherwise engaged, the Poles carried out a minor revolution led by the more liberal of their nobility. One of their aims was to weaken the influence of Russia and to protect themselves against further Russian encroachments; so they turned to Prussia for help. The Prussians were willing to give it – but at the price of Danzig and Thorn. The demand led, in turn and by stages, to renewed demands on Poland by Russia and Austria. Thus the Triple Alliance broke up and Prussia, Russia and Austria – though deeply divided over Germany, the Netherlands and Turkey – were able once more, by further partitions in 1793 and 1795, to compose their differences at the expense of the luckless Poles.

But nothing had been finally resolved and, as the age of revolution opened, the countries of Europe were faced with problems in their international relations which the Revolution and the wars that followed would open up afresh, and to which new – though strictly temporary – solutions would be found in the peace treaties attending the Vienna Settlement of 1815. Such vistas, however, lie far beyond the scope of the present volume. All we can do here is to draw up a provisional balance-sheet to indicate how far the contests of the seventy-five years between Utrecht and the outbreak of the Revolution had altered the map of Europe and the world as we saw it in the opening chapter of our book. Within Europe itself, Russia had driven westwards up to the Baltic and the River Dniester and southwards into the Black Sea and the Crimea; the main losers had been the declining northern and eastern powers, the Swedes, the Poles and Turks. Prussia had doubled her population, mainly by her eastern expansion at the Poles' and Austrians' expense; having by the treaty of Nystad (1721) acquired a few Swedish and German slices of territory to the north and west, she had by the death of Frederick (1786) added to these the far more substantial provinces of Silesia and Polish (or West) Prussia to the east. France had acquired Corsica from Genoa in 1768–9 and Spain had recovered Minorca from

6 The Western expansion of Russia under Peter I and Catherine II

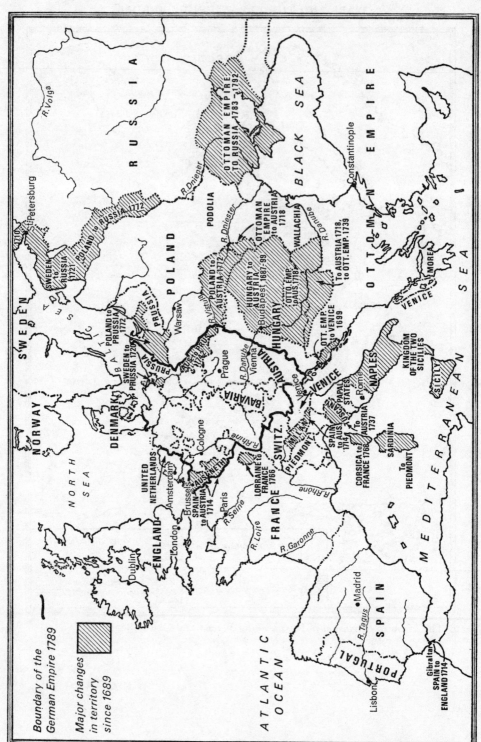

Legend (bottom left):

Boundary of the
German Empire 1789

Major changes
in territory
since 1689

Map labels:

RUSSIA
R. Volga
R. Dnieper
SWEDEN
NORWAY
St Petersburg
SWEDEN to RUSSIA 1721
POLAND to RUSSIA 1772
POLAND
PODOLIA
R. Dniester
OTTOMAN EMPIRE 1783–1792 TO RUSSIA
BLACK SEA
OTTOMAN EMPIRE
Constantinople
WALLACHIA
R. Danube
OTTOMAN EMPIRE 1718 TO AUSTRIA
To AUSTRIA 1718, to OTT. EMP. 1739
POLAND to AUSTRIA 1772
HUNGARY to AUSTRIA 1687–99
Budapest
OTT. EMP. 1718 to AUS.
OTT. EMP. to VENICE 1699
OTT. EMP. to VENICE
VENICE
MOREA
Warsaw
R. Vistula
PRUSSIA
POLAND to PRUSSIA 1772
SWEDEN to PRUSSIA 1720
BALTIC SEA
NORTH SEA
DENMARK
PRUSSIA
E. PRUSSIA
Prague
Vienna
R. Danube
AUSTRIA
HUNGARY
BAVARIA
SWITZ.
Venice
VENICE
PAPAL STATES
Rome
NAPLES
KINGDOM OF THE TWO SICILIES
SICILY
MEDITERRANEAN SEA
SARDINIA
To PIEDMONT
CORSICA to FRANCE 1768
SPAIN to AUS. 1714
To AUSTRIA 1737
MILAN
PIEDMONT
R. Rhône
LORRAINE to FRANCE 1766
UNITED NETHERLANDS
Amsterdam
Brussels
SPAIN to AUSTRIA 1714
AUS. NETH.
Cologne
R. Rhine
Paris
R. Seine
FRANCE
R. Loire
R. Garonne
ENGLAND
London
Dublin
ATLANTIC OCEAN
SPAIN
Madrid
R. Tagus
PORTUGAL
Lisbon
Gibraltar SPAIN to ENGLAND 1714

7 Europe in 1789

England in 1783. Austria had, in succession, been a winner and a loser; but she had lost far more than she had gained. Her loss of Silesia had been offset by her gain of Galicia from the Poles in 1772 and a small slice of Bavaria in 1779; but meanwhile she had returned Serbia and Wallachia to the Turks (Treaty of Belgrade, 1739) and lost The Two Sicilies and Parma and Piacenza to Don Carlos and Don Philip by the successive treaties of Vienna and Aix-la-Chapelle. So the main changes made in Europe had been to add to the territories of Russia, Prussia and the Spanish Bourbons at the expense of the Austrians, Turks and Poles.

Outside Europe Britain had, in spite of the final loss of her American colonies, maintained her ascendancy over the other maritime and colonial powers. The gains she had made had been mainly at France's expense. Spain and Portugal had (for the time being) retained their South American Empires, though at the cost of opening their trade to the British: Spain through the *asiento des negros* conceded at Utrecht and Portugal through the earlier Methuen treaty of 1703. Spain moreover had added to her colonial possessions; for her loss of Florida to England in 1763 had been more than offset by the gain of Cuba and the Philippines and of the greater part of Louisiana. Britain had, meanwhile, in her long duel with France, acquired Acadia, Newfoundland and Hudson's Bay in 1713 and gone on, through the treaty of Paris, to extend her dominion over Canada, to add further islands in the Caribbean and to remove France from all but a tenuous hold on India. Thus the Paris treaty marked the peak of Britain's colonial ascendancy before the Napoleonic wars. There followed the loss of the American colonies, which was of course a serious reverse, though not as serious as George III and his ministers had been ready to believe. For one thing, she retained her trade with the former colonists and France certainly emerged from the encounter more badly mauled than Britain. But Britain had the further consolation that no rival would be able to step into her shoes. For the Americans, in declaring their independence of England, served notice on the old colonial system as a whole. Thus an important precedent had been established that would, in the near future, have more dramatic and more immediate consequences for the Portuguese and Spaniards in South America than for the English or the French.

But the expansion of Europe had proceeded by other means as well. It was not only through colonial wars and the exchange of territories between one or other of the great colonial powers that Europe had thrust outwards into other continents by land and sea. This had also been accomplished by new voyages of discovery, which with the aid of new methods of scientific navigation made it possible for Europeans to open up vast new areas of the globe. In the north, a Dane, Christian Behring, reached the straits that bear his name and discovered the north-west American coast and the Aleutian Islands between 1720 and 1741; while

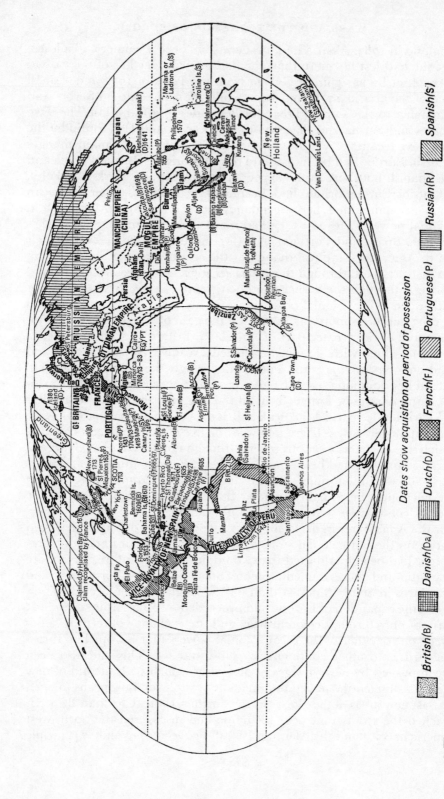

Dates show acquisition or period of possession

British(B)   Danish(Da)   Dutch(D)   French(F)   Portuguese(P)   Russian(R)   Spanish(S)

8 The world: Europe overseas, 1714

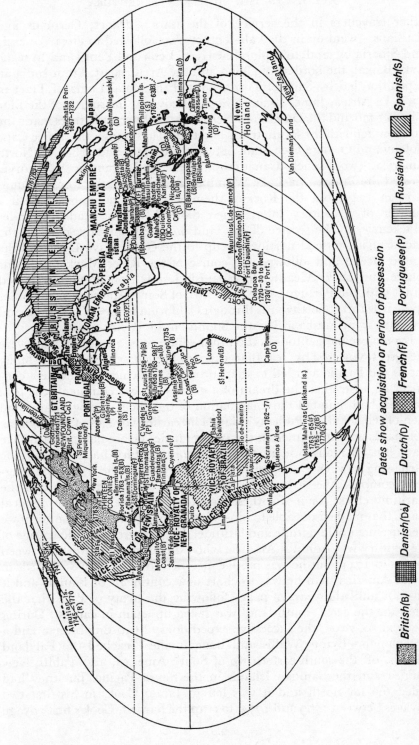

9 The world: Europe overseas, 1763

Dates show acquisition or period of possession

British(B)　　Danish(Da)　　Dutch(D)　　French(F)　　Portuguese(P)　　Russian(R)　　Spanish(S)

Europe overseas

other travellers in the service of the tsars – Danes, Germans and Russians – went on in the half-century that followed to cross Caucasia and Siberia by land, to explore the rivers Lena and Yenisi and to reach Lake Baikal, the borders of China and the Arctic coast. From India an expedition led by Samuel Turner visited the Dalai Lama of Tibet in 1783. In Africa, James Bruce, a Scot, discovered the source of the Blue Nile in 1770 and the Dutchman Hermanus Hubner and others made the first contact with the Bantu tribes and travelled through the future Cape Colony and Orange Free State between the 1750s and 1780s. In North America, two French Canadians, Pierre and François Vérendrye, crossed the Prairies via Lake Winnipeg and reached the Rocky Mountains in 1743; but the Rockies themselves were not crossed until a quarter of a century later, when Samuel Hearne and Alexander Mackenzie, in the service of the Hudson Bay Company, reached the Pacific coast, pushed northwards up to the Great Slave Lake and the Arctic Ocean and followed the course of the River Mackenzie to its source and back. Meanwhile, Spanish Jesuits from Paraguay joined hands with the Portuguese in the centre of South America; while other Spaniards thrust northwards through California to meet Canadians and Russians from Alaska at Nootka Sound on the Pacific coast.

Even more momentous in their immediate consequences at least were the great voyages by sea that carried Frenchmen and Englishmen across the Pacific and led to the European settlement of the new continent of Australia. The dream of a great southern continent, the *terra australis*, had haunted the imagination of travellers, cartographers and men of science since Ptolemy's day. The earlier voyages of Portuguese, Spaniards and Dutchmen in the two centuries before had prepared the way; but its realisation in the eighteenth century had to await the harnessing of science to navigation: in particular, the use of the magnetic compass, the sextant, Borda's 'circle', the chronometer and the maritime clock; for it was these, together with the new astronomical maps, that made it possible to pin-point a ship's position by the accurate measurement of longitude and latitude. The first great Pacific voyage of the century was Admiral Anson's, who sailed round the world between 1740 and 1744; but he was more concerned to harass the Spaniards in South America than he was to chart new continents or islands, and it was not until the years of peace following the treaty of Paris that the quest for the great 'south-land' was taken up again in earnest. During the next six years, the successive expeditions of two Englishmen and a Frenchman – Byron, Wallis and Bougainville – reached the Falkland Islands, off the south-eastern tip of South America, and Tahiti, New Guinea and the Samoan Islands in the South Pacific. But they had sailed too far north and it was left to James Cook, in his first two voyages between 1769 and 1774, to reap the harvest. Cook's first voyage

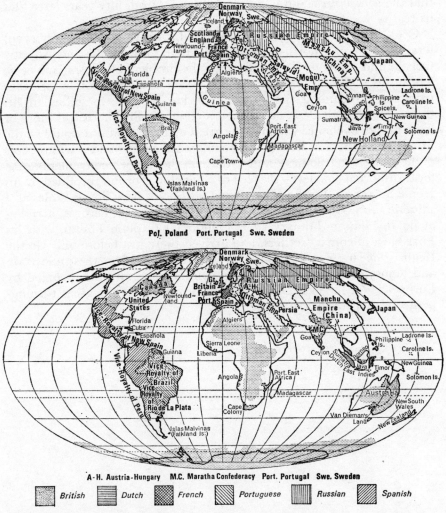

10 Expanding knowledge of the world, 1700 (top) and 1800

was equipped by the Royal Society of London as a scientific expedition. Accompanied by an astronomer, a botanist and a naturalist, he sailed to Tahiti, where he spent four months plotting the transit and eclipse of Venus; he went on to sail round the northern island of New Zealand and to land on the east coast of Australia, which he surveyed, named New South Wales and claimed for Britain. But the existence of a separate southern continent was still in doubt; so he was sent out again in 1772 to explore the matter further. This time, he sailed across 50,000 miles of Pacific Ocean, circumnavigated New Zealand for a second time, re-visited Tahiti and, on his return to England in 1774, reported that the *terra australis* did not exist. It was not until fifty years later that its reality was finally confirmed.

Cook's third voyage (which ended in his death at Hawaii in 1779) was in search of a north-west passage linking the Pacific and Atlantic Oceans and threw no further light on the problem of Australia. Yet he left an invaluable collection of maps which made it possible for other navigators, including the Frenchman La Pérouse, to follow in his tracks. So, though Cook had staked a claim for Britain, it was more or less a matter of chance which of the great maritime nations would be the first to settle the new land he had explored. For England it was the loss of the American colonies – and with them the loss of a convenient home for transported convicts – that led to a decision. For Pitt, prodded by his Home Secretary, Lord Sydney, fixed on Cook's New South Wales as a suitable successor. And chance would have it that La Pérouse, arriving at Botany Bay in January 1789, found that Captain Phillip, with his First Fleet of convict settlers, had arrived there just before him. So the English once more stole a march on the French and from these uncertain and inauspicious beginnings a new continent began to be peopled by Europeans on the eve of what was to prove one of the great turning-points of their history at home.

CHAPTER 15

EPILOGUE: WHY WAS THERE A REVOLUTION IN FRANCE?

A history of Europe in the eighteenth century, particularly one that is carried up to 1789, can hardly escape the impact of the pending revolution in France. Implicitly or explicitly, it will almost inevitably pose the question: why did the century end in revolution and why, specifically, in France? These, or similar, questions have been asked by succeeding generations of writers and historians, and the answers given have naturally reflected, to a greater or a lesser degree, the generation and country to which they belonged and their approval or disapproval of the event. The first writer of note to comment on it was Edward Burke, who, though neither a Frenchman nor a historian, left in his *Reflections on the Revolution in France* a record that has influenced the views of many people since. To Burke, the French society that we pictured in some of our earlier chapters was by no means antipathetic: in fact, it only needed a few comparatively minor adjustments to put it right. The Revolution could not, therefore, in his opinion, be the outcome of a genuine and widespread feeling for reform, but rather of the machinations of a few: he instances, in particular, the clique of literary men and *philosophes* who had long been sniping at the established church, and the jumped-up moneyed interest, eager to settle accounts with the older aristocracy. And in the wake of these, he argued, followed the 'mob' or 'swinish multitude', eager for loot and incapable of holding any views of their own. Thus the Revolution, having no roots in legitimate dissatisfaction, was the child of the conspiracy of a few. This 'conspiracy' explanation has been taken up by other writers since: by the Abbé Barruel in the 1790s, by Hippolyte Taine in the 1870s and by Auguste Cochin in the 1920s. In short, it has found favour with many to whom the Revolution has appeared as an evil from start to finish and who have consequently, in order to explain its origins, fastened on a variety of scapegoats, including Freemasons, Jews, *illuminati*, Committees of Thirty, 'literary cabals' and disgruntled lawyers.

Those who favoured the Revolution, however, have naturally tended

243

to explain it in somewhat different terms: it could be explained either as a legitimate political protest against the tyrannies and restrictions of the *ancien régime,* or as a social protest of depressed or impoverished classes. The liberal historians of the Restoration – writers like Thiers, and Mignet, or Madame de Staël – saw it mainly in the former light. The motives that prompted them in their day to demand a more liberal constitution, or charter, from Louis XVIII and Charles X were basically the same as those which, a generation earlier, had prompted the revolutionaries of 1789 to draft a Declaration of the Rights of Man and to demand a constitution from Louis XVI. Thus, the Revolution was seen essentially as a political movement from 'the top', promoted by the 'respectable' classes of the nation for the redress of long-standing grievances and the reform of outmoded institutions. 'When a reform becomes necessary,' wrote Mignet, 'and the moment to achieve it has arrived, nothing can stand in its way and everything serves its progress.'[1] This liberal or Whiggish explanation, too, with its emphasis on an almost inevitable progression in institutions and ideas, has found plenty of adherents down to the present day. So we find Francis Parkman, in a history first written seventy-five years ago, describing mid-century French society as 'an aggregate of disjointed parts, held together by a meshwork of arbitrary power, itself touched with decay', which was 'drifting slowly and unconsciously towards the cataclysm of the Revolution'.[2]

Jules Michelet, the great French historian of the 1840s, took a different view. He also sympathised with the revolutionaries of 1789; but, being a republican and a democrat, he saw the Revolution as a far more drastic surgical operation than Mignet, Thiers or Madame de Staël. In his pages it becomes a spontaneous and regenerative upsurge of the whole French nation against the despotism, growing poverty and injustice of the *ancien régime*: something, in fact, like the spontaneous outbreak of popular hope and hatred portrayed by Dickens in the opening chapters of *A Tale of Two Cities*. And as it is the common people – the peasants and city poor – that have suffered most from the cruelty and injustice of kings and aristocrats, for Michelet 'the people', far from being a passive instrument in the hands of other groups, is the real and living hero of the play. This view of the Revolution as a spontaneous, angry outburst of a whole people against poverty and oppression has, until recent times, probably been more influential than any other.

Yet none of these early explanations, for all their influence and literary brilliance, will appear entirely adequate to us today. Basically, they are too simple and one-sided; and this, in these days of social science and mass psychology, and with our experience of later and even more dramatic revolutions, effectively rules them out of court. Burke's 'conspiracy' theory, for example, can only be acceptable if we are willing to believe that a convulsion of such magnitude could, regardless of other factors, be switched on at the whim of a handful of men. Thiers's and Mignet's version, with its focus on the upper classes, is likely to command more respect; but theirs, too, is an élitist view which takes little or no account of the people as a whole. Michelet obviously fares better for, unlike his predecessors, he places 'the people' at the centre of his stage and presents the Revolution as something more than a mere transfer of power between political groups. Yet his notion of revolution as a spontaneous revolt of the 'miserable' and deprived obviously has its limitations. Tocqueville, who wrote a few years later, was the first to point them out. For, he asked, if France was so poor and becoming poorer, how does this accord with the expansion of her trade and industry, her record of administrative reform and the growing prosperity of her agriculture, commercial centres and middle classes? Moreover, he adds, the peasants, far from wallowing in poverty, backwardness and unrelieved squalor, or being bound by servitude to their lords' domain, had (in most cases) won their freedom, were becoming literate and had already become proprietors of one-third of the land of France. Why then, asks Tocqueville pointedly, was there a revolution in France, and not in Austria, Bohemia, Prussia, Poland, Hungary or Russia, where the people – and the peasants, in particular – were evidently far more impoverished and oppressed? And, in answering his own question, he put forward, in the place of Michelet's *thèse de la misère*, a 'prosperity' explanation of his own. It was precisely, he argued, because the middle classes were becoming richer and more conscious of their social importance and because the peasants were becoming free, literate and prosperous that the old feudal survivals and aristocratic privileges appeared all the more vexatious and intolerable. For, he concludes, 'It is not always by going from bad to worse that a society falls into revolution . . . Feudalism at the height of its power had not inspired Frenchmen with so much hatred as it did on the eve of its eclipse. The slightest acts of arbitrary power under Louis XVI seemed less easy to endure than all the despotism of Louis XIV.'[3]

There is little doubt that Tocqueville's comments have been a source of inspiration to many historians who have written since his day. They are especially illuminating in that they remind us that revolutions – as opposed to food riots and peasant rebellions – seldom if ever take the form of mere spontaneous outbreaks against tyranny, oppression or utter destitution: both the experience and the hope of something better are important factors in the event. So although Michelet's views command respect (as we shall see), it is on Tocqueville's analysis rather than his that later enquiry has tended to be built. To be built on, but not to be swallowed whole; for brilliant as it is, recent research and our experience of later revolutions suggest that it does not go far enough and does not take account of all the factors which, taken in combination, made for a revolution in France alone among the European states. For if kings and ministers were (as Tocqueville assures us) of such a reforming disposition, why did their reforms stop short – and *have* to stop short – of giving a more general satisfaction? And if the middle classes were becoming gradually more prosperous and more confident of their role in society, why should they suddenly feel the urge to resort to open rebellion against a system which they had hitherto supported? Again, if the peasants were acquiring land and gradually freeing themselves of the last vestiges of personal servitude, why should they, in 1789, revert to forms of rebellion that had not been seen in France for the past seventy years? Further, how did the ideas of the Enlightenment (to which Tocqueville, like Burke, accords considerable importance), after being propagated by the writers, journalists, Parlements and fashionable salon clientèle, begin to grip the minds of the poorer townsmen, if not the peasantry? What were the actual circumstances out of which the Revolution arose, and how did a revolt of disgruntled magistrates and nobles become transformed into a revolution of the 'middling' and lower classes of town and countryside? And were these factors peculiar to France, and therefore inapplicable to other countries? These are some of the further questions we shall now attempt to answer.

To begin with France, with her government and institutions. We have already seen that the system of government devised by Louis xiv had, under his successors, lost a great deal of its vigour and its ability to maintain the loyalty and respect of their subjects. This, as we saw, was due in part to the indolence and personal failings of Louis xv and, in part, to the tendency of the bureaucracy, staffed largely by privileged office-holders, to become almost a law unto itself. Meanwhile, as the middle classes became more prosperous and more self-important, they could hardly fail to become more resentful of the extravagance, inefficiencies and petty tyranny of a court and government to whose upkeep they largely contributed but over which they had no control. Yet Louis xvi, on ascending the throne, was eager to bring about substantial reforms in the administration, to reduce the expenditure of the court, to free trade of petty restrictions, to ease the tax-burdens of the peasants and promote a measure of self-government by means of local assemblies in the provinces. Unlike his predecessor, he had a high sense of personal responsibility; besides, in Turgot he had a minister who enjoyed the esteem and affection of both the 'enlightened' and the industrious middle classes. Yet the whole scheme collapsed and Turgot was out of office after a couple of years. Why? Because Turgot's reforms, though welcome to the middle classes, ran counter to the vested interests of the Parlements, the higher clergy and aristocratic factions at court. In this his experience, as we have seen, was similar to that of Machault and

Maupeou before him and of Calonne, Brienne and Necker after him; and it proved once more (as we have said already) that no far-reaching measures of reform were possible, however well-meaning the King or honest and able his ministers, so long as the privileged orders were left in possession of their powers, through the Parlements or their influence at court, to obstruct their operation. These then were the limits beyond which reform could not go – sufficient to whet the appetite of some, to irritate others and to satisfy none. Sufficient, too, to draw further hatred on the privileged orders and contempt on the monarchy that appeared to shield them.

The French middle classes, for all their rising wealth, had other grievances besides. Among them were the obstacles to the free exercise of trade and manufacture by onerous internal tolls and duties (exacted by both state and private interest) and the inquisitions of armies of government inspectors. Another was their failure to realise social ambitions commensurate with their wealth. We have seen that merchants and financiers, enriched by banking, manufacture and colonial trade, often sought to crown their careers by the purchase, for themselves or their descendants, of hereditary offices of state or commissions in the army. It has long been argued by historians – by Lavisse, Mathiez, Lefebvre, Elinor Barber, Franklin Ford and others – that these avenues to preferment began to be closed in the latter part of the eighteenth century; and we have seen that several Parlements (notably those of Aix, Nancy, Grenoble, Toulouse and Rennes) were, from the 1760s on, slamming their doors against middle-class intruders; and that, with very few exceptions, noble birth had, by 1789, become the sole essential qualification for holding high office in the army, church or administration. Thus, paradoxically, writes M. Godechot, 'the more numerous, the wealthier and better educated the French bourgeoisie became, the scarcer became the number of governmental and administrative posts to which they could aspire'.[4] And this, it has been said, sharply contrasted with that *règne de vile bourgeoisie* that Saint-Simon complained of in Louis xiv's time and, by thwarting middle-class ambitions at a crucial stage, goaded them into opposition to the *ancien régime*. Recently, such views have met with a cross-fire of criticism: some have insisted that the *privilégiés* were never quite as privileged as they have seemed; others that, on the contrary, their privileges were considerable at all times but no more so at the end of the century than they were at the beginning; while Miss Behrens strikes a balance between the two by insisting that 'though the avenues leading to the heights of prestige and power were, in the last stages of the ascent, harder to climb at the end of the eighteenth century than earlier, entrance to them . . . was easier than in the past'.[5] In consequence, it may well be that the old view will have to be modified in some respects: it is possible, for example, that Louis xiv promoted fewer bourgeois to offices and bishoprics than Saint-Simon claimed, that some Parlements (as in Paris) were less restrictive of bourgeois ambition than the rest, and that the notorious army law of 1781 was directed more against the recently *anoblis* than the wealthy merchant class. But none of this alters the fact that the French bourgeoisie at the end of the century were suffering from an increasing sense of indignity and humiliation at the hands of government and aristocracy. It was not just a matter of doors becoming progressively closed but of doors being closed at all at a time when their rising wealth and importance led them to believe that all doors should be kept wide open. To many, even among those who had no intention of investing in commissions in the army, the terms of the law of 1781 must have appeared as an intolerable affront; and the Marquis de Chérin, who hoped the law would do the nobility some good, nevertheless thought it must be humiliating for the Third Estate.[6] So the resentment and grievances were both genuine enough; but in history, as Tocqueville reminds us, it is resentment that is often the more important of the two. Yet it is perhaps the more remarkable that the French middle classes – if we except the writers, pamphleteers and journalists among them – waited so long before giving it political expression. It was only when prodded into action by the Parlements, the high clergy and nobility that they began seriously to lay claim to social equality and a share in government.

Again, growing peasant prosperity was by no means as universal as Tocqueville appears to suggest. While one in three of the French peasants owned their land outright, the larger part of these proprietors owned tiny parcels of land that even in years of good harvest were quite insufficient to feed their families. There were, too, the even greater number of share-croppers and landless labourers, who purchased their bread in the market and who could never, even under the most favourable of circumstances, hope to have more than the most meagre of shares in rural prosperity. The small proprietors, poor tenants and cottagers had the added grievance that improving landlords and wealthy peasants, stimulated by the urge to increase agricultural production, were enclosing fields and commons and encroaching on the villagers' traditional rights of gleaning and pasture. A more general grievance was one already noted in an earlier chapter: the recent tendency of landlords (whether noble or bourgeois) to rake up old rights attaching to their lands and to impose new or added obligations to those already exacted from their peasants. This is what the peasants, in their *cahiers* of 1789, called a revival of feudalism and what most French historians have termed a part of the 'feudal reaction' of the age. Alfred Cobban, however, objected to the use of this term on the grounds that what the landlords were doing was 'less a reversion to the past than the application to old relationships of new business techniques'.[7] This may well be so; but the peasants were not inclined to draw such fine distinctions and to them feudalism appeared even more obnoxious when dressed up in a new and unfamiliar garb.

Further, Tocqueville failed to notice what only recent research has brought to light: that it was precisely in these closing years of the *ancien régime* that the general prosperity of agriculture was grinding to a halt. This developed in two stages. After 1778, the year France entered the American War, there was a recession as the result of which prices fell – gradually in most industrial and farm products, but reaching crisis proportions in wines and textiles. During these years, the net profits of small tenant farmers, peasant proprietors, wine-growers and other share-croppers tended, because of the heavy and sustained toll of tax, tithe and seigneurial exaction, to fall out of all proportion to the fall in prices, while large landed proprietors were cushioned against loss by means of their 'feudal' revenues. Then, on top of this cyclical depression, came the sudden catastrophe of 1787–9, which took the form of bad harvests and shortage, with the price of wheat doubling within two years in the main productive regions of the north and reaching record levels in twenty-seven of the thirty-two *généralités* in mid-summer 1789. The crisis hit the bulk of the peasantry both as producers and as consumers: as wine-growers, dairy-farmers or wheat-growers. From agriculture it spread to industry; and unemployment, already developing from the 'Free Trade' treaty of 1786 with England, reached disastrous proportions in Paris and the textile centres of Lyons and the north. Another result was that wage-earners and all small consumers, in both villages and towns, were compelled by the rapid rise in food prices to increase their daily expenditure on bread to amounts far beyond their means. Thus peasants and urban craftsmen and workers were drawn together in common hostility to government, landlords, merchants and speculators; and these classes entered the Revolution in a context of increasing poverty and hardship rather than of prosperity. In this sense at least, modern research has tended to justify Michelet rather than Tocqueville.[8]

But, of course, it needed more than economic hardship, social discontent and the frustration of political and social ambitions to make a revolution. To give cohesion to the discontents and aspirations of widely varying social classes there had to be some unifying body of ideas, a common vocabulary of hope and protest, something, in short, like a common 'revolutionary psychology' or pattern of 'generalised beliefs'. In the revolutions of our day, this ideological preparation has been the concern of political parties; but there were no such parties in eighteenth-century France. In this case, the ground was prepared in the first instance by the writers of the Enlightenment. It was they who, as Burke and Tocqueville both noted, weakened the ideological defences of the *ancien régime*. The ideas of Montesquieu, Voltaire, Rousseau and of many others were, as we have seen, being widely disseminated and absorbed by an eager reading public, both aristocratic and middle-class. It had become fashionable, even among the clergy, to be sceptical and 'irreligious'; and the writings of Voltaire had combined with the struggles within the church itself (Gallicans against Jesuits and Jansenists and Richerists against the increasing authority of bishops) to expose the church to indifference, contempt or hostility. We have noted that Parisians demonstrated against their Archbishop over the *billets de confessions* in the 1750s (see page 128); and Hardy, the bookseller-diarist of the university quarter in Paris, reported similar expressions of anticlericalism in his *Journal* in the 1780s. Meanwhile, such terms as 'citizen', 'nation', 'social contract', 'general will' and the 'rights of man' – soon to be followed by the *'tiers état'* (or 'third estate') – were entering into a common political vocabulary. This was partly the work of the pamphleteers of the Third Estate in 1788 and 1789; but, long before that, the ground had been well and truly prepared by the tracts and Remonstrances published by the Parlements who, in their prolonged duel from the 1750s onwards with ministerial 'despotism', quoted freely, and often indiscriminately, from the writings of Montesquieu and Rousseau and other 'philosophical' critics of the day. What was new in all this activity was that the Parlements were not just writing political tracts as the *philosophes* had done, but were deliberately setting out to mould public opinion and to marshal active public support in their struggles with the crown.

However, when all this has been said, it is still doubtful if (say) in January 1787 any intelligent Frenchman or foreign observer could have found good reason to predict that a revolution was close at hand, and still less to foretell the form that such a revolution would take. It is easy for us, with our superior knowledge after the event, to see that such reasons existed; yet, even so, there was still an important element lacking. It still needed a spark or 'trigger' to cause an explosion of any kind; and it needed a second spark to bring about the particular alignments of 1789.

The first spark was the government's declaration of bankruptcy following the American war. Opinions may vary as to the extent of the influence of the American Revolution and of its Declaration of Independence on the course of events in France; but there can be no two opinions about the cataclysmic results that flowed from France's participation in the war. Calonne, the current Controller General, estimated a deficit of 112 million livres, which represented nearly a quarter of the total state revenue; so it called for drastic remedies. In the event, it was decided to abandon the old procedures and invite an assembly of *notables* to consider a number of stop-gap measures to meet the crisis. It was this, as we have seen in an earlier chapter, that provoked the *révolte nobiliaire* of 1787–8, which ended in the defeat of the Ministry and in a total victory for the Parlements and aristocracy; above all the government had been forced to concede that the States General (on which both Parlements and nobility pinned their hopes) should be summoned after all. So, in September 1788, as the Paris Parlement returned in triumph to the capital, it looked as if the prophecy reported by Arthur Young a few months before might be fulfilled: that 'some great revolution in the government' would follow that was likely to 'add to the scale of the nobility and clergy'. So a belief in 'revolution', provoked by the success of the nobility's challenge to government, was already in the air; but the form that revolution took when it broke out was, as we know, of quite a different kind. Why was this? Briefly, it was because the promise of the States General compelled the contending parties to define their aims and take up new positions. The bourgeoisie, or the *tiers état*, hitherto divided between the supporters and opponents of ministerial reform, now found it expedient, once the States General was called, to close their ranks and present a programme of their own. The Parlements and nobility, however, who entertained quite different hopes from the meeting of the Estates, were also compelled to put their cards on the table and to show that the 'liberties' that they looked for were not the same as those of the *tiers* or of the nation at large. In consequence, the aristocracy and clergy, far from increasing the support they had already won, began rapidly to lose it; and Mallet du Pan, a Swiss observer, noted only four months after the *révolte nobiliaire* was over that the position in France had radically changed: the question at issue (he wrote) was no longer a constitutional contest between the King and the privileged classes with popular support, but 'a war between the Third Estate and the other two orders'. The position changed again after the States General met at Versailles in May 1789. Now the King, faced with the irreconcilable claims of nobility and Third Estate, chose to support the former, called in troops to Versailles and prepared to disperse the National Assembly (as the *tiers* had now become) by force of arms. This *coup* was averted by the intervention of the *menu peuple* and lesser bourgeoisie of Paris. Meanwhile the peasants, stirred by both economic and political crises, had begun to take direct action of their own; and it was an association of these forces – middle classes, urban *menu peuple* and peasants, with liberal–aristocratic support – that carried through the first stage of the revolution in France in the summer of 1789.

The French Revolution appears, then, to have been the outcome of a combination of factors, both long-term and short-term, that arose from the conditions of the *ancien régime*. The long-standing grievances of peasants, townsmen and bourgeoisie; the frustration of rising hopes among wealthy bourgeois and peasants; the insolvency and break-down of government; a growing 'feudal reaction'; the claims and intransigence of aristocracy; the propagation of radical ideas among wide sections of the people; a sharp economic and financial crisis; and the successive 'triggers' of state bankruptcy, aristocratic revolt and popular rebellion: these all played their part. Were these factors peculiar to France? Considered in isolation, the answer must be no. If we leave aside the ultimate 'triggers', similar tensions, crises and frustrations appear, in one form or another, in several other European countries at this time. Why then was there a revolution of this kind in France and nowhere else? Or we may put the question in another way and ask, as M. Godechot does after reviewing the riots and uprisings in large cities like London, Brussels and Amsterdam in the 1780s: 'Why was it that the riots which broke out in foreign capitals, notably in London, did not entail the collapse of the old régime or the capitulation of the royal or aristocratic power before the insurgent masses?'[9]

It would be ingenuous, of course, to imagine that a recipe for revolution in one country would be equally or exactly applicable to any other. Yet it is perhaps reasonable to argue that a similar combination of factors would in any two countries (of broadly similar size) have broadly similar results; and, conversely, that it is the absence of such a combination rather than the absence of any one or other of the factors that may help to explain why France had a revolution in 1789 and other countries did not. In the states of eastern Europe – in Russia, Poland, Hungary, Austria and Bohemia – the status and general conditions of the peasantry were far inferior, as we have seen, to those in France; and we have seen plenty of evidence that grievance was matched with widespread discontent. Yet, in these countries, peasant rebellion – even of such a magnitude as Pugachev's in Russia – tended to remain out on a limb; and this was partly (though not solely) because in none of these countries was there a sufficiently developed middle or intermediate class to give it support or to help it develop an articulate language of revolt or the hope of a better future. The Austrian experience was, in this respect, a little different from the Russian; for Joseph II's reforms raised hopes and provoked rebellions that, while they were on a less massive scale than Pugachev's, may in the long run have been a greater danger to the absolute monarchy than all the peasant outbreaks in the reign of Catherine the Great. In some countries, too – in Austria, Sweden and Poland – the challenge of aristocracy was even more sustained and persistent than it was in France; but in Sweden and Poland, though it enjoyed a prolonged period of triumph, it failed to unite the nation against the crown, and the King in the first case and foreign intervention in the second brought it to heel after 1772. Again, Austria was a special case; for Joseph almost lost his throne at the hands of the

Hungarian nobility; but it was only in the Belgian provinces, as we have seen, that a national revolution developed that declared for independence and expelled the Austrian troops.

In Spain, the condition of the common people was, once again, probably far worse than they were in France: there were the armies of beggars in Madrid and other cities; and the poverty and depression of the land-workers on the great *latifundia* of the south far exceeded those recorded in the French peasant *cahiers* of 1789 or in the *Travels* of Arthur Young. Moreover the Spanish nobility retained privileges that were just as onerous as those of the French; and the corporate nature of Spanish society, with its proliferation of regional and particular-interest groups, proved, as we have seen, to be an intractable problem that defeated the well-intentioned plans of the reforming ministers of Charles III. But there was no middle class mature enough or powerful enough to dispute the social ascendancy of the landed classes; nor was there a widely diffused body of 'enlightened' ideas to question the old-established notions of authority in society, church or state. There was no aristocratic challenge to monarchy on anything but a regional scale; the church remained a firm and widely respected pillar of the monarchist state; so there was at no time under Charles III a crisis of government such as that which overtook France under Louis XVI.

In Prussia, feudal survivals and the bureaucratic state combined to prop up the nobility, crush the peasants and keep the middle classes in their proper stations. The latter in fact had few outlets for such energies as they possessed: the paths to social advancement under Frederick II were strictly circumscribed; the nobility were paid subsidies to retain their estates; and even the growth of industry was hampered by taxes, mercantilist restrictions and the prolonged crises of the 1760s and 1780s. Meanwhile, the condition of the people, for all the claims of enlightened despotism, continued to grow worse: the peasantry, both east and west of the Elbe, remained enserfed; and grain prices (following a pattern not unlike the French) almost doubled between 1750 and 1800, while wages rose by a third or a half.[10] So there were plenty of grounds for dissatisfaction. Yet there was no deep sense of injustice or frustration of hopes, and the old hierarchical social order – so firmly implanted in Germany as a whole – remained virtually unimpaired. Nowhere perhaps outside France did the ideas of the Enlightenment circulate as widely; but they tended to be directed into literary channels – to cluster round cults of nature, 'sensibility' or language – and were rarely put to the political uses to which they were put in France in the 1780s. So lower- and middle-class dissatisfaction was absorbed, and there was no crisis of authority and no effective challenge to privilege or monarchy.

So far, it will be noted that the factors most conspicuously absent have been a substantial middle class and a widely circulated *corpus* of radical-political ideas. This was in fact the case with all the countries of eastern, northern and southern Europe (the sole exception here being Italy north of the Po). So they were confined to the West: apart from France, to Holland, Belgium, parts of Switzerland, and Britain. In none of these, as we have observed already, were the middle classes and middle-class attitudes as developed as they were in Britain; and it has been argued (by Godechot, Butterfield and others) that, around the year 1780, Britain found herself in something like a revolutionary situation. It was the time of the first phase of the industrial revolution, of the Volunteers and Grattan's Parliament in Ireland, the Gordon Riots, a renewed challenge by aristocratic and middle-class reformers, and a critical stage in the American War. Yet it all ended quietly: there was no fundamental crisis of government, and the established authority emerged – with minor modifications in Ireland – more solidly entrenched than ever before. Some have argued that the result was due to the soothing effects of Methodism, which served to cool passions and draw the sting of violent protest.[11] It seems more likely, however, that the key factor was the attitude of the middle classes. For them the vista of rising prosperity appeared to lie wide open; there was little of that deep-felt social frustration in the face of aristocratic privilege and arrogance that was so evident in France; and when it came to the point (in the early 1780s), they had no more intention of throwing in their lot with riotous miners, weavers or petty consumers than they had with an 'aristocratic reaction'. So they pinned their hopes on Pitt and George III and, momentarily at least, abandoned reform for continued prosperity.

The challenge to authority was in fact far more serious in Belgium, Holland and Geneva than it was in England; why this was so, however, will not be further considered here. In Belgium, as we noted, all three estates – clergy, nobility and gilds – joined forces and, with the aid of the middle-class democrats led by Vonck, expelled the Austrians and proclaimed a United States of Belgium. But once this had been accomplished, the Estates party turned on their democratic allies, drove them out and forced many of them to seek refuge in France. Thus an aristocratic revolt, when faced with the consequences of a national revolutionary uprising, had turned to counter-revolution. In Holland, the Patriots' rebellion against the Stadholder and city patriciates never went so far; and we have seen that, after the withdrawal of French support and Amsterdam's resistance to the Prussians, the movement rapidly collapsed. In Geneva alone, there was a popular revolution in the 1780s that actually preceded the one in France. But Geneva was a small city state and the combined movement of *bourgeois* and *natifs* (unique of its kind in Europe at the time) stood little chance of success when the French, responding to the ruling *citoyens'* appeal, sent an army in to crush it.

The tables, of course, were turned when the French themselves, in the summer of 1789, took the path of revolution; and it is no coincidence that, under the impact of the events in France, several of these western countries (the Rhineland and Piedmont as well as Belgium, Holland and Geneva) should find themselves in new revolutionary situations in the 1790s. In others – in Germany (outside Prussia), Poland, southern Italy and parts of Spain – it may be argued that the 'revolutions' that followed later were the result of French military occupation rather than of the mere force of the French example or of the Declaration of the Rights of Man. But this is another story and takes us, once again, far beyond the limits of this book.

NOTES

I COUNTRIES AND POPULATION

1 Quoted by Raymond Carr, *Spain 1808–1939*, Oxford 1966, p.3.
2 Lionel Rothkrug, *Opposition to Louis XIV. The Political and Social Origins of the French Enlightenment*, Princeton 1965, pp.98, 455–6.
3 E.N.Williams, *The Ancien Régime in Europe*, London 1970, p.6.
4 William Coxe, *Travels in Poland, Russia, Sweden and Denmark*, 5 vols, London 1802, IV, p.14.
5 *Hansard*, 8 May 1753, p.1320.
6 For the above see H.G.Habbakuk, 'Population, Commerce and Economic Ideas', in *New Cambridge Modern History*, VIII, pp.25–6, 714–15; A.Armengaud, 'Population in Europe 1700–1914', in *Fontana Economic History of Europe*, vol. 3, ed. C.M.Cipolla (London 1970), pp.6–12; H.Moller, *Population Movements in Modern European History*, New York 1964, p.5; M.Reinhard, A.Armengaud, J.Dupaquier, *Histoire générale de la population mondiale*, Paris 1968, pp.202–69; A.Braudel and C.F.Labrousse, *Histoire économique et sociale de la France*, II, 1660–1789, Paris 1970, pp.17–21; A.Soboul, *La France à la veille de la Révolution*, I, *Économie et société*, Paris 1969, pp.43–5.
7 For varying opinions see Habbakuk, in *New Cambridge Modern History*, pp.26–33; Armengaud, in *Fontana Economic History*, pp.16–56; A.Sauvy, *La population. Sa mesure, ses mouvements, ses lois*, Paris 1961, pp.83–4; Reinhard, Armengaud, Dupaquier, *Histoire Générale*; Braudel and Labrousse, *Histoire Économique*, II, pp.20–1; C.Hill, *Reformation to Industrial Revolution*, London 1969, pp.254–8; J.T.Krause, 'Some Aspects of Population Change, 1690–1790', in *Land, Labour and Population in the Industrial Revolution*, eds. E.L.Jones and G.E.Mingay, London 1967, pp.187–93; P. Goubert, 'Historical Demography and the Reinterpretation of Early Modern History: A Research Review', in *Journal of Interdisciplinary History*, I (1), 1970, pp.37–48; T.McKeown and R.G.Brown, 'The Interpretation of the Rise of Population in England and Wales', *Central African Journal of Medicine*, XV (8), 1969, pp.187–90.
8 See Braudel and Labrousse, *Histoire Économique*, II, pp.20–1.
9 Habbakuk, in *New Cambridge Modern History*, p.30.
10 Goubert, 'Historical Demography', p.45.
11 Armengaud, in *Fontana Economic History*, p.42.
12 Quoted by Habbakuk in *New Cambridge Modern History*, p.33.

2 LAND AND PEASANTS

1 For much of what follows see A. de Maddalena, 'Rural Europe 1500–1750', in *Fontana Economic History of Europe*, vol. 2, pp.36–66.
2 For opposing views as to whether the real agricultural revolution in England started in the mid-eighteenth century or a century before, see J.D.Chambers and G.E.Mingay, *The Agricultural Revolution 1750–1880*, New York 1966; and E.Kerridge, *The Agricultural Revolution*, London 1967.
3 David Landes, 'Technological Change and Industrial Development in Western Europe, 1750–1914', *Camb. Econ. History of Europe*, VI, p.308.
4 Marc Bloch, *French Rural History*, London 1966, pp.219–33.
5 Coxe, *Travels*, V, p.10.
6 Coxe, *Travels*, I, p.246.
7 Maddalena, in *Fontana Economic History*, pp.41–2, 63–5.
8 Arthur Young, *Travels in France during the Years 1787–1788–1789*, ed. J. Kaplow, New York 1969, pp.15–16.
9 Quoted by Williams, *Ancien Régime*, p. 277.
10 Quoted by Richard Herr, *The Eighteenth-Century Revolution in Spain*, Princeton 1958, pp.99, 96.
11 Map in Herr, *Revolution in Spain*,
12 Coxe, *Travels*, IV, p.27; V, pp.104–5.
13 Maddalena, in *Fontana Economic History*, p.32.
14 Coxe, *Travels*, I, p.114.
15 Coxe, *Travels*, III, pp.152–3.

3 INDUSTRY AND TRADE

1 Quoted by E.J.Hobsbawm, *Industry and Empire*, London 1969, pp.25–6.
2 Daniel Defoe, *A Tour through the Whole Island of Great Britain*, 2 vols, London 1962, II, p.242.
3 C.H.Wilson, 'The Growth of Overseas Commerce and European Manufacture', in *New Cambridge Modern History*, VII, p.44.
4 Quoted by R.and E.Forster, *European Society in the Eighteenth Century*, New York 1970, p.231.
5 A.Soboul, *La France à la veille de la Révolution*, I, pp.126–7, 141.
6 Defoe, *A Tour*, II, pp.193–5.
7 Quoted by Herr, *Revolution in Spain*, p.147.
8 R. Portal, *L'Oural au XVIIIe siècle*, Paris 1950, pp.157–9.
9 Phyllis Deane, 'The Industrial Revolution in England 1700–1914', in *Fontana Economic History of Europe*, vol. 4, pp.20–1.
10 Hobsbawm, *Industry and Empire*, p.51.
11 Paul Bairoch, 'Agriculture and the Industrial Revolution 1790–1914', in *Fontana Economic History of Europe*, vol. 3, pp.49–62; Bertrand Gille, 'Banks and Industrialisation in Europe 1730–1914', in *Fontana Economic History of Europe*, vol. 3, pp.7–8.

12 See F.Crouzet, 'England and France in the Eighteenth Century: A Comparative Analysis of two Economic Growths', in *The Causes of the Industrial Revolution in England*, ed. R.M.Hartwell, London 1967, p.171.

13 David Landes, in *Cambridge Economic History of Europe*, VI, pp.281–6.

4 CITIES

1 City population figures, here and elsewhere, are from R.Mols, *Introduction à la démographie historique des villes d'Europe du XIVᵉ au XVIIIᵉ siècle*, 3 vols, Louvain 1955, II, pp.508–40; Reinhard, Armengaud, Dupaquier, *Histoire générale de la population mondiale*, pp.209–69; Adna F.Weber, *The Growth of Cities in the Nineteenth Century*, New York 1963, pp.236–7, 449–50.

2 Quoted in *The Cambridge History of Poland*, eds. W.F.Reddaway *et al.*, Cambridge 1951, p.75.

3 Landes, in *Cambridge Economic History*, p.284.

4 E.A.Wrigley, 'A Simple Model of London's Importance in Changing English Society and Economy 1650–1750', *Past and Present*, 37, 1967, pp.49–50.

5 Defoe, *A Tour*, I, p.324; W.F.Reddaway, *A History of Europe 1715–1814*, London 1954, p.28; M.D.George, *London Life in the Eighteenth Century*, London 1966, p.318.

6 Frederick II, King of Prussia, *Memoirs of the House of Brandenburg*, 2 vols, London 1758–68, I, pp.283–90.

7 Defoe, *A Tour*, II, pp.299–300.

8 Letter of 22 August 1716; quoted by W.H.Bruford, *Germany in the Eighteenth Century. The Social Background of the Literary Revival*, Cambridge 1935, p.97.

9 J.McManners, *French Ecclesiastical Society under the Ancien Régime. A Study of Angers in the Eighteenth Century*, Manchester 1960, pp.1–7.

10 Defoe, *A Tour*, II, pp.300, 334–5.

11 Defoe, *A Tour*, II, pp.255–6.

12 M.Reinhard, 'Paris pendant la Révolution', *Les Cours de Sorbonne*, 2 vols, Paris n.d., II, p.44.

13 R.Davis, *The Rise of the English Shipping Industry*, London 1962, p.390.

14 Y.Le Moigne, 'Population et subsistances à Strasbourg au XVIIIᵉ siècle', in *Contributions à l'histoire démographique de la Révolution française*, 1962; quoted by Soboul, *La France*, I, p.50.

15 Wrigley, in *Past and Present*, p.46; and the *Listener*, 6 July 1967, p.7.

16 G.Mauco, *Les migrations ouvrières en France au début du XIXᵉ siècle*, Paris 1932, pp.29–31.

17 Bruford, *Germany in the Eighteenth Century*, p.98.

18 J.Kaplow, *Elbeuf during the Revolutionary Period. History and Social Structure*, Baltimore 1964, p.84.

19 R.Forster, *The Nobility of Toulouse in the Eighteenth Century. A Social and Economic Study*, Baltimore 1960, p.36; G.Lefebvre, *Études orléanaises, I. Contribution à l'étude des structures sociales à la fin du XVIIIᵉ siècle*, Paris 1962, p.228.

20 Quoted by M.D.George, 'London and the Life of the Town', in *Johnson's England*, ed. A.S.Turberville, 2 vols, London 1965, I, p.175.
21 J.V.von Archenholtz, *A View of the British Constitution and the Manners and Customs of the People of England*, 1794, pp.119, 132.

5 SOCIETY AND ARISTOCRACY

1 H.J.Habbakuk, 'England', in *The European Nobility in the Eighteenth Century*, ed. A.Goodwin, 1953, pp.3–4.
2 Coxe, *Travels*, I, pp. 304–15.
3 R. and E.Forster, *European Society*, pp.74–5.
4 G.E.Mingay, *English Landed Society in the Eighteenth Century*, London and Toronto, pp.19–23.
5 C.B.A.Behrens, *The Ancien Régime*, London 1967, p.73.
6 A.de Tocqueville, *The Old Régime and the French Revolution*, New York 1955, p.91.
7 D.Defoe, *The Complete English Tradesman*, London 1726.
8 Mingay, *English Landed Society*, pp.26–9.
9 Behrens, *Ancien Régime*, pp.73–5.
10 Landes, in *Cambridge Economic History*, p.303n.
11 Quoted by Landes, in *Cambridge Economic History*, p.303.

6 GOVERNMENT

1 *The Letters and Works of Lady Mary Wortley Montagu*, ed. Lord Wharncliffe, 2 vols, London 1908, II, p.160.
2 *Seven Britons in Imperial Russia, 1698–1812,* ed. P.Putnam, Princeton 1952, pp.145–58.
3 Quoted by Behrens, *Ancien Régime*, p.85.
4 Coxe, *Travels*, IV, pp.111–30.
5 Quoted by Christopher Hill, *Reformation to Industrial Revolution*, London 1969, p.218.
6 Quoted by W.Oechsli, *History of Switzerland 1499–1914*, Cambridge 1922, p.257.

7 BUREAUCRACY

1 Quoted by M.S.Anderson, *Europe in the Eighteenth Century 1713–1783*, London 1962, p.93.
2 Quoted by Behrens, *Ancien Régime*, p.100.
3 J.H.Bosher, *The Single Duty Project*, London 1964.
4 H.Rosenberg, *Bureaucracy, Aristocracy and Autocracy. The Prussian Experience 1660–1815*, Cambridge, Mass. 1958, pp.175ff.
5 Carr, *Spain*, p.63.
6 Carr, *Spain*, pp.62–4.
7 J.H.Bosher, *French Finances 1770–1795*, Cambridge 1970, *passim*.

8 CHURCH, STATE AND SOCIETY

1 Quoted by G.R.Cragg, *The Church in the Age of Reason 1648–1789*, London 1962, p.211.
2 Coxe, *Travels*, I, p.318.
3 Coxe, *Travels*, III, pp.141–2.
4 Quoted by Carr, *Spain*, p.45.
5 Quoted by Soboul, *La France*, I, p.103.
6 A.Latreille, *L'Église catholique et la Révolution française*, Paris 1946, pp.40–1.
7 Quoted by S.E.Ayling, *The Georgian Century 1714–1837*, London 1966, p.319.
8 Coxe, *Travels*, III, pp.142–5.
9 Young, *Travels*, p.452.
10 Quoted by Behrens, *Ancien Régime*, p.10.

9 THE ARTS

1 Quoted by Anderson, *Europe*, p.303.
2 Quoted by E.Préclin, *Le XVIIIe siècle. II. Les forces internationales*, Paris 1952, p.707.
3 See Préclin, *Le XVIIIe siècle*, pp.754–7.
4 Hill, *Reformation*, p.281; and see F. Antal, *Hogarth*, 1961.
5 R.Mandrou, *De la culture populaire aux XVIIe et XVIIIe siècles. La bibliothèque bleue de Troyes*, Paris 1964, pp.1–14.
6 H.Koht, *Les luttes des paysans en Norvège du XVIe au XIXe siècle*, Paris 1929, pp.178–88.

10 ENLIGHTENMENT

1 Quoted by A.V.Judges, 'Educational Ideas, Practice and Institutions', in *New Cambridge Modern History*, VIII, p.143.
2 Quoted by P.Gay, *The Enlightenment. An Interpretation*, New York 1966, p.12.
3 Gay, *Enlightenment*, p.312.
4 Adam Smith, *The Wealth of Nations*, ed. James E.Thorold Rogers, 2 vols, Oxford 1880, II, pp.208–17.
5 For the 'social diffusion' of these ideas see N.Hampson, *The Enlightenment*, London 1968, pp.132–46.
6 Hampson, *Enlightenment*, p.134.
7 Herr, *Eighteenth-Century Revolution*, p.196.
8 Hampson, *Enlightenment*, p.138.
9 See D.Mornet, *Les origines intellectuelles de la Révolution française (1715–1787)*, Paris 1947, pp.281–308.
10 Peter F.Sugar, 'The Influence of the Enlightenment and the French Revolution in Eighteenth Century Hungary', *Journal of Central European Affairs*, XVII (1958), pp.332–3.

11 H.Brunschwig, *La crise de l'état prussien à la fin du XVIIIe siècle et la genèse de la mentalité romantique*, Paris 1947, pp.42–6.
12 Gay, *Enlightenment*, p.20.

11 THE STRUGGLE FOR CONTROL OF THE STATE

1 See Ingvar Andersson, *A History of Sweden*, London 1956, pp.273–81; and Denise Aimé, 'La révolution suédoise de 1772', in *La Révolution française*, Paris 1937, pp.144–54.
2 But see John B.Owen, *The Rise of the Pelhams*, London 1957, pp.294–7.
3 Cited by N.C.Phillips, *Yorkshire and English National Politics 1783–1784*, Christchurch, N.Z. 1961, p.60.
4 See R.R.Palmer, *The Age of the Democratic Revolution*, vol. 1, New York 1959, pp.341–57; E.Tassier, *Les démocrates belges de 1789*, Brussels 1930.
5 Wilhelm Oechsli, *History of Switzerland 1499–1914*, Cambridge 1933, pp.277–85.
6 R.B.McDowell, *Irish Public Opinion 1750–1800*, London 1944, p.45.
7 McDowell, *Irish Public Opinion*, p.51.

12 THE POPULAR CHALLENGE

1 G.M.Trevelyan, *England in the Age of Johnson*, London 1920, p.7.
2 Portal, *L'Oural*, Paris 1950, pp.315–29.
3 C.-E.Labrousse, *Esquisse du mouvement des prix et des revenus en France au XVIIIe siècle*, 2 vols, Paris 1933; *La Crise de l'économie française à la fin de l'Ancien Régime et au début de la Révolution*, Paris 1944.
4 E.J.Hobsbawm, 'The Machine-Breakers', *Past and Present*, February 1952, pp.55–70.
5 D.Mornet, *Origines*, pp.444–8.
6 Labrousse, *Esquisse*, II, pp.597–608.
7 Mornet, *Origines*, pp.444–8.
8 G.Rudé, *Paris and London in the Eighteenth Century*, London 1970, pp.55–6.
9 Edward P.Thompson, 'The Moral Economy of the English Crowd in the Eighteenth Century', *Past and Present*, May 1971, pp.71–136.
10 For a discussion of the evidence, see Edgar Faure, *La disgrâce de Turgot*, Paris 1961, pp.293–318.
11 I am, however, persuaded by Dr Walter Shelton, author of a recent PhD thesis on the English riots of 1766, that the hostility of the local gentry to grain-merchants served to prolong them.
12 E.J.Hobsbawm, *Primitive Rebels*, Manchester 1959, pp.114–16.
13 J.Godechot, *The Taking of the Bastille*, London 1970, p.18.
14 See, for example, Louis Chevalier, *Classes laborieuses et classes dangereuses à Paris dans la première moitié du dix-neuvième siècle*, Paris 1958.
15 Hobsbawm, *Primitive Rebels*, p.115.
16 Godechot, *Taking of the Bastille*, pp.5ff.

17 Godechot, *France and the Atlantic Revolution of the Eighteenth Century, 1770–1799*, p.3.

18 For a recent paper, however, that (contrary to the opinion here expressed) firmly places the Pugachev rebellion within the context of the 'Atlantic' or 'Democratic' revolution of the West, see Paul Dukes, 'Russia and the Eighteenth Century Revolution', *History*, 118, October 1971, pp.371–86.

13 DIPLOMACY AND WARFARE

1 Quoted by Anderson, *Europe*, p.130.
2 R.Mousnier, C.-E.Labrousse, M.Bouloiseau, *Le XVIIIᵉ siècle. L'Époque des 'Lumières' (1715–1815)*, Paris 1967, p.216.
3 E.N.Williams, *Ancien Régime*, p.3.
4 Anderson, *Europe*, p.131.
5 E.Wangermann, *From Joseph II to the Jacobin Trials*, Oxford 1959, p.30.
6 A.Vagts, *A History of Militarism*, London 1959, p.72.
7 Anderson, *Europe*, p.146.
8 Anderson, *Europe*, p.149.

14 WARS AND THE EXPANSION OF EUROPE

1 Francis Parkman, *Montcalm and Wolfe*, new ed., Toronto 1964, p.253.

15 EPILOGUE: WHY WAS THERE A REVOLUTION IN FRANCE?

1 F.A.M.Mignet, *History of the French Revolution from 1789 to 1814*, London 1915, p.1.
2 Parkman, *Montcalm and Wolfe*, pp.27, 24.
3 A.de Tocqueville, *The Ancien Régime and the French Revolution*, Oxford 1937, p.186.
4 Godechot, *Taking of the Bastille*, p.51.
5 Behrens, *Ancien Régime*, p.71. For the traditional view, see, *inter alia*, E.Lavisse (ed.), *Histoire de France depuis les origines jusqu'à la Révolution*, IX (1), Paris 1910, pp.399–400; E.G.Barber, *The Bourgeoisie in 18th-Century France*, Princeton 1955, pp.112–25; Braudel and Labrousse, *Histoire Économique*, II, pp.643–4; Soboul, *La France*, I, pp.183–5. For a revisionist view, see F.Furet, 'Le catéchisme révolutionnaire', *Annales*, March–April 1971, 2, pp.273–5. For a more comprehensive summary of the revisionist case and the literature on which it is based, I am indebted to Professor David Bien, who has kindly allowed me to see a first draft of an unpublished article, 'Social Mobility in Eighteenth-Century France'. The debate will, presumably, go on.
6 Barber, *Bourgeoisie*, p.123.
7 A.Cobban, *The Social Interpretation of the French Revolution*, London 1964, p.123.
8 See, in particular, Labrousse, *Esquisse*, II, pp.637–42; *Crise*, pp.ix–xli, 625.

9 Godechot, *Taking of the Bastille*, p.xxiv.
10 Helen P.Siebel, 'Enlightened Despotism and the Crisis of Society in Germany', *Enlightenment Essays*, I (3–4), Chicago 1970, pp.151–68.
11 See R.F.Wearmouth, *Methodism and the Common People of the Eighteenth Century*, London 1945, p.265. E. Halévy's similar argument applies, more particularly, to the early nineteenth century.

1713   Treaty of Utrecht
      Papal Bull *Unigenitus*
      Pragmatic Sanction (Austria)
1715   Regency in France
      Jacobite Rebellion
      Palladian architecture in England
1716   Austro-Turkish war
      Septennial Act in England
1717   Triple Alliance: Britain, France, United Provinces
1718   Treaty of Passarowitz: Austria, Turkey
1719   Peerage Bill defeated in England
      Defoe's *Robinson Crusoe*
1720   Law financial scandal in France
      South Sea Bubble in England
      'Aristocratic' *coup d'état* in Sweden
1721   Treaty of Nystad: Russia, Sweden
      First inoculations against smallpox
      Montesquieu's *Lettres persanes*
1722   Peter I's Table of Ranks in Russia
      General Directory in Prussia
      Walpole First Lord of the Treasury
      Ostend Company
1723   Duc de Bourbon's Ministry in France
1725   First Treaty of Vienna: Austria, Spain
      Vico's *Scienza nuova*
1726   Cardinal Fleury's Ministry in France
      Swift's *Gulliver's Travels*
1727   Death of Newton
1728   Gay's *Beggar's Opera*
1730   Zinzendorf and Moravian Brethren at Herrnhut
1731   Second Treaty of Vienna: Britain, UP, Spain, Austria
      Tull's *Horse-hoeing Husbandry*
1733   War of Polish Succession
      First Family Compact: France, Spain

Walpole's Excise Bill withdrawn
Kay's 'Flying Shuttle'
Pope's *Essay on Man*
1734 Voltaire's *Lettres philosophiques*
1735 Abraham Darby smelts iron from coke
Linnaeus's *Systema naturae*
Hogarth's *Rake's Progress*
1736 Russian's capture Azov from Turks
Porteous riots in Scotland; 'Gin' riots in London
1738 Wesley's first Methodist association
1739 Treaty of Belgrade: Russia, Austria, Turkey
Anglo-Spanish war ('Jenkins's Ear')
1740 Frederick II invades Silesia
Richardson's *Pamela*
1741 Russo-Swedish war
1742 Fall of Walpole
Treaty of Berlin: Austria, Prussia
1743 Death of Fleury
Second Family Compact
1744 France at war with England and Austria
1745 Jacobite Rebellion
British capture Louisbourg
Madame de Pompadour at Versailles
1746 French capture Madras
Diderot's *Pensées philosophiques*
1747 Orangist *coup d'état* in United Provinces
1748 Treaty of Aix-la-Chapelle
Ruins of Pompeii discovered
Montesquieu's *De l'esprit des lois*
1749 *Vingtième* tax imposed by Controller General Machault in France
Huntsman smelts steel in England
Diderot's *Lettre sur les aveugles*
Fielding's *Tom Jones*
1750 Pombal chief minister in Portugal
Voltaire at Potsdam
1751 Diderot's and d'Alembert's *Encyclopédie*, vol. I
Hogarth's *Gin Lane*
1752 Place Stanislas built in Nancy
1753 *Billets de confession* at Paris
Kaunitz Chancellor of Austria
1754 Condillac's *Traité des sensations*
1755 Expulsion of Jesuits from Paraguay
Rousseau's *Discours sur l'origine de l'inégalité*
Winckelmann's *On the Imitation of Greek Painting and Sculpture*
1756 Seven Years War
1757 Pitt–Newcastle Ministry in England
Clive's victory at Plassey
Battles of Rossbach and Leuthen

1758   Duc de Choiseul chief minister in France
       British recapture Louisbourg
       Quesnay's *Tableau économique*
1759   Fall of Quebec to British
       Jesuits expelled from Portugal
       Voltaire's *Candide*
1760   Capitulation of Montreal
       Council of State in Austria
       Bakewell's stockbreeding in England
       Rousseau's *La Nouvelle Héloïse*
1761   Third Family Compact
       Resignation of Pitt
       Brindley's Bridgwater Canal
1762   Calas affair in France
       Rousseau's *Émile* and *Du contrat social*
       Gluck's *Orfeo ed Euridice*
1763   Peace of Paris: Britain, France, Spain
       Peace of Hubertusburg: Austria, Prussia
       Wilkes and *North Briton* affair in England
1764   Expulsion of Jesuits from France
       Beccaria's *Of Crimes and Punishments*
       Voltaire's *Dictionnaire philosophique*
       Hargreaves's 'Spinning jenny'
1765   Joseph II elected Holy Roman Emperor
1766   Aranda chief minister of Charles III in Spain
       Lessing's *Laocoon*
1768   Russo-Turkish war
       French purchase of Corsica
       Burgher rebellion in Geneva
       Wilkes elected MP for Middlesex
       Cook's first voyage to Australia
1769   Arkwright's 'water-frame'
       Royal Crescent, Bath
1770   Fall of Choiseul
       Lord North chief minister in England
       Struensee in Denmark
1771   Parlement of Paris exiled by Maupeou
1772   First Partition of Poland
       Gustavus III's *coup d'état* in Sweden
       Cook's second voyage
1773   Boston Tea Party
       Pugachev rebellion in Russia
       Society of Jesus dissolved by Clement XIV
1774   Treaty of Kutchuk-Kainardji: Russia, Turkey
       Quebec Act
       Priestley discovers oxygen
       Turgot Controller General in France
       Goethe's *Werther*

1775   American War of Independence
1776   American Declaration of Independence
       Fall of Turgot
       Cook's third voyage
       Watt's steam-engine
       Adam Smith's *Wealth of Nations*
1777   Necker Director General of Finance in France
1778   France enters American war
       Death of Pitt, Rousseau, Voltaire
       Buffon's *Les Époques de la nature*
1779   Crompton's 'Mule'
1780   Gordon Riots in London
1781   Further rebellion in Geneva
       Joseph II's peasant reform in Austria
       Watt's rotary steam-engine
       Kant's *Critique of Pure Reason*
1782   End of Lord North's Ministry
       France crushes revolution in Geneva
1783   Treaty of Versailles ends American war
       Russia annexes Crimea
       Younger Pitt Prime Minister
       Peasant revolt in Bohemia
       Lavoisier's analysis of water
1784   Fox's India Bill
       Pitt's second Ministry
       Cort's 'puddling' process (iron)
1785   Catherine II's Charter to the Nobility
       Cartwright's power-loom
       Mozart's *Marriage of Figaro*
1786   Anglo-French 'free-trade' treaty
       Lofthuus affair in Norway
1787   Russo-Turkish war
       Meeting of Assembly of Notables in France
       Triple Alliance: Britain, Prussia, UP
       'Patriot' challenge in United Provinces
       Wilkinson's first iron boat
       Lagrange's *Mécanique analytique*
       Mozart's *Don Juan*
1788   Austro-Turkish war
       Treaties of Berlin and The Hague: UP, Prussia, Britain
       'Aristocratic revolt' in France
       Convict settlement at Botany Bay
       Kant's *Critique of Practical Reason*
1789   Estates General at Versailles
       Fall of Bastille and outbreak of French Revolution
       Belgian revolt against Austria
       Blake's *Songs of Innocence*

RULERS OF EUROPE, 1713-89

France
Louis xv   1715
Louis xvi   1744-92

Great Britain
George i   1714
George ii   1727
George iii 1760-1820

Habsburg Monarchy
Charles vi   1711
Maria Theresa   1740
{Maria Theresa
{Joseph ii   1765
Joseph ii   1780-90

Italy
Popes Clement xi   1700
       Innocent xiii 1721
       Benedict xiii 1724
       Clement xii   1730
       Benedict xiv   1740
       Clement xiii   1758
       Clement xiv   1769-74
       Pius vi   1775-99
Sardinia Victor Amedeus ii
          (as King of Sicily)   1713
          (as King of Sardinia)   1720
          Charles Emmanuel iii   1740
          Victor Amedeus iii   1773-96

Poland
Augustus ii   1697
Augustus iii   1733
Stanislas I (Leszcinski)   1763
Stanislas ii (Poniatowski) 1764-94

Portugal

John v 1706
Joseph i 1750
Maria i 1777–95

Prussia

Frederick William i 1713
Frederick ii 1740
Frederick William ii 1786–97

Russia

Peter i 1689
Catherine i 1725
Peter ii 1727
Anna 1730–40
Elizabeth 1741
Peter iii 1762
Catherine ii 1762–96

Scandinavia

Denmark–Norway	Frederick iv	1699
	Christian vi	1730
	Frederick v	1746
	Christian vii	1766–1808
Sweden	Charles xii	1697–1718
	Frederick i	1720
	Adolphus Frederick	1751
	Gustavus iii	1771–92

Spain

Philip v 1700
Ferdinand vi 1746
Charles iii 1759
Charles iv 1788–1808

Ottoman Empire

Ahmed iii 1703
Mahmud i 1730
Othman iii 1754
Mustapha iii 1757
Abdul Hamid i 1774–89

BIBLIOGRAPHY

Of the vast bibliography of the period only a comparatively small selection of English, American and French titles will be given here. A useful guide is that by J.S.Bromley and A.Goodwin, eds, *A Select List of Works on Europe and Europe Overseas 1715–1815* (1956). Also to be recommended is the Select Bibliography in E.N.Williams, *The Ancien Régime in France: Government and Society in the Major States 1648–1789* (1970), pp.527–62. Students should also consult *A Bibliography of Modern History*, ed. John Roach (1968), as well as bibliographies in the volumes marked * in the paragraph that follows.

Among the numerous general histories of eighteenth-century Europe I have found M.S.Anderson's *Europe in the Eighteenth century 1713–1783* (1961) as useful as any. In addition, the following may be recommended: R.R. Palmer, *The Age of the Democratic Revolution: A Political History of Europe and America*, vol. I: *The Challenge* (1969); M.Beloff, *The Age of Absolutism 1660–1815* (1954); R.Mousnier, C.-E.Labrousse and M.Bouloiseau, *Le XVIIIᵉ siècle. L'époque des 'lumières' (1715–1815)* (1967); L.Krieger, *Kings and Philosophers 1689–1789* (1970); and three volumes in the Langer series (The Rise of Modern Europe): P.Roberts, *The Quest for Security 1715–1740* (1947); W.L.Dorn, *Competition for Empire 1740–1763* (1940); and L.Gershoy, *From Despotism to Revolution 1763–1789* (1944). Most useful, too, are the relevant volumes in the French *Clio* series by E.Préclin and V.-L.Tapié, *Le XVIIIᵉ siècle* (2 vols); and, in the rival *Peuples et Civilisations* series, those by P.Muret – *La prépondérance anglaise 1715–1763* (1949) – and P.Sagnac – *La fin de l'Ancien Régime et la Révolution américaine 1763–1789* (1952). The student should also be familiar with the appropriate chapters in vols VII and VIII of *The New Cambridge Modern History* (1957, 1965).

Among the general histories of individual countries the following may be recommended, though some with rather more enthusiasm than others:

Austrian Empire: R.J.Kerner, *Bohemia in the 18th Century* (1932); H.Marczali, *Hungary in the 18th Century* (1910).
Belgium: H.Pirenne, *Histoire de Belgique*, vol. 5 (1926).
Denmark, Norway, Sweden: L.Krabbe, *Histoire de Danemark* (1950); T.K.Derry, *A Short History of Norway* (1957); I.Andersson, *History of Sweden* (1956); B.J.Hovde, *The Scandinavian Countries 1720–1865* (2 vols, 1948).
France: A.Cobban, *A History of Modern France*, vol. I, *1715–1789* (1961); D. Dakin, *Turgot and the Ancien Régime* (1965); G.Duby and R.Mandrou,

History of French Civilisation (1966); E.Lavisse (ed.), *Histoire de France depuis les origines jusqu'à la Révolution*, vols 8–9 (1909–10); J.Lough, *An Introduction to 18th-Century France* (1960).

Germany, Prussia: W.H.Bruford, *Germany in the 18th Century* (1935); F.L. Carsten, *The Origins of Prussia* (1950).

Great Britain: B.Williams, *The Whig Supremacy 1714–1760* (1962); and J.Steven Watson, *The Reign of George III 1760–1815* (1960) – both in the Oxford History of England. See also D.Marshall, *Eighteenth-Century England* (1962); J.H.Plumb, *England in the 18th Century* (1966); and, in the Pelican Economic History of Britain, Christopher Hill, *Reformation to Industrial Revolution* (1967); and E.J.Hobsbawm, *Industry and Empire* (1969).

Italy: L.Salvatorelli, *A Concise History of Italy* (1940).

Poland: The Cambridge History of Poland, eds W.F.Reddaway *et al.*, vol. 2 (1951).

Russia: P.Milioukov, C.Seignobos and L.Eisenmann, *Histoire de Russie*, vols 2–3 (1932–3); B.H.Sumner, *Peter the Great and the Emergence of Russia* (1950); G.S.Thomson, *Catherine the Great and the Expansion of Russia* (1947).

Spain: R.Herr, *The 18th-Century Revolution in Spain* (1958); and the excellent opening chapters in R.Carr, *Spain 1808–1939* (1966).

Switzerland: E.Bonjour, H.S.Offler and G.R.Potter, *A Short History of Switzerland* (1952); W.Oechsli, *History of Switzerland 1499–1914* (1922).

Turkey-in-Europe: H.A.R.Gibb and R.Bowen, *Islamic Society in the West. I. Islamic Society in the 18th Century* (1950–7); B.Lewis, *The Emergence of Modern Turkey* (1968), chaps 1–3.

United Provinces (Holland): G.J.Renier, *The Dutch Nation. A Historical Study* (1944); B.H.M.Vlekke, *The Evolution of the Dutch Nation* (1945).

Population and growth of cities may be studied in M.Reinhard, A. Armengaud and J.Dupaquier, *Histoire générale de la population mondiale* (1968); R.Mols, *Introduction à la démographie historique des villes d'Europe* (3 vols, 1954–6); H.Moller, *Population Movements in Modern History* (1964); and A.Armengaud, 'Population in Europe 1700–1914', in *Fontana Economic History of Europe*, ed. C.M.Cipolla, vol. 3 (1970).

In the considerable literature on economic development, the following general histories are recommended: *Fontana Economic History of Europe* (see above), which, though not yet completed, already has valuable studies by A.de Maddalena on agriculture (vol. 2), Phyllis Deane and P.Bairoch on industrial revolution (vols 3 and 4), and B.Gille on banking (vol. 3); also S.B.Clough and C.W.Cole, *Economic History of Europe* (1952); A.Biernie, *An Economic History of Europe 1760–1932* (1962); and W.Bowden, M.Karpovitch and A.P.Usher, *Economic History of Europe since 1750* (1937). For agriculture and the 'agricultural revolution' see, in addition to Maddalena (above), B.H.Slicher van Bath, *The Agrarian History of Western Europe 500–1850* (1963); J.D.Chambers and G.E.Mingay, *The Agricultural Revolution 1750–1880* (1966); E.Kerridge, *The Agricultural Revolution* (1967); Marc Bloch, *French Rural History. An Essay on its Basic Characteristics* (1966); A.

Braudel and C.-E.Labrousse, *Histoire économique et sociale de la France*, vol. 2, *1660-1789* (1970); and H.Sée, *Esquisse d'une histoire du régime agraire en France aux 18e et 19e siècles* (1921). For the eighteenth-century industrial revolution the standard work is still P.Mantoux, *The Industrial Revolution of the 18th Century* (1928), though now admirably supplemented on a European scale in David S.Landes, *Unbound Prometheus* (1969). See also (mainly for England) W.O.Henderson, *Britain and Industrial Europe 1750-1850* (1966); T.S.Ashton, *An Economic History of England. The 18th Century* (1955); and R.M.Hartwell, *The Causes of the Industrial Revolution in England* (1967); and (for Russia) R.Portal, *L'Oural au XVIIIe siècle* (1950). For mercantilism, see E.Heckscher, *Mercantilism* (2 vols, 1956); and for prices and wages in France, two masterly studies by C.-E.Labrousse, *Esquisse du mouvement des prix et des revenus en France au dix-huitième siècle* (2 vols, 1933), and *La crise de l'économie française à la fin de l'Ancien Régime et au début de la Révolution* (1944).

A bird's-eye view of European society is given by R. and E.Forster (eds) in their *European Society in the Eighteenth Century* (1970). For aristocracy, see A.Goodwin (ed.), *The European Nobility in the Eighteenth Century* (1963); R. Forster, *The Nobility of Toulouse* (1960); F.L.Ford, *Robe and Sword. The Regrouping of the French Aristocracy after Louis XV* (1953); and G.E.Mingay, *English Landed Society in the Eighteenth Century* (1963). For the peasantry, in addition to Braudel and Labrousse, Bloch (above), see E.M.Link, *The Emancipation of the Austrian Peasant 1740-1798* (1949); A.Young, *Travels in France 1787-1789* (various editions); J.Blum, 'The Rise of Serfdom in Eastern Europe', *American Historical Review*, LXII (1957); G.T.Robinson, *Rural Russia under the Old Régime* (1932); and H.Koht, *Les luttes des paysans en Norvège du XVIe au XIXe siècle* (1929). For society in different countries see (for France) C.B.A.Behrens, *The Ancien Régime* (1967); R.Mandrou, *L'histoire de la civilisation française aux XVIIe et XVIIIe siècles* (1958); P.Sagnac, *La formation de la société française moderne* (2 vols, 1946); A.Soboul, *La France à la veille de la Révolution. Economie et Société* (1969); and A.de Tocqueville's great classic, *The Ancien Régime and the French Revolution* (several editions). For German society see Bruford (above) and R.Brunschwig, *Crise de l'état prussien à la fin du 18e siècle et la genèse de la mentalité romantique* (1947); for Russia, see P. Putnam (ed.), *Seven Britons in Imperial Russia 1698-1812* (1952); and, for Britain, see two books by M.D.George, *England in Transition* (1953) and *London Life in the Eighteenth Century* (1966), of which the latter is a masterpiece of its kind.

For government and administration, see the works of Anderson, Beloff, Krieger, Palmer and Tocqueville cited above; also E.Barker, *The Development of the Public Service in Western Europe 1660-1930* (1945). In addition, see (for Prussia) H.Rosenberg, *Bureaucracy, Aristocracy and Autocracy. The Prussian Experience 1660-1815* (1958); (for France) John H.Bosher, *French Finances 1770-1795* (1970); (for Russia) M.Raeff, *Plans for Political Reform in Imperial Russia 1730-1905* (1966); and (for Britain) R.Pares, *Limited Monarchy in Great Britain* (Historical Association pamphlet, 1957). Enlightened Despotism has been a favourite field for many writers. In addition to its treatment by Anderson, Krieger and Palmer (above), the following may be recommended: F.Hartung, *Enlightened Despotism* (Historical Association, 1957); S.Andrews,

Enlightened Despotism (1967); G.Bruun, *The Enlightened Despots* (1967). More inspiring are E.Wangermann, *From Joseph II to the Jacobin Trials* (1959); and Helen Siebel's 'Enlightened Despotism and the Crisis of Society in Germany', *Enlightenment Essays*, I (1970). In addition, there are numerous individual studies of 'despots', among them: P.Dukes, *Catherine the Great and the Russian Nobility* (1967); G.P.Gooch, *Frederick the Great* (1947); Paul P.Bernard, *Joseph II* (1968); F. Fejtö, *Un Habsbourg révolutionnaire. Joseph II* (1953); and (with ample reservations) M.Chele, *Dictator of Portugal. Life of the Marquis of Pombal* (1938).

For a brief but comprehensive treatment of religious affairs, the reader is referred to G.R.Cragg's *The Church in the Age of Reason 1648–1789* (1962). Other studies, on a national scale, include N.Sykes, *Church and State in England in the Eighteenth Century* (1934); and A.L.Drummond, *German Protestantism since Luther* (1951). Of greater interest are a number of studies on France: R.R.Palmer, *Catholics and Unbelievers in Eighteenth Century France* (1934); J. McManners, *French Ecclesiastical Society under the Ancien Régime* (1960); B.C. Poland, *French Protestantism and the French Revolution* (1957); and A.Latreille, *L'église catholique et la Révolution française* (1946). On Freemasonry, an interesting short study is R.Le Forestier's *La franc-maçonnerie templière et occultiste aux 18e et 19e siècles* (1970).

The Enlightenment has, like Enlightened Despotism, attracted a large number of scholars and writers. Of these only a handful will be cited here: N.Hampson, *The Enlightenment* (1968); P.Gay, *The Enlightenment. An Interpretation* (1966); K.Martin, *French Liberal Thought in the Eighteenth Century* (1954); and A.Cobban, *In Search of Humanity* (1960). The most original study has probably been D.Mornet's *Les origines intellectuelles de la Révolution française* (1947); while new ground has also been broken, in a more modest way, by R.Mandrou in his *De la culture populaire aux 17e et 18e siècles. La bibliothèque bleue de Troyes* (1964). For an imaginative and scholarly study of education in France, see G.Snyders' *La pédagogie en France aux 17e et 18e siècles* (1965); and, for the history of the sciences, see J.D.Bernal's *Science in History* (1954); A.R.Hall's *Scientific Revolution 1500–1800* (1954); and A.Wolf's *A History of Science, Technology and Philosophy in the 18th century* (1952).

Another well-trodden field is that of the arts and literature. There are, however, remarkably few studies that cover Europe as a whole: among them are P.Lavedan's *Histoire de l'art*, vol. 2 (1944); L.Réau's *Histoire universelle des arts*, vol. 3 (1936); and the same author's somewhat chauvinistic *L'Europe française au siècle des lumières* (1933). More readable are N.L.B.Pevsner's *Outline of European Architecture* (1960); Sir John Summerson's essay on English architecture, *Georgian England* (1962); and Ian Watt's *The Rise of the Novel. Studies in Defoe, Richardson and Fielding* (1966). Also to be recommended is A.S.Turberville (ed.), *Johnson's England* (2 vols, 1965).

In the growing literature on the social and political conflicts of the latter part of the century, the following may be mentioned in addition to the works of Koht, Oechsli, Palmer, Wangermann cited above: D.Aimé, 'La révolution suédoise de 1772', in *La Révolution française* (1937); I.R.Christie, *Wilkes, Wyvill and Reform* (1962); J.Egret, *La pré-révolution française, 1787–1788* (1962); J.Godechot, *The Taking of the Bastille. July 14th, 1789* (1970), ch. 1; P.Harsin,

La révolution liégeoise de 1789 (1953); S.Maccoby, *English Radicalism 1762–85* (1955); R.B.McDowell, *Irish Public Opinion 1750–1800* (1944); R.Portal, 'La révolte de Pugachev', *Études d'histoire moderne et contemporaine*, I (1947); M.Raeff, 'Pugachev's Rebellion', in R.Forster and J.P.Greene, *Pre-Conditions of Revolution in Early Modern Europe* (1970); G.Rudé, *Paris and London in the Eighteenth Century. Studies in Popular Protest* (1970); S.Tassier, *Les démocrates belges de 1789* (1930); E.Chapuisat, *La prise d'armes de 1782 à Genève* (1932); E.J.Hobsbawm, 'The Machine-Breakers', *Past and Present* (1952); and E.P. Thompson, 'The Moral Economy of the English Crowd in the Eighteenth Century', *Past and Present* (1971).

Finally wars, diplomacy, international relations and European expansion – to which such little space has been devoted in this volume – may be studied in the tendentious, but highly readable, opening chapters of A.Sorel, *Europe and the French Revolution. The Political Tradition of the Old Régime* (1969), which is only one of the eight volumes that appeared in French in the 1880s; A.Vagts, *A History of Militarism* (1959); G.Zeller, *Histoire des relations internationales. Les temps modernes. De Louis XIV à 1789* (1955); and Glyndwr Williams, *The Expansion of Europe in the 18th Century* (1966).

INDEX

Abbeville, woollen industry at, 47, 50
academies, emergence of, 140; as channels
  of communication, 167, 168; function
  of provincial, 167
Acadia see Nova Scotia
Acton, Lord John, 97
Adam, James, 68, 139, 145, 149
Adam, Robert, 68, 139, 145, 149
Adams, John, 190
administration, training for, 105; survival
  of amateurs in, 106; need for creation
  of professional class for, 106; in Sweden,
  106, 110; in Russia, 106–7, 116; in
  Prussia, 106–7, 116; in the Austrian
  Empire, 108–9, 117; in Spain, 109–10,
  118; in France, 110–12, 116; in Britain,
  112–13, 115; problems of and steps
  towards greater efficiency, 113; reforms
  in, 118–19; see also bureaucracy
Adrian, Patriarch, 124
Africa Company (Britain), 41, 42
Africa, West, European trade in, 41
agriculture, 14, 20, 26–7; improved
  methods, 14, 16, 17; relation of
  geographical features to, 20, 21–2;
  'agrarian revolution', 3, 22–7;
  communication of ideas and practices,
  23; enclosure and land-clearance
  (Britain), 24, 25, 37; (France), 24–5;
  backward areas, 26–7; distribution of
  farming land, 28, 29; decline of in
  France in years before Revolution, 249;
  see also individual countries
Agriculture, Board of (Britain), 24;
  (France), 24
Ahmed III, Ottoman Sultan, 86
Aix-la-Chapelle, treaty of, 122, 208, 227,
  237
Alba, Dukes of, 71
Alberoni, Giulio, 222
Alembert, Jean d', 134, 154, 162
Altamira, Conde de, 70
American War of Independence, 53, 140,
  183, 188–9, 208, 209, 211, 218, 222, 231

Americas, Dutch, British and French
  trade in, 39, 40, 41
Amsterdam, 39, 42, 43; population, 54;
  government of, 66; Jewish community in,
  131
Anglicans, Anglicanism, 121, 123, 124, 129
Anna, Empress of Russia, 28, 36, 75, 87,
  107
Anne of England, 121, 124, 178
Anson, Admiral George, 220, 240
Antwerp, 42
Anzin Mining Company, 47, 49
Aragon, integration of, 110, 117
Aranda, Count of, 99, 123, 136, 162–3
architecture, 139, 140–2, 143, 144, 145,
  147–8, 149
Arenberg, Duke of, 70
Argenson, Marquis d', 112, 210
aristocracy, nobility, 'aristocratic' society:
  in social structure of cities, 62, 63;
  analysis of, 69; in Britain, 69, 70, 72,
  73; in France, 70, 73–4 82, 178; in
  Spain, 70, 71; in Eastern Europe, 70–1,
  72, 87; in Italy, 72; status, privileges
  and obligations of, 73, (Britain) 73, 76,
  (France) 73–4, (Spain) 74, (Sweden)
  75, 76, (Italy) 74, 75–6, (Belgium) 74,
  (Germany) 74, (Eastern Europe) 74–5,
  76, 178, (Switzerland) 76, (Ottoman
  Empire) 86; absorption of banking and
  merchant classes into, 77, 80, 81;
  political power, 86, 87, 88, 175, 176,
  177–8 181; role in church, 124–5; as
  patrons of arts, 147, 148–9; patronage
  of Enlightenment, 164, 165; political
  defeat in Sweden, 177; tensions between
  monarchy and, 181–5
aristocratic revolt, révolte nobiliaire, 183–4,
  251, 254
Arkwright, Sir Richard, 51
Armengaud, A., 15, 17, 18
armies, 215–19; see military technique
  and individual countries
Artois, Comte d', 164

T   277

Sacheverell, Dr Henry, 121
Sade, Marquis de, 135, 169
Sainte-Geneviève, church of, Paris, 139
Saint-Germain, Comte de, 215
Saint-Pierre, Bernardin de, 151, 210
Saint-Simon, Claude Henri de Rouvroy,
  Duc de, 78, 90, 178, 181, 247, 248
Salamanca, churches, 148
Sales, Delisle de, 135
Salvador, Joseph, 131
Salzburg, churches in, 148
Sandemanians, 130
Savoy, Duchy of, 223
Saxe, Maréchal de, 216, 217, 218, 227
Saxony, feudalism in, 34; invasion of by
  Frederick II, 209, 227; surrender of by
  Prussia, 228
Scandinavia, emergence of national
  literature, 140; and see Denmark,
  Norway, Sweden
Schlegel, August Wilhelm, 140
Schleswig-Holstein, 21
science, 153–4, 156–7, 164, 168, 170
Scienza nuova (Vico), 154
Scotland, 57, 58, 66; literary awakening
  in, 146; interest in ideas of Adam Smith,
  165; universities, 168; rising of 'The
  Fifteen', 179; rising of 'The Forty-Five',
  179
Ségur, Chancellor, 178
Sephardic Jews, 130, 131
Serbia, 9
serfs, serfdom, 28, 30, 31–2, 33–4, 35–6,
  48, 49, 75, 97, 98, 100; see also individual
  countries
serva padrona, La (Pergolesi), 143
Seven Years War, 39, 48, 119, 168, 208,
  216, 222, 227–8, 229
Shelley, Percy Bysshe, 140
Sheraton, Thomas, 149
Sheremetev family, 28
Sheridan, Richard Brinsley, 139
Siberia, movement of Russians into, 19
Sicily, Austrian surrender of, 223
Siena, University, 168
Silesia, invasion of by Frederick II, 209, 225
Smith, Adam, 154, 158, 161, 162, 165,
  168, 170, 211
Smollett, Tobias George, 147
Snorri Sturluson, 146, 151
Society of Jesus see Jesuits
Society for the Promotion of Agriculture
  (Russia), 26
Socinians, 130, 137
Sorbonne, the, 167
Soufflot, Jacques Germain, 139, 141
Southcott, Joanna, 137
South Sea 'Bubble', 42

South Sea Company (Britain), 41, 42
Spain, geography and relation to national
  character, 7, 8, 9; growth of population,
  12–13; agriculture, 21, 22, 29–30;
  distribution of land, 30; feudalism, 32–3;
  textile production, 47; cities, 54, 55, 59
  and see separate entries; aristocracy, 70,
  71, 74, 253; government, 85, 91;
  reforms of Charles II, 99; expulsion of
  Jesuits from, 99, 136; administration and
  bureaucracy, 104, 105, 109–10, 117,
  (reforms of Charles III), 110–11, 118;
  taxation, 113; church and clergy, 121,
  122, 124, 125, 127; concordats of 1737
  and 1753, 123; religious schism, 128;
  Jewish communities, 130; the arts,
  139, 140, 143, 144, 147; import of
  French culture, 144, 161; patronage of
  the Enlightenment, 165; the press, 157;
  decline of absolute monarchy, 176;
  riots, 202, 203, 204; the army, 215;
  the navy, 219–20; warfare and
  expansion, 222, 231, 237; colonial
  possessions, 239; poverty of
  land-workers, 252
Spanish Succession, War of the, 38–9, 91,
  195, 211, 212, 219
Spectator (London), 167
'spinning jennies', 50, 51
Squillace riots, 202
Staatskanzlei (Austria), 109
Staatsrat (Austria), 109
Staël, Madame de, 244
Stamitz, Johann Wenzel Anton, 146
St Andrews, University of, 168
Sterne, Laurence, 142
steam-engines (Watt), 50, 51
Stock Exchanges, founding of, 42
Stockholm, treaty of, 8; population of, 55
St Petersburg, 55, 57; growth of, 54;
  development and improvement, 67;
  merchant class, 77
Straffpatent, the, 35
Strasbourg, 42, 61, 66
Strawberry Hill, residence of Horace
  Walpole, 141, 149
Strikes, industrial disputes, 64, 198–9
Struensee, Johann, 99, 101, 176
Strutt, Jedediah, 80
Sturm und Drang, 139, 145
Sweden, decline as military power, 9, 213;
  population, 11, 12; birth and death
  rates, 15, 17; agriculture, 20, 26;
  merchant navy, 41; stagnation of
  industry, 48; aristocracy, 75, 76, 175,
  178; government, 85, 92–3; creation
  of professional bureaucracy, 106; the
  arts, 140; French cultural influence,